# The Bipolar WAVES Workbook

FIND YOUR BIPOLAR STRESS ZONE

*Philip Van Ostrander*

Third Edition October 2021

All rights reserved

Copyright © 2021 by Philip Van Ostrander

philipvanostrander.com

This book or parts thereof may not be reproduced in any form without expressed written permission. No part of this publication may be reproduced, distributed, or transmitted in any form or by any means, including photocopying, recording, or other electronic or mechanical methods, without the prior written permission of the author, except in the case of brief quotations.

This workbook is a hybrid work of creative fiction and nonfiction. The author did not diagnose anyone with a mental or physical illness mentioned in this workbook. Health care professionals have diagnosed all people referenced in this workbook with bipolar disorder (BD). The author is only giving his observations and opinions based on his experience of living with multiple mental and physical illnesses. Any resemblance to actual events, situations, conditions, or people living or dead is entirely coincidental.

ISBN: 978-0-578-87770-9 (paperback)

# Disclaimers

By agreeing to this Disclaimer, you, the reader, acknowledge you have read and understood all ten clauses.

Do not read this workbook If you do not agree to all the terms in this Disclaimer

The author intends to encourage people with bipolar disorder (BD) illness to seek treatment early on from mental health care professionals.

1. Work of Creative Nonfiction
This workbook is a work of creative nonfiction and is dedicated to people with bipolar (BP). The workbook spans the lives of two brothers from childhood until 75 years old. The characters in the examples of cases of bipolar are a hybrid of fiction and nonfiction.

Chapter 2 covers my life story with bipolar disorder (BD) and other illnesses; visions and premonitions are the creation of the author's imagination. Some characters in Chapters 4, 5, 6, and 7 represent real people with the same diagnosis of BD, but some situations are not factual and only a product of the author's imagination.

2. This workbook is only a product of the author.
The author of this workbook has not discussed the contents of this workbook with anyone before publication. My brother has not reviewed this workbook. The author alone has written every word of

this workbook. The author has not consulted or sought advice from any health care provider, including the author's psychiatrist.

3 The author is not a Medical or Mental Health Provider.
The author is not a medical provider or mental health provider. This workbook book is not a substitute for the medical advice of physicians. The reader should regularly consult a physician in matters relating to his/her health and particularly concerning any symptoms that may require diagnosis or medical attention. You should never delay seeking competent medical advice from a health care professional. The ideas, charts, and suggestions contained in this workbook are not a substitute for consulting a competent psychiatrist.

The WAVES Chart and other information in this book are not based on a scientific study. The charts were created and designed by the author. The author intends to offer information that may help readers in the quest for a better quality of life.

4. Mental Health Providers.
The author's opinions at times are critical of the treatment provided by health care professionals but by no means reflect poorly on the entire mental health care system. The author of this workbook is not a mental health care provider and does not prescribe or advise the use of any form of treatment for medical, physical, emotional, or mental illness.

The author has not diagnosed anyone in this book with a mental disorder. Psychiatrists have diagnosed all the people with BD mentioned in Chapters 4-through 7. The workbook's intent is to encourage people with BD to seek treatment from a mental health care professional.

5. Personal Responsibility.
If the reader uses any information in this book for themselves or

anyone else, the author accepts no responsibility for any harm whatsoever. Readers of this workbook are solely responsible for their mental and physical healthcare. The author does not accept any responsibility for any adverse effects readers may claim to have, whether directly or indirectly, from the information in this workbook.

6. No Guarantee.
There is no guarantee expressed or implied that the information in this workbook would be helpful.

7. Assumption of Risk.
As with many experiences in life, some events may involve some risk. The reader assumes all risks, including the possibility of death. The writer is not responsible for any injury, damage, or even death allegedly arising from any information in this workbook.

8. Indemnification.
The reader shall indemnify, completely hold harmless, and release the author from and against all claims, allegations, actions, obligations, losses, suits, demands, damages, liabilities, settlements, and judgments.

9. Limit of Liability/Warranty.
The author makes no representations or warranties concerning the content of this book. The information in this book is not guaranteed or warranted to produce any particular results and may not be suitable for every individual. If you are under a psychiatrist's care, he/she may be able to advise you about the information described in this book. If you are not under a psychiatrist's care perhaps, you should consult a health care professional about the information described in this workbook. The information in this book is not meant to replace sound advice from a competent psychiatrist.

10. Small Claims Court.
If you have a valid claim, you must file a claim in small claims court as determined by the author, but before making any claim, please contact the author to resolve any issues.

# Acknowledgments

First, I want to acknowledge our mother for her tough and courageous stand to provide for us while enduring many hardships along the way.

I wish to thank my brother for his support throughout my entire life.

I thank our two sons for putting up with my sometimes-bizarre behavior for so many years.

I thank our extended family for their love and support for many years as we learned to stick together.

Thanks to the leader of the Bipolar Disorder Support (BDS)Group for her courage and dedication. She is helping hundreds of people with BD to lead better lives.

Many thanks to my psychiatrist for keeping me stable on effective medications for many years.

I would also like to recognize my 1st love. I wish you and your family joy, love, and happiness.

I want to thank my 2nd love for her support and caring as I was learning to love again. She endured hardships when just a child in

*Philip Van Ostrander*

war-torn Europe and then dedicated her life to helping less fortunate people in America.

Finally, I want to thank my wife in my life for the love, caring, unrelenting patience, and kindness toward our entire family.

# Preface

I have been working on this workbook between bad spells, as I call prolonged bipolar disorder (BD) episodes, for over ten years. I have stopped and started publishing this workbook more times than I want to admit.

I believe everything happens for a reason, and the pandemic and other factors drove me to finally publish this workbook. Forgive my rough and scattered writing style; as you will see, I do not have command of my writing skills. After years of delays, I decided this workbook may help people, especially people struggling with BD. I named the workbook The Bipolar WAVES Workbook. The name WAVES represents the never-ending cycles of waves in the ocean. Ocean WAVES crashing onto the shoreline could also be a symbol for someone living with BD and represent a mental crash.

The President of The United States, Trump (POTUS), declared a National Emergency in March 2020; it is now the fall of 2020, and the pandemic is destroying the fabric of our nation. People young and old are waking up to the reality our nation will be changed forever. For over four decades, I have been very concerned about the growing political division in our nation has become more divided every day. Lately, I have come to the conclusion we are at war with the pandemic but also at war within our own nation. We have a war raging within our country between what I call the Radical American Democrats (RAD) nation and the Main Street American or the MSA nation.

# Table of Contents

Disclaimers ............................................................................. iii
Acknowledgments .................................................................. vii
Preface ................................................................................... ix

Introduction ............................................................................ 1
Chapter 1  Developing the WAVES Chart ................................ 5
Chapter 2  My just another bipolar story ............................... 21
         Stage 1 Life on the Farm ............................................ 22
         Stage 2 Our teenage years .......................................... 26
         Stage 3 Life in our college years ................................ 33
         Stage 4 Life with Careers and Family ....................... 46
         Stage 5 Life in the '70s ............................................... 55
         Stage 6 Life in the '80s ............................................. 105
         Stage 7 Recovery- Life after 50 on lithium ............. 124
         Stage 8 Discovery-A Bipolar Disorder Support
             (BDS) group ................................................. 135
         Stage 9 Nature was my way of pursuing
             happiness ..................................................... 156
         Stage 10 My past life returns after I awoke
             from amnesia ............................................... 185
         Stage 11 The Great Outdoors was our path to
             happiness .................................................... 212
         Stage 12 My spiritual growth has taken a lifetime ..... 257
         Stage 13 The pandemic is here ................................. 301
         Stage 14 The Teardrops attempt to speak out ......... 334
         Stage 15 Wake up! Your nation is at war ................. 364

Chapter 3   How to Use the WAVES Chart .................................. 387
Chapter 4   The tragic story of Jack and JoJo ............................ 409
Chapter 5   Erika's Career and Job Story.................................... 425
Chapter 6   My brother Stu's Story ........................................... 433
Chapter 7   Henry's Marriage and Job Story...............................451
Chapter 8   Find your Bipolar Stress Zone ................................. 459
Chapter 9   My WAVES Chart..................................................... 463
Appendices.................................................................................491
        Appendix A The Bipolar WAVES Stress Chart .......... 491
        Section 1 WAVES Chart—Lifestyles Disorders,
            Illnesses, Addictions............................................... 492
        Section 2 WAVES Chart—Careers, Jobs, and
            Relationships.......................................................... 493
        Section 3 WAVES Chart—Marriage and Family....... 494
        Section 4 WAVES Chart—Personal Situations ......... 495
        Section 5 WAVES Chart—The 7 WAVES
            Stress Zones............................................................ 496
        The Bipolar lifestyle ..................................................... 502
        Physical Illnesses.......................................................... 504
        Mental Disorders........................................................... 504
        Addictions...................................................................... 505
        Careers and Jobs .......................................................... 506
        Relationships and Dating .............................................510
        Marriage and Family .................................................... 516
        Personal situations ....................................................... 520
        Appendix B .................................................................... 529
Bibliography .............................................................................537

# Introduction

THE BIPOLAR WAVES WORKBOOK HAS three main goals, to help people with bipolar disorder (BD), tell my bipolar story, and voice my concerns about the future of America. Oh, and finally, I want to voice my opinions on why extraterrestrials or ETs are visiting planet Earth and the role they will play in the future of the human race.

The primary goal of the WAVES Workbook is to help all people with BD to Identify and determine the chance of a serious BD episode or, even worse outcome, suicide. The Bipolar WAVES Stress Chart in Appendix A is used to "Find your Bipolar Stress Zone." I named the chart WAVES to represent the never-ending cycles or waves of mania and depression found in most cases of BD.

The second goal of this workbook is to tell my story. Both my brother Stu and I lived very different lives socially, but we both have a diagnosis of BD in common.

If you want to bypass my bipolar story in Chapter 2, you can go to Chapter 3. Chapter 2 of this workbook is a very long BD story about two brothers born with BD. Throughout this workbook, I will refer to my brother Stu and me as we. We are about a year apart and are now over 75 years of age.

In many ways, my story is just another BD story, except both my brother and I did not get diagnosed with BD until midlife or around

50 years old. Now many people define a midlife crisis as a time of deep emotional turmoil and confusion. Our midlife crisis was just ending from 50 years of chaos and setbacks before we got effective treatment for BD.

Again, my just another bipolar Story in Chapter 2 can be bypassed and go directly to Chapter 3. However, understanding how my brother and I lived for over 75 years with BD may encourage other people to get help early on and avoid decades of setbacks and challenges.

Encouraging people to get help early on in life is one of the main goals of this workbook. Although this workbook follows the lives of my brother and me, our story is told from my point of view, and I am solely responsible for its content. In addition to living with bipolar, I also lived over four decades in a state of amnesia.

Chapter 1 is about how The Bipolar WAVES Stress Chart was developed and is an essential part of this workbook. The Bipolar WAVES Stress Chart or WAVES Chart for short is a list of abnormal stressful situations, conditions, and events unique to anyone with BD.

For example, the abnormal stresses of losing a job, losing family support, and then finding yourself homeless. I claim when all these stressful events occur, during a year or more, it can trigger a BD episode. When all your stress points are simply added up, you find your Stress zone. Unfortunately, the higher your score on the WAVES Chart of this workbook puts you at a higher risk for serious mental and physical issues.

Most people I have met with BD, including myself, do not seek pity but want the public, friends, employers, and family members to respect them and not ridicule or shame them for having a mental illness.

For anyone with BD, The Bipolar WAVES Workbook" will help you to "Find your Bipolar Stress Zone." In this workbook, I am going to use The Bipolar WAVES Stress Chart, or WAVES Chart for short is used to measure the mental and physical stresses bipolar Illness can have on our lives based on many unique life situations and events.

The WAVES Chart takes into account the many stages and events in the life of someone with BD and the treatment or mistreatment of them. The WAVES Chart covers many mental and physical illnesses and addictions. It also includes many stages of life, including Relationships, Careers & Jobs, Marriage, Family, and other situations in life.

The third main goal of this workbook is to voice my concerns about the path our nation is on and some dire predictions regarding the fate of our nation. This path has forced me to look at the history of our nation and the world. Following this path, I discovered our nation's short history involving wars, drugs, immigration, corruption, politics, pandemics, and little-known emergency laws of our Democracy would end in its destruction from within.

For years I have been very concerned about the growing political division in our nation. Lately, I have come to the conclusion we are at war with the pandemic but also in a war within our nation. We now have a war raging between two very different ideologies, the Democrats and the Republicans, for the soul of our nation. The war here is between what I call the Radical American Democrats (RADs) nation and the Main Street American or MSA nation.

Another path I have followed from a very young age is nature's role in living on planet Earth. I believe our nation will not survive unless we follow the fundamental laws of nature. These three paths will converge to arrive at my dire prediction regarding our nation's future. Again, I also have an opinion about extraterrestrials (ETs) and the role they will play in the evolution or destruction of the human race.

Again, it is not necessary to read my story in Chapter 2 to use the WAVES Workbook, although it will provide the reasons why I think our nation is on a dangerous path.

CHAPTER 1

# Developing the WAVES Chart

THE BIPOLAR WAVES STRESS CHART or WAVES Chart for short is an integral part of the Bipolar WAVES Workbook.

This workbook and accompanying charts are from the perspective of someone that has BD. I recognize family, loved ones, and caregivers are under tremendous stress when living with and caring for someone with mental illness, especially BD mental illness.

I also recognize many people I will present later with other physical and mental illnesses can also struggle a lifetime with even higher levels of pain and stress—for example, people I have met like Sabrina with schizophrenia and Owen with the physical pain of Cerebral Palsy.

### I joined a Bipolar Disorder Support (BDS) group

I was not diagnosed and treated for BD until mid-life or about 50 years old. My brother Stu was diagnosed and treated with lithium in Florida in 1992. After our family returned from Florida in 1992 to our home in PA., I found a psychiatrist and also was treated with lithium.

I began to study and learn more about BD from books, articles, and searching on the internet. By 1995 the information on the internet was expanding exponentially, and I read many articles online about mental illness. I also had an older DSM manual [(American Psychiatric Association, 1987) to learn more about many mental illnesses.

About five years after I was diagnosed with BD, I found a Bipolar Disorder Support (BDS) group. When I began to hear firsthand stories from people with BD, it confirmed my claim just how stressful and complicated life can become. I found navigating the many stages of life while dealing with unrelenting cycles of BD is very challenging at best.

The stats were grim because I learned for one out of five people with BD, life gets too much to handle, and sadly, life is cut short by suicide. When I realized for many others with BD, their lifespan is cut short by about nine years. These stats confirmed my claim people with BD endure enormous stress in their lives. These tragic realities are what The Bipolar WAVES Workbook is attempting to identify and help prevent.

## The WAVES Workbook assumptions

This workbook is not based on a scientific study but on my experience and observations of living with BD for over 75 years. I also had many insights and observations from attending the BDS group for over 15 years. This workbook makes several assumptions regarding the mental health status of someone with BD.

Number 1. The BD illness is the most significant factor in the life of someone with BD. People live a lifetime with the illness. This workbook assumes BD is more important than all other mental illnesses like anxiety or personality disorders.

There are exceptions to this rule, perhaps someone with both schizophrenia and bipolar; schizophrenia may be a more significant mental illness.

Number 2. People with BD do not live "Normal" lives. I define "Normal" as someone without any mental disorders. Normal also includes the families and loved ones who do not have any history of mental illness. A "Normal" person may resolve a crisis with short-term "Normal" responses and never affect their lives with extremely high levels of stress. In other words, a "Normal" person has no stress due to mental illness. I put the word "Normal" in quotes if someone has no mental illness of any kind.

Number 3. People with BD can live one of two different lifestyles, stable and unstable. I want to make the point if someone is not diagnosed with BD or is diagnosed with BD but is not receiving effective treatment, this is an unstable BD lifestyle. For this workbook, a person treated with effective medications leads a stable BD normal lifestyle. There are exceptions, some people do not need psychiatric medications and are stable, but I understand this is rare.

Number 4. I have not taken into account a psychiatric diagnosis of BD I, BD-II, or mixed states of BD. I have not included a rapid cycling form of mood disorders. When I refer to stable or unstable, it refers to my definition of a BD lifestyle and not a DSM [(American Psychiatric Association, 1987) official diagnosis of a mental disorder.

Number 5. The WAVES Chart only applies to adults and not children or teens. I thought about creating a separate category for old people but was afraid of age discrimination lawsuits, just kidding. Many children and teens have other unique situations that may cause stress, for example, being bullied by classmates for their sexual orientation.

Number 6. Stable people on effective medications may experience psychotic episodes due to extremely high stressful situations or very low-stress levels. Due to the nature of our illness, some people may experience a psychotic episode for no apparent reason. It's the reality of the illness. Also, an unstable person may not be at risk for a psychotic episode because they have very few stresses in their lives. Therefore, the WAVES Chart attempts to determine the chances of a BD episode for both BD lifestyles.

Number 7. Some *people* with BD struggle with what I call an unworthy syndrome. After I accepted my diagnosis of BD, I also needed to acknowledge I was emotionally and verbally abused by my family from the age of 5. I was also sexually abused by a teenager at the age of 8. So, in my case, I was a victim of childhood abuse in addition to BD. These two conditions led to a case of what I call unworthy syndrome.

After attending a Bipolar Disorder Support or (BDS) group for over 15 years, I noticed many people were also abused and rejected by family and loved ones. Statistically, over 90 percent of marriages end in divorce if one spouse is diagnosed with BD. I claim for many people with BD; divorce is a form of abandonment. I also contend years of experiencing BD, divorce, rejection, ridicule, and many other forms of abuse can lead to a condition I call an unworthy syndrome.

This condition is not an official psychiatric disorder listed in the DSM manual. (American Psychiatric Association, 1987)

I felt I was not worthy of being loved by anyone from a very young age. I came to the grim conclusion, like many people in the BD group, I also felt the same way, unworthy of being loved.

I believe my unworthy syndrome started shortly after my father died of a heart attack when I was only five years old. Managing my feelings of not feeling loved has been very challenging; I think it will be a lifelong issue for me to manage, much like BD.

Number 8. I refer to bad spells throughout the workbook. I define bad spells as episodes of BD, plus other issues. Issues like my unworthy syndrome, amnesia, past traumatic recollections, and alcoholism. Then mixed feelings of guilt, shame, and abandonment started when I was a very young child. I needed to deal with severe cases of SAD in the winter months. In my case, I was a victim of emotional and sexual abuse from about the age of 5. So, I claim after I was diagnosed and treated for BD, I also needed to also deal with childhood abuse plus several other mental issues. These bad spells lasted for weeks, sometimes for months at a time.

Number 9. I was in a state of amnesia for over 45 years. I met a young woman named Maria I call my 1st love. We met on Nantucket when I was about 17, and I fell madly in love with her. After the tragic event on Nantucket, we broke up when I was 22 years old during my senior year in college. I was so distraught I went into a state of amnesia for over 45 years. I awoke from amnesia over 45 years later when I was 70 years old.

I was remembering and reliving the tragic events of the past triggered some very stressful and painful past recollections of when I was 22 years old.

Number 10. The stress points I have given for each life situation on the WAVES Chart can be different depending on the person scoring the chart. For example, if you feel bankruptcy is more stressful, then you could score the points on the WAVES Chart even higher.

Number 11 Of course, you can add new life situations or conditions to the WAVES Chart and assign points based on your experiences over the past year or more. The pandemic is one situation that needs to be evaluated and assigned stress points. For example, the pandemic is not listed on the WAVES Chart but needs to be included as a very stressful situation for most people with BD.

Number 12.-The focus of The Bipolar WAVES Workbook is on people with BD. In other words, this workbook is from the perspective of someone living with BD.

Number 13. This workbook defines treatment as any method that will make a person with BD stable. Treatment may include pills, injections, magnetic therapy, and other forms of treatment.

Number 14. The purpose of this workbook is not to diagnose people with BD but determine the overall stress on people with BD. I am not diagnosing anyone with BD because their psychiatrist has already determined they have been diagnosed with BD. This workbook only determines the overall stress and other factors on people with BD.

Number 15. Many times, the stresses accumulate over time to create a crisis. I call this condition the accumulative BD stress factor.

## What the Bipolar WAVES Workbook is not

This workbook is not a scientific study of BD. The workbook findings are not the result of years of research by a highly esteemed research institute. I did not consult any health care professionals, but everyone mentioned in this workbook has been diagnosed with BD by a psychiatrist. I have based the findings only on my experience and observations and from living with bipolar for over 75 years.

## What if I am "Normal" and don't have a mental illness?

For this workbook, I use the word "Normal" in quotes to indicate someone without bipolar or has any other mental illness in their entire family.

Well, if you are fortunate enough not to have BD or any history of mental illness in your family, you may not need the WAVES

Workbook. Perhaps you know a friend or loved one that may have BD mental illness; in that case, you may want to use the WAVES Workbook to learn and understand the abnormal stresses on people with mental illness, especially BD mental illness.

Other people may want to use the WAVES Workbook to learn more about the abnormal stresses on people with mental illness, especially BD mental illness. Perhaps you have a loved one that has BD; you may want to learn and understand how many stressful situations may affect their behavior.

## Bipolar has one of two lifestyles Stable and Unstable

When I use the term treatment, I mean someone on effective medications from a competent psychiatrist for over a year.

When I use the word, mistreatment means a person with BD that is getting toxic meds or ineffective meds from a psychiatrist or health care professional. Mistreatment includes harmful procedures or techniques that are counterproductive.

This workbook attempts to illustrate the vast difference in stress levels of good effective treatment can have on everyone with BD, including families and loved ones. Generally, I call someone taking effective medications stable, but of course, this may be oversimplifying a complex mental illness. I define "unstable" as someone that is not on effective medications or is not taking any psychiatric meds.

I define effective treatment as any method, procedure, or treatment that will stabilize someone with BD. Any treatment may include pills, injections, magnetic therapy, or another effective method.

For this workbook, I assume people with BD may have either BD I, BD-II, or other mood disorders.

Again, I do not diagnose anyone with BD because their psychiatrist has already determined they have BD. This workbook only determines the overall stress on people with BD.

## I am stable on no meds

Some people diagnosed with BD claim they are stable even if they are not on any psychiatric medications (meds). These people may claim they have never had a psychotic episode and do not need any meds. Well, I argue you may think you are stable, but for the same life situations as a stable person, you have significantly higher stress in your life. You have no way to control the episodes of mania and depression, so for this workbook, I define your lifestyle as an unstable BD lifestyle. You may also feel you are stable because you have very few stressors in your life.

There are always exceptions to the rule. I understand some people with BD do not need psychiatric medications and are stable, but this is rare.

So, what is my answer for someone with BD that says, "I am stable on no meds." I say you potentially have a fatal illness that could end your life prematurely, especially if not treated effectively.

## A lifetime of stress on people with bipolar

I believe most people living with BD have a constant lifelong level of stress. I call this Lifetime Bipolar Stress Level (LBSL) or Lifetime LBSL for short. This level of stress stays with a person for a lifetime, but the level of stress depends on whether a person is stable or unstable.

I assign different Lifetime (LBSL) points to stable and unstable. Furthermore, many stressful situations can have an additive effect on people with BD illness over time. I call this the Stress Level Score (SLS), and this score can determine if someone is at risk of a serious mental breakdown. The SLS score will determine what stress zone level of someone that has BD.

Now this score is not a scientific study but derived from my experience and observations from living with BD for over 75 years.

## *Troubling Statistics about Bipolar Disorders*

I do not like to cite statistics about mood disorders, but the Depression and Bipolar Support Alliance [(The Depression & Bipolar Support Alliance (DBSA) dbsalliance.org) website lists many troubling statistics about mood disorders, but I will only cite a few statistics for this workbook.

Another study found as many as one in five patients or about 20% with BD commit suicide. [(National Institute of Mental Health, n.d.). I could not find what percentage of these people with BD were untreated for BD. My hope, if people with BD get treatment early on, the risk of suicide will become much less. This is one goal of the workbook to bring down the tragic loss by suicide.

Another study found that people with BD results in 9.2 years reduction in expected life span [(The Depression & Bipolar Support Alliance (DBSA) dbsalliance.org) of people with BD.

According to the article "Managing Bipolar Disorder" in Psychology Today (Managing Bipolar Disorder, 2003), an estimated 90 percent of marriages end in divorce.

These are very sad statistics; ninety percent of marriages end in divorce if one spouse has BD.

These stats are very troubling because many times, treatments with antidepressants and unproven medicines do not improve a person's quality of life.

I like to site only a few stats from many studies for the WAVES Workbook. Number one, people with BD have a 9.2-year reduction in the expected life span. Second, as many as one in five people with BD commit suicide. The third stat is ninety percent of marriages end in divorce if one spouse has BD.

## *Bipolar illness can be fatal*

So, I guess you could say in many ways; BD can be a deadly illness, much like a drug addiction if not treated effectively by a professional.

I believe abnormal physical and mental stress can negatively affect all areas or stages of people's lives, including jobs, relationships, marriages, and even life expectancy.

By using the WAVES Chart in Appendix A, these unique, abnormal stresses in life can be objectively measured to predict the chance of a psychotic breakdown or, even worse outcome, suicide.

Furthermore, I claim without proper treatment, BD can be deadly. This may be a bold statement, but it is time we need to treat BD as a potentially fatal illness similar to drug addiction.

The average life span of a male in the US is 76 years old. [(OECD, n.d.) People with BD live about nine years less than the average male. This means; statistically, I would not live life past (76 minus 9) or 67 years old. Sometimes Stu and I joke we are living on borrowed time, meaning we beat the odds by living past 67.

The main reasons I have lived past 67 are getting treatment, engaging in less risk-taking, getting and keeping sober, and using effective meds. This lifestyle has not been carefree, but I have avoided highly stressful situations for the past 25 years. I have challenges and setbacks like most people with BD, but my quality of life has vastly improved after treatment.

## Unique life situations that apply to a bipolar lifestyle

After living with a diagnosis of BD for over seven decades, I noticed I had far greater stress in my life than "Normal" people, but I did not have a way to measure my life stresses. I had no way to determine if I was at risk of a mental breakdown or, worse, severe depression or at risk of suicide. Therefore, I set out to find a way to measure the total stress on someone with BD illness.

I could not find a way to predict at what level of stress someone has at any given time in his/her or her life. After observing many different life situations in my life and others with BD, I recorded life situations in a journal that apply to someone with a diagnosis of BD. For example, I noticed many people that have BD also had a family history of BD and other serious mental illnesses in their family. I call these conditions unique because someone with BD needs to deal with highly stressful external situations in addition to dealing with their own mental illness.

Also, many families had substance and alcohol abuse in the family. These issues were the case in our family; not only did my brother have BD, but several family members also had a history of alcoholism. Also, I had other mental disorders, so I needed to include other disorders to get a total picture of my total stress level.

I began to expand a list of life situations that applied only to people with mental illness but realized the stresses were far more significant if someone was not successfully treated for BD. After attending the Bipolar Disorder Support (BDS) group for over 15 years, I noticed far greater pressure on people with no treatment or ineffective treatment for the same life situations. For example, the tasks required for getting and keeping a job were much more difficult for someone with BD if they were not stable. After I had a list of unique stressful life situations, I assigned points to each situation, condition, or event, but it still did not give an accurate assessment of the stresses on someone living with bipolar.

Even if the person with BD has no stressful life situations, I claim people with BD have a constant lifetime level of stress in their lives, meaning their stress level is never zero. I call this Lifetime Bipolar Stress Level (LBSL) or Lifetime LBSL, but I noticed this Lifetime LBSL is much higher for someone without proper treatment or is unstable on meds or has no mental health care. Therefore, I assigned a Lifetime (LBSL) twice that of someone that is stable on meds and has a sound support system.

I assigned a Lifetime (LBSL) of 65 points for someone stable and a Lifetime LBSL of 130 to someone who is unstable or not on any meds.

How did I assign a Lifetime (LBSL) of 65 for someone stable on meds? These stress points are based on The Holmes and Rahe Life Stress Scale in Appendix B.

The Holmes and Rahe Chart [(Holmes & Rahe, 1967) has been referenced for many years now. It gave a score of 53 out of 100 for someone with a physical illness. The chart does not take into account any mental illness; therefore, I assigned a higher score for someone mentally stable on medications at 65 points. I assumed someone without proper meds has a score double that of a stable person with BD or a score of 130 points.

I arrived at these numbers because both my brother and I lived until midlife in an unstable BD lifestyle until we finally got proper treatment. We only became stable after getting effective meds and support. We determined in our own experiences living without proper medications was twice as stressful before we got good psychiatric meds and therapy.

Now many of these life situations are common to many "Normal" people, but in combination with the diagnosis of bipolar can make these stressful situations unique. For example, a "Normal" person with no history of mental illness may find family conflicts somewhat stressful, but someone with BD conflicts with members of the family can be overwhelming, especially if one or more family members also have a history of mental illness.

To make the living conditions even more complicated and stressful, both spouses and siblings may be either unstable or stable.

## *The accumulative BD stress factors*

I claim harmful, stressful conditions and events in the lives of people with BD have an accumulative effect on people with mental illness, especially BD mental illness. If these events and situations do not get resolved, the pent-up emotions can lead to a psychotic breakdown. Perhaps these stressors may have been building up throughout an hour, days, months, or even years, especially if not treated effectively. These events may cause a person to "snap" for no apparent reason, but if you look deeper into their history, many accumulative BD stress factors may be the reason.

I also claim these accumulative BD stress factors do not occur in most "Normal" people because they resolve conflicts differently, especially when several events happen all at the same time. Many "Normal" people can prioritize stressful situations and make rational decisions to solve stressful events. Many "Normal" people, even people in the health care field, cannot understand people with BD cannot resolve these so-called "simple" everyday tasks.

From a "Normal" person's perspective, it is hard to understand why someone with BD finds losing and finding another job can be so overwhelming. Many times, it results in giving up finding work after several job losses. Of course, this leads to family conflicts, shaming, and criticizing the person with BD.

## Living an Unstable Bipolar Lifestyle
I think many people associate unstable with people with BD illness doing bizarre and crazy things when having a full-blown manic episode, but I claim you can also be very unstable in a severe depression. I remember those dark days in a desperate state of depression, and I was not stable. I was very unstable in my thoughts and actions. Out in public, I probably appeared just to be withdrawn and unhappy like many "Normal" people, and I did not appear to be mentally ill at all.

I call this way living an unstable BD lifestyle, a life of setbacks, and perhaps bizarre and unstable behavior. The cycles of uncontrolled mania followed by deep, prolonged depressions made our lives unbearable. Many times, our unpredictable cycles of BD made our families and loved ones want to abandon us, and sometimes they did.

## Living a Stable Bipolar normal lifestyle
After we got stable on lithium, we did not have any severe episodes of mania or depression, but we learned if we became too manic or depressed, we went to our psychiatrist and got a medication adjustment to become stable again. We also learned to stay on our mood stabilizers to help protect us from dangerous and unpredictable highs or lows. We both feel getting stable was the number one reason for us to live a more productive life. Just staying sober alone did not make our quality of life any better.

By effective treatment, I mean taking effective meds, having a good support system, being emotionally stable, and being on meds for about a year or more. I think even if you are under good treatment, life situations may put a BD normal individual into a very stressful, chaotic life situation with possible life-threatening consequences.

## The workbook has one chart for two types of BD Lifestyle

I wanted to design the WAVES Chart to show how life situations unique to someone with BD can dramatically affect their quality of life. I wanted to develop the WAVES Chart to predict the occurrence of tragic life events such as a full-blown manic or a dangerous suicidal depression type episode.

The sum of all the harmful life situations and events I refer to as a Stress Level Score or (SLS). I wanted anyone to easily calculate their total Stress Level Score (SLS) and evaluate their chances of risk to themselves or others.

Using this Stress Level Score (SLS), they or their loved ones could then determine their BP Stress Zone. Depending on the SLS score, a person could be in one of 7 BP stress Zones. The 7 zones correspond to low levels of stress to Extreme Emergencies; level 7 requires immediate attention.

The person's WAVES stress zone level would tell how high their stress level is and what risks they pose to themselves or others. Based on the WAVES stress zone level, they or a loved one can then decide to get help based on their stress zone level.

## Bipolar lifestyles are not easy to chart

When developing the WAVE Chart for this workbook, I tried to simplify many BD issues. As I got deeper into explaining the various unique life situations for the WAVES Chart, I discovered BD is a very complex and complicated illness because it affects so many people and so many stages of life. It usually starts to affect our lives in our youth and then relationships, jobs, careers, marriage, family, physical illness, and many other areas of life.

Also, I claim these stresses are far more significant for people with BD if not stable and under good psychiatric care. Therefore, all these conditions can be unique to someone with mental illness, but the level of stress still depends on whether they are stable or unstable.

I came to the conclusion I needed two separate WAVES charts, a chart for stable people and a second chart for unstable people with BD. I decided to combine two charts into one chart. I am aware that combining two charts into one WAVES Chart may be a bit confusing, but I needed a way to emphasize the vast difference between a stable and unstable BD lifestyle.

Chapter 2 is my very long bipolar (BP) story. It is not necessary to read my story to use the Bipolar WAVES Workbook, but my story may explain many challenges and situations my family and I have experienced over 75 years. My story is quite lengthy because it covers over 75 years.

You can bypass my long bipolar (BP) story in Chapter 2 and go to Chapter 3. Chapter 3 has a summary of how to use the BP Chart. Chapters 4 through 7 are examples of people living with BD. Chapter 8 wants people with BD to determine their WAVES Stress level by using the WAVES Chart. In Chapter 9, I calculate my BP stress zone level and list some ways I use to manage my BD and other disorders.

CHAPTER 2

# My just another bipolar story

I WANT TO MAKE IT clear this is my story, and no one else has helped me write this story of my life; I take full responsibility for its content.

In many ways, my story is just another bipolar story with two notable exceptions. It is difficult to tell my story of living with bipolar (BD) without including my brother Stu. Throughout this workbook, I will refer to both my brother and me as we. We are now both over 75 years old, born about a year apart, and share many things in common, including a diagnosis of BD but not until around midlife.

Because I needed to account for over 75 years, I like to think of my life as having over a dozen stages. Separating my story into stages made it easier for me to organize and tell my story in chronological order. I also used what I call placeholders to help me segment my story chronologically because I lost my place often.

Chapter 2 is my story, the many emotional challenges, and setbacks both my brother and I experienced, like many other people with BD. People do not need to read my story to use the Bipolar WAVES Chart, but it may encourage people with BD to decide to find help early on and not wait until mid-life.

So, the first exception is I have a brother Stu with BD, and we did not get effective treatment until midlife or until about 50 years old.

Another exception that makes my life unique; I lived in a state of amnesia for over four decades, starting in my early 20's.

# Stage 1 Life on the Farm

My brother Stu and I were brought up on a small farm in the early '40s in New England (NE). I was fascinated with nature from an early age. One day I came across a large ant hill on the side of a sand pile near the barn. I could see all the rooms and tunnels and how the tiny ants all worked together to bring food into the nest. I wondered if someone, maybe a giant, was looking down on me and thinking, look at all those little people all running around; they don't even know we are watching them. My father even noticed the anthill as he walked by one day. I returned the next day to discover the anthill was gone, and only a few ants were running around without a home.

The next memory I have on the farm, my father was driving a tractor. Stu and I were on the back of the tractor. A lime spreader was towed behind the tractor, and clouds of lime dust were everywhere. Then I remember both my brother and me seeing my father sitting up in bed; he was talking to us, I knew it was important, but I could not understand what he was saying to us.

The next thing I remember, I watched two old ladies get out of a car in our driveway. They were dressed in heavy winter coats, and they both carried large pocketbooks over their arms. I thought they were just visiting us.

Then it was summertime, and a local farmer in an old pickup truck pulled into our yard. The man got out of the truck and spoke to us; he said, "I am sorry your father died of a heart attack." I ran back to the house, and I asked my mother if our father had died of a heart attack. She was at the kitchen sink; she turned around and told me he did die and was buried in the small cemetery just above our farm.

After our father died, our grandmother and her sister stayed with us while our mother worked uptown. Our home life became very stressful for our entire family. My father's death was just the start of our dysfunctional family life.

My mother's mother, Grammy, and her sister, whom we called Aunt Maddie, moved in with us to stay. I thought they would both move out, but that was just my wish and not my reality. We also had an older brother, Harold, who was about six years older than us. My brother Stu became my Aunt Maddie's favorite, and Harold was my mother's pride and Joy.

Our mother suddenly became a widow at 40 years old with five dependents and a farm to maintain. It was very confusing because I only learned our father passed away a year after our father died of a heart attack. I thought my father was going to return; I had no closure. We put a daisy chain on our father's grave every year around Father's Day.

My father's death was just the start of our dysfunctional family life. My brother Stu became my Aunt Maddie's favorite, and Harold was my mother's pride and Joy.

A teenager moved in down the street and wanted to play with me; after a few weeks, he coaxed me into the barn, pulled my pants down, and touched my genitals. Another time he pulled down my pants and told me to lie down and put his mouth on my genitals. That day I told him I would tell my mother. He visited the farm several times, but I stayed away from him. I was upset and afraid of him, but I needed the attention until he molested me, then I felt betrayed and angry.

After my father died, I felt very stressed about everything. The farm became more of a burden after our septic tank went bad. Then our source of water went bad to the farmhouse; we needed to get clean water. Before we drilled a well, we would drive to a place where natural spring water came right out of the side of a hill. We filled up huge jugs of water right from the spring. Then we needed to drill a well to get a good source of drinking water for the farmhouse.

I remember a man came to the farm; he picked up two sticks from the ground. With just a stick in each hand, he walked around until both the sticks pointed to the ground, then he told us to dig the well only at that exact spot. After drilling several hundred feet down, they hit a source of pure good clear water. Well, after the water douser located a source of water, an artesian well with two sticks, I did not question how he did it; it just worked out well, get the pun.

My brother and I had symptoms and behavior patterns of BD at a very young age. Without a father, I became moodier and more prone to have fits of anger. I was constantly being harassed and shamed for my behavior; I could not change without some professional help. No one protected me from criticism, especially Aunt Maddie.

When we were about ten years old, Stu and I camped in the woods by ourselves. I loved to camp; I felt independent and away from my chaotic home life. Stu didn't like camping, but I convinced him to go with me anyway. Sometimes on a hot summer day, I escaped to the top of a hill where I spent the day watching hawks as they soared effortlessly just below the white puffy clouds. I came home when I heard the dinner cow bell.

I felt alone and abandoned from a very young age. Spending time in nature was my way of escaping the realities of my life. I used my time spent outdoors without criticism from my Aunt Maddie. Mother Nature became my therapy, my escape from the verbal abuse from my family. I was not physically abused, but my family treated me unfairly. Stu was always right in my aunt's eyes. I was always moody and different, told not to feel that way and not be so sensitive about everything.

We had farmhands to do the chores, but after a few years, my mother could not even afford a farmhand. Harold and our mother were left to do most of the heavy farm work. Our grandmother and Aunt Maddie did not do any farm work. Stu and I fed the chickens and gathered eggs. Harold did most of the milking of the cows and cleaning out the stalls. Most people don't know how difficult and time-consuming milking a cow can be. In the summer, we had to hire help to harvest the hay and put bales of hay in the hayloft.

We grew all kinds of vegetables, and our mother canned many of the crops for the winter. Our grandmother and Aunt Maddie did not drive, so our mother had to cart them around to doctor's appointments.

Life on the farm was very hard for my mother and Harold, but we had everything we needed to be self-sufficient. Stu and I were too young to do most of the heavy work, so we had the freedom to build forts in the woods and go fishing down at the local pond. I loved the sense of freedom and peace; on the farm is where I learned to love and respect nature.

In the spring, I loved to see crystal clear water flow down the stream past our farmhouse. I watched the meadows come alive with hundreds of different plants, flowers, bees, and butterflies.

Without our father, the farm was in disrepair and required major work. Our mother worked the farm and a full-time job for six years after our father died, and then it became too much work for her to keep up. Harold found a job at a local chicken farm. My brother and I were too young to operate the farm equipment.

We lived a very frugal lifestyle; we only had enough money for the bare essentials; we didn't even own a TV. I learned to fix things like a broken bike I found in the barn, but it didn't even have rubber tires; we rode our only bike on the bare rims. Stu became the destroyer, and I became the fixer. We always had good food, a warm house, and clothes on our backs. All we had were a few pairs of dungarees, a few t-shirts, warm boots, a winter coat, and a suit and tie for church and special occasions.

We were required to go to church every Sunday, but I did not believe in organized religion, period. I remember confronting the pastor when I was about eleven and asking him, "Why can't we speak directly to God?" He told me in a stern voice, "You just need to believe in the church teachings."

I was upset that the church constantly asked our mother for money. I felt we needed the money more than the church. I did not believe in the church teachings. I didn't know what I believed in, but I did love the outdoors and nature. I guess my belief in nature was becoming my religion.

## Stage 2 Our teenage years
After our mother sold the farm, she bought a large white house in town; I called it a white elephant. The house was white and too big to maintain. We bought a big Black and White (B&W) TV for my grandmother and Aunt Maddie to watch soap operas all day long.

One of my first unforgettable experiences, after we moved uptown, was at a local small print shop. We hung out at a print shop after school on days when the weather was cold and rainy. One day the printer had a large box of negatives delivered to his shop. He started to develop very large Black and White (B&W) pictures from WW II negatives. The printer told us the pictures were from Germany from WW II, and some pictures were of the Holocaust. These were not just a few pictures but 100s of very large pictures that showed the grotesque images of the war. These were not small 4 x 6-inch pictures but large, the size of a big magazine page. Some pictures showed piles of rotting corpses and men, women, and children in line to die in Nazi gas chambers. Every time I went back to the print shop, the printer had more gruesome and horrific pictures of the war. After several more visits, I never went back to the print shop, but the images were forever burned into my mind.

I had a recurrent nightmare of one picture of a German SS soldier standing on the backs of men, women, and children as they lie face down in a long trench. He was shooting them in the back with a pistol.

I could not deny these pictures were actual pictures of real people being slaughtered by their own people. I was so confused; how could one man coerce a nation to allow such horrific acts against their own people. The pictures haunted me for years after I first saw the realities of war. I saw how pure evil could result in millions of people killed in the cruelest and most inhumane ways imaginable.

After we moved uptown, I lost the sense of freedom and peace I experienced on the farm. Stu quickly made friends and hung out with several kids around town. Of course, we all started to smoke cigarettes and meet other troubled teens. I was more of a loner and loved to hang out in the woods with other kids.

## Greg becomes my best friend

I met a kid named Greg, and he became my friend shortly after we moved uptown. We spent our time hanging out in the woods, along the railroad tracks, and at the junkyard. I quickly became best friends with Greg; he lived only two streets over from our house. We both got paper routes, and in the winter, we would walk three miles in the bitter cold to deliver newspapers along our paper routes out of town. On very cold days, we would stop at the last house on our paper route and talk to the old lady until we warmed up to head back home. She had an old coal stove that heated her house to over 80 degrees, even on the coldest winter day.

Summers, we would ride our bikes on the paper route; each of us would take one side of the street and then ride back our bikes along the railroad tracks, hang out around the ponds and streams on the way back home. Greg was not as academic as his other brothers and sisters. I think that was one reason we got to be the best of friends.

Both Greg and I were the black sheep of our families. We were not good students and did not get recognition, but then again, we were lazy and had no direction in life. Greg's brothers and sisters all did well in school. I was criticized and ridiculed by my family for being moody and different.

After a few years, Stu began to party at one of his friend's houses. His friend's mother did not want kids riding around town with older kids and getting into trouble. One night, Stu got so drunk he blacked out. This was the first but not the last time Stu drank until he passed out from alcohol intoxication.

I continued to be an avid nature lover of outdoor activities, camping, hiking, canoeing, and just hanging out with the kids at the lake and along the railroad tracks.

I met a local guy named Joe at the pool hall, who lived about a mile out of town, and we hung out at the local junkyard. We began to smoke and learned to drive old cars up the dirt back roads around our farm. Anyone could get cigarettes from the cigarette machine at the junkyard just put a quarter in the slot, and out came a pack; you even got a penny back in the wrapper.

Joe was several years older than our crowd, but he had a car and could get liquor any time of the day or night. Joe became my role model, he could fix cars, and he had girlfriends in several towns. He had what you might call a one-way open relationship with many girls. I don't think they knew of his two-timing ways. Joe began to drink, drive drunk, buy beer any time day or night; of course, that is when everyone in our group started to drink hard liquor.

Both Stu and I had several undiagnosed disorders, including alcoholism, learning, personality, hoarding, anxiety, and other disorders, all operating under the major bipolar disorder.

Our home life was very chaotic and stressful because our mother became an alcoholic when we were in high school, and we had no father in our lives to discipline or guide us in our teenage years and beyond.

### What happened to my whistle?
One morning I woke up with severe pain on the left side of my face. The left side of my face was severely distorted as if someone pushed up my cheek into my face, and it was very painful. I went to the family doctor, and he had no idea what caused the deformity. He referred me to the Mass General Hospital in Boston. I got very upset, thinking I would die or may become severely disabled for the rest of my life. A few days later, we drove into the Mass General Hospital in Boston; a doctor took one look at my face and said I have Bell's Palsy. It is a facial paralysis caused by a virus infection of the nerves

in the side of my neck. He said there was no cure or treatment that would help. He told me it would hurt for maybe a year or more and may get better after time. I was relieved that I would not die, but I must live with my face deformed in my teen years and possibly for the rest of my life.

My smile was very crooked and very noticeable, and when I tried to smile, it turned into a weird smirk. I could not even whistle. After a while, I thought people saw me as a weirdo, so I stopped smiling altogether.

The first year I felt very abandoned and lost within the family. I felt no one cared about my pain. I was very self-conscious of my smile and knew I had to cover it up. I was very self-conscious because it was very noticeable. I was afraid I would be ridiculed even further if I said how painful it was for me.

## I felt my father guiding me

I felt my father abandon me even though I knew he died of a heart attack years ago. Sometimes I would sense that he was guiding me and helping me in bad times. I would call my father my spirit guide. Maybe I felt my father was the only one in the family that truly loved me, and of course, he was gone.

I had a girlfriend in high school, her name was Martha, but my relationship with her was at times rocky. My drinking and moody behavior interfered with having a close relationship with her. I'm afraid to say that at times I mistreated Martha as well as other friends. I did not physically abuse her or other people but was moody and had a quick temper when I felt rejected by anyone. I am afraid I treated Martha like I felt my family treated me.

I invited Martha and her friends to my birthday party at our house. The girls arrived, and we had friendly conversations about school.

The guys arrived after a few beers, and the conversation became crude, rude and vulgar; all the girls got up and left within an hour. I got so drunk I blacked out on the kitchen floor. Stu considered calling the cops, but we were all underage. By now, both Stu and I had blackouts from alcohol; we later learned this was a major sign of alcoholism.

Our mother was drunk before the party even started and went up to bed. After my birthday party disaster, I did not invite anyone I did not know well to visit our house.

Throughout high school, our crowd drank and became juvenile delinquents, so to speak. We were out-of-control teenagers who came and left home as we pleased after we got our driver's licenses. Just a few weeks after Stu got his driver's license, Stu crashed our family car racing his friend. He didn't even get a speeding ticket. Our mother had to drive around town in Stu's old Ford coupe. I was severely criticized for not helping Stu repair our family car.

## I found my 1st love on Nantucket

Harold found a job in the summer as a cook, and I started to work as a dishwasher at the same well-known restaurant on Nantucket. Our mother encouraged us to get out of our hometown summers to stay out of trouble. For the next two summers, Harold, Stu, and I got jobs at the same restaurant on Nantucket. The following year we all had cars, not the best situation for out-of-control teenagers. Stu was a wild and crazy kid racing cars and finding wild parties with the Nantucket yacht club crowd.

I found my first love on Nantucket after meeting her at a beach party. She was visiting a family on the other side of the island. Her name was Maria, and I fell for her after our first kiss. She lived in Boston, and I wanted to see her during the winter.

After graduating from high school, I didn't know what to do with my life. Our mother enrolled me in a state college; behind my back, I told her I had no desire to go to college. I was lazy and wanted to skip college and find a fun job on Cape Cod.

I wanted to date Maria in Boston on my days off. I found a job all right on Cape Cod but ended up working seven days a week in a dirty, downright stinking kitchen. The boss introduced me to Tommy; he was about 30 years old. Tommy is Puerto Rican and has a badly deformed leg but was very friendly and kind to everyone. The boss treated Tommy like dirt.

Then I met my roommate Jake. He was a real mean-looking man, maybe 6"2 inches tall and 350 lbs. I can tell you one thing you don't want to mess with Jake; he looks like a real mean dude, and he had the scars to prove it. I can only imagine if he went into a rage, he could throw a refrigerator at you. It was the first time I got to know anyone Black, and I was glad he was kind and protective toward me.

I was the only one with a car, so every Saturday night, my roommate Jake and Tommy went to a hidden all-night club back in the woods on Cape Cod. I was underage, but Tommy knew the owners of the club. I had a dark tan and could almost fit in with the crowd, but I was underage.

The club was hidden deep in the pine barons of Cape Cod. They called it a club, but it was just a wild and lawless bar; many fights never saw a cop. Jake told me to watch out because most of the guys carried knives. Most nights, several fights would break out, and they would be pushed out the front door into the parking lot to finish the fight; the band kept on playing. I was much younger than most guys at the club. A few times, some guy would want to start a fight with me, but Jake was very protective. All Jake needed to do was walk over and ask me, "Is this guy bothering you?" Conflict resolved.

Mostly Black and Puerto Rican people came to the club, and everyone knew how to drink all night long. The band would play non-stop all night, and the dance floor was so crowded I could not turn around to get a drink at the bar. The beat of Rhythm & Blues (R&B) music was so soulful; the band had everyone up dancing, young, old, Black, and Brown. By midnight no one was sitting down; everyone was on the dance floor. Even Tommy, with his badly deformed leg, danced all night long; it was a no-judgment zone.

At first, I was very self-conscious, but Tommy eventually coaxed me into dancing with a women friend of his in the back of the bar. Surprisingly by the end of the summer, I actually liked to dance to R&B music; it made me forget all my problems for more than just a few hours. We came back to the restaurant at dawn and got a few hours of sleep. We were all hung over on Sunday after our all-nighter, but our boss never said a word.

At the end of the summer, we got stopped by the police coming back from the bar. Tommy and Jake were dead drunk in the back seat. A few days after I got home, I got a notice from the DMV. I lost my driver's license for a year for underage drinking. I was lucky they could have given me a DUI. It was a summer from hell, and I decided to start college in the fall. I did not get a chance to see Maria in Boston all summer.

## Stage 3 Life in our college years
A few days after I got back from Nantucket, I packed up, and then my mother drove me to college. I found my small room in the dorm, and I began my freshman year of college. Kids warned me it was a difficult college, and many kids did not graduate. I was concerned because I did not have the best grades in high school, and some of the kids had top honors in their high school graduating class.

The entire freshman class needed to stay in the dorm. Another disappointment, I lost my driver's license for a year, so I could not see Maria in Boston, an hour's drive from the college. A few days later, I met my roommate; he was a short kid with a big brain. He graduated first in his class from a local, very wealthy town around Boston.

The Dean of the college talked to our freshman class at the start of the first semester. He said, look to your right, then look to your left; only one of you will graduate. I was very worried because I was not the best and brightest in the class. How could I compete with all the smart kids?

College was very stressful. I could not study in the dorm. Kids went wild without parental supervision. My roommate was up all-night visiting kids all over the dorm. Somehow, he was getting A's on most of the courses; I was determined to graduate and decided to go to the library right after dinner to study until it closed at 11 PM.

I swear, my roommate never studied even one hour a night, and he aced most of the exams. The word got out from the upperclassmen; the sophomore year was much harder than the freshman year. I think if they had told me that when I first arrived at college, I might have dropped out after the first exam. Well, I am kidding because I was determined to graduate.

At the end of the first semester, about half the class dropped out or flunked out. I had the advantage of going to many all-night drinking beach parties on Nantucket and the wild all-night club on Cape Cod. I did not need to risk graduation for a few dumb parties. Besides, I could never find a better club band than the one hidden in the pine barons of Cape Cod.

The cold war with Russia was becoming very dangerous, with so many nuclear warheads ready to be fired at the East Coast. President

Eisenhower, nicknamed Ike, was the top General during WW II. I remember he went to the concentration camps after the war. I saw a picture of him with the troops at one of the concentration camps. Of course, I remembered those horrific B&W prints at the print shop of the Holocaust. I respected Ike because all the troops respected his honesty and leadership.

When he left office in 1961, he gave a speech on live TV to the American people. He warned the American people that what he called the Military-Industrial Complex (MIC) could become so powerful and be a risk to our country. I thought it was very odd at the time because he was the top commander during WW II.

College life went on; I was studying 6 hours a night in the library. Stu went to a party school in Boston. At 18, I registered for military service and got an official draft card that could draft me into the Army. I was fortunate because college students had a waiver from being drafted into the Army. Several kids went into the Navy and Marines to avoid being drafted into the Army.

Without a car, I could not date Maria in Boston. We basically drifted apart, but I still loved her. I met a kid with a car at college, and we went to Stu's drunken college parties in Boston a few times. Christmas and New Year were celebrated around our hometown with more keg parties and more drunken all-nighter parties.

## A Catholic becomes President

Politics became a popular topic when John F Kennedy (JFK) ran for President. He was a Senator from our home state of Massachusetts and was from a very Catholic and wealthy family. Some people thought a Catholic president would be beholden to the Vatican and not our country, but his charm, wit, and charisma quickly overcame many criticisms. Like many people, especially Catholics, he was what the country needed to inspire our nation to be more Patriotic.

I felt the freedom I had experienced on the farm, the freedom to attempt any project without the fear of war.

JFK won the election but had some obstacles to overcome when Russia attempted to place nuclear missiles in Cuba. Russia backed down, but with the reality of WW-III looming, I lost some of my optimism. I thought we would never be at war again.

Some people began to accuse JFK of being reckless and a danger to our national interests. Rumors circulated he was going to start armed conflicts with Cuba after the Cuban missile crisis. His famous speech when he asked, "Do not ask what your country can do for you but what you can do for your country," helped unify the entire nation.

We saw a Russian-built satellite orbiting the planet, and JFK announced we would land a man on the moon by the end of the decade.

After my miserable dirty job on Cape Cod, I decided to get a job on Nantucket during the summer. I got my driver's license back in the spring. I wanted to get away from college and party all summer. Both Stu and I found good-paying jobs working at a well-known restaurant on Nantucket. Our nights were spent at beach parties house parties with some very rich summer people. Harold was older and had his own circle of friends.

I did not want to admit it, but Nantucket lured me back; it was a thousand miles from civilization. There was only one traffic light on the entire island. People rode bicycles to the beach and around town. We spent our days off on the beach. Almost every night, you could find a beach party somewhere on the island. I guess I did fall in love with the natural beauty of the island. Nantucket became my spiritual oasis from life. I did not watch any TV the entire summer.

I forgot college, my severe depression and I am afraid the most important person in my life, my 1st love Maria.

I made a few friends from the restaurant, but I was more of a loner. I did crash almost every party on the Island, especially if there was a free keg of beer. I remember one lavish house party where the champagne flowed like water, and everything ended up in the pool, including most of the kids and all the patio furniture. I had sex with a few girls I met at beach parties on the island, but it was just sex, no real attraction. I was still deeply in love and maybe hopelessly in love with Maria.

I lived on very little money all through college and became very frugal. Stu made a lot of money as a waiter and went manic most of the summers. He was a risk-taker; he risked his life by racing old fast cars over the dirt roads and moors around the island.

## Our voyage around Nantucket

After a long night of drinking at a beach party, Stu and I had an idea to sail around Nantucket Island. Stu borrowed, well, took a very small sailboat from a member he met at the yacht club. Stu assured me the small sailboat was unsinkable. We started our voyage at 4 AM in the very small sailboat; we planned to sail nonstop around Nantucket. Without even getting a weather report, it was a very dangerous journey. Boston weather reports were practically useless anyway, never accurate.

We were both drunk and manic when we headed out but quickly sobered up by the time we arrived back at the restaurant 16 hours later. Our boss fired both of us on the spot but let us work until the end of the summer. After coming down from our high, on the high seas, I realized we both cheated deaths.

A few weeks later, a storm sank the little sailboat; all you could see was the mainmast sticking up out of water. We cheated death; if we capsized, the chances of survival in a very small sailboat were slim at best. The swells were four feet high, and if our sailboat capsized out in the open Atlantic Ocean, both captains would have gone down with the ship.

I felt my spirit guide was with us that day. I was brought up in a religious household and did not believe in organized religion, but I always believed in a higher power. Maybe my understanding of nature when just a kid taught me there must be a higher power that created everything I saw in nature and out in the universe.

Stu and I often recount the dangers of that voyage around Nantucket and other risks we took before we got properly treated for BD. Many times, I felt the presence of my father guiding me through difficult times. I called my father my spiritual guide; he was working a double shift that day to help us sail around the Nantucket Island.

## JFK's assassin shot on live TV

I was in a history class at college when a man came in and took our professor aside and whispered something in his ear. He turned white as a sheet and told us President Kennedy was killed in Dallas. We all left the classroom in disbelief.

I went home and was watching TV and saw his assassin, Oswald, shot on live TV while being transported to jail. Rumors spread to several other people who may have been involved in the crime of the century. Oswald was a man that may have ties to the criminal underworld. I guess I became suspect of the government's role in covering up the entire tragic event. We all witnessed Lyndon Johnson being sworn in as President on the Air Force One heading back to DC. I never liked Lyndon Johnson. He was more of a politician, and for a while, I thought he might have been involved with the assassination of JFK because he was from Texas.

Other conspiracy theories began to surface; he was shot in retaliation for JFK confronting Russia? I saw Oswald, his assassin, being buried without being proven guilty. I lost some confidence and the feeling our country was not safe from threats from abroad and at home. After President Johnson ordered the bombing of Vietnam, I lost trust in him and in our government.

Thanksgiving weekend, all the kids were home from college, and we went down to the pool hall in town. I noticed the kid that sexually molested me on the farm playing pool with some young kids. I got very angry. I knew for sure was molesting kids from the pool hall. He was a lot older, but I wanted to lure him outside and beat the living crap out of him. When I get angry, my adrenalin rises, and I get very strong, but I did not want an assault and battery charge for starting a fight.

I set up a date with Maria in Boston on our Thanksgiving break. Maria was living with two roommates, so we could not make out at her place. I did not have any money to have dinner at a restaurant, so we parked along the Charles River. Our date did not go as planned. I think I was too stressed out to even talk to her. She seemed distant and did not want to make out. I was disappointed, but I still loved her, maybe a lot more than I wanted to admit.

College was a very traumatic time in my life, and I had a very difficult time completing courses to graduate. I was close to having a nervous breakdown and almost flunked out of college several times. I did not know I had a reading and writing disability since grade school. I had to study 6 hours a night to pass courses; I was living on the edge of a cliff, ready to jump off after just one more stressful situation. I also had violent outbursts of anger and a moody personality at a very young age. If I had a psychiatric evaluation in college, I would have been placed under immediate psychiatric care.

My brother has a very outgoing personality and often had lasting bouts of mania followed by very severe depressions. I believe he has a diagnosis of BD I, and I have BD-II. My mood swings were more hypomanic, and my depressions more agitated and moodier. Episodes of BD and alcoholism destroyed my relationships with guys, gals, family members, and co-workers.

During the summer, Greg got a girl pregnant at a party in our hometown. His father gave him an ultimatum, marry the girl or go into the service. I stood by while Greg made his decision to join the service rather than be drafted into the Army. The pregnant girl went to a home for girls to have the baby.

I could not contact Greg after he got assigned to military bases all over the globe. Rumors circulated the Army was considering drafting more kids right out of high school into the Army. I was thankful I was in college and planned to stay in college. College kids got a draft deferment until they graduated from college. Some kids made college a career just to avoid the draft.

## The Civil Rights Act

President Johnson signed the Civil Rights Act in 1964. In 1965, there was a march in Selma, Alabama. Dr. King and 600 other civil rights activists led the march to protest Blacks had the basic right to vote. People in the march faced brutal attacks by state troopers. John Lewis, a future congressman from Georgia, was one civil rights leader that marched in the protests.

I was in college during all the protests and conflicts in the south during the '60s. I was struggling to pass finals and other college courses. I was still studying in the basement of our college library, 1000 miles from the civil rights marches and conflicts.

I did not even have a TV at the time. I was working on Nantucket summers, and we did not have one Black or minority working at the restaurant. Most of the summer help was college kids, and some were very wealthy. I do think many White people in the north did not understand the hardships of many Black people. I, along with most students in our college or on Nantucket, did not talk politics.

After working on Cape Cod with Tommy and Jake after high school, it did give me a different view of race relations in our nation. Minorities did have a much harder time getting and keeping jobs compared to many White people.

## *My tragic breakup with my 1st love*

After taking my final exams, I needed to forget my stressful life at college. I was lured back into finding a summer job on Nantucket. I arrived on Nantucket without a job and stayed at Stu's place. A few days later, I found a good job as a short-order cook. Stu and his friend started a car wash business on Nantucket. I found a place to stay at a small guest house in town. The landlady let me stay on the back porch of her guest house for only $5 a week.

I made very good money, but I worked seven days a week from 7 AM until 3 pm with no day off. Stu often said our Nantucket's lifestyle was not real, and leaving the island was like going back into the real world again. As the summer wound down, I became a little lonely and looked forward to seeing Maria in Boston after returning from Nantucket.

I got a notice from college; I needed to be in class only two days after leaving Nantucket. That meant I would have no time to be with Maria in Boston before classes began at college.

I made a hasty decision to invite Maria to Nantucket. We never did have sex, and I wanted the intimacy and closeness we had together.

I wanted to go to the beach with her after work, have sex and make out with her all night long under the stars.

I was delighted when she agreed to come to Nantucket, but soon after she agreed to visit me, I had a bad feeling; it was a bad decision. She arrived, and things went from bad to worse. She was staying at a house with ten waitresses from swanky colleges that did not treat her with kindness.

I was working from 7 AM until 3 PM every day and was exhausted after working every day all summer. The weather turned cold, and then a frigid cold front came down from Canada. I was freezing cold sleeping on the back porch of the guest house. I woke up with a sore throat and a throbbing headache. I was feeling sicker all day at work.

One night we found an isolated shack on the other side of the island. As we began to make out, she questioned if I had lost a testicle. Of course, I immediately knew she was having sex with some guy and became very angry. On the drive back to town, Maria told me she loved me, and I replied in a jealous rage, "I don't love you."

A few days later, we both were very sick with a high fever. I went to a doctor and got antibiotics and verbally criticized her for not going to the doctor with me. The next morning, we were scheduled to leave the island on the first ferry to the mainland. Stu's jeep was in line to get on the first ferry to go back to the mainland. We arrived at the dock too late to get the first ferry. Maria kept on telling me she just wanted to go home. In a fit of anger, I told her to go home with Stu. I watched her leave with Stu on the first ferry.

I left on the next ferry and arrived home several hours later. I immediately called Maria in Boston; her mother answered the phone. She told me in a stern voice, "Maria does not want to talk to you."

I started college classes two days after returning from Nantucket and had no time to visit Maria in Boston, an hour's drive from the college. A few weeks after I started the fall semester, Maria sent me a Dear John letter formally ending our relationship.

My state of mind was overcome with grief and sadness over losing the girl I had loved since a teenager. I could not sleep or study, the images of her making love to him were tormenting me both day and night, and I questioned if she was telling me the truth. I had to find out what was going on. Was she dating this guy for months and never mentioned it to me?

Late one night, I could not sleep and decided to visit Maria at her apartment in Boston. I arrived at her apartment at 2 AM and knocked on the door. I heard her say, "He is here." I kept on knocking harder; I needed to know the truth. All of a sudden, a guy came out and closed the door behind him. He said we needed to talk. I was in a state of shock and was weak in the knees as we went down to an all-night diner to talk.

He told me he had been dating Maria for a while and he loved her. Somehow, I was not angry at him but felt betrayed and emotionally heartbroken by Maria. I told him I thought we were meant to be together. At the end of our conversation, I told him I needed to talk to Maria.

On the way back to college, I felt isolated and so all alone; I had no one to share my story with. Greg was far away in some outpost on the other side of the world, but I did find out the truth, my truth, Maria was dating this guy long before she visited me on Nantucket. I felt she was cheating on me and did not want to tell me she was in a serious relationship with a guy in Boston.

I decided not to contact Maria any longer because I felt she betrayed me; the trust was forever broken. A few months later, I ended up having a life-threatening BD episode that put me into a state of amnesia or repressed memory.

I did not want to admit it at the time, but I did verbally abuse her after learning she was having sex with some guy. All my insecurity and inferiority issues came to the surface all at the same time. The extreme stress of college, my feelings of abandonment since a child, the heartbreak and pain of rejection, and the effects of my untreated BD illness ended our relationship forever.

In order to survive the most tragic event in my life, I needed to forget how badly I mistreated her. I also had to block out another truth; I was to blame for the entire incident. The end result of all these tragic events happening all at the same time put me in a state of amnesia.

The workbook is designed to identify these types of life-threatening events of people with BD. Identifying life-threatening events or situations is one reason I have become a strong advocate for getting treatment early on. Anyway, my jealous rage and intense anger toward Maria destroyed my relationship with her forever.

As I am looking back, I believe if I had the support of a good psychiatrist and was treated effectively for my BD and personality issues, I might have weathered the storm and saved our relationship. Maria was not at fault. I was responsible for the entire breakup. The only way I may have survived my crisis was by getting an emergency intervention.

I don't know if amnesia is a correct psychiatric diagnosis, but I hope you get the idea. The more psychiatric term might be some other disorder, but I use the term in a state of amnesia to describe the time I was in a state of not consciously remembering the tragic events.

I call the time after I came out of amnesia my past period. I believe my past traumatic recollections of the breakup with Maria and childhood abuse will never end and will require an ongoing process of healing over time. As time goes on, my past recollections of the tragic events of the breakup with Maria have become much less frequent and stressful. Now I believe the childhood abuse I endured from about the age of 5 is a more significant factor in my life.

These types of traumatic, life-threatening events don't need to happen. Perhaps the workbook may help people better understand the incredible mental stress that can occur during a life crisis involving the loss of a loved one in combination with BD.

This unstable BD lifestyle in our youth and college resulted in over 20 years of living a life of reckless behavior, severe stress, alcoholism, driving when drunk, blackouts, abusive behavior, verbal abuse, neglect, and in my case, and the many painful past recollections after I *awoke from amnesia.*

It was the height of the cold war with Russia, and I could not contact Greg; he was on active duty for months at a time. I felt everyone in my life was leaving me. If Greg had been around during this traumatic period in my life, I might have weathered the storm and not have gone into a state of amnesia after the breakup.

My life started to become a psycho-thriller that even a good psychiatrist would need decades to unravel, and that is what happened after I went into a state of amnesia. Our chaotic childhood, teen, and college years were just the beginning of another 25 years of struggling with bouts of depression followed by mood swings of mania. It was not a good way to start our adult lives with careers and family obligations in front of us.

I often look back and wonder how my life would be different if I had the support of my friend Greg or people in our Bipolar Disorder Support or BDS group. Of course, I would not discover the bipolar disorder support (BDS) group for another 30 years.

When I met unstable young people at our BDS group, I strongly urged young people to become and stay stable. I am sure some members of the BDS group get tired of my beating the drum to find a good psychiatrist and become stable early on in life.

## Stage 4 Life with Careers and Family

Our carefree but chaotic younger years ended with my brother Stu marrying his high school sweetheart, starting a family, and beginning a new stressful but successful sales career.

I barely graduated from college and then faced being drafted into the Army. Stu's wife Denise got pregnant, and he became ineligible to be drafted into the military.

Maybe seeing those horrific pictures of the Holocaust when I was only 12 years old convinced me I could not go to war. After graduation, I traveled to the West Coast with a couple in a VW Beetle and found work that gave me a draft deferment. I found a job in Seattle, and the stress began just a few months after starting the job. The weather was dismal, along with my mood.

The following spring, I woke up to see the sunlight coming through my bedroom window for the first time since the fall. I went out on the pouch and started talking to the girl next door. We could see the snow-capped mountain of Mt Rainier in the distance. For over six months, if it was not raining, the sky was overcast. I felt trapped and close to having a mental breakdown, but I was thankful I had a military deferment.

I became friends with a guy at work named Shawn from Ireland, and he said Ireland had similar weather. He was looking for a job in Southern CA. I was envious of his situation because he didn't need a draft deferment because he was not a US citizen. He planned to save several thousand dollars and buy a small farm in Ireland. The summer weather was mostly sunny; I joined a tennis club and played several times a week. I planned to join a bowling league in the fall.

In the fall, I became seriously depressed. I started to drink weekends at sleazy bars and learned to pick up women for one-night stands at seedy motels. I would go to the bars with my married co-workers to pick up women. I saw guys cheating on their wives and their wives cheating on their husbands. I had a very grim view of marriage and ever finding a good, trustworthy mate. Some nights I would cry on the way back to my apartment as the Seattle rain poured down on the windshield of my car.

At this point, I did not know I had a life-changing event just a few years earlier. I had no conscious memory of emotionally and verbally abusing Maria. I was drowning my sorrow in liquor and sex with women that also had drinking and probably serious emotional problems.

### I wanted to comfort her, but I did not

I picked up a woman at a Country & Western (C&W) bar, and we went to a cheap motel. She told me she wanted to drive her car to the motel because she was cheating on her husband. We had sex, and I was too drunk to drive home.

In the morning, she was sad and crying, and I asked her if she was ok. She replied, "My husband does not want me anymore" I wanted to hold her and tell her everything would be ok, but I did not hold her, and I did not believe everything was going to be ok. We left the motel without even saying goodbye.

I was not sympathetic to her pain and feelings of betrayal and rejection. Now I know I unconsciously remembered my sad and tragic breakup with my 1st love Maria. Her comment, "My husband does not want me anymore," was what I felt Maria was saying to me during our breakup. I think the most painful part of our breakup was when Maria would not talk to me. I did feel she just told me, "Go away, I don't want you anymore."

After my tragic breakup with Maria, I entered a state of amnesia; I was incapable of expressing my true emotions. My intense grief and sorrow were buried deep in my mind in a case of amnesia.

My friend Shawn from Ireland found a good job in sunny Southern California. He invited me down to visit him, and I came back to Seattle even more depressed with my life.

## Massive troop buildup in Vietnam

Reports of the Army was drafting kids right out of high school, it was true. Some college students burned their draft cards in protest, but the government threatened to deny them college deferments.

Reports of heavy bombing raids in North Vietnam further raised my fear I could be drafted at any time. The military was looking for anyone that could hold a rifle. Reports of kids being sent to the front lines within days of being drafted made me anxious and quite depressed. What would I do if I got a draft notice to serve in the Army?

One nightly TV broadcast showed a B 52 carpet bombing targets on the ground for miles. I knew thousands of innocent people on the ground were killed because we could not distinguish the enemy from the general population. The Pentagon told the press almost 400,000 troops were now in the war zone, and just a matter of time until we would declare a certain victory.

Mohammed Ali, the greatest boxer of all time, became a draft resister and lost his heavyweight title belt and his ability to fight professionally. I had to admire his courage because he probably would not be sent to the front lines. I remembered back in 1964 when he won the heavyweight title, and he was about my age.

Martin Luther King (MLK), a civil rights leader, began to protest the war because the military was drafting poorer Black teens. He was right; many Black kids were drafted right after graduation from high school as other kids, including myself, got college and job deferments.

I remember one civil rights leader commented it was only 100 years ago we fought the Civil War, and our government was still mistreating Blacks. He was right; the Civil War started around 1865, not that long ago.

## A real UFO incidence in Canada?

A coworker from Montreal, Canada, mentioned a story about a UFO that crashed in the ocean near Shag Harbor in Canada. He thought the crash had something to do with the Vietnam War and submarines. The story caught my interest; we followed the story.

He heard several people report a plane crashed near Shag Harbor, Canada. At first, the plane was reported to have crashed into the water near Shag Harbor. I do not believe many UFO stories, but the Canadian Navy officially referred to the object as a UFO. There were several other UFO sightings in the area at the time.

I did not believe any UFO stories from the US, but when the Canadian officials called the craft a UFO, it caught my attention. Several stories seemed to confirm there was a UFO on the bottom of the harbor, and the naval ships monitored the UFO for several days. Then a report came out; another UFO was seen near the first UFO and apparently repaired the downed UFO. Then both UFOs came out of the water and flew away.

This story seemed to be an actual UFO encounter because our government was not involved, and no one covered up the incident. Our military most likely would have explained the incident as two submarines that mysteriously flew out of the water back up into the universe. I do not know why our government will not tell the public the truth about UFOs. When our military covers up real UFO sightings, then the credibility of all departments of our government is suspect.

I thought of Greg and wondered if he was in combat in Vietnam. Did this incident have something to do with the massive buildup of troops in Vietnam? For obvious reasons, I believed reports from Canadian officials over our own.

## Stu's lavish lifestyle in the fast lane

Stu had a career as a salesman in a well-known fortune 500 company, but his stresses began to accumulate after starting a family and dealing with family obligations. Stu's high-stress, high-paying job resulted in excessive spending sprees and then deep depressions. Shortly after he was married, he purchased cars, houses, and boats. He had years of living on the edge managing a career and family responsibilities. He drank to excess to medicate the stresses of his extravagant lifestyle and "treat" his BD mental illness.

Stu was kind enough to invite me to his place during the Christmas holidays, Stu's family always celebrated Christmas with gifts, good food plenty of drinks, and we all had a great time. He bought a small farm with a beautiful farmhouse. His wife, Denise, fixed it up to look picture-perfect. Stu talked about starting a sailing club and was looking for a boatyard to convert to a yacht club.

I started to feel very sad about how my life was going; here, Stu had a pretty wife, a nice house, and great kids. I wasn't even dating anyone and was afraid my company was going to go out of business at any time.

## A volunteer Doctor tells us what is happening in Vietnam

I met a doctor along with several other guys at the bar during a Christmas party. He gave us a reality check about what was actually happening in Vietnam. He volunteered to be a medical doctor on the front lines for six months. The doctor described the horrors of innocent Vietnamese men, women, and children being killed in their villages. He described food being taken from Vietnamese families for little or no reason. Food was taken even if our troops just suspected the villagers aided the North Vietnamese (NV).

He called the military and contractors corrupt; many were making millions by selling pot, alcohol, and prostitution to the troops. He said one high-ranking officer told him the military and civilian contractors did not want the war to end.

Back in high school, I respected President Eisenhower; they called him Ike. At the time, I thought he would make a great father, the father I never had; I was looking for anyone to look up to at that time in my life. I remember he talked about the Military-Industrial Complex (MIC) and how they could become too powerful. I admired Ike and listened very carefully to his warning. I was only a teenager at the time and needed to carry my official draft card. Now I understood what he was warning us about; the MIC was real, and it was becoming too powerful.

Again, I was relieved I was not drafted because, from those horrific pictures of the Holocaust, I knew atrocities were happening on both sides of the war. I did not know about the corruption and crimes against humanity or how high up the command it went.

## I found a job in New Jersey
The work in Seattle was ending, and I got a job offer in South Jersey with a draft deferment. I packed up my stuff and drove 3000 miles to New Jersey. After a month on the job, I could tell my new job was worse than my previous job, but I had a draft deferment. I went to a Christmas party at my new supervisor's home. Everyone was very friendly, and I made it a priority not to get drunk.

## The Tet Offensive
After the Christmas party, I did not find any joy in my life. I spent New Year's Eve alone in my apartment. A few weeks after New Year's, an all-out attack by the Viet Cong (VC) was across South Vietnam. This included security areas around Saigon and other military outposts across South Vietnam.

The news implied the attacks were the beginning of the end of the Vietnam War. The scope of the secret invasion was a major military victory for the VC. Apparently, guns, ammo, and other weapons of war were smuggled into Vietnam undetected by our military. The VC dressed in civilian clothes moved weapons and supplies right under the noses of our security forces. It was obvious at this point we were losing the war, and the VC was not going to surrender under any conditions.

## Martin Luther King was assassinated
Martin Luther King was assassinated, followed by JFK's brother Robert Kennedy. Demonstrations against the war continued, and the troop buildup was estimated to be almost 500,000 troops. The military promised a troop withdrawal starting in the summer.

President Johnson announced he would not seek another term, and Richard Nixon became our next President.

President Richard M. Nixon announced a new Vietnam policy called the Nixon Doctrine. This doctrine expected the Vietnamese military to fight for their own country. In November 1969, more than 260,000 anti-Vietnam war demonstrators marched on Washington, D.C., to peacefully protest the Vietnam War.

## Crimes against humanity., the My Lia Massacre

I did not want to believe the reports of American troops murdering unarmed Vietnamese people near the northern coast of South Vietnam. The story was front-page news around the world. A platoon entered one of the village's four hamlets. They were on a search and destroy mission. Instead of finding guerrillas, they found unarmed villagers, most of them women, children, and old men. They proceeded to set huts on fire and murdered some 500 unarmed civilians, including 50 children under four years old.

The myth we were fighting the communists for a just and noble cause evaporated into thin air. It was becoming clear we were not winning a victory over the Viet Cong.

I was astounded that the My Lia Massacre incident was covered up for more than a year. The graphic scenes and pictures of dead innocent men, women, and children were aired on TV for several weeks. I was ashamed and horrified our military was so cruel and sadistic. Like the horrific war crimes of WW II, the My Lia Massacre was indeed many crimes against humanity.

I had those graphic images of the Holocaust burned into my mind when I was only 12 years old. I wondered if there were more horrific stories hidden from the public. That volunteer doctor I met at a Christmas party told us atrocities were happening in Vietnam.

After the My Lia Massacre, I believe both the American people and the GIs did lose the will to fight. President Johnson was defeated and did not run for a second term. Many people at home treated the GI coming back from the war with anger and rage. I did not blame the troops; our military created a culture of hate toward the VC and the South Vietnamese people. Our troops were caught in the crossfire, so to speak; no one won the war.

I had my justification for avoiding the draft all along, but I had guilt and shame. I was a coward and did not actively protest the war. After listening to the volunteer doctors' firsthand knowledge of the atrocities, I did not have the courage to actively protest the war.

The press announced the VC body count almost every day on the nightly news. I sat on the couch and knew lies were told; we were not winning the war; at one point, we had 500,000 troops in Vietnam. The war was a waste of our young people's lives and our money on bombs, planes, and misery for everyone. It was reported over 30,000 GIs had died, and many more were disabled either physically or mentally.

Marvin Gay released his timely What's Goin On album. His words spoke volumes about how Black and Brown mothers and young kids suffered during the war. The words talked about the truth of how Black and Brown kids were only judged by their long hair and the color of their skin. The song was honest, and the message I got was, "War was not the answer; only love will conquer hate.".

Marvin was killed by his father and may have had other problems. Marvin's death was a tragic loss of a true artist. I could never have guessed he grew up in an abusive household.

### The moon landing was a positive event
On July 20, 1969, we landed on the moon. I was in a severe depression and could not experience the excitement like my co-workers. I was still worried about being drafted into the military.

I did not go back to New England for Christmas. So, the '60s took me from four difficult years in college and then to four stressful years of work in Seattle and then back east to South Jersey.

At a 1970 New Year's Eve party with just a few people, I hardly knew we all got very drunk. I had hoped the '70s would be a better decade for everyone.

## Stage 5 Life in the '70s
I woke up on New Years' Day in someone's apartment with a colossal hangover and found a few glasses of tomato juice to bring myself back into reality. The '70s began with more massive protests against the Vietnam War.

In June of 1971, the New York Times published the Pentagon papers. The Pentagon sought to cover up the report, but the Supreme Court ruled in favor of giving first Amendment rights to the paper to release the report.

This paper exposed everything the doctor told us years earlier at a cocktail party in Seattle. The Pentagon lied about the success of the war effort. The killing of innocent men, women, and children was covered up by the high-level Pentagon brass. My suspicions the military did cover up misdeeds were true all along. Stu was also struggling with his BD illness.

Stu was also having problems with starting a family and holding down a very stressful job as a salesman for a Fortune 500 company.

He had three kids, a beautiful wife, real estate, sailboats, yacht club dues, and needed to live a very high lifestyle to keep up with his affluent co-workers. Yes, some people had high-paying jobs with Fortune 500 corporations but were expected to live very upscale lifestyles. Nice homes and encouraged to belong to golf clubs, to name a few of the expected upper-class lifestyles of the rich and not-so-famous.

Stu did not fit the ideal affluent dedicated company man profile. Stu was battling alcoholism and severe bouts of depression. When manic, he would buy houses, invest in real estate, race sailboats and start projects he could not finish. When depressed, he would abandon or not complete projects and eventually sought help but never found it. I had the same character flaws but didn't have the cash to afford as many expensive projects. You know we do call our serious mental issues just character flaws.

Work at my new job in South Jersey was hopeless, and within a year, the management closed the division, and I got a layoff notice. I went to a singles bar that weekend and was in a drunken blackout as I drove back to my apartment. The cops stopped me for drunk driving; I was sure I would lose my license and get a DUI, but the cops realized I was out of a job and gave me a break. They told me to park off the side of the road until morning, but if I did not, the police would go to my apartment and charge me with a DUI. I sobered up by the morning, drove back to my apartment, and went to bed. I woke up sometime in the late afternoon and realized all my money was gone. I had over a hundred dollars in my wallet, and I suspected bartenders and waitresses found a way for me to spend it all in one night. I needed to wake up to the fact I drank to reach a blackout state several times; I was a certified alcoholic. I justified my blackout; it was alright because I was out of a job.

## Our entire team was transferred to Texas

After finding another job in Philly, our entire team was transferred to Texas. Texas was just another place to drink all night at honky-tonk bars on weekends and pick up women for one-night stands.

By now, most of my co-workers were married with families. Some of my co-workers in Texas were very conservative family guys that did not openly cheat on their wives as far as I could tell. They invited all the members of our Philly team to their BBQs and gave us a real Texas welcome.

I was alone again to hang out at the Country and Western bars, but the social atmosphere was not like Seattle's free love scene. I was tired of the bar scene and was a very lonely and seriously troubled guy at this point in my life. I was so distraught and depressed. I would cry on the way back to my apartment. I had these bad spells, as I call them. I felt isolated, depressed, and very lonely for weeks at a time.

Yes, I knew I was depressed but also worried I had some deadly disease the doctors could not diagnose. I went to several doctors, but they could not find anything wrong with me. Now I know now I was struggling with several issues, namely abandonment, BD, amnesia, and alcoholism. I had serious abandonment issues from a young age. I had felt isolated and emotionally abused since childhood. After I entered a state of amnesia, I had an unconscious fear of getting emotionally close to any woman for fear I would face rejection again. But the most significant issue was not discovering and treating my BP. How would I ever recover from all my personal issues and live long enough to talk about them?

Without any warning, the company closed the plant in Texas. I was very upset with upper management. They transferred our entire team to Texas from Philly a year earlier. Our team members from

Philly bought new houses, cars, and put their kids in new schools. Within a year, we all lost our jobs and any respect for the company.

## Something was not right

I was hopelessly depressed, almost suicidal, and an alcoholic. I had no idea what was affecting my life. I never even met someone with a known serious mental illness, except my brother, and I just thought he just had several annoying character flaws.

Well, to clarify, I probably did know several people around our hometown that had some form of mental illness, but they never admitted it openly to our group of misfits and alcoholics.

Now I do remember a guy named Ziggy, but that's another story. Ziggy was a prime example of someone that needed to be in some sort of treatment early on. He was the kid we joked "He's crazy" behind his back, but no one offered to help him. At that point, we couldn't even help ourselves. As an advocate to get people with mental illness treatment early, he needed treatment of some kind of help years earlier.

Here I was, a young guy in the prime of my life struggling to keep a highly stressful job. I had a good job and a career in my chosen field, but something was not right with my life. I thought when I graduated from college, I would lead a more productive and happy life, but the stress of starting a new career in a new city became overwhelming.

I had another six-month assignment in Pittsburg, Pa, and then I moved back to Philly and collected unemployment benefits. After my unemployment benefits ran out, I found another dead-end job.

## I did not care if I lived or died

The new job was making me even more depressed, and at one point, I did not care if I lived or died. I don't know why I returned to Philly, but something told me that it was my place to settle down. Within six months, I was collecting unemployment benefits again. I just zoned out for several months, went to the park in the summer, and spent time in my apartment until winter arrived around November. After several months of living on unemployment benefits, I found myself broke and in a state of despair, even worse than depression. The military went on a lottery system, and I was not worried about the draft any longer.

My unemployment benefits were just about up, and I found another job at an employment agency. The entire country was in a steep downturn with high unemployment. Here I was trying to find other people jobs while I became very distraught and flat broke. I called employers all day long, trying to find someone else a job. This desperate frame of mind drove me to seek professional help. Perhaps I did have a deadly physical illness?

I went to another doctor a few blocks from my apartment. She ordered some lab tests. A few days later, she said my physical health was excellent and referred me to a psychiatrist. Several weeks went by, I was ashamed and in denial I had any type of mental illness. I had never even known anyone with a mental illness at the time except my brother Stu, and I thought he was just your average risk-taking maniac with several serious and annoying character flaws.

I had hoped when the stresses of college life ended, my life would be "Normal." Relationships went nowhere; I was depressed about everything in my life. I had very few dates, and after a few more bad dating experiences, I stopped looking for a mate or even a friend. Like my mother, I started to drink to excess, and life became intolerable. I did not even have the sexual energy or desire to hang out in sleazy bars looking for one-night stands with women any longer.

I was slowly sinking into a severe prolonged depression, and my boss noticed my moody and other bizarre and inappropriate behavior. It was at a holiday party, I was acting inappropriate, and after too many drinks, I was sure my co-workers were talking behind my back. I felt like an old car, broken down on the side of the road as my other "Normal" co-workers went speeding past me. They had good relationships, marriages, and "Normal" lifestyles. I was envious of a "Normal" happy couple in our office, leading a fairy tale lifestyle. Why couldn't I live the same fairy tale life?

At this point, I called the psychiatrist and got an appointment, but it was not for another month. I was in denial and did not want to admit it was a mental condition. I could not sleep or concentrate on anything, but it was not a physical illness; according to my doctor, my labs and vital signs were perfect, but I did not care if I lived or died.

I was not suicidal but knew I was spiraling down into a dark place no one wanted to enter. I was afraid I would never come out of this state of mind. Finally, I went to the psychiatrist, and he recommended group psychotherapy and treated me with Valium.

## I attended group psychotherapy sessions

Under my psychiatrist's recommendation, I attended a group psychotherapy session every week, but it was very expensive. I did not want to use my company's health insurance for fear they would discover I had a mental illness, so I paid out of pocket.

Now, this was a hard decision. I was frugal all my life, so I was desperate to feel better at any cost. I went to the first session, and after a few minutes, I was sure I was in the wrong group. The first person to speak was a young woman named Sabrina, and she told us she has schizophrenia. I did not believe her because she didn't act crazy. After the group session ended, I wanted to avoid Sabrina and quietly left the meeting room.

Several people admitted they were alcoholics. I reasoned I was not an alcoholic because I did not drink alone like my mother. In the next session, I questioned why I was in group psychotherapy with very mentally ill people? Several people had no jobs and lived with their parents. Many were severely depressed, but no one talked about having BD or other mental illnesses except Sabrina. Several people in the group mentioned they were on several medications, but the psychiatrist asked us not to disclose the names of our medications.

I called these sessions group psychotherapy because a psychiatrist was present to oversee the group, but he just observed and did not actively participate unless some conflicts came up. I found the group very intimidating, and I was very uncomfortable. I felt the psychiatrist was just looking on and judging my every word.

Before the next session, I told a woman I was taking Valium; I did ask her what meds she was taking. She told me, in a stern voice, "I cannot discuss my medications." I thought that perhaps I was right; everyone was on anti-psychotic meds for schizophrenia. That would explain why our psychiatrist did not want us to disclose our meds to people in the psychotherapy group.

At the next group psychotherapy session, I avoided talking to Sabrina again, even though she was honest, but her thoughts seemed bizarre and a bit mixed up and scattered. She told us she had thoughts that were not true. Then she told us she had hallucinations frequently and had no way to determine if they were real. At that point, I was very afraid I was schizophrenic. She then said, "I was reincarnated from a previous life. I was a peasant from ancient times and came back to live in this body".

I thought she really is insane, but I have heard people do remember a past life recollection, usually a few years after they arrive on this planet. I remembered a story of a young girl who told people she lived in another town in her past life. She visited the small town, and it was exactly how she described it. Now I began to listen to Sabrina with less skepticism and thought maybe she wasn't as crazy as I first thought. Perhaps was experiencing things outside the realm of our consciousness.

It showed how biased I was toward people with serious mental illness. Sabrina was being honest and told us exactly how life was treating her. She knew she had a serious mental illness and was trying to cope with life the best way she could. I did imagine someone with schizophrenia having very bizarre and crazy behavior. I had a stereotype of a crazed, delusional maniac wielding a butcher knife and hallucinating about seeing a large toad attacking them.

I thought Sabrina did know we all had serious mental issues and wanted us to talk openly about our experiences living with mental illness. She was actively participating in the sessions, and I was in denial and taking up space. Most of us thought we were just depressed, and we would go back to live a "Normal" lifestyle after group psychotherapy.

From what I know now about mental illness, I would have been more sympathetic toward Sabrina and perhaps become her crazy friend. Isn't it sad? Did I miss an opportunity to learn about schizophrenia? I also missed an opportunity to discover and perhaps better understand my mental illnesses. I did have some of the behavior patterns and scattered thoughts like Sabrina, but I did not want to admit that to anyone, including myself.

I do know I have a personality disorder or disorders, but I still claim BD is the most important issue I have faced to date. Notice I don't rule out discovering another mental illness.

I did not think the group psychotherapy sessions were beneficial. I am just depressed, and Sabrina is a crazy schizophrenic; that was my thinking at the time. Sometimes when I am feeling sorry for myself, I think of Sabrina and what kind of life she is having now. I would be more compassionate and empathetic towards her very difficult situation.

I did not participate in the group because I thought I was not seriously physically or mentally ill. I told the group I was very depressed caused by my stressful job. I became paranoid and thought everyone in the group had schizophrenia, including me. I even thought, at one point, Sabrina was embedded in the group to inform us we were all schizophrenic. Perhaps our psychiatrist wanted to give us all anti-psychotic meds, and that is why he did not want us to disclose our meds to the group. Of course, no one could talk about the effectiveness of our medications, and no one wanted to be critical of the psychiatrist.

After several weeks, I did not think the group psychotherapy sessions were beneficial, and I became very guarded in what I said to the group and my psychiatrist.

I got books on schizophrenia and thought it was the most difficult of any mental illness. It was not wise to study schizophrenia; the more I learned, the more convinced I had schizophrenia. The more I learned, the more paranoid I became. I bought an old outdated [(American Psychiatric Association, 1987) (DSM) from a used book store and began to study all the mental disorders. I was determined to self-diagnose my mental illness. That was also a mistake like many others in my life; I convinced myself I had all the mental disorders listed in the DSM manual, but I never did zero in on the possibility of having BD, so much for self-diagnosis.

Now looking back at Sabrina's situation reminded me of some of the symptoms of my schizophrenic thoughts and behavior. I did have some of the symptoms of schizophrenic personality traits.

Back then, I did not want to face the grim reality of having a more serious diagnosis than "just" depression. A diagnosis of depression was more socially acceptable than the emotionally charged label of bipolar or, even worse, schizophrenia. I remember back when I was in my teens, the words, "He's crazy, "were whispered behind Ziggy's back. Ziggy was the wild and crazy kid in our hometown.

I told the doctor I was not feeling any better and could not afford the sessions. He said in a stern voice," You are not ready to drop out of the group." I did not take his advice. I now believe psychiatrists should inform patients why they are taking certain meds and the possible toxic side effects. The side effects were listed on a sheet of paper but did not spell out all the toxic effects. I also think my psychiatrist should have explained in general terms my diagnosis and his treatment plan. I spent weeks assuming I was schizophrenic.

I don't understand why I never knew my prognosis or his treatment plan. I don't think Valium was the right treatment plan. Sabrina somehow knew she was diagnosed with schizophrenia and was working to find a way to help herself. She was not seeking pity or sympathy, but she was trying to understand and cope with her illness.

My depression did not improve, and I went to about eight doctors over eight months that prescribed harmful and very toxic drugs. Some doctors wanted to put me back on Valium even after I told them Valium did not make me feel better. I experienced hallucinations after taking one antipsychotic medication. I knew then what Sabrina was dealing with; I was terrified and thought the psychiatrist had given me psychedelic LSD mistreatments instead of meds for my undiagnosed BD disorder. Well, that was a joke, but maybe LSD would have been a more effective treatment than the ineffective toxic meds I was taking at the time. I stopped looking for a "cure" and stopped looking for another psychiatrist.

At this point, I was desperate for a "cure," but I did not want to try illegal drugs. Many people were experimenting with illegal drugs, but I knew I had a very addictive personality and would lead to my demise. It was a miracle I did not get hooked on crack cocaine or the worst crystal meth.

I don't want to be overly critical of the health care system, but perhaps psychiatrists should treat mentally ill people with more respect, discuss treatment options, and be honest and open with patients. At the BDS group, people talked openly about their illness and stressors in their lives. Of course, all the people in the BDS group were diagnosed with BD and under a psychiatrist's care.

I do have some type of personality disorder, and perhaps the psychiatrist did diagnose my personality disorder correctly but missed my BD and case of repressed memory, amnesia, and addiction to alcohol. The Bipolar WAVES Workbook attempts to identify these destructive behavior patterns and situations unique to people with BD. This is why early diagnosis and treatments are so important.

Sometimes I think how my life would have been different if treated for all my issues back then. It may have taken a psychoanalyst years at the cost of half a million dollars to sort through all my psychiatric issues. I had personality disorders, abandonment issues, alcoholism, amnesia, BD probably a few more.

I think if I had a good psychoanalyst, he or she could have unraveled some issues of my chaotic life. If a doctor had not diagnosed my BD, my life might have remained the same. My brother and I think treating our BD illness has been the most important overriding factor in our lives.

## Christmas in New England was not the same

Christmas came, and I visited Stu in New England. Stu didn't seem to be the Stu I had known in my past visits; he seemed to be very angry and upset. He yelled at the kids and didn't seem to enjoy life as he did years earlier. He was drinking a lot of beer and seemed to be under a lot of stress at his job. His company was expecting him to meet higher sales quotas while decreasing his sales territory at the same time.

I came home to my apartment and thought our whole family was in crisis. My mother was an incurable alcoholic, Stu was all messed up, and our older brother did not offer to help us. We had very little contact with Harold and his wife after a Nantucket incident, but that's another story.

Without proper treatment, the stresses built up, and we both had severe suicidal depressions. Stu also was driven to seek help for his deep depressions. He was also living an unstable BD lifestyle and going to a psychiatrist for severe depression. He was afraid his company would find out he had a mental illness. He needed to hide everything from his boss and co-workers. He avoided business meetings with other coworkers. He even snuck into the back door of his pharmacy to pick up his meds. None of his meds were helping Stu either.

We lived what I call an unstable bipolar lifestyle before proper treatment. We lived every day in a state of turmoil and very high-stress levels. Perhaps our doctors did diagnose our illness correctly as BD, but without effective medications, the quality of our lives did not improve; some medications caused us to get harmful mistreatment instead of effective treatment.

## Stu and his hippie lifestyle

A year later, Stu was living in the fast lane again, making big money but having even bigger problems. He convinced his boss to give him a yearlong sabbatical to study in Europe. I asked him what he was going to study. He said he was not taking any courses; he wanted to drop out and live a hippy lifestyle.

He told me his boss approved a year sabbatical, and his entire family was scheduled to leave the following month. He said they wanted to leave as soon as possible before his manager changed his mind. I said, "You mean your bosses found out you were going to Europe to live a hippie lifestyle?" He said, "Oh no, I have no plans to study abroad, just travel abroad." I was happy for him but very concerned about the kids traveling abroad.

He packed up his whole family, including their toddler, and arrived in Europe. He had no intention of going to Europe to further his education; he bought a van and toured Europe for one year. He wanted to live the hippie lifestyle as he described it to me. He said they had a budget of $9000; I was a bit envious of his lavish so-called hippie lifestyle because I was earning less than $9,000 a year back then.

For several years, life went on, and I drifted between jobs thinking my life would be different in another city or state. At other times, I thought a new job or even career change could make my life better. I found a good, less stressful job with a local company and thought I found a new career to last a lifetime. I never wanted another high-stress 60 hours a week job ever again.

## A UFO invasion in the South
Several sightings of UFO sightings were made across the country in 1973. The Vietnam War was winding down, and I thought UFO stories were a distraction from what was going on in the Pentagon. The Pentagon did not come out and disclose or deny if UFOs were real; the tabloids and the press made jokes and ridiculed the stories of the victims or abductees.

In October, another story caught my eye. An older man and his young fishing partner claimed they were abducted by aliens and went up into a spaceship. The aliens performed some sort of investigation or examination of some type and returned both of them to earth. I made a joke of the abduction, but I was suspicious of any military story. I thought at the time those guys most likely were drinking too much southern white lighting alcohol.

## *I met a guy named Dean*
I still went out to meet women at bars but no longer picked up women for one-night stands. Now I dated women I met at nightclubs. Nightclub sounds much better than a sleazy bar; it was a step above taking desperate measures just to have one-night stands. On the second date, I would ask my date if she liked sex. Yes, this was very shallow, indeed, but I did it anyway. Some women were not offended, and other nice women never answered my calls.

During the winter, I had dates almost every weekend but wanted to have open relationships with all the women I dated. Most women also wanted just casual sex and no long-term relationship. Some women were professionals and worked 60 hours a week for months at a time; others traveled and had no time to establish long-term relationships. I called these open relationships', no commitment, just casual sex called "friends with benefits."

I managed to get through the winter and looked forward to spending time at the shore. One weekend, I met a guy named Dean at a public tennis court at the shore. He told me about the shore house he rented with four other people. He said they were looking for someone to buy a share in the summer rental. I went back to Dean's house, met two guys and two gals, and made the decision to buy a share that night. The house was older and run down, and well, to be honest, it was more like a weather-beaten old shack.

Dean was a "serial dater"; he had a different date every week. He could not commit, but the women I met were fine gals. They had both looks and brains and would be good mates for life. I was no better; I did not want to commit to a relationship either. I was not a serial dater; I wanted an open relationship. I would meet a woman at the shore and make a date during the week in Philly. I would ask her on the second date if she liked sex. I know this was tasteless and crude, but I needed to know if I had any chance of sex, very shallow indeed. I didn't want to tell my dates. I was very frugal either, but I was. I would make the first date for lunch or a drink after work. Now I can admit I was frugal, cheap, and had no class at all.

I began to have a better social life meeting new women but wanted to have open relationships. I did not want to begin to date someone and then meet someone else and carry on a secret relationship. Even though I was single in Seattle, I watched marriages destroyed by infidelity; I did not want to live that dishonest lifestyle.

## Stu returned from Europe

I was so busy I didn't even have time to call Stu and ask him how his trip to Europe went. He said they had a great time but was glad to be back. He said they went to almost all the European countries in Europe and Eastern Europe.

He said his boss was angry, and I asked him why? Stu said, "Because I tricked him into giving me a sabbatical to study in Europe." His boss gave him a poor territory and increased his quotas to make it more difficult for him. He said the job was getting very stressful; he needed to work all day long just to meet his quotas.

I did question how hard he worked; he was making a lot of money every year. He was not making the money he made years ago; he had a bigger territory and more companies in his territory. He said he had a new woman boss who required detailed expense reports to be filled out and turned in on time. He said, "The job is driving me crazy, but I plan to sail out to Nantucket for a week. The boys are happy they all have motorcycles. I joined another yacht club. I want to get into racing sailboats".

After I hung up, I felt very envious of his lifestyle; he's making big bucks with his company, and I'm barely making ends meet.

After Stu was in treatment, he realized he got high, meaning manic, whenever he got a lot of money. After treatment, Stu recognized having fast money was a trigger for him to go into a manic phase of BD.

When he returned from Europe, his boss cut down his territory in half, and his income was also cut in half. These are the types of misguided decisions people make with BD. A few months later, his job became intolerable, and he quit before he got fired.

## I decided to go on vacation to Europe then moved to California

After Stu came back from Europe with stories of all the places he visited, I also saved up to plan a vacation to Holland, Paris, and England. I admit I was envious of his adventures in Europe. My budget was under $1000 dollars, not $9000. I had a great time and thought my life was finally "Normal" at last. I was elated and, well, a little manic when I arrived back in Philadelphia.

Shortly after returning from Europe, I went into a long hypomanic cycle of BD. During this prolonged manic episode, I decided to go to school in California. The school in California assured me I could get a good-paying job close to the school and a high-paying job after graduation.

I quit my low-stress job drove 3000 miles in 6 days and entered school the following week. After several weeks in LA, I became severely depressed again and could not explain why I moved across the country. This bizarre behavior was what I now call now a bad spell. A mix of BD, no logical explanation, a rash spur-of-the-moment decision hoping a new location or new career could lead to a "Normal" life.

I loved the LA weather but hated the congested traffic on the eight-lane freeways, but the worst was the thick smog most days. Some days the smog was so bad my eyes got irritated and swollen—no lush forests with 70-foot trees like in PA.

The school did not have any good-paying jobs, and I was flat broke. I found a nighttime job as a courier driving a van and delivering packages to businesses around Hollywood from 10 pm to 3 am. The first stop was the busy bus station in LA. I struck up a friendship with the ticket master; we would watch kids arrive from all over the country with hippy tie-dyed clothes, long hair, and guitars slung over their shoulders.

My boss was a former manager of a famous LA nightclub. He was a player in the Hollywood scene; he knew producers directors and introduced me to the corruption and depravity of the Hollywood movers and shakers.

I was introduced to a TV game show host by my boss at a bar near Hollywood. No greeting; he just walked off to find influential people to help his fame and fortune. I was told so-called important people, producers, and directors picked up kids along Hollywood Boulevard. The decadent lifestyles of the rich and famous are being exposed in the media now, but their decadent behavior was hidden in plain sight back then.

## My near-death experience and near-fatal car crash

One morning I was so ill I could not get out of bed. Our landlady, who was a kind nurse, came over to see me. She said it was probably the Hong Kong flu and could be very serious if not treated soon. I had to believe her; she was about 80 years old and had a lifetime of experience with the Hong Kong flu. The next day I was getting weaker and could not get out of bed. I felt I had a 200-pound weight on my chest. Our nurse, as we fondly called her, ordered me to go to the hospital. I drove myself over to the UCLA hospital.

A few hours later, I was informed I needed a heart procedure to rule out a heart attack. They rushed me into the operating room, put tubes in my arms, hooked me up to a heart monitor, and started the procedure. After a few minutes, I felt like I was going to pass out, and then I heard a flat-line loud tone on the heart monitor. I floated into a bright light and felt like heaven, but unfortunately, no angels were there to greet me. I quickly came back into the operating room.

A few hours later, one of the guys from the operating room said I had died, but for only a few minutes on the operating table. Some people call my experience a near-death experience, but I call it a death experience. After that death experience, I did not have any fear of dying, but I was a bit concerned because no angels were there to greet me.

Very late one night, I was driving back to my place about 3 AM and was run off the road by someone driving in the wrong direction on a six-lane Hollywood freeway. To prevent a fatal head-on crash, I went into a drainage ditch. I called my boss on my CB radio. He was more concerned about the condition of the van than my physical condition.

I took this near-fatal head-on crash experience as another sign from my spirit guide to move back to Philly. Between my near-fatal head-on collision on the Hollywood freeway and the near-death experience in the hospital, it was time to pack up and leave LA.

I left my notice to leave my courier job the next day; I told the school I needed to drop out for a semester. I packed up my VW van and drove back 3000 miles across the country to Philly.

## I needed to reevaluate my life again

After I arrived in Philly, I called my previous boss to get my old job back, but they hired someone else for my old job. I needed to reevaluate my life again; I was beginning to make friends in Philly and got real lasting friendships with guys and gals. I loved the shore house, and our members all got along. Why did I make such a hasty decision to go to California? I felt Philly was the place I should be, and it feels like home to me now.

At the time, I could not understand why I made such a hasty decision to go to school in LA. As they say, everything happens for a reason; I may have been killed on an LA freeway become a drug addict. I might have never attended the bipolar support group or met caring and kind people in Philly. My life kept repeating, going into hypomania, spending money to excess, ending up broke again, then going back into a depression, and then starting the same cycle all over again. I was fortunate I found another low-stress low, paying job in downtown Philly.

One bright spot after coming back to Philly, Dean wanted to rent a shore house again, and I signed up for a share. My best guy friend, Dean, dated a lot of women and was starting up a DJ business. He always met nice women but always found something was wrong with them.

Dean was a good friend, and we joined a private nightclub in center city, Philly. We would meet women at bars or church groups in the winter and invite them to the nightclub. I loved the nightlife; disco fever was everywhere. So, we went clubbing at the shore in the summer and at the nightclub scene in the winter. I loved the nightlife;

the disco club scene was the place to meet and socialize. You know, I never found a better live club band than the one on Cape Cod. That R&B band kept everyone dancing till dawn.

## A midnight bike ride in Central Park

I would go to single social events around town, and one night, I met a woman from France named Maria. We did not have a sexual relationship but quickly became very good friends. We would meet downtown and go to lunch and talk about life in the city. She met a guy from France named Ethan. I could tell she was falling madly in love with him after dating him for only a few weeks.

She joined a very active bike club, and I recommended a good but expensive bike. A few months later, my friend Maria's bike club was planning a trip to New York City. They planned a midnight bike ride in Central Park. I thought that was a great idea, what a unique experience. I had my VW bus to bring our bikes to New York City. So, we got to New York City, and we found about 25 people from several different bike clubs around NYC, NJ, and PA.

We all gathered just outside Central Park about midnight. The Central Park was dimly lit, but we all headed out and got maybe 10 minutes into the park; we witnessed homeless people on benches and other homeless people sleeping under cardboard boxes.

We then heard the sound of motorcycles all around us; some were getting closer to our group. That's when I got very worried and anxious; we had no self-defense against robbery or worse. Then we heard loud screams of someone being attacked or hurt, and I began to feel fear of being attacked ourselves. When we heard people in the woods right behind our path, we decided to end our trip and went out of the park in a hurry. I was very afraid a gang of motorcycle riders might attack us. Back then, we had no way of calling the police.

We all met at an all-night coffee shop and talked about our death-defying bike ride through Central Park. My friend Maria and I loved the excitement and experience of visiting New York City. I struck up a conversation with a woman named Dawn from NYC. She was attractive, but I did not ask her if she liked sex, just kidding. She was very friendly and invited me to visit her sometime in NYC. She said she had an apartment in Greenwich Village and told me it was run down but very cheap. She said it was in a rent-controlled building and only cost $75 a month. I am always impressed with frugality and told her we need to set up a date. I looked forward to getting to know her better.

### I visited Dawn and the King Tut exhibit in NYC
A few weeks later, I called Dawn and asked if I could visit her in New York City. I did not want to assume I was going to stay with her overnight. She said she was going to visit her girlfriend out on Long Island for the weekend, but she said I was welcome to stay for the night.

It was great weather, much less humid than a few weeks earlier, and I decided to go anyway. She reminded me again she had a very small apartment, and we would need to sleep together, but she did not want to have sex.

I went to her apartment, and it was a rundown building but in the heart of the Village. I climbed up six flights of stairs and got to her apartment; her entire apartment was just one room, about 12' x 12'. We went out to dinner and had a few drinks at an outdoor café and then went to a jazz nightclub near the Village. I must say the Village has a vibe all its own, sophisticated yet bohemian.

I asked her if she had met anyone over the summer, and she said she had met a girl at the end of the summer and was going to stay with her over the weekend. I assumed she was going to have a sexual relationship with her. We talked about being bisexual and discovering our sexual identity. I admitted my sexual identity was another thing I had been struggling with all my life. I told her it was the first time I had talked openly to anyone about being bisexual.

We talked about the high crime in the city and how the city was going to get out of debt. I noticed that almost every other high rise had a for lease or for sale sign; we walked past a brownstone for sale for $100,000. We talked about Trump's conflict with city hall over giving him free real estate tax benefits for years in exchange for building skyscrapers. She was very upset millionaires were getting tax breaks, and the working middle class was left with paying the city bills.

All Dawn wanted to talk about was what was happening in "the city," meaning Manhattan. She never asked about Philly or where I went on vacation in the summer. She did not have any interest in visiting Philly. I must say New Yorkers are politically savvy, very direct, and say what they think. I learned people in the "city", namely Manhattan, live in sort of a bubble, and they don't want to even consider living anywhere else on the planet Earth except, of course, the "city" meaning Manhattan.

It was after midnight, and on the way back to the Village, I noticed hundreds of huge rats and trash piled up everywhere. Philly had lots of trash but much smaller rats. I will admit I was afraid we would not make it back to Dawn's apartment without either being robbed or attacked but a thousand rats. I never knew rats could be as large as small cats.

The sleeping arrangement was quite cramped; she had a Murphy bed that folded out of the wall. We got up late and went to brunch at a typical New York City deli and had bagels and lox; she left to take the train to her girlfriend's house out on Long Island.

I spent the day sightseeing, went from Wall Street to Battery Park back to Central Park, and walked around for hours. I could not believe that the scary midnight bike ride we took through Central Park was a once-in-a-lifetime misadventure. What were we thinking? I really thought we were going to be robbed at knifepoint by biker gangs that night.

It was a beautiful day for a long walk in the park, and the atmosphere was vibrant and exciting as I became just another NYC tourist. By the afternoon, I was exhausted; I walked past a very large billboard for the Egyptian Tutankhamen or King Tut exhibit at the Met Museum of Art.

I thought it might be interesting, but when I got to the ticket counter, an older woman told me in a low, gruff voice, "All the tickets were gone long ago." I guess I did not believe her, so I pleaded my case. I said, "I just arrived from Philly and cannot return to NYC before the exhibit ends." Then a much younger and much more attractive gal told me they might have a ticket if someone left one at the booth. I then asked her, "I hope you a not offended; I think you are very attractive." Sure enough, she had a ticket someone just left off, and I was glad they did not even charge me, but I think they wanted a donation. Perhaps she felt sorry for me, an out-of-town tourist all alone in the Big Apple.

I entered a strange world of mystery and mysticism. The 5500-year-old artifacts made me question everything about the human race. Were these treasures of an Egyptian Pharaoh's human or beings from another planet? The brilliant colors the exquisite attention to detail of every artifact were unbelievable.

The inscriptions on the walls told a story of going into the afterlife. I noticed many Egyptian Pharaohs had elongated heads. Their belief in the afterlife was so interesting; did they have some actual contact with the beings in the afterlife? I thought some present-day mediums claim to be in contact with spirits, dead people from the other side. I did have a feeling I went over the other side briefly after my death experience in LA years ago. I discovered our spirit does not end with death here on earth.

On the train back to Philly, I thought about the pyramids and how it took thousands of men to place a million heavy blocks of solid granite to build each pyramid. I questioned if the Egyptians did ask extraterrestrials () ETs to help lay the heavy blocks with such precision. Why were the pyramids even built? I also questioned, could their gods be from another world or galaxy? I arrived back in Philly after my brief tour of NYC and started work the next day.

## I forgot her name

About a month later, I met a woman at a singles event, and she invited me back to her apartment. The sex was great and, in the morning, I could not remember her first name. All I could remember was she had a very Russian-sounding last name, but I forgot her first name. I want to say she had a very long, difficult Russian first name to pronounce. Her first name had dots over the letters, but I have to tell you the truth she had a very short first name, and I was embarrassed I forgot it.

She recognized I had forgotten her first name and told me her name was Iva; she quickly forgave me. The sex was great; she was very sensual, and I felt comfortable just being around her. She had a European way about her; she was quiet but very sensual and down to earth.

There was something about her I liked after sleeping with her the first night. We spent several hours in bed in the morning, and I felt very accepted and relaxed around her; she made brunch, and I wanted to know more about her. She said she came to America when she was eight years old from Eastern Europe. Then she abruptly changed the subject and told me she has several long-term relationships with other men and wants to be honest with me right from the start. She said she didn't want to cheat or sneak around behind my back. I think she was also telling me she does not want me to keep my other relationships a secret from her. I didn't say anything, but I felt the same way; I also wanted a completely open relationship.

I found her honesty a real change for the women I've met to date. It's not just casual sex; she wants long-term caring relationships. She doesn't seem to care about money, fancy cars, or houses and lives a very modest lifestyle. She doesn't even wear a lot of makeup or fancy jewelry, either. She didn't even ask me what I do for a living, and I didn't ask her either. I don't know what we were talking about, but we talked for hours.

I left her apartment and hoped she wanted to see me again. I thought maybe she was the reason why I came back to Philly, and just maybe she has come into my life for a reason. For the first time, I did not feel threatened by Iva and was willing to risk a long-term sexual relationship with her. She was not just "A friend with benefits." It was more like having "an honest, intimate friend with the best benefits."

She called me during the week and asked me to come over to her place for the weekend; I told her I was planning to go to our shore house and invited her to come with me for the weekend. I told her our place was a little run down, and she just laughed; Iva was not materialistic and was grateful for everything in her life. We had a very special time together. She met some of the members of our shore house.

I think it was the first time I ever had an intimate relationship with anyone. I told her if she ever needed me to "just call." She said she would do the same for me. It was very important for me to have someone I could trust and comfort me. I know it sounds like I was desperately in need of closeness and intimacy, but intimacy was what I craved from a very young age. Our relationship was based on trust, sex, and knowing we could comfort each other at any time we needed it. My relationship with Iva was a bit odd because I never felt jealous of men in her other open relationships.

I went to the shore house the following weekend alone, and two members of the house questioned me about my relationship with Iva. I told them she was just a new "Friend with benefits" that I had just met a few weeks ago. One of the guys turned around and said: "Looks to me; she is a little more than just a friend with benefits." That weekend I did think of Iva and didn't enjoy clubbing as usual, but the summer was coming to an end.

## Sharing our childhood was unspeakable
The following weekend I stayed at Iva's apartment and continued to talk about our lives, but she was hesitant to talk about her childhood. I said something like, "It must have been difficult living in Europe during the war.". She just said in a matter-of-fact tone, "The Russians treated us like dirt, and when the Germans came, they murdered innocent men, women, and children." I did not need to ask any more details of what happened to her in war-torn Europe. Sharing our childhood experiences was literally unspeakable.

Maybe I was trying to ask too many personal questions because, from those B&W pictures of the Holocaust, I knew she probably witnessed many unspeakable crimes against humanity.

Another weekend we went to Valley Green Park near Iva's apartment. The stream reminded me of the stream that ran through our farm in New England. I mentioned I grew up on a farm until I was 12 years old, and then we moved uptown. She became very distant and solemn, like she was reliving something in her mind but could not speak. A few minutes later, she was back to being the kind and quiet Iva.

I refrained from mentioning our childhood ever again. Of course, I never mentioned those horrific B&W pictures of the Holocaust. I think we both had very traumatic events happen in our lives, she had tragic memories of WW II, and I had the traumatic breakup with Maria. My tragedy was still hidden in a case of amnesia, and maybe hers was too.

Iva and I would never talk about our childhood. I did not want to talk about my emotional abuse and was ashamed to talk about it with anyone. My childhood on the farm was some of the best times and worse times. I am sure Iva's childhood was also one of the worst times for her.

Sometimes I wondered what happened to Iva's parents. I wanted to know if she had brothers or sisters. We both had an unspoken rule never to speak about our childhoods. I never discussed my tragic breakup with my friend Maria because I was in a state of amnesia.

## I bought a row house in the inner city

Philly was becoming more violent, and crime was on the rise but not as bad as in New York City. In July 1977, a blackout in New York City resulted in massive looting and violent conduct during its twenty-five-hour duration. This event was downplayed in the national media, but I take these events as another cover-up by the government and the media. This event told me Philly could also erupt into anarchy within hours of a crisis like a blackout.

I had been renting apartments for years and wanted to own a place of my own. Leases, damage deposits, security deposits, and the hassle of moving every few years left me with a stack of rent receipts and no savings in the bank. I also wanted a place to start a business, and a one-room apartment wasn't going to do it.

Socially and career-wise, my life was getting better. I was living a single life with much less stress from my work. I wasn't looking for a high-tech job where I worked 60 hours a week anymore with deadlines and management breathing down my neck.

I bought a low-cost HUD row house in a less than desirable part of Philly. I paid $6500, but even I needed to borrow money to buy it. I got a loan from a bank after I threatened them with a lawsuit. I learned many banks engaged in Zip Code profiling; many banks did not give loans to anyone living within certain Zip codes.

My row house was a duplex, and I rented the first-floor apartment to a young White couple to cover my mortgage payment. I was now basically living rent-free. Our neighborhood was a mix of several ethnic groups, and we all respected one another. We had several Asian and Hispanic families and two Black families in our block. The only White people on our block were me and the young couple on the first floor. Two-row houses were vacant and boarded up, but I was told not violent or crime-ridden like other parts of Philly. Many nights the nightly local news reported violent acts of stabbings and robberies across the city.

I decided the only way out of my financial situation was to start my own business, so I started to work on three business projects at the same time. This decision was a disaster both financially and for my mental health.

## The family next door was trapped in poverty

Shortly after I moved into my row house, I struck up a conversation with the guy next door. His name was Blake; he was African American had six kids, all under seven years old. He had a significant other, but she was not around most of the time. He was struggling to make ends meet. Then I noticed he had visitors all hours of the night, and I suspected he was dealing drugs. My conversations with Blake became less frequent, and I suspected he was using and dealing drugs. A few months later, he was arrested on drug charges and went to jail.

I don't want to judge people's actions because selling drugs was Blake's way out of poverty. He could not improve his family's quality of life by staying on government assistance. Buy selling drugs; he could probably make enough money in one night instead of working a month-on-a-day job, and besides, who would take care of his six kids.

After Blake went to prison, the drug house was run by a guy not related to Blake; I called him the boss. A woman moved in to take care of the kids, and she told me the boss was not a member of Blake's family and implied I should not mess with him. This new guy, the boss, was a nonsense businessman type and didn't want to acknowledge I even existed. One day I was fixing my van out front, and he came out and said: "What are you looking at?" Not friendly at all; it was obvious this guy was sent by someone to take charge and run the drug house operation 24/7.

Blake spent about a year in prison; he didn't talk to me as often after he came back from prison. It was obvious his house was taken over by higher-level drug dealers, gangs, or the mob.

I can see now how drugs can quickly take over anyone's life; you start off using drugs but then cannot afford to support your drug habit, then you need to deal drugs to support your drug habit. You land up in jail, and then bigger dealers or gangs take over your territory.

After the dealers controlled the block, Blake never went back to jail. I did not judge Blake; I did realize his entire family was dependent on using and dealing drugs. Of course, with his arrest record of using or dealing in drugs, he was effectively unemployable. Now his entire family was trapped in poverty and deep into the drug culture.

At this point, I was very concerned the mob was taking over the streets and the drug house next door. Many nights the national news showed mob hits in many areas of Philly. I heard the mob did not deal with drugs, but that did not make me feel any more secure. I was becoming street-savvy, but I was in denial of the dangers I faced every day and night. One Asian family moved out abruptly after one of their kids was seriously injured in a street fight.

One night a row house a few doors down was on fire at 2 AM, and the fire was ruled suspicious. Rumor had it; the owners may have been police informants. This was a strong incentive for me not to talk to the police, period.

I was so impressed the fire department was on the scene in five minutes and took charge, asking us if anyone was living in the house, true professionals. At this point, I was worried about everything. Was I going to be thought of as an informant? After the suspicious fire down the block, I did know now what they could do with informants.

The young couple downstairs moved out. Our block was going down fast after several other families moved out, and their houses were boarded up. At this point, no one moved into our block, and the trash and blight were becoming an eyesore.

My friend Maria moved in with her parents in a better neighborhood; it is unfortunate our block was so dangerous while her block was relatively safe and only 20 blocks away. My friend Maria was still dating Ethan, the guy from France, and I was very happy for her. She would share intimate details of her relationship, and I knew he was more than just a boyfriend. I also began to share intimate details of my relationship with Iva. We probably acted like silly high school kids talking about our first sexual relationships.

My friend Maria had a wild streak and had a friend, a bad biker boyfriend, before I met her. They rode 1500 miles to Florida and 1500 miles back. She told me it was the best sex she ever had on the trip to Florida. That's what I liked about her very open about sex and a little bit wild.

It was unfortunate I was still in a state of amnesia because I knew I could talk to her about anything. I did not even connect the fact my friend Maria and my 1st love had the same first name. I confided in my friend Maria about my close relationship with Iva. She mentioned Iva could be my soul mate several times.

Maria was my best woman friend, and I wanted to meet this guy from France. I did not want her to get hurt if he dropped her for someone else and went back to France without her. I brought up my concerns about Ethan several times, but she acted a bit defensive; I don't think she wanted me to even meet Ethan.

I finally met Maria's boyfriend from France at our private nightclub downtown. While my friend Maria talked with her friends at a table, I struck a conversation with Ethan at the bar; he told me he worked as a social director for singles cruise ship line. Within minutes, we began to talk openly about our sexual lifestyles. I told him I was in open relationships with several women. Knowing he had to be a player on a cruise ship, we began to talk openly about his single life. He told me he had sex with hundreds of women he met on the singles cruise ships. I began to like this guy, but now I was a little annoyed, well envious because he was bragging about his wild sex lifestyle; I gave up I could not top his wild and open sex lifestyle.

I got it; Ethan was a charming guy with a French accent and had no problem getting any women he met in bed. I told him I was envious of his single lifestyle and told him my friend Maria was my best friend. I was happy she found someone that would treat her right. I made the point he should treat her right. He was a player for sure, but my friend Maria also had her wild side. I thought maybe it was a good match.

I was holding down a full-time job and working on three businesses all at the same time. I was developing a startup online business website to sell computer products. The online website was years ahead of its time. I wrote the software to run the online business and published a trade magazine to sell computer products. I would come home from work, take a nap for a few hours, and then work on my three businesses until 1 or 2 AM. My friend Maria and Hayley would help me bundle the magazines to be shipped out to computer clubs across the country.

## Yet another hidden disorder in plain sight, hoarding

I was starting to buy any and all computer parts, printers, memory, disk drives, anything to list on my online computer website. The problem, I did not have an online website ready to list the products. When I moved into the row house, I had an entire basement to collect and store things to list on my unfinished website. I began to pick up stuff off-the-street, lamps, tools, tables. My rationale, I could fix them and sell them on the website. I was in denial; I had yet another disorder, hoarding.

## Iva was becoming a very important person in my life

I began to realize Iva was becoming a very important person in my life, but I did not want to admit it to anyone, including myself. Sometimes you meet someone very special, and Iva was certainly that person. I had a lasting connection with her from the first night I met her. We got together during the week, and I continued to have open relationships with several other women, but it was just for casual sex after I met Iva.

Iva visited me at my row house a few times, but only during the day; I could sense she did not want to spend the night. Now I realize the inner-city environment probably reminded her of her life in war-torn Europe. After a few months, I was glad she wanted me to stay at her place. I had an anytime-open invitation to stay with her.

On weekends our block looked like a 4$^{th}$ of July parade coming down our street. Cars drove by my row house all night with people coming in and out of the drug house next door. Sometimes White people with nice expensive cars from the suburbs would back up around the block while drug users scored their dope. I planned to be away almost every weekend at the shore in the summer. I planned to stay at someone's apartment on the weekends in the winter.

## The alternative lifestyle movement

After I returned to Philly and bought the row house, I found Iva and a few new friends; I became involved in the alternative lifestyle movement. I attended an alternative lifestyle convention at a fancy hotel in Philly and came across a class in a small meeting room on "How to live a less stressful life." The speaker introduced The Holmes and Rahe Life Stress Scale. [(Holmes & Rahe, 1967) Refer to Appendix B.

The Holmes and Rahe Life Stress Scale predicted your chance of having a physical illness based on 43 life events. I was fascinated by how you could predict your risk of having a physical illness just by filling out a simple questionnaire. I scored a moderate risk of having a serious physical illness, and I kept the chart among my papers, and I scored my risk of physical illness from time to time. The chart, however, did not take into account any mental illnesses.

Many of the classes at the conference were aimed at alternative lifestyles like organic farming, vegetarian diets, yoga, acupuncture, meditation, and many other alternative ways of living. This back-to-nature lifestyle did fit with my love of nature and living a simple life. Having grown up on a farm, I could identify with living a back-to-nature lifestyle.

## I joined the open relationships lifestyle movement
I walked past another meeting room that had a sign outside, "Join the open relationship lifestyle movement" I was in an open relationship with Iva and signed up. I entered the room and felt right at home; you could tell the people were laid back and didn't bug you with a lot of questions like "how much do you make per year?" Or "what kind of car do you drive." If someone asked me where I summer and I could tell them at the shore in an old run-down shack. The group was called the Open Lifestyles group, or OLS for short.

The truth was I was ashamed of my life; I didn't have any money in the bank and was living in a less than marginal neighborhood in Philly. I didn't want to admit my relationship with Iva became very important as time went by, but unconsciously I was afraid of falling in love with her.

I was still in a state of amnesia and could not understand why I was so terrified of falling in love with Iva. She was my lifeline to learning to trust a woman and not to be afraid of seeking comfort, love, and affection. I was always so afraid of experiencing the overwhelming grief and sadness of rejection again.

To my surprise, no one in the group asked me any personal questions; they just seemed to accept me. They spoke very honestly and seemed very friendly without being too curious about my personal life. The people in the group seemed very normal I met Bob and

Stacy, and they talked about how an open relationship lifestyle can make life better for you and your significant other.

I told Bob about my relationship with Iva and said, "I know it was working for me." Then he said, "An open relationship could make sexual relationships honest instead of hiding your sexuality; both women and men want to have better sex but want to keep an intimate relationship only with their partner. Most people in the group all like sex and want their partner to enjoy a better sex life". He mentioned they had weekly nude massage sessions.

## I kept OLS group sex parties a secret from Iva

Well, I liked this group, maybe I can ask Iva, but we have good sex together; I don't know how our sex life could be any better. I met a woman named Lois at the meeting and asked her what she thought of the group. She also had a good vibe; we exchanged phone numbers. I got information about when they had their next meeting

## The Awake spiritual growth presentations

The next meeting room at the conference had a sign "Find your purpose in life" A woman was passing out brochures on the course called Awake. She wanted people to come to their presentation held every week in an upscale downtown hotel. I had no idea of my purpose in life but thought it might be important to find it.

I questioned how one course could help me find my purpose in life. At that time in my life, I was critical of everything in my life except, of course, myself. I took their brochure back to my apartment with me.

A few weeks later, I found the Awake brochure staring at me on the coffee table. Maybe this was a sign; I went to my first presentation, where they explained the outline of the course. The people seemed very friendly, and I was impressed because they did not ask me a lot of personal questions;

I hate it when people want to know your profession, what type of car you drive, or where I summer. If someone asked me any questions, I would tell them, "Look, I'm between jobs, and I drive an old beat-up VW," both would be true." Oh, and I summer at the shore in a rundown shack."

Nosey people are not cool, but I was impressed by their friendly and honest style. I was very attracted to the people at the presentations but frankly was afraid it might be a cult of some type. The women at the meeting did not wear lots of makeup or flashy fancy jewelry. The only drawback was the cost. The cost to take the course cost was several hundred dollars. With my firm policy of being very frugal but not cheap, the cost was a deal-breaker.

The following week I met a woman from Calcutta, India, at the Awake presentation. She was asking people to take the Awake spiritual growth course. She said many people attending the course found purpose and meaning in their lives. She said many people that took the course had breakthroughs and rapid spiritual growth in just a few days and not years.

When the presentation ended, I went up to her, and we talked for a while. She wore a beautiful, full-length embroidered dress, and she was so calm and self-confident, a beautiful person both inside and out. I finally asked her in a sarcastic tone of voice, "Well, what is the meaning of life?" She gave me the most inspirational and spiritual answer, but all I could remember from our conversation was her saying, "Find your purpose in life and be kind to everyone." A guy at the presentation said she had an old soul. I didn't think she was that old and wondered if I even had a soul.

Most other members of the group had similar viewpoints of respect and talked about finding true meaning in their lives. I liked the fact the Awake course was not based on any one organized religion, so I decided to take the course.

People told me I would learn valuable life lessons from the wisdom passed down from many religions and philosophers throughout the ages. Someone told me the course taught we all had free will; I was always perfectly fine with anything free.

The presentations were given every week to explain what the Awake course was all about and get you to sign up for the course. I was drawn to the atmosphere and good vibes I felt from everyone at the presentations. Several people had taken the course and said it was very spiritual and taught them valuable life lessons. Several people told me they did experience spiritual growth during the intense five-day course.

At that point, I guess I was attending to meet nice people, especially women. After several weeks I was using the weekly presentations to meet very nice women. I would get a woman's name and telephone numbers and then make a date during the week. The Awake presentations turned into my personal dating service. Several of the staff began to question my motives after they saw me every week at the presentations but never signed up to take the course. Some presenters also picked up my policy of being frugal at any cost. Several times I wanted to know if they had discounted memberships.

I still spent time with Iva during the week or anytime we needed a little comfort time together. We had a pact if we ever needed to comfort each other, just call anytime. I mentioned the Awake course several times to Iva, but she had no interest.

## Nude massage sessions

I was interested in the open lifestyle group or OLS group and called Lois, the woman I met at the conference. I asked her if she was interested in going to a nude massage session. She didn't commit. She gave me Stacy's number, and at that point, I thought we were getting the runaround, but they did not want to pressure anyone to join the OLS group.

I found out about the next nude massage session from Bob, and I called Lois again to see if she wanted to go with me to check it out. This time she did commit to going. We were excited and a little anxious at the same time. We arrived at a townhouse in a nice neighborhood in Philly. The people I met were hippy types, very laid back, get the pun, I did get the "free Love" vibe from everyone I met that night. There was no shirt and tie business suit types at this massage session; everyone was completely nude. Without any clothes or jewelry, people were basically stripped; get the pun on words, of any status symbols. Men did not wear fancy watches or jewelry. The women did not wear lots of makeup, watches, dyed hair, wigs, fancy jewelry, or even false breast implants either. The dress code was simple; everyone wore nothing.

Both Lois and I loved the closeness of the group and planned to go back the following week. I became friends with Lois, and I felt a bond with everyone in the group. There were rules, no clothes, no drugs or alcohol allowed, but that was about it. Oh, and an unwritten rule, no sex during the massage session.

## The drug house next door only got worse

It was only a few years after I bought the row house in Philly, and the dangerous conditions only got worse. The drug house next door was going full blast, and drug users stopped by and drove by all night long. Several times the cops blocked off our block but only arrested the drug users.

I came back late one night and could not park my car on our block; a dozen police cars blocked off our street. I saw the drug house boss sitting on their front stoop as the cops rounded up the drug users; I never saw the drug raid aired on the local news or in the newspaper.

I never called the cops because I knew someone was protecting the drug dealers, and I may be called out as a snitch. I instinctively knew what drug dealers do to a snitch. I was becoming street-savvy and accepted; this was the drug culture in some neighborhoods in Philly. Blake, the owner of the row house, was not around as often, and I noticed a new, much older guy was running the house operation. Blake's kids, I assumed, lived with their mother, but I did not want to ask anyone personal questions. The boss was a mean-looking dude. He was a business type of guy; he never seemed to be on drugs or alcohol like many people in the neighborhood.

Before the drug house became very active, people in the neighborhood got along and respected each other. The family next door struggled to survive. I always respected Blake and his family, and they respected me, but I could see the drugs were taking a toll on everyone, including me. After several African Americans, Hispanic, and Asian families moved out, several houses were boarded up and left vacant. The neighborhood looked like a war zone.

Back in the mid 70' I noticed people in Philly respected other people's lifestyles but didn't invite you over for dinner, but that was ok. Now when I travel down to Philly, minorities do not even acknowledge my presence as they walk by. Now I feel a deep distrust of the minorities toward the White people and vice versa.

I learned years ago it was respectful to acknowledge everyone by just a nod or other friendly gesture. The reality of living in a poorer neighborhood in the inner city was clear. Without skills or education, many minorities and uneducated White people got trapped in the drug culture and welfare system with little chance of escape.

A few years later, I detected a foul odor coming from the drug house next door. Now know it was a meth lab right next door. A meth lab was very dangerous and could blow up the entire block at any time. If I was desperate to feel better, I might have tried meth, and that would have been my death sentence.

I don't want to make a joke about other people's misfortune, but I am bitter that nothing is done for the people addicted to drugs in our country. Back then, many people out in the suburbs were very righteous and critical of poor people addicted to drugs or alcohol, but now the drug culture is flooding our entire country, and nothing is being done to prevent drug use.

I noticed many White people in fancy cars from New Jersey were stopping by the drug house, and I concluded the drug bosses were expanding their territory to all parts of Philly and even into New Jersey. I became very concerned drugs were draining our entire nation of cash, and many times the reason is an addiction to drugs. Perhaps I was in denial of the dangers of the drug epidemic because I was living at ground zero, but now it is clear we are losing the war on drugs.

I don't know why I didn't try any drugs; all I needed to do was open my front door and stick out my hand with a five-dollar bill, and I would have a few addictive pills or a baggie of heroin or meth in my hand in a matter of a few seconds or less.

I think my relationship with Iva, Greg, my friend Maria and the people I met at the Awake presentations may have saved my life from a lifetime of drug use. At that time in my life, I was still struggling with alcoholism and BD, although I was spending more time with people that were not alcoholics or drug users. I was very fortunate; I was surrounded by friends that were not addicted to drugs. Several people at the Awake presentation were hippies and smoked pot, but I never detected the use of any hard drugs.

Stu often talks about young kids in AA, many are also drug addicts, but Stu said you would never know by just talking to them. Alcohol addiction to alcohol can easily be detected from 5 feet away.

At that time, I was desperate for a "cure," but I did not want to try illegal drugs. I saw what devastation drug addiction did to entire families. Many people at work were experimenting with illegal drugs, but I knew I had a very addictive personality and would lead to my demise. It was a miracle I did not get hooked on crack cocaine or even the worst crystal meth.

This was a very dangerous and stressful situation; The WAVES Chart has an entry for living in a crime-ridden area.

## I got invited to an OLS sex party
A few months later, I was invited to an OLS sex party. I called Lois during the week and asked her if she wanted to go to a sex party. She said she was busy, and I called another woman on the member's list. We never met, but she agreed to go. Trust was very important, especially for women, and that's why many women loved the OLS group. We arrived at a large stone house in a nice Philly neighborhood. The basement had a large hot tub, and things got pretty hot soon after people arrived, but I won't go into details.

After the closeness, I experienced the OLS Group's sex parties nude massage sessions; the Awake presentations seemed a bit timid, but the Awake presentations lured me back. Maybe I did need to find my purpose in life? I definitely needed to grow spiritually.

## I met Hayley, a woman with two small kids

The following week I went to another Awake presentation and met a woman named Hayley at the sign-in table. We struck up a conversation; she told me she works as a yoga instructor. She looked very European, had beautiful olive skin, and had an upbeat personality. I was interested in getting to know her and asked her where she lives, and she said in a Greek neighborhood of Philly. As usual, I got her number and set up a date for the following weekend.

We hit it off right from the start and had something in common. We were both very frugal. I stayed at her place on our first date. She was a single mother and had two young boys. After a few months, I bonded with her boys, Haley, and I took them to a nearby playground. We all spent time at a park riding our bikes and eating at fast food places. I thought at one point; I was the father to them I never had.

Hayley became my friend, but she had some issues; at times, she would be moody and distant and then become isolated by reading everything and ignoring people around her, including her kids and me. She had hundreds of old magazines and newspapers scattered around her apartment. I could not be too critical of her because I knew I was also a hoarder and had a few more issues of my own.

You could say we had an up-and-down relationship. When I was up, she was down, and when I was down, she was up, but we needed each other for emotional support. We became friends and slept together at her place, but I also had open sexual relationships with other women.

## My dates were afraid to stay overnight

I had a date with a woman I met at the Awake presentation a few weeks earlier. I had to admit I used the presentations as my personal dating service, very shallow and cheap. One weekend I took my date down to Philly to the Italian market several blocks away from my row house. The Italian market is an open-air market and has all types of vendors selling all types of food, farm produce, and dry goods, including the famous Philly cheese steak. We had dinner at the famous Melrose diner in south Philly. It was about 11 pm when we arrived back at my row house.

After just a few minutes, she became anxious and asked to go back to her apartment. I did not question her decision, and we went back to stay at her place. Perhaps I was in denial of the dangers of living in my drug-infested neighborhood? By now, many of the row houses were boarded up after several families had just abandoned their row houses and moved out of the neighborhood. I bought my row house after the previous family had just moved out, and HUD was left to sell it.

I tried to invite other dates back to the row house for a sleepover, but after a few more bad incidents, I gave up. I did not bring anyone back to the row house to stay overnight, including Hayley. Iva mentioned she visited people in depressed areas of the city as a social worker but never after dark. I took the hint and did not want her to stay at my row house.

Hayley would come over days, but she was afraid to bring the kids to stay overnight. Nights in the hood became violent in parts of the city, but our neighborhood was relatively quiet except for the drug traffic, especially on the weekends.

Now I suspected the drug house was probably the reason our block was off-limits for criminals, the drug dealer next door probably put out the word on the street not to mess around with people our block. I was afraid my row house could be firebombed by rival drug dealers. I never did remove the thick heavy piece of plywood over the front door. I was in denial of how stressful living in a neighborhood controlled by drug dealers was.

I found safer places to stay overnight, especially over the weekends, when the drug traffic was nonstop all night long. Now drugs were being passed out right outside my front door; maybe I was fortunate I didn't speak to people in the drug house any longer.

I woke up one very cold winter morning and noticed my old car was gone. I called the police to report my car stolen, but they didn't seem to want to fill out the paperwork. I took the bus to work, and when I got home, I got a message on my answering machine. They found my car abandoned about three miles away from my row house. They told me it was probably used by some kids to avoid the cold weather or to move drugs around the city. It took me two hours to take three different busses to pick up my car.

## I needed to find a solution to all my problems

After attending several, well many Awake presentations, I began to embrace the simple message of respect and kindness. I realized I could no longer keep highly stressful jobs and decided to find even less stressful work. Every high-tech job eventually created too much stress, and I usually quit before I got fired. I was striving to gain wealth and status, but it was not getting me either. I needed to find a solution to all my problems soon.

I still worked on all three businesses I started after moving into the row house, but I was too busy attending the OLS parties, massage sessions, and meeting people at the Awake presentations. I thought I was making progress in the businesses, but the personal computer industry was growing and changing so fast I could not keep pace with the technology. Hardware and software systems were obsolete after just a few years, sometimes even months.

## I decided to take the Awake spiritual growth course

As usual, I procrastinated for several months; then, I decided to take the Awake course. Maybe the kind woman from Calcutta was right; I could find my purpose in life and find out what was wrong with me at the same time. I could have both problems solved in just a few days for the same price. That was my motto, be frugal at some cost, but never at a high cost. Hayley and I took the course at the same time for support.

The course began in a very large ballroom in an upscale hotel in Philadelphia. Here I was with a group of maybe 60 "Normal" people. The group facilitator asked everyone to commit to completing the course and not just drop out. I thought this guy was psychic; he was reading my mind; I do have a long history of quitting before I complete many projects.

The course began, and I thought I was in an intensive, very large, intensive group psychotherapy session. After a few hours, it then became like a boot camp for psychos, and the group facilitators were not kind and gentle at all. Maybe it was a cult?

The facilitator acted more like a driven psycho cult leader than a spiritual growth group facilitator. Apparently, the object of the course was to tear down your ego then build it back up with an entirely new outlook on life. My ego was certainly being dragged down, but would it ever come back up to find a new outlook on life?

The course introduced several concepts from religions around the world. Most believed in a higher power or God. I always believed in higher power from a very young age but not in any organized religion. One principle I experienced in my life, I had a spiritual guide and a belief in a higher power. Many times, I felt my father's presence guiding and protecting me. I guess my spiritual guide was on vacation during the entire course.

The course used powerful music to bring up emotions and feelings to reveal what was causing roadblocks in your life. One of the goals of the course was to unblock the repressed emotions and allow you to grow emotionally and spiritually. I always loved music and even listened to classical music in college, but the music did not bring up repressed emotions, and I did not feel free. I did not feel any change at all. I felt the course cost me several hundred dollars; it definitely was not free.

Some people did uncover repressed emotions that have been buried for years. I did not. The group facilitator confronted me in one session; he asked me, "What is your problem?" I could not answer him; I knew something was wrong with me, and I expected he would tell me what was wrong with me. That's the reason I took the course to find out my problem; also,

I was worried I wasn't getting anything from the course after spending hundreds of dollars. In one process, I learned I was basically selfish and did not want to give unless I got something in return. That was my frugal policy, don't give unless I get something in return, but that was obviously not working for me.

Finding out that truth was not why I took the course; I did not want to hear that I did have selfish issues as well. I didn't want to admit it was the truth. I could see many people in the group were getting far more out of the course. Many people in the course could use guided meditation to resolve deep emotional issues; I could not. I was disappointed, and I thought the course would at least tell me what was wrong with me and find my purpose in life. That was the main reason I took the course.

In one process, the group facilitator had all the participants attempt to use what they called remote viewing. We all sat in a chair and concentrated on an object, distant location, or people in another place. One guy had a remote viewing of his grandparents in Italy at an outdoor gathering at an unfamiliar place. He could see everyone at the gathering, some people he did not even know. He called his grandparents the following day, and indeed they were at a gathering at a place he had never been before.

The group facilitator talked about incarnation; we come from another dimension, for lack of a better word. The facilitator said people pick their own parents. He also talked about remembering your past life before birth.

Of course, I thought of Sabrina, who told us she was reincarnated from a peasant in ancient times.

I remembered a story of a young girl in England that claimed she came from a small village in another life. She described the village in great detail. When she visited the village, it was exactly as she described it.

These concepts were not entirely impossible except picking our own parents. From my death experience, I learned when we die, our spirit or consciousness leaves our body and does pass over to the other side, as I call it.

The day after the course ended, I did learn something from the Awake course. Well, I learned I was basically selfish and did not give unless I got something in return. I didn't want to hear that at that time in my life. My thinking went; if the Awake course could not find my purpose in life, maybe I don't have a purpose. It never occurred to me I needed to discover I had an untreated mental illness and other issues first and then find my purpose in life. This is what the course taught many people to look deep inside your core beliefs, into your soul to find your unique meaning and purpose in your life. I sure did not look deep enough to find my inner soul; I just found more confusion, resentment, and frustration in my life.

Most people came out of the course feeling better about themselves and their outlook on life. Many people in the group had dramatic emotional breakthroughs and did grow spiritually; I did not.

On the last day of the course, the facilitators told us we might feel all kinds of emotions for a few days after the course and not make any major changes in your life. The only emotion I felt was disappointment. I did not find out what was wrong with me and definitely did not find my purpose in life.

## What if I was treated for my bipolar disorder (BD)?
Again, I believe if I were treated for my BD, the Awake course would have been far more valuable; I might have had breakthroughs on several issues I was hiding for years. I may have discovered I had a case of amnesia starting in my early 20's. The consequences of being in a state of amnesia for so long still does affect my thoughts and probably always will. I still have "what if "questions to this day.

I can see now; my amnesia prevented me from having lasting long-term relationships with women until I met Iva. After my devastating breakup with Maria, I had an unconscious fear of ever falling in love again, but the most harmful belief, I was not lovable. After I felt my 1$^{st}$ love abandoned me, I felt unlovable, unworthy of being loved by anyone. I had a very difficult condition to live with from a very young age.

Iva was the one person that taught me I could love again, but I denied I loved her. Iva did not want a family, and after my relationship with Hayley and her kids, I knew I wanted a family, but I did not have a love relationship with Hayley. Of course, I still did not resolve my true relationship with Maria because I was still in a state of amnesia.

Several weeks after I took the course, I did feel better about my life in general and had to confront some truths; I was selfish, self-centered, maybe a little too frugal, let's face it, I was cheap. My character flaws were a problem, but I could not discover my core problem was, of course, my constant struggle with BD and my hidden case of amnesia, plus a few other issues like alcoholism.

The reason was obvious, I was mentally ill, but after a dozen psychiatrists, no one could tell me what mental illness I was struggling with all my life. I get a bit upset when I think about the ineffective treatment I have received for years. If my psychiatrist had sat me down and told me I had BD, I might have accepted my illness and been more receptive to treatment. Sabrina seemed to accept her diagnosis of schizophrenia and was coping with her illness with courage and openness.

If you have trouble with your car and go to a dozen repair shops and they overcharge you but don't fix the problem, won't most people give up trying to find another expensive mechanic that won't fix your car?

I was looking for the Awake course to solve my problems, and nothing seemed to help me. Years earlier, I studied books and manuals to find my diagnosis but ended up even more confused and discouraged with my life. From the meds I took back then, I don't believe they diagnosed my mental illness correctly. I was attempting to cure my illness without medicine. From my experience at the BD group years later, it took years for some psychiatrists to arrive at a correct diagnosis of BD. It appears that, years ago, BD was it was a very difficult illness to diagnose and treat; both my brother and I was exhibit number 1. Early-on treatment is what I am working on for people with BD to get early detection and effective treatment.

I believe the WAVES Workbook may help people with BD understand they are living with several stressful situations they may not be aware of. The WAVES Chart lists many unique situations common to people with BD. Perhaps a health care provider could help someone fill out the WAVES Chart if someone has BD. Spending a few minutes with a psychiatrist does not give an accurate picture of a true lifestyle. It is only a snapshot of their life and not a long-range picture of many stressful events happening in their lives now and in the past. In my case, I finally went to a psychiatrist after being severely depressed for several months. Severe depression is what drove me to my first psychiatrist years ago. My psychiatrist at the time did not discover the many cycles of manic behavior I experienced for years, like moving to LA and a case of amnesia.

I began to socialize more and be a little bit more generous but not extravagant. I was learning not to spend money on meaningless projects. The Awake course taught me about the law of abundance and many other valuable life lessons that I could not fully grasp at the time. Even today, many concepts I learned at the Awake course have helped me at times. The principle everything happens for a reason comes to mind.

## The OLS parties got even wilder
The OLS parties got even more sexual as time went by. There was no pressure to participate, and the women could accept or reject advances. It became more recreational, like tennis or golf but a lot more fun. I'm sure someone today would videotape the parties, and it would go viral on the internet.

The OLS group sex parties were a no-judgment zone for people to express their sexuality and discover their sexual identities. It was also a place to experience their sexual fantasies live and in person. After attending several parties, I had to accept I was bisexual. I was attracted to women but also to several men. At the OLS group, I did find my true bisexual identity after struggling with it for decades.

A few months after one wild party, I learned several people in New York City were diagnosed with some type of an autoimmune disease later called AIDS. It was all over the news; it was a Sexually Transmitted Disease (STD), and it was incurable. A deadly disease was a wake-up call for the OLS group members to be more responsible. People from across the country attended the OLS sex parties.

A few months later, I contracted a Sexually Transmitted Disease STD at one wild OLS party and went to my doctor. He scolded me for my open, unprotected sex lifestyle and warned me of the deadly autoimmune virus, later called AIDS. He looked me straight in the eye and said: "There is no cure.".

I was very concerned I might have given the deadly virus to Iva, Hayley, Iva, or others. I was very disturbed by the possibility of any of us contracting the fatal illness. I never did tell Iva about the OLS parties. I stopped going to the OLS sex parties but continued to go to the nude massage sessions.

## Stage 6 Life in the '80s

After over 15 years of dating, nightclubbing, picking up women in sleazy bars for one-night stands, I was ready to stay a bachelor. I found it challenging to meet women but far more difficult to find attractive and kind women. I'm afraid I was not the most attractive mate either was an understatement at best, but I won't go into all my character flaws again.

I lost interest in finding a mate, but after my relationship with Hayley and her kids, I knew I wanted a family. When Hayley and I were not colliding with each other in one of our moody cycles, we got along just fine. For most of the time, our mood cycles were not in sync with each other. When I was up, she was down and vice versa. We even went on a short weekend vacation to the Jersey

Shore with the kids and acted like a normal family. I accepted I was bisexual but did not live an open bisexual lifestyle except during the OLS parties.

Iva did not want to have children. I mentioned I wanted to have a family a few times, but she did not respond. I was taking advantage of my "just call" relationship with Iva and thought, in a sense, we were married but in an open marriage. I felt we would always be together on a physical and spiritual level but could not admit it to myself. We always had unprotected sex; I wondered what would happen if she got pregnant. I kept my secret sex life with the OLS group hidden even from Iva.

## I met a very attractive and kind woman

I met a very attractive and kind woman named Nicole at a Sunday night dance for singles in Philadelphia. We danced, and I asked her for her phone number. I could tell she was kind, honest, and attractive. Yes, I did ask her if she liked sex on our second date, and she was not offended as far as I could tell. Maybe I found someone very special?

On our first date, we had dinner at a nice restaurant, and she ordered the least expensive entree on the menu. I hope you don't think that was the only reason I was attracted to her, but we did have a frugal, modest lifestyle in common. That night I committed to making this new relationship work. I was afraid I would be too moody or say something inappropriate like I had done in the past. Maybe I might say," Would you like to have sex with everyone at our OLS sex parties?" or some other totally inappropriate remark.

I called Lois, my friend from the OLS group, and told her I was in a monogamous relationship with someone I had recently met. I dropped out of my secret OLS lifestyle.

Iva called me one night, and I told her I was in a monogamous relationship with a woman I had just met. When I hung up, I had a sinking feeling I may have made yet another serious error in judgment. Iva and I made a pact to comfort each other. We had our rule, "just call." I thought if my new relationship with Nicole didn't work out, I might have lost Iva's trust forever. I am afraid my attitude was very selfish and shallow thinking on my part.

## *I married Nicole*

Nicole and I traveled to New England to visit my brother's family. We visited my mother at her cottage on Cape Cod. We spent some time on Cape Cod; I was finally living a "Normal" lifestyle. Nicole and I had several things in common she also wanted a family. She also was fiscally conservative; of course, I call that frugal but not cheap. We dated for a year before I asked her to marry me. Things went well. I had a good-paying job in the city, but I was harassed at work.

I still kept on spending money on all three businesses but was falling behind trying to keep up with the fast-paced PC industry. The IBM personal computer was introduced and overnight became the industry standard. My projects were designed around different older hardware and software. My projects were effectively obsolete before I finished them.

We were living in my row house in a changing neighborhood in the city. As the drug dealers gained control of our block, life became stressful and outright dangerous. We bought a very expensive but very old house in a small town outside the city.

We decided to start a family, and life became even more difficult because I needed to commute one hour each way into Philly every workday. Nicole became pregnant but, after seven months, had a complication with the pregnancy and needed to go on bed rest at our new house. As the contractions became more frequent, the doctor ordered her to go on bed rest at the hospital in Philly.

The constant conflict between management and the workers became intolerable. I was having problems even keeping my low-stress job but could not quit; I had financial obligations, our mortgage on our new house. I also had the stress of Nicole on bed rest in the hospital. I was being harassed at the job and afraid of having a nervous breakdown, but I needed to stay strong and remain calm when I visited Nicole after work.

Christmas arrived, and the doctors would not allow Nicole to go home. I was dealing with too many stressors, staying at the row house weekdays, the job, and visiting Nicole in the hospital on bed rest.

I did not know how Nicole could lie flat on her back for days then weeks. On New Year's Eve, we ordered out at a famous seafood restaurant in North Philly. I went up to pick up our take-out diner in North Philly in a very bad part of the city.

I came out of the restaurant, and the car would not start. I broke down sobbing for several minutes; I had finally reached my breaking point and needed to pull myself together and deal with all the setbacks in my life. Here I was in a very dangerous part of town late at night with a car that would not start. I tried to get out and jump the car by pushing it, but no luck.

I got back in the car and broke down again in tears. At that point, a young Black teen knocked on the car window and asked if I needed a push. Three young Black kids pushed the car until it started, and I went back to the row house to get our other car. I was physically and emotionally exhausted but felt the Philly motto of "The City of Brotherly Love" was alive and well. Nicole questioned what took me so long, and I told her about the three Black kids giving me a push to start our car. A month later, Ryan was born, and we started to settle down in our new home in the suburbs.

### Can't sell row house

We still had the row house in the hood in Philly and our new but very 70-year-old house in the suburbs. We decided to sell the row house, but after a year, no one even came to even inspect the property. When I told people the location, they quickly ended our conversation. It was years since I bought the row house, and the drug house was still in operation.

Owning two properties was becoming overwhelming. I decided to rent the row house to an African American woman I worked with at my job in the city. She was very kind and very religious and even helped me with my business. I was upfront and told her about the drug house next door. She told me the crime in her old neighborhood was so bad she needed to leave her crime-ridden block because she had a teenage daughter.

The Philly mob was still at war with each other, but the feds were closing in. Several higher-up-level mob bosses were jailed, but the drug house next door was still in operation. I had hoped the drug house was part of the mob or gangs and would be shut down by the feds permanently, no such luck.

After I was married for several years, my life had more even turmoil than my single lifestyle. Again, I hoped I would find the stability of marriage and find joy and happiness. The stress of a job, mortgages, baby, and in-laws created an enormous amount of stress for our family. The marriage obligations started to pile up, and I began to drink after work and often alone whenever I got a chance. I was fortunate; Nicole stood by me, and I received good health care from her employer. I had a good support system but still struggled with the cycles of highs and lows of BD.

I was so busy with the job in the city, the row house, and our new house I had very little time for the three businesses I started years earlier. By 1983 the IBM PC was the industry standard, and I needed to upgrade both hardware and software to develop a website and then online business.

My printer of the computer trade magazine convinced me to stop publication, and I did. This decision to continue to spend money on not one but two failing businesses was crazy, and I admit a little bit insane. I was dealing with dozens of highly stressful life situations and continued to pour hundreds of dollars into a failing business. This is the classic definition of insanity.

The WAVES Chart identifies these situations that can cause dangerous levels of stress. My stress levels kept getting higher every year until something needed to snap to release the mental, emotional, and physical stress I was under at the time.

This is a point I am trying to emphasize; everyone has their breaking point, but it happens more often and quicker if dealing with an unstable case of BD. The WAVES Chart attempts to identify these dangerous life situations before people reach their breaking point. Ideally, the goal of the workbook is to find dangerous situations long before a catastrophic psychotic episode. Sometimes it is hard for me to comprehend how my brother and I lived without lithium. I guess we didn't live but just struggled to survive to get past the next setback or crisis.

It was many years since I met Sabrina in the group psychotherapy sessions, and I often wondered how she is dealing with schizophrenia. I felt if she could survive schizophrenia, I couldn't complain about my mental issues. I felt empathy for her dealing with schizophrenia; in my opinion, it is the most difficult of all mental illnesses. She described hallucinations and delusions several times she came to the group psychotherapy sessions. The most alarming part of her illness was she could not determine real events from imaginary events—what a difficult way to live life.

As Stu and I approached mid-life, my brother and I struggled to lead even a semi "Normal" life. We endured many years of setbacks, including near bankruptcy, marriage conflicts, family conflicts, divorce, business failures, and other stressful life situations.

Our chaotic lives went on for decades before we got any relief from our constant, never-ending cycles of mania followed by episodes of devastating, life-threatening depressions. Oh, we both enjoyed the manic highs when we felt relief from the depressive cycles, but it seemed the higher the highs, the lower the lows; we had no way to escape our unstable BD lifestyles.

Thanks to Nicole, my life was bearable; she could see I was struggling with emotional issues but tried to support and accept my constant erratic behavior. The worst of times was when I was having a severe moody depression when nothing seemed to help my mood.

Summer arrived, and Nicole convinced me to attend the Music Fest in Bethlehem. The 10-day music festival did bring me out of my hopeless depression. The music and positive atmosphere lifted my spirits, and we planned to attend the music festival the following year. The last prolonged episode was longer than just a BD episode. I call it a bad spell. A bad spell was a combination of anxiety, mixed states of BD, and several stressful life situations over several weeks and even months. I hit rock bottom; I was never going to feel better.

## Stu gets stopped going 120 MPH
Stu called me and told me he got stopped going 120 miles per hour on a highway in MA. He said he lost his driver's license indefinitely and had a serious DUI case in front of him. He was afraid of jail time.

Denise had to drive him to his clients and other appointments. The court ordered him to go to AA or face jail time. After about a year, he became sober and attended AA meetings regularly.

## The stock market dropped over 500 points
In October 1987, the stock market dropped over 500 points. The New York Stock Exchange reported a record 22% drop. It was heading for another Great Depression-like 1929.

Shortly after the stock market took a dive, the banks called in loans on Stu's businesses and his real estate properties. A year later, his wife Denise filed for divorce. My brother Stu lost his business, his marriage of 20 years to divorce, lost the family home, and his self-confidence to be a good salesman. By midlife, Stu lost nearly everything, including his family's support, and was planning his suicide. The only thing he had left was his sobriety and AA for support.

Greg came to visit us; he was in good health and was married to a nice woman from Hawaii. We talked about our drinking days in our hometown. He was in contact with several of our classmates, and we talked about his difficult decision to go into the service instead of marrying the girl that he got pregnant with. I told him it was a very difficult time for both of us, and I was glad he was my best friend back in those difficult years. I told him it was hard for me to lose my best friend and have no contact for years at a time.

## Stu went up to Nantucket
The following summer Stu, went up to Nantucket to make money to pay his alimony of $1600 a month. At the car wash, Stu only made $399 a week, and that left him with only $4 a month to live on. Well, that's a bit dramatic, but he did play his trumpet on Main Street some evenings just for the fun of it and made a few dollars with his faithful dog Buster at his side.

## Is Stu planning another suicide attempt?

He told me he thought about drinking again and said he was regularly going to AA meetings. The following spring went he went up to New England and decided to sail his sailboat solo back to Florida to live on. When he told me that, I thought it was very risky and might be another suicide attempt several years ago while going 120 mph in a drunken blackout. I thought our trip around Nantucket years ago was risky, but sailing solo all the way from New England to Florida solo was a little bit over the top. I don't think either one of us would have sailed around Nantucket solo.

Stu arrived in Florida two months after leaving New England. I called him, and he told me he arrived in Florida after a few risky misadventures. I asked him, "What misadventures?" He said a guy sailed with him down past Cape Cod, but after he got lost a few times and then ran aground, his shipmate decided to take the bus back to Maine. Then he said, "That was just the beginning of my solo trip."

Stu said sailing was a way to find himself and reevaluate his life again. He told me he was sorry he did not have better navigation gear because he got lost several times. He went on with some very tall tales on his voyage all the way to Florida. I asked him if he ever found himself, and he said: "No, I was lost most of the entire trip."

At one small fishing village, a Captain warned Stu he needed to follow out the fishing boats on the high tide at 4 AM. He was warned several times he needed to go out of the harbor on a high tide at 4 am, but he could not get his engine started and headed out at 6 AM. Of course, he ran aground and needed to be towed off the sandbar.

He told the fishermen he was in a hurry to get to Florida. I said, "You had years to sail to Florida, didn't you"? Oh yes, he said, but I was always in a hurry to get places, but I never even knew where I was going. My reply, "Yes, you are always in a hurry to get where you are going, but how did you even know where you were?" Remember, you got caught going 120 mph on the freeway to get home and told the cops you were in a hurry.

Well, I thought that was a good tall sailor tale. Stu said he was lost most of the entire voyage. He would enter a little fishing village and read the transoms on the stern of the fishing boats to find out where he was before docking his boat. He called it transom navigation. You read the names of the seaside harbors off the transoms of boats; if you saw a boat named "Lady Luck out of Top Sail, NC," you sailed into Top Sail, North Carolina. I guess he didn't find himself; lost at sea was a metaphor for both of our lives at that point.

I was thankful he reached Florida but still questioned the risk he took sailing solo down the Atlantic Coast for over 1500 miles. Stu settled into his new lifestyle living on his sailboat, and I thought it was a very inexpensive way to stay in Florida. He was still sober, attending AA meetings regularly but was living on his sailboat at a local marina surrounded by homeless people with drug and alcohol problems.

Stu planned to start a sailing school in Florida and spend his summers in New England. The following summer, he drove up to New England packed all his sailing gear, sails, anchors, and motors to bring down to Florida.

When he arrived at our house, he had a huge trailer filled with motorboat parts and sailing gear for his new sailing school business. He told us his trailer was so overloaded the New Jersey State Police would not let him drive on the New Jersey Turnpike. I never saw so much junk on one trailer and mentioned it looked like Noah's ark. I can't complain about his junk collecting. I have the same character flaw; it's a hereditary trait from our father's side of the family.

I felt a bit guilty he was having such a difficult time; we could not help him financially, we had a huge mortgage, and I was so dysfunctional I was no help even to myself.

## Stu was rear-ended by a tractor-trailer but found Buster

Stu headed out for Florida, towing his overloaded trailer. He was driving down I-95 in the middle of the night through North Carolina and was hit in the rear by a tractor-trailer. The tractor-trailer driver thought he fell asleep and hit Stu's trailer from behind, damaging Stu's junk, I mean the valuable sailing gear. Stu got the tow truck driver to hoist his junk back onto his trailer, and he headed to Florida. After Stu got to Florida, he filed a claim with the truck driver's insurance company for the loss of $15,000.

The insurance company refused to pay Stu for his losses, but Stu located the trucking company in Florida; he got a broken motor from the accident and walked into the trucking companies' president's office. After showing the president of the company a broken motor, he told him he could not start his sailing school without the insurance money. The president made their insurance company release a check for $15,000 to pay for Stu's losses.

Stu cashed the check for 15,000 and started to look for a place to live. He found a very small cottage for $15,000 near Homestead, Florida. Under the towns Homestead Act, cities were giving awards to many people incentives to live in low-cost housing. The Homestead Act gave him the right to live in the city without paying any property taxes for long as he lived in the house. Stu now had a place to stay and his sailboat school for income.

Shortly after Stu moved into his cottage, a dog showed up at his door. Stu said the dog looked at him as if to say, "Do you need a friend?" Stu found a friend and named him Buster, and Buster found a place to call home.

## Stu met a Floridian named Lara

Stu was meeting women at AA meetings and had good support from people at AA meetings. He met a woman named Lara at a BBQ one night. They started to see each other and quickly became more than just friends. Stu finally found a good time to tell her he had a mental illness, and she seemed to accept his illness. She had doctor's appointments quite often but would never tell Stu about her illness. After a few months, she finally told Stu she had a rare form of cancer with no standard treatment. She found a research hospital in Orlando that treated her cancer-free of charge in exchange for experimental drug treatments. Getting to her doctor's appointments 100 miles away was challenging, but Lara also loved the Atlantic Ocean.

Stu got his sailing school business up and running, not making enough money to pay all his bills, and certainly couldn't pay the $1600 a month alimony to Denise. He was still depressed; he had no steady income, no healthcare insurance, and is living day-to-day, trying to make money with the sailing school. He thought about taking groups out on sunset cruises around the harbor.

I called Stu a few weeks later and asked them how the sailing lessons business was going for him. He said he decided to take more groups of people out on sunset cruises to make up for lost income from the sailing school.

## I left the job in the city and put the row house up for sale

Nicole had a successful part-time job with a good income and good family health care benefits. I told my wife I needed to leave the job in the city before I got fired for bizarre behavior. I was showing the symptoms of a severe stress disorder. I had one hour to commute into the city, eight hours of being harassed on the dead-end job, and another hour in bumper-to-bumper traffic to get back home.

I was still renting the row house to Violet, and she always paid the rent on time; she told me her daughter was getting into trouble in the neighborhood but said she was not on drugs.

The news had stories of the mob wars in Philly almost every night on the local and national news. Everyone knew the mob was involved in drugs, loan sharking, gambling, and extortion. I stayed away from the South Street Farmers Market in South Philly, where many of the mob guys hung out. I was paranoid; I could be targeted as an informant or member of a rival mob. Well, I was not worried about the mob as much as the drug dealer next door targeting me as an informant.

## Hayley decided to move back to the Midwest

Hayley decided to move back to the Midwest; she came to our house, and I gave Hayley and the boys a big hug. I always wanted to be a good dad to them. I felt I had let them down as my father did to me. I should have spent more time with them after I heard they wanted a father mentor from Big Brother.

One night I came home from work late, I was walking home in the dark from the train station, and I was attacked from behind only ten blocks from our house in the suburbs. A White guy about 30 years old jumped me from behind, I fought him off, but I was badly shaken. So much for the safe suburbs; I filed a report with the police. How ironic; I lived in the row house in Philly for ten years and was never robbed or attacked in the dark coming back to my row house.

I was becoming very distraught, commuting 2 hours by train, 8 hours at I job I despised every day. My business plans were not working out. The job was getting more stressful every day. My boss still was harassing me almost daily. I told Nicole I was afraid I was going to blow up at one of the abusive supervisors at work and be fired. Nicole thought it was a good time to quit before I got fired. I told Nicole shortly after I met her; I wanted to leave the dead-end job and start a business.

I complained to Nicole I could not tolerate the job in the city any longer. Nicole understood my concerns, and I put in my resignation the following Monday. After I quit the job in the city, I was desperate to sell the row house.

## I worked on my business after I quit the job in the city

I started work on my business full-time. Just like many experts in the computer industry predicted, the IBM personal computer was popular shortly after its introduction. Most of my software and personal computers became obsolete.

I went to flea markets and trade shows to sell my old computers, but no one wanted the old first-generation PCs. I went to a large Trenton Computer Festival in New Jersey and brought thousands of dollars' worth of old computer equipment to sell. I only sold a couple of old computer systems for 20 cents on the dollar. I brought copies of my computer trade magazine to pass out at the show, hoping to get listings to put in the magazine and put online on my website.

## I stopped publishing the trade magazine

Several weeks after the Trenton Computer Festival, I only got a few listings to put in the trade magazine. I met with the printer to publish the next issue of the magazine. He told me his company is making money on every issue I published, but he has to be honest with me. He recommended I stop printing the magazine. He told me to stop publishing the trade magazine two years ago; he thought it was a bad idea.

I took his advice and stopped the publication of the next issue. Now I needed to concentrate on the online business and become a computer reseller.

We decided to put Ryan in daycare to allow me to work full-time on the business. Daycare informed us Ryan's behavior is very disruptive, and he won't take a nap. In the mornings, it took me half an hour to get him up to go into day care. Nicole is working the night shift, and our time together is becoming less as I struggle to get the business off the ground.

## What happened to Iva after WW II?

In November of 1989, I watched as the Berlin wall fell. I thought of Iva again after seeing the Berlin Wall fall on live TV, allowing German citizens to pass freely between East and West Germany for the first time since the end of WW II.

Iva was about my age and was only three years old in 1945 when WW II ended. Iva came to America when she was only 8. I wonder if she escaped to West Germany and then came to America as a refugee. You know, I never even knew if she became a US citizen, and I didn't care. I never asked her anything about her life before she arrived in America. I am sure she would teach us all the tragic lessons of any war. I know she witnessed horrendous events because she never spoke about her life in war-torn Europe. Throughout all the suffering, she was such a compassionate woman and treated everyone with respect and kindness. She never thought of herself as a victim, and I treated her as a kind and true survivor.

Perhaps I should contact her now and learn more about her past, but I have enough to worry about in my life right now.

I hope we can have a better relationship with Russia in the future. From the WW II battles, I saw the Russians were fearless fighters. I remember seeing war films of the battle of Stalingrad, where the Russian troops fought the Germans block by block until the Russian troops eventually surrounded the Germans. The Russians did not fall back for the rest of the war.

After and during WW II, Russia acquired many small countries, even dividing East and West Germany. Iva was living in one of those small defenseless countries taken over by the Russians. All this conflict led to the Cold War. I remember the Cold War back in the '60s when we were in the arms race. I think we had well over 6000 nuclear bombs; it was a terrifying global threat to our entire planet.

## We decided to have one more child; we named him Matt

Ryan was in elementary school, and home life became tolerable, so we decided to have another child. Nicole was approaching an age where it became a risk to have another child. We both knew the risk of premature labor and possible miscarriage, but we took the chance. Everything went well until the 7$^{th}$ month. Nicole went into premature labor, but our new baby boy was healthy; we named him Matthew or Matt.

## Tragedy on our row house doorsteps

I got a call one morning at our house in the suburbs, and a neighbor on our block in Philly told me Violet's daughter was stabbed in the back on the stoop (steps) in front of our row house and died at the hospital.

I felt so guilty about the tragic death of her daughter. I called Violet and asked her if I could help in any way. I offered her free rent for as long as she wanted to stay. She was a very deeply religious woman and accepted her daughter's death was in God's hands. I went to her church and signed the prayer book, but I was too ashamed or, more honestly, too afraid to attend her daughter's service. Violet moved out shortly after her daughter's tragic death. I should never have rented the apartment to Violet and her daughter. This was yet another regret I had in my life.

### I sold the row house as a rent to own
I waited a few months to rent the second-floor apartment, but I did not want to leave it vacant. I rented the second-floor apartment to four college students. They also told me our neighborhood was far more secure than the area around their own campus in North Philly. They seemed to be good kids, but I could smell weed several times I went down to work on the house. Weed did not bother me, but other drugs did. All four of the kids seemed very responsible and paid the rent right on time.

After several months, I gave them an offer they could not pass up. I sold the row house as a rent to buy property over several years. I took a chance; they were good kids. The rents around their campus in north Philly were hundreds of dollars per month; all four kids could all buy our row house for the same as monthly rent on just one apartment. When they split the rent, they were living almost rent-free and buying our row house at the same time.

It took five years to sell the row house after we bought our new but old house in the suburbs. If our row house were in a different neighborhood, it would have been sold years earlier.

### My hoarding addiction expands into the suburbs
Now that we sold the row house, I needed to move stuff out of the basement. In hindsight, I should have cleared out the stuff after we bought the duplex in the suburbs. Most of the computers and parts were obsolete even before we moved into our house in the suburbs.

The stuff was only worth pennies on the dollar, but I moved it all into the basement of our new house using our small car and dozens of trips back and forth to the row house. I planned to go to flea markets, and computer shows to sell the computer stuff. I sold very little at the flea markets but began buying more modern computers and repairing them. I was much better at fixing than selling computers.

## I built a garage for the computer business

I was not going to give up on my online shopping website. I convinced Nicole we needed a garage to start my online business. The garage was completed in six months. I moved all the computers to the new garage. I justified the cost of the garage; I needed to secure my inventory. Sometimes I would have more than $10,000 of inventory. I set up the computer server in the garage but only had two phone lines coming into the garage.

I was way over my head; I needed someone to design the online network and run the online business while I was busy designing the online software.

I sold a few computers locally but teaching people to use them was a very time-consuming chore. The computer software was difficult to learn or teach. I was not a good salesman or instructor. Becoming a computer retailer was not going to happen. I was determined to sell computers on my own online computer website.

## I closed all my businesses, and we moved to Florida

Now I was free to devote all my time to the businesses. I worked 60 hours a week on the two businesses I started when we lived in the city. After the IBM personal computer was released, all my computer hardware and software needed to be updated to be competitive. I needed to spend thousands of dollars on upgrading my hardware and software to stay in business.

Summer came, and Nicole took Ryan and Matt up to my mother's place in NE. I stayed home and worked on my business every day until midnight.

Our new garage was filled with new and old computer parts, books, printers, and assorted office equipment. A year later, my $10,000 in inventory was only worth at the most 1000 dollars.

Between family obligations and my BD issues, I was overwhelmed again. A year later, my accountant told me to close all the businesses. I had lost thousands of dollars with no chance of ever making a profit. I had some good business ideas but could not make any of them a success.

In July, we went to visit Nicole's parents on the West Coast of Florida. After a few weeks, we decided to move down to Tampa for one year. I flew back to PA, stored our furniture in the garage, rented our place, packed up my work van, and drove to Tampa all within two weeks.

This was another hypo manic BD episode. After a few months in Florida, I was depressed and started to drink to excess. I could not find any computer-related work, and it did not make sense to put Matt in daycare; besides, we needed someone to watch Ryan after school. Nicole and the kids loved the Florida lifestyle. This move was just another repeat of my hasty move to LA many years earlier.

I spiraled downward into another black hole fueled by several setbacks and alcoholism. I was experiencing guilt and shame for the business failures after spending thousands of dollars when in a hypo manic state of mind. Our marriage was in jeopardy, and I was not responsible enough to care for our children, let alone our family. My life was a series of failures and disappointments for both my family and myself.

We decided I would stay at home and become a househusband; I was relieved in a way because I avoided the stressful tasks of getting and keeping a job. It did not make any sense to put the kids in daycare because of the high cost of daycare. We were living on the West Coast of Florida, and Stu lived on the East Coast about a hundred miles apart; I was so messed up I didn't even want to visit him.

This "I don't care if I live or die" attitude was not uncommon; several times when I was severely depressed, I would lose contact with Stu. We would lose contact for months until we felt better. The WAVES Chart lists several job-related stressors and financial issues that can accumulate and lead to a psychotic episode.

My friend Maria married Ethan, and they moved to France. She was a person I could talk to about my setbacks. She sent me letters after we moved to Florida, but I never replied to her letters or postcards. I was so ashamed of my life and didn't even bother to contact her after we became such close friends for so many years. My BD illness was taking its toll on my mental health and on our marriage. I found postcards from my friend Maria in France, but they did not have a return address. Sadly, I lost all contact with my friend Maria after she moved to France.

## Stage 7 Recovery-Life after 50 on lithium
My life in Florida became more difficult because I was drinking before dinner and trying to cover it up. I was severely depressed and was not taking proper care of Matt during the day. I was not paying attention to the kids' or Nicole's needs. Being neglected is what I accused my family of how I was treated for years. Now I was treating my family like I was treated when living with my family. Nicole was sleeping during the day, and after dinner, we would go to a park.

Our new tenant at our house in PA abruptly moved out without any notice. This was just another hassle in my confused and messed-up life. We could not afford to stay in Florida with a very high mortgage payment on our house in PA.

Stu arrived at our place in Florida, and he was flat broke. I felt guilty we could not help him financially; we had a huge mortgage payment on our house in PA in addition to paying rent on the apartment in Florida.

I was so upset and depressed. I wanted to move back to PA. I made a deal with Nicole if we moved back to our home in PA. I would stop drinking. Nicole left her notice at her job, and we packed up and drove nonstop to South of the Border. The kids were asleep in the car, so we continued and drove nonstop back to our home in PA.

I did stop drinking cold turkey; I had no other choice after I hit rock bottom. I went to a few AA meetings but thought my alcoholism was not the primary cause of my chaotic and frankly miserable life. I convinced myself maybe I was not an alcoholic; after all, my proof, I stopped drinking after we returned from Florida.

## Stu meets a fellow sailor that is a psychiatrist

Several months later, I called Stu to see how his sailing school was doing in Florida? He said he scheduled a cruise with a party of five to go out for a sunset cruise one evening. One older man on the cruise said he was a doctor and had sailed racing yachts for years all around the Caribbean. Stu struck up a conversation with him about his sailing adventures, and he quickly became friends with the doctor. Stu said his name was Dr. Freed, and he was a multimillionaire that had owned very large racing yachts years ago.

After a while, they got to know each other better. Dr. Freed told Stu he thought he could help Stu because he has been treating many patients with medications. He told Stu many people had dramatic changes in their lives. Some people were released from mental hospitals that had been institutionalized for years. Dr. Freed also told Stu he would help him at no cost, and he would provide him medicine and psychiatric care.

After Stu told me about his doctor friend, I did not think anyone could help Stu. He had been in and out of psychiatric hospitals and even told he needed ECT or shock therapy as a last resort to help his depressions. Stu said he felt better after two weeks of receiving treatment with lithium.

Shortly after his remarkable recovery from years of many cycles of mania and depression, he was stable on lithium in just a few weeks. After I learned about his rapid recovery, I found a psychiatrist in our area, who also treated me with lithium.

Here, we are both about 50 years old; let's say at mid-life and just receiving effective treatment with lithium. One definition of a mid-life crisis is a deep emotional crisis. Well, if that's the case, Stu and I had been in a deep emotional mid-life crisis from birth.

So, at mid-life were properly treated for bipolar and given an effective med, lithium. Maybe years ago, our doctors accurately diagnosed our mental illnesses as BD, but without proper medical treatment, we were both very unstable.

I began to learn more about mood disorders from books and magazines. I also referred to the old edition of the DSM [ American Psychiatric Association, 1987) to learn more about all types of mental illnesses.

Although other disorders were still with us, treatment with lithium meant some control over our lives and a path to acceptance and healing. We learned to manage our lives better, and I began to recover from decades of alcohol abuse.

## The 1992 Rodney King LA riots

The nightly news showed a Black man named Rodney King severely beaten by several police officers in the streets of LA. The savage beating of an unarmed Black man was an example of police brutality, plain and simple.

I was busy dealing with my family issues, but the press and the entire nation were fixated on the Rodney King trial. The cops went on trial, and all were found not guilty.

Living in the inner city for over ten years, I realized a lot of these violent acts occur. The beating was shown every night on the national news for everyone to witness. It was obvious the police used excessive force in order to punish an African-American.

The trial ended, and every cop was exonerated of all the charges in the beating of Rodney King. Now I support the police, but this verdict was unjust on many levels. The trial was held in another city, and the jurors were not Rodney King's peers. The trial was originally set in LA, but the police attorneys thought the police could not get a fair trial in Los Angeles, so they moved the trial out of the city.

Several days riots continued all across the city, and hundreds of buildings were burned down. Riots and looting continued for many days and nights. People were shown looting many businesses in broad daylight.

Back when I lived in LA, I went to Compton with a Hispanic guy to pick up a car and was warned it was a very violent place at night. He did not need to tell me that. I sensed the tension and realized the Hispanic community could also explode into riots if the cops abused anyone in the hood as they did with Rodney King.

Back in the '70s, when I was in LA, I sensed real hostility between cops and the African American community. After all the police officers were acquitted of all the charges, the riots and looting lasted for days.

## Talk shows advise, "Don't marry someone with a mental illness."

I was watching daytime TV one day, and the topic was how to have a happy married life. The host said the number one rule for a happy life is "Don't marry someone with a mental illness." The words "Don't marry someone with a mental illness" were in big, bold letters across the entire TV screen. A feeling of sadness came over me, and it was the truth; it is a difficult life for some people to marry someone with a mental illness. The talk show host then said, "If you find out the person has a mental illness, run away," some people in the audience laughed softly. I guess it was said as a joke, but it was no joke to me.

I felt very sad; they were basically telling people never to fall in love with a mentally ill person. So, someone with a mental illness should never fall in love because the partner will run away? This attitude toward the mentally ill upset me greatly, but I needed to learn more about mental illness, not just run away. A few days later, I came to the conclusion I needed to learn more about mental illness before I could talk to other people about BD.

## Here is lesson 101 for anyone with mental illness

My psychiatrist moved his practice a half an hour away, and he only spent five minutes of his time writing another prescription. For several days my anxiety got a lot worse, I thought I was going insane, but I prefer crazy. I called my psychiatrist, but he didn't call me back. I called the next day, I left a message on his answering machine, and I asked for the doctor on call. No response.

During the night, I was having what was what I would call a severe panic attack, a dire emotional crisis. Again, my psychiatrist still did not call me back; no one was on call to take my repeated calls for help.

I could not sit still or sleep; from studying several articles, this behavior was a symptom of a serious mental illness of some kind. After several hours I told Nicole I needed to go over to our local psychiatric hospital. After an evaluation, they put me in the partial day program. The partial is a two-week daytime program to evaluate and stabilize my condition. The hospital has a psychiatrist on hand around the clock; you can just ask to see a psychiatrist any time, day or night.

A few days later, the psychiatrist determined I was not taking the right dose of my mood stabilizer, lithium. I don't know what happened; I was embarrassed to go back to the partial day program. I thought I was taking lithium every day, so I was concerned lithium was no longer working. After just a few days on the right dose of lithium, I was back feeling stable again. Lithium was an almost magic pill. How could a little pill change my moods so dramatically in just a few days? After that psychodrama, I made a commitment to say on my psychiatric meds.

So, here is lesson 101 for anyone with mental illness; if your psychiatrist does not call you back within a few hours, find a new psychiatrist or go to an emergency room of any hospital. A few days later, I found a psychiatrist closer to our house. All this psychodrama convinced me everyone with mental illness needs to become stable early on and stay on meds to remain stable. After my panic attack, it took me only a few days to become stable again, thanks to our excellent doctors at our psychiatric hospital.

## Stu started a halfway house
During this time, Stu started a halfway house in Florida for people with addictions to drugs and alcohol. Dr freed bought a house close to his place to start a sober house. Stu became very active in AA and the 12 Step program, and he learned to make amends for past misdeeds and began a path to healing.

I was a bit envious of Stu because he was helping people with drug and alcohol problems and starting a good business with his psychiatrist and friend Dr. Freed. I had no direction in my life and began to feel like a burden on our family and a failure to myself. To make matters even worse, my sexual drive was lacking, and I felt ashamed I was becoming incapable of having sex. I had learned my sexual identity was bisexual years ago but had no sexual desire to live a bisexual lifestyle.

## I kicked into my college study mode
After getting a diagnosis of BD, I felt relieved in a way and yet sad at the same time. I began to understand many reasons for our behavior over the past 50 years. I had studied mental illness years ago after attending group psychotherapy but couldn't self-diagnose my mental illness. Now it was clear Stu and I most likely have textbook classic cases of bipolar disorder. I could not understand why doctors could not diagnose our BD disorder much earlier in life. Then I thought perhaps they did, but there was no effective treatment back then.

## My psychiatrist recommended a talk therapist
A few years later, I had my BD under control but was having other emotional problems. I would complain to my psychiatrist I was anxious. He recommended I see a talk therapist. I was worried about talking about my childhood and all those abandonment issues. I was ashamed to talk about my failures, job losses, and thousands of dollars on failed projects.

At that time, I was still in a state of amnesia and did not want to deal with both my hidden case of amnesia and abandonment issues. I had a bad experience with group psychotherapy years earlier. Over the years, I did go to about a dozen, maybe more family doctors, a few more psychiatrists, and not one of them mentioned a mood disorder. I was beginning to heal from some of the painful wounds of my past, but I was sure talk therapy was not my path to enlightenment.

## I turned over ownership of the row house

The college kids I sold the row house were now young adults. They paid off the entire amount owed on our row house in the city. The college kids were not kids any longer; they were all young professionals and had good jobs in the city. They only missed a few payments the entire time. I didn't even go back to the row house. It was a chapter in my life; I would rather just forget.

I owned in the row house for ten stressful years, and the drug house next door was still in operation. If the row house was in a different section of the city, it could be a very frugal way for Nicole and me to live. After Ryan reached school age, it would be very difficult to live anywhere in the city; the schools were a disaster. However, the taxes and maintenance of the row house were just a fraction of the upkeep and mortgage costs of our old house in the suburbs. That was my frugal at any cost model, very frugal but may have cost us our lives in a more crime-ridden part of the city.

## I need to deal with my hoarding disorder

I was still going to flea markets to sell computers, but I bought computers that needed repairs for just a few dollars. Sometimes all they needed was to replace the memory. I was not making a lot of money but was not losing thousands of dollars as I did on the three businesses I started years ago. I was not honestly dealing with my obsessive-compulsive disorder to hoard stuff; I enjoyed fixing things.

## Stu invited us to Nantucket
The following summer, Stu invited us to Nantucket and found us a place to stay outside of town at no cost, and we had a blast. He worked at the car rental agency at the airport, and he borrowed a jeep to take us out to Great Point. Great Point was at the tip of the island, only accessible by jeep. The boys had a blast driving the Jeep over the sand all the way out to Great Point. We went surf fishing, caught several bluefish, and made a campfire on the beach.

The wild natural beauty of the island was very exciting and calming at the same time. That night we went out to Main Street watched Stu play his trumpet just for fun and make a few dollars. He always had his dog Buster with him at all times.

You know, all the time we spent on our trip to Nantucket, I never remembered my tragic breakup with Maria. My memory of that entire tragic event was buried deep in my mind in a case of amnesia.

## Stu gets a free ride in a Medivac helicopter
The following Christmas, Stu was flying up to New England to visit his girlfriend to have sex. I mean, go out to dinner. On the plane, he began to feel nauseous and had chest pains. He landed in Boston and got on a bus to his son's place on the North Shore. He ignored the symptoms, but the chest pain got so bad he had to tell the bus driver. The bus driver stopped the bus along the highway and called 911. The EMTs arrived and said it was critical he gets to the ER as soon as possible they suspected a heart attack. They flew him by helicopter to a nearby hospital and took him into the operating room. The doctors performed a test and proceeded to unblock an artery in his heart. Anyway, at the end of the procedures, they abruptly stopped and said he was okay and sent him to the recovery room. In the recovery room, they said he could be released, and he could go home.

Apparently, the hospital found out he didn't have health care insurance. He got a bill from the hospital for $34,000 and another bill for the helicopter ride for $15,000. I told him this is the type of thing guys do to have sex; it's a life and death decision. I experienced several shallow experiences to get dates in Seattle. Sometimes I took desperate measures just to find companionship; I mean a one-night stand. I asked him if he died?" I said, "I think that was the same procedure I had in LA when I had my near-death experience."

Our adventures sometimes turn into misadventures. When Stu told me that story, I had to laugh, but it wasn't funny at the time; he could have "checked out" for good, as my mother called it. I call these adventures misadventures because most are timed badly and could end with a very tragic outcome. Maybe you need to be a bit mentally ill to understand our bipolar lifestyle; sometimes, it's humorous to us but to no one else.

At times we do laugh at the stupid things we do, like Stu crashing our family car and trying to put a new body on it in our driveway. Sometimes we make complete fools of ourselves and have a good belly laugh, but our behavior was not funny to the people around us. Stu called us intentionally dysfunctional and mentally ill idiots. I don't know about being intentionally dysfunctional, but we didn't have free will to do whatever we wanted to do. Before treatment, we were at the mercy of where our BD illness took us.

## Stu's very serious health emergency
During some routine blood work at the hospital, they found Stu had an abnormal prostate. When he went back to Florida, he was told he needed surgery, but like many men, they don't want to have any surgery. He was told several times but wanted a second opinion. After going to several doctors, they advised radiation therapy instead of surgery because of the risk of having another heart attack.

After several visits, they implanted markers to start the radiation treatments. I was busy and thought it was just a routine procedure, so I did not call him for a few days. I could not get in contact with him for a week. I finally got through to the hospital, and he told me the near-death experience from complications with the radiation treatment.

He went home after one treatment and thought he had just the flu, but his temperature rose to over 104 degrees in a matter of a few hours. His neighbor came to visit him and immediately called 911. He was rushed to the emergency room and got IV treatment with antibiotics for several hours, but his condition was even getting worse. Around midnight the infectious disease doctor was called into the hospital. He was put on a very strong drug to control a blood infection. A few days later, they told him he came very close to dying of a very serious blood infection.

Family life became tolerable, and I continued to take my meds for BD. Ryan was about to enter high school, and Matt was doing well in elementary school. Looking back, I think it was a good idea to move back from Florida years ago. The schools in our area are excellent, and the kids are making lasting friendships. Ryan has joined the high school band and is learning to play the trumpet. His Uncle Stu also learned to play trumpet when he was in high school.

## Ryan has been diagnosed with ADHD

About a year later, Ryan was diagnosed as having ADHD. Ryan's behavior in school is becoming erratic, and I suspect he may have serious emotional problems. However, I was reluctant to tag him with a case of BD just because I had been diagnosed with it myself.

We are getting reports from the school, and the truant officer suspects drug use. Ryan never comes back from school and spends his time at a friend's house a few streets over. Nicole doesn't want him to take any toxic meds until he is diagnosed by a competent psychiatrist. Ryan's high school administration recommended he attend an alternative high school for troubled kids. At this point, Ryan is considered an at-risk teen and is heading down the road to become a part of the legal system.

### My psychiatrist recommended a talk therapist
A few years later, I had my BD under control but was having other emotional problems. I would complain to my psychiatrist I was anxious. He recommended I see a talk therapist. I was worried about talking about my childhood and all those abandonment issues. I was ashamed to talk about my failures, sexual abuse, job losses, and squandering thousands of dollars on failed projects.

At that time, I was still in a state of amnesia and did not want to deal with both my hidden case of amnesia and abandonment issues. I had a bad experience with group psychotherapy years earlier.

Over the years, I did go to about six, maybe more family doctors and a dozen more psychiatrists, not one of them mentioned a mood disorder. I was beginning to heal from some of the painful wounds of my past, but I was sure talk therapy was not my path to enlightenment, so to speak.

## Stage 8 Discovery—A Bipolar Disorder Support (BDS) group
For the past five years, I have studied articles and learned as much as I could about my bipolar disorder. Stu was more interested in helping people with alcohol and drug addictions. He started a halfway house in Florida.

As I sat in my psychiatrist's office, I picked up a brochure about a bipolar disorder support (BDS) group in our area. I must say, I thought I had a vast amount of knowledge about anything and everything bipolar; I did not think I needed to attend a support group. Then I thought I could tell my very long and sad story to the BD group. I could tell the group Stu, and I did not get diagnosed with BD until we were about 50 years old.

So, I decided to attend the next BDS group meeting. Before I went to the first meeting, I had my BD sob story ready to tell the group. At my very first meeting, I quickly realized my life was relatively stress-free compared to many people in the group. Some people in the group lost jobs, marriage problems, divorces, physical and mental abuses by friends, family, and coworkers. I heard stories of the setbacks and hardships of many people in the BD group at my very first meeting.

I was fortunate I had a safe and good home life and a wife that supported my struggle with BD and other issues. No one in the BD group was spared rich, poor, young and old, White, Black, Brown, we all struggled with the highs and lows of our bipolar illness.

I soon realized people without good treatment had much more stress and conflict in their lives. I also noted people were living with the illness their entire life and not just after they reached adulthood. Although for some people, a crisis triggered a psychotic episode later in life, the symptoms of BD started very early in life. That was the case for both my brother and me, he had more bouts of mania, and I had more agitated moody depressions from an early age. Many people agreed they had BD episodes from a very young age. Many people acted out used alcohol and drugs. Some people got diagnosed with ADHD at an early age, and others had oppositional defiant behavior after pre-teen.

Like my brother and I, other people did not get a diagnosis of BD until later on in life. I became an advocate for people to get treatment for BD early on. I praised young people in the group who got diagnosed early on in life. I told my story of the consequences of not getting help until mid-life.

I became very active in the BDS group. My observations provided a basis for many of the insights into what I call the bipolar lifestyle. Attending the BDS group was certainly an eye-opener for me. Why were so many people struggling with BD? The lives of most people were chaotic and frankly depressing for me to witness. Many people lost jobs, homes, and even support from families and friends. I was peering into the lives of people struggling with many problems unique to BD. I was humbled by seeing how most people handled such difficult living and working conditions.

I noticed many people who came to the group looked worn out from years of stress and hardships of living with BD. I also looked worn out as well after battling BD and alcoholism for decades. I wasn't taking care of myself; I had my own issues, but compared to other people, my life was tolerable.

Some of us had multiple mental issues and addictions. The only positive ray of hope was we all understood each other and bonded because we all experienced the same illness. We treated each other with respect and kindness. We tried to be non-judgmental because we did not know when our next BD episode would take place. You notice I said when and not if the next BD episode would happen.

If a member asked for help, we offered advice. Sometimes we just listened to members tell their stories. I found a second home after attending the BDS group. It was a safe environment after years of rejection I experienced in my childhood. We also discussed the pros and cons of certain meds for BD. We did not share meds but learned about side effects and the effectiveness of good vs. harmful meds.

Our group leader Rosie had a "good doc" list of good psychiatrists in the area. The "good doc" list proved to be very valuable for many people. We advised many members to get a second opinion from psychiatrists on the "good doc" list. Some people essentially got mistreatment instead of good treatment. One woman was taking six psych meds and arrived at the meeting acting like a zombie. Needless to say, we strongly advised her to get a second opinion from a psychiatrist on Rosie's "good doc" list.

I tell people in the BD group my story when I went to our psychiatric hospital during a severe panic attack. My psychiatrist at the time did not call me back after several days. The psychiatric hospital recommended a new psychiatrist. I got an appointment the following day. We are very fortunate to have a first-class psychiatric hospital in our area. I pitch my message to people in the BD group to use our great psychiatric hospital to get and stay stable early on in life.

I began to see more young people coming to the BDS group meetings; our leader Rosie and the founder of the BDS group showed sympathy and kindness toward everyone that came to the sessions. Many people were in crisis and had no healthcare. She found them psychiatric care from local county assistance programs. Rosie even got people free medicine from the drug companies. I admire her patience and commitment to helping all people with mental illness. Many people resisted treatment, but after seeing other people get much better, they usually accepted their illness. Accepting you have a lifetime mental illness is very difficult for most people.

## Starting a Journal

Our group leader Rosie is a very good writer and encouraged people to keep a diary; she wrote several articles about the BDS group in the local papers. She also wrote several books. I talked to several women who found it therapeutic to keep a diary. They relied on their diary to examine thoughts and emotions and detect patterns of when they were manic or depressed. For example, someone may have a depressive episode after spending time with an abusive relative.

At first, I rejected the idea of a diary because I could hardly write a complete sentence. As more people attended the sessions, I found it very difficult to remember people's names, so I started to take brief notes about the different issues people were having with BD. I did not want to call my notes a diary because a diary sounded too girlish, so I called my collection of notes a journal. A journal sounds more like an important self-study official document. I guess that is what I was writing an emotional self-study of my life, just kidding.

## No one appeared to lead a "Normal" life

After attending the group for several years, I had more questions than answers about our BD illness. Why were we all experiencing such a difficult time trying to lead "Normal" lives? After several years, I had stacks of notes from many of the sessions in my journal. No one seemed to lead a "Normal" life. I concluded most people would never lead a normal life; it is more of a BD normal life, as I call it.

At first, I thought only my brother and I struggled with BD illness. I came to the conclusion most people in our group had far more challenges in their lives than either my brother or me. The only major difference was we lived 50 years or until mid-life before we got proper treatment for our bipolar disorders.

## I developed the Bipolar WAVES Stress Chart

I started a list of many situations and events that caused unique and abnormal stress in people's lives. I developed the Bipolar WAVES Stress Chart for people with BD. The Bipolar WAVES Stress Chart is in Appendix A.

I began to question from a philosophical point of view why we are living with such a devastating illness. It is so unfair; why are we born with these challenges? This is a question I have asked myself many times, especially when I am depressed and feel sorry for myself. Then my mantra repeats, "Why me; it is so unfair my friends and family do not understand the challenges I face every day."

Then I remembered Sabrina, the woman living with schizophrenia. She could have complained about how unfair it was living with schizophrenia. She was trying to cope with her illness and was attempting to get us to talk about our mental issues. Sabrina was trying to help us all deal with our illness, but I was not trying to help her.

I did not show Sabrina respect or kindness after I met her at the group psychotherapy sessions; I avoided contact with her because I did not accept my shortcomings and learned to be kind to her. She did have some bizarre thoughts and behavior. I was not helping her cope with her devastating illness. However, she had a free and unique personality, and I wish now I had taken the time to become her friend.

I did not know or understand at that time what I needed to do, help other people cope with BD. Now I look back at those dark days and nights and realize doctors were not treating my most destructive mental illness, my BD illness. I think if I were stable on effective BD medications, the group psychotherapy sessions would be very beneficial because, as I learned 25 years later, I was also dealing with personality, stress disorders, alcohol abuse, amnesia, and other issues.

Years ago, I learned an anti-depression medication for my depression was probably not a drug of choice for people with BD mental illness and could cause more harm than good. I also think I do have personality disorders, and it probably was not good med for my other mental issues. Ideally, I needed to get treatment early on in life for my BD illness before other issues compounded to cause much bigger problems.

### I was abused and neglected since a child was a common theme

After I regularly attended the BDS group for several years, I noticed a common pattern. A common theme was, "Since a child, I was mistreated by many people, ridiculed, verbally abused, shunned and shamed by family and friends."

I noticed many people had poor self-esteem; no one really cared if they left or stayed in a relationship or a job. Statistics supported my claim about 90 percent of marriages end in divorce if one spouse has BD.

The shame and guilt of having a serious mental illness made some people feel worthless and not loved or lovable. I had similar feelings, unworthy of being loved by anyone. I almost don't want to admit it, but I did not have anyone tell me they loved me when I was a child.

### I have bad spells, cycles of BD, plus feelings of unworthiness

I came to the conclusion my BD was a major problem, but I also had other issues that prevented me from feeling loved by anyone. I call these prolonged periods of mixed emotions, depression, anxiety, and shame bad spells. After I was diagnosed with BD and put on lithium several years ago now, I did not experience major cycles of mania or depression any longer, but something else was causing anxiety and feelings I was a failure. For some reason, I did not deserve to be successful. My emotional struggle to publish the workbook was just one example. Then all of a sudden, I realized I have been struggling with dual conditions most of my life, my BD disorder, plus deep feelings of unworthiness. I needed to put a name to my deep feelings of unworthiness; I named my dual condition my unworthy syndrome.

## Ryan was diagnosed with ADHD, again

Our oldest son Ryan was always causing problems at school and at home. The school guidance counselor advised us to take him to a child psychologist. He was diagnosed with ADHD and put on a medicine to help him to focus better during classes at school. They told us he had oppositional defiant behavior. We did not need to go to a child psychologist to figure that one out; we argued and fought with him over the most trivial things you could ever imagine.

When Ryan was about 11, he wanted to pick a fight with everyone in the family. He was out of control and very unstable. Nicole and I sat him down in a chair, scolded, and ridiculed him for his behavior. After a few minutes, I realized he could not help being out of control; he was struggling with some type of disorder. We needed to get him to a competent child psychiatrist and not a school guidance counselor.

I was diagnosed with BD several years earlier but did not want to forever brand him for having a serious mental illness. I no longer could be in denial; he could have more than just ADHD, and we needed to get him to a good psychiatrist and hope he would be diagnosed correctly and, if necessary, get effective medications. He needed to find a way to become stable. It was very easy to label Ryan as a BD kid. I guess I was diagnosing his condition as BD without taking him to a competent psychiatrist.

In high school, he was in trouble in classes and skipped school. The school's truant officer suspected he was using drugs. We did not want to believe him, ignored the officers' warning, and let him roam around unsupervised after school. At times, we did not know where he was, but maybe we just needed some peace and quiet from all the turmoil we had at home.

Of course, I was also having issues with my mood disorder. I was still a househusband and working on our then 85-year-old house. Nicole was working nights, and our lives were tolerable but not ideal. I did all the grocery shopping and cooking and kept track of the kids. I did not consider getting a job because Nicole was sleeping during the day, and someone needed to keep track of our boys, especially Ryan.

Ryan had many of the same behavior problems young people in the BDS group mentioned at meetings. He acted out, was probably using drugs, and was diagnosed with ADHD at an early age. He also exhibited oppositional defiant behavior as a pre-teen.

Ryan has very few office visits, and I was afraid some psychiatrist was going to just assume he had BD because I was diagnosed with BD. His diagnosis was very vague, but he is smart and can solve technical problems. Perhaps he can overcome the challenges he will face later on in life without any mental healthcare.

You know I criticize Ryan, but both Stu and I had even more bizarre behavior when we were Ryan's age. Maybe I am trying to project my diagnosis of BD onto Ryan.

## Labeling someone as bipolar is very serious

I want to make it clear, in this workbook, I do not diagnose anyone with BD, and I am not a health care professional. The consequences of labeling someone as BD is a very serious charge without proper analysis by a competent psychiatrist. I understand many health care professionals say it is very difficult to diagnose someone with BD.

Once someone is branded with a mental illness, it stays with them for a lifetime. Generally, a diagnosis of any mental illness cannot be reversed and stays on your profile within the health care system. Years ago, I thought my visits to a psychiatrist were confidential, but the electronic age has changed all that. Now I am afraid the patient-doctor confidentiality does not exist any longer; I can assume my records are on many databases.

I also want to make the point many people could meet the threshold of having a mental illness according to the DSM manual. Many different types of disorders could be called serious mental illness, depression, anxiety, phobias, and many other conditions that could qualify as mental illness.

Millions of people have temporary life situations that could be called mental illnesses, but are they? So, I believe a diagnosis of any mental illness must be made by a competent, preferably board-certified psychiatrist. However, if depression or other condition only lasts a short period of time and then the crisis is over, should it be diagnosed as a lifelong mental illness?

The DSM manual warns any mental illness must be made by competent professionals.

## I found a "Cautionary Statement" regarding diagnosis

I referred to the DSM [(American Psychiatric Association, 1987) again to find out if my unworthy disorder is an actual psychiatric disorder. I could not find my unworthy disorder in the manual. However, I found a "Cautionary Statement" regarding diagnostic criteria of mental illnesses.

The statement reads in part:

"The specified diagnostic criteria for each mental disorder are offered as guidelines for making diagnoses since it has been demonstrated that the use of such criteria enhances agreement among clinicians and investigators. The proper use of these criteria requires specialized clinical training that provides both a body of knowledge and clinical skills."

The statement goes on for several more paragraphs about how the DSM should be used to classify mental disorders. I don't think the words of this cautionary statement are strong enough to warn, a misdiagnosis by a psychiatrist could harm a patient for life. A misdiagnosis could prevent someone from getting a job or running for political office. A misdiagnosis will prevent someone from using their 2$^{nd}$ Amendment right to own a firearm.

I also came across a possible explanation of the difficulty I have in reading and writing English. I discovered I might have Developmental Expressive Writing and reading disorder. The discovery of this disorder is no surprise; I have struggled with reading and writing the English language from grade school right through college. Now I have lost count of the number of disorders I am living with today.

I put the DSM manual on the back shelf because every time I look something up, I discover yet another mental disorder.

A few weeks later, Ryan told us he was not mentally ill and refused treatment. After a month, he announced he was not taking his meds. I must admit I was trying to label his behavior as bipolar, but perhaps I was projecting my mental illness onto Ryan.

After high school, he drifted between several jobs and even took courses at our local community college but dropped out after a semester. Spending several hundred dollars on college was just the beginning of years of supporting Ryan financially.

Nicole was still working nights, so I needed to be at home nights to keep track of the boys. I thought I might find a part-time job, but at this time, my computer skills were not in demand, meaning obsolete. I would need to be re-educated to learn a new skill. If the truth is told, I dreaded finding a job.

Our neighbor up the street found a secure job with the state, and he thought I might qualify for a job at his state agency division. I calculated all the taxes we would owe. I would be working for less than 7 dollars per hour. Nicole was earning almost triple what I would be earning at the state job.

The WAVES Chart has several entries for finding and keeping a job. Many everyday tasks are very difficult for people with BD.

## Matt was responsible from a young age

Our youngest son Matt did well in school. He was always independent and responsible enough to complete projects on time. When I was his age, I was quite the opposite. I rarely, if ever, completed projects on time and was not responsible enough to shovel the driveway after a snowstorm.

As time went on, I realized Ryan is handicapped may be dealing with personal problems and not a serious mental illness. It was unfair to compare him to Matt. But at the same time, we did not give Matt the attention he deserved; we spent most of our time dealing with both Ryan's and my issues.

At one point, I needed to get away from Ryan's frustrating and annoying behavior. I was so frustrated with Ryan. I needed a break. Matt and I went up to visit my mother in NE. We had a great time crabbing and fishing in the bays along the shore. After crabbing, we would go down to a clam shack and have the best clam rolls I had ever tasted anywhere. I realized then just how much time and effort we spent dealing with both my and Ryan's mental issues. As we packed up to leave, my mother took me aside and apologized for not protecting me from Aunt Maddie. I did not respond to her apology; I thought her apology was a few decades too late to make any difference in my life.

After a very bad summer storm, the creek behind our house overflowed into our backyard. After the storm, we had a big pile of debris in our backyard. Matt was out near the big pile of wood and noticed a kitten crying for help on the top of the pile of debris. He begged Nicole to keep the little kitten, but Nicole resisted having any pet. We set up a tent in the back lawn, and the kids all loved the kitten and fed her milk and other treats. After a few nights, Nicole gave in, and we adopted a little black kitten and named her Liberty.

## Matt is doing well in school and is a very responsible teenager

We all went out for breakfast at a local diner uptown, and as we were leaving, Matt asked the cashier if they had any work. The owner said, "Not now, but I will take your name." A woman waiting to pay her check speaks up and says to Matt, "I have some work at our shop." Matt always looked older than his age; he was tall and presented himself well even as a pre-teen. I had to tell the woman he was not quite old enough for a part-time shop job. A few weeks later, the owner of the breakfast cafe called and offered him a job.

He went to work at 8 am on weekends and was always on time. The owners knew Matt was a nice kid and treated him like family. Actually, the family that owned the breakfast place treated all the kids like family.

## Ryan has a bad spell

About then, Ryan went into a bad depression, and we did not know what to do. He refused treatment, and he got agitated and very moody as I had done at his age. Every time we mentioned he needed help, he stormed out of the house. Now the challenge was to get Ryan to my psychiatrist and hope he would figure out how to make him feel better. I cannot tell you how frustrating our situation was with Ryan; he has access to my excellent psychiatrist only three miles away that would find a way to help him. I hope he can get help in five weeks, not wait five decades like Stu and me.

Perhaps I was attempting to be a homegrown amateur psychiatrist, but if he went psychotic, we would need to have him involuntary admitted to a hospital for evaluation. Having Ryan involuntary admitted to a hospital may have been counterproductive because he may have been so resentful he might never seek help.

Although it is tempting, I do not want to claim Ryan has BD. He has only had a few visits to a psychiatrist; I don't think anyone should be diagnosed with a serious mental illness after only two or three visits. Perhaps my psychiatrist is projecting my BD illness onto Ryan. All throughout this workbook, I am very careful not to diagnose anyone with BD.

The WAVES Chart is a good way to identify unique situations common to many people if they are diagnosed with BD.

## Our family vacation to the Southwest

Nicole and I thought it was a good time to take a family vacation to the southwest part of the country. I thought most people go to California, but unless they drive across the country, they don't see the great width and breadth of our great country.

We all flew to Las Vegas and rented a van. We drove from Las Vegas to the Hoover dam, then down to Sedona, Arizona, and eventually returned to Las Vegas and back home. The natural beauty surrounding the mountains in the Southwest was a very spiritual experience for me. We stopped at a few tourist attractions along the highway.

I questioned if the Indigenous people should be called the American Indians, and so I began to name all Indigenous people in North America as Native Indian people.

You know, when I was a kid, I watched hundreds of TV shows that portrayed the American Indians as savage enemies of our nation. I wish I had the chance back then to learn more about the very spiritual way tribes lived their lives. We call North America our country, but some Native Indian peoples see North America as their nation; we only occupy their sacred native lands.

One difference I observed about the Native Indian culture is they believed the earth and nature as sacred. I felt I could easily blend in with their lifestyle and culture.

I did see many organized religions as a business, especially the Catholic Church. The church strongly encouraged our mother to send them to cash in numbered envelopes. I was tempted to take money out of the offering basket as it was passed in front of me at church. I thought the church should help us; we could not afford to help them.

### President Clinton was acquitted
In February of 1999 – President Clinton was acquitted by the U.S. Senate in the Monica Lewinsky scandal. The Senate trial needed a 2/3 majority to convict. Although he did commit perjury, the trial ended with a not guilty verdict. I personally did not see the charges

as important enough to remove the POTUS from office. In March, the Dow Jones Industrial Average closed above 10,000 for the first time. The healthy economy may have been the reason the POTUS was not removed from office.

## 9/11, 2001, and the US Patriot Act

On September 11, 2001, the World Trade Center in New York City was attacked. It was a wake-up call that radical terrorists could threaten our way of life. The attack on the twin towers woke up the country to the dangers of foreign militant terrorist groups that wanted to harm us.

Of course, I was afraid we might be attacked again and fight a ground war within our country. The horrific images of the Holocaust came up again, knowing more innocent men, women, and children would die. I have always been very critical of our involvement in the Vietnam War, and this attack on the Twin Towers may lead to an endless war in the Middle East.

In October 2001, House Resolution 3162, or the US Patriot Act, was overwhelmingly passed by Congress and was signed into law the next day by President Bush. The Patriot Act of 2001 was written to balance civil liberties and national security concerns.

The surveillance of people that would harm our country was expanded greatly after 9/11, and most people thought the government should collect any and all personal data. After all, if you had nothing to hide, you should not object to any privacy concerns.

The Patriots Act allowed the government to intrude on the privacy of any citizen if the government had probable cause. It allowed the police to enter your home without probable cause and not notify you if they found you were a threat to the government. My feeling was the government had lied to the public for years about our actions in the Vietnam War and could use this Act to spy on law-abiding citizens of our country. Could the government obtain personal information on ordinary citizens and then use the information to get favors, bribe, or blackmail anyone? Were my thoughts insane and unthinkable? Well, I had these insane, but I prefer crazy thoughts.

The mastermind behind the 9/11 attack was a radical terrorist named Osama Bin Laden. I understood his agenda was to punish all Americans because we were occupying parts of the Middle East. I remembered a terrorist attack on the World Trade Center that was bombed back in 1993, but only a few people died. Was it the same group that was responsible for the 9/11 attack vowing revenge?

## The Pentagon blamed Osama Bin Laden for the 9/11 attack

In October 2001, the US forces launched an attack in Afghanistan on the Taliban and al-Qaida terrorists. Kabul was taken in November, and an interim government was formed to stabilize the region.

I was concerned the Afghanistan conflict would turn into another Vietnam. Our troops occupy another foreign country among terrorists that hate America. We cannot speak their language or understand their customs. After months of intense searching, we still could not capture Osama Bin Laden.

I do worry about our security forces using the Patriot Act to spy on Patriots as well as on terrorists. I am sure some terrorist cells are hiding in plain sight across the globe.

I did not know much about the Middle East but wondered how a small group of rebels could attack our nation. Of course, those B&W pictures of WW II came into my mind. For years I worried some crisis could be used at any time to trigger a declaration of war. Some people warned the military-industrial complex or MIC could start a conflict, and we could be drawn into another prolonged war, much like Vietnam. How could we worry about a few thousand terrorists? Because we should?

President Bush decided to blame Saddam Hussein for the 9/11 attack on the Twin Towers in NYC. The justification was not clear to me, but Congress was told Iraq had weapons of mass destruction. President Bush declared a "War on Terror" in response to the 9/11 attack.

So, then the US invaded Iraq and toppled Saddam Hussein, triggering protests abroad. As the bombs dropped on Bagdad, I was overcome with sadness because, like in all wars, innocent men, women, and children would die horrific, painful deaths.

Reports Iraq soldiers changed uniforms to street clothes and melted into the general population. Weren't these the same circumstances we fought in during the Vietnam War? We could not distinguish the VC from the peaceful Vietnamese. Ever since the Pentagon Papers were released exposing the cover-ups during the Vietnam War, I have been skeptical of the Pentagon's involvement in any conflict.

About a year later, reports the terrorists that planned the 9/11 attack were Saudi and not Iraq citizens. A report came out terrorists learned to fly airplanes somewhere in Florida and only wanted to learn how to take off and not land. One flight training school instructor reported the odd occurrence to the FBI, but the incident was never followed up. Weapons of mass destruction were never found in Iraq. Some experts warned sending our troops into the Middle East was like walking into a field of quicksand.

## Our mother passed peacefully at the assisted-living home

Our mother passed peacefully at the assisted-living facility. We all went to the gravesite to see her put to rest beside my father. Joe's ex-wife Jody and her friend Penny came to pay their respects to our mother. The small graveyard was just across the street from our old farm, and I remembered back to the time when Stu and I put daisy chains on our father's grave.

I often thought my father was my spirit guide over the years; I needed to believe someone cared for me. Our mother said she wanted to be buried alongside our father. I think it was appropriate he was next to his farm all the years. He wanted to live a simple life after the stock market crash of 1929. Our mother said he sought to be independent of the financial system and bought the farm in 1935.

I thought back to what a hard life my mother had to deal with our mental health issues, also, two old ladies that provided very little support. Our mother put us all through college. With the stresses of high school and college, Stu crashed our family car and her battle with alcoholism. She was relatively young when my father died and left her with five dependents. He did not leave our mother with any life insurance benefits, only the farm. She supported all of us on a meager salary. She kept the farm going for another six years after our father died suddenly from a heart attack.

Our mother always provided us with the basics of good food and shelter. We ate better than a lot of kids around town, but we never got that push car we always wanted when we were kids. We never let her forget the disappointment we had every Christmas; it was just a guilt trip on our mother for years. A few years before she died, I did accept an apology for not protecting me from my Aunt Maddie's verbal abuse, but I thought her apology was a little too late to make any difference in my life.

Our mother did not have BD, but if you look at the WAVES Chart, our mother would be at a high-stress level zone most of the time. We had to deal with her alcoholism, but she was the most giving and generous mother, especially when she was sober. When sober, she had an entirely different personality; I think back in high school when she dealt with Stu crashing the family car and our reckless behavior during our drinking sprees.

We could not afford a nursing home for my grandmother, and she took care of our grandmother when she was dying of cancer. She took care of all our grandmothers' health needs. We even had my grandmother's viewing at our house in the formal parlor room. Our lives moved along, and the threat of terrorists attacking our homeland became much less of an issue.

## What! A Navy pilot encountered a Tic-Tac near San Diego

I have not been following UFOs closely lately, but in 2004 a short TV segment seemed real for some reason. I learned years ago; the Pentagon did not allow any active or inactive military to talk about any space ships or aliens under severe penalty. The report described the Tic-Tac shaped UFO objects as a UFO that moved erratically and then disappeared. Now I have heard the military attempts to cover up UFO sightings by claiming they are natural phenomena like cloud formations. They called the Roswell incident a weather balloon. I remember a farmer saved a piece of the crash debris and said he could not fold or tear the material; it snapped back into its original shape. But really, the military could have come up with a better explanation (cover-up) of the sighting than a UFO shaped like a Tic-Tac. By showing the actual video of the UFO, the Navy came a step closer to a full disclosure event. A full disclosure event is where actual aliens arrive in a spaceship and step out and communicate with human beings on planet Earth.

## Did Hurricane Katrina trigger a local State of Emergency?

In 2005 a massive hurricane was bearing down on the New Orleans area of Louisiana, and the local weather report warned of catastrophic destruction. As the hurricane approached the gulf coast, there was no time to evacuate all residents in the path of the hurricane. Parts of New Orleans are below sea level, and when the levees broke, hundreds of homes flooded, and many people needed to be evacuated by helicopter from rooftops and others by boats.

The death toll was over 1800, and a state of emergency was declared for the area. The emergency response teams were overwhelmed, and people fled to the Superdome; over 1 million people were evacuated from the hurricane, and the damage was in the billions of dollars.

After the storm passed, emergency response teams were overwhelmed and went door to door to evacuate people in the flood zone.

A week later, an investigative reporter aired a segment questioning why guns were taken from everyone during and after the hurricane. The reporter showed a huge pile of guns about five feet high on the ground. The reporter then asked the guard, "Were these guns illegally taken from people?" The guard quickly replied something like, "In a disaster, the rules are suspended to protect the people."

That ended the 90-second segment. I never saw another follow-up story on the legality of confiscating legal and illegal guns from US citizens. Shouldn't the legal guns be returned to law-abiding citizens to protect themselves and their families? Apparently, under the State of Emergency, the 2$^{nd}$ amendment is suspended until the emergency is over.

I never learned when the emergency rules under an emergency were declared or lifted. Was it even constitutional to confiscate legal guns from law-abiding citizens? After Hurricane Katrina, was a local National Emergency Law declared or was it what I call a local Secret State of Emergency (SSE)? The press and the government kept the incident a secret from the public.

## Stage 9 Nature was my way of pursuing happiness

Ryan met a nice woman named Jane, and within a year, Jane was pregnant. Ryan was so angry I thought he was going pack up and move away. I offered my only words of wisdom; everything happens for a reason and that he may not understand the reason at the time. A few months later, he accepted the fact he was going to become a father.

After spending several years attending Rosie's BDS group and finding a new, better mood stabilizer for my BD, things got better for our family and me. Matt was a responsible teenager, and Ryan was well sort of finding his way through life. Ryan was acting more responsible, knowing he would soon be a father.

We were all waiting in anticipation of our first grandchild to be born in the spring. Ryan was getting excited about the birth of their baby. Ryan accepted the fact that Jane was going to have the baby, and he was going to be a father; he started to plan for her arrival.

Ryan found a good steady job with a local high-tech company, and they trained him to become an IT technician. This on-the-job training was equivalent to a technical computer science degree at a community college. He moved out and got an apartment of his own. I was very excited about him being independent and taking responsibility for their baby. I told Nicole I was afraid of Ryan's future because he was not in treatment; he was not stable but unstable. However, I gave up trying to diagnose Ryan's problem; maybe I was projecting my mental illness onto Ryan.

Early in 2006, Jane delivered a healthy baby girl Bonnie with Ryan in attendance, and we all visited her in the hospital. Ryan was a nervous wreck; he was so excited to see Bonnie born. Finally, he was a dad. He was very protective of Bonnie and wouldn't even let the nurses take her back to the nursery.

As time went on, I realized Bonnie was sent to him for a reason. I think she stopped him from becoming a selfish kid and possibly a drug addict. Ryan finally found something to love in his life. Before she was born, he was talking about moving to Arizona and starting a new life. That might have been the beginning of the end of Ryan's life. I had moved several times, and without proper treatment, I was living with the same unstable mental illnesses and personal problems only at a different physical address.

We were the proud grandparents of a beautiful little baby girl and accepted Jane's family into our family. I was so proud of Ryan because he was becoming a responsible father to Bonnie and Jane's other kids as well. As his high-tech job, rent payments, and family obligations piled up, he became more stressed out.

After a year, Ryan wanted to leave his good-paying job and get a part-time job. He left his steady job and moved back in with us after his lease was up in his apartment.

Ryan found a part-time job. Now Nicole was living with two problem children; I meant to say, adults. Sometimes his behavior was infuriating because I was living with another me when I was his age. We tolerated his behavior in large part because we loved to spend time with Bonnie. At this point, I needed to get out of the house every day and find something besides living with an incarnation of my younger self, very disturbing indeed.

### I found kayaking my escape into nature

One afternoon Nicole and I went up to a county lake about an hour's drive from home. We rented a two-person or tandem kayak and paddled around the peaceful and calm lake. Nicole, of course, loved the peace and quiet, and we decided to buy two single kayaks. Happiness was finally within our reach. I was hooked on the freedom and living free again, enjoying the Great Outdoors.

Other than the cost of a camper and the kayak, an outdoor vacation was a very low-cost way to vacation. Campgrounds had a low cost per night fees, and the cost to maintain a kayak was zero, with no fuel and no upkeep. Maybe that was what attracted us to outdoor life, almost free and a simple, frugal lifestyle. I bought a nice kayak to use for both rivers and lakes.

Kayaking was my escape to nature and from the chaos of my home life. A few hours of kayaking on the Delaware River reset my psycho mind; I mean my psyche. I was ready to deal with the tasks of maintaining our 95-year-old house and ignore the irresponsible behavior of Ryan.

## I had regrets about our finances
Nicole was the sole breadwinner for over fifteen years, and I was telling myself I was too old to start working again. By now, it was almost 15 years since Stu and I were properly treated for BD, and I became the house husband. I am sure some neighbors thought I was a loafer, but I was grateful my meds kept working, and I was reasonably stable. I am sure many people thought, what is wrong with Ryan's dad? He seems healthy but never goes to work.

The guy up the street was ready to retire and collect a good pension from his state job. Years ago, he wanted me to get a state job in his government agency. Now I signed up for Medicare, but the benefits were not anything like retiring from a government job. I had regrets I didn't find job years ago and began to feel guilty about our finances, but it was too late to start over. Nicole was also getting older and had several more years to retire. Nicole was having a difficult time working nights and on the weekends. Her workload increased, but she still got several weeks of paid vacation every year. I could see it is very hard to work nights; you need to reverse your sleep patterns on the days off and then switch back to work a night shift.

## Stu meets Willy and learns the 4 rules to live by

After Stu went back to Florida, he became friends with Willy, a very tall Black man, 6 foot 6, and people called him the Mayor Willy of the county park. Willy listened to alcoholics, and drug users tell their stories. Willy was not an alcoholic or a drug user but a preacher, as Stu described him to me. Stu said he could cite verses of the Bible but could not read or write English.

Stu said he was learning Willy's simple words of wisdom "Find your purpose in life through prayer to your higher power, and he will tell you what to do." I thought his message was so simple it must be true.

Willy was from rural Mississippi and had a sorted past, but that's a whole other story. Willy told Stu all he needed to do in this life was follow four very simple rules.

| Willy's 4 rules to live by |
| --- |
| Rule Number 1 Learn to be kind |
| Rule Number 2 Be kind |
| Rule Number 3 Be kind to everyone |
| Rule Number 4 Don't expect people to be kind to you |

I noticed Willy did not say a happy life without challenges or setbacks, even if you follow these four rules to live by. Willy's life was filled with many challenges, especially throughout his childhood, but that is a story that should be told.

I never met Willy, but I had a sense he was truly a deeply religious man who practiced what he preached every day, all day.

## I was still in denial I had a hoarding disorder

Over the years, I had gone to flea markets, and computer shows to sell computer equipment. Now, most of my computer stuff was obsolete. Stuff I could have sold at a profit a few years ago was now worth very little. I was still in denial I had a hoarding issue. Now, our house and garage were full of old business equipment, computer desks, desktops, and office equipment. Even Stu, the poster child for picking-up stuff on the street, was shaming me; what a hypocrite.

I decided to rent a big dumpster and just junk all the obsolete desktop computers. Everyone was buying laptops, and no one wanted bulky old desktop computers. The local trash collector would not take any electronic equipment. I rented a dumpster and filled it with over 50 outdated desktop computers and a ton of heavy office equipment. I was finally getting rid of the hardware I clung to for years.

I had a hard time emotionally letting go of my dream to start an online website. My idea of an online shopping website years ago was ahead of its time; now, many online shopping websites have become very profitable.

## Tis the season for politics

The election season for President of our great country was starting to get some coverage, and on the Democratic side was Hillary. Hillary, the wife of President Clinton, was not my favorite woman politician. I thought she felt entitled to become the first woman president of the US.

I remembered as the first lady, she tried to get a sweeping health care bill passed, and I did not like her behind-closed-door tactics to get her agenda passed in Congress. She was not appointed to any position in the Clinton administration. Apparently, she just set up an office in the White House.

An African American Freshman Senator from Illinois, Barrack Obama, was getting some press by his words of "Hope and Change." He had a degree from Harvard and spoke eloquently about the challenges we faced in our country, especially race relations between the African Americans and the White citizens of the country. I was never impressed with Ivy League college-educated guys; I worked with on Nantucket years ago. Many kids had book knowledge but no practical skills.

## I needed two major operations

By 2007 I had good management of my mood disorder by finding a good psychiatrist and regularly attending Rosie's BDS group nearby.

For over 15 years, I had been on a mood stabilizer called lithium, but our group leader Rosie warned us prolonged use could result in damaging side effects. Rosie had her kidneys damaged by lithium after taking very heavy doses of lithium for several years. She was told she may need a kidney transplant or may need to go on kidney dialysis. After her experience, I got regular lithium levels to prevent long-term irreversible kidney damage.

At the same time, however, my diabetes was not being managed well, and I had neuropathy in the right leg. I'm afraid I was not taking care of my physical health. After over 30 years of abusing alcohol and 20 years of smoking two packs of cigarettes a day, I was living with the consequences of neglecting my physical health.

A routine visit to my primary care physician (PCP) indicated I had an abnormal prostate. So, my family doctor referred me to a urologist connected with a local hospital. I got an appointment and am sitting in the waiting room waiting to see the urologist, and I overheard two guys talking about their treatment experience for their prostate cancer.

One guy had a complication with a prostate biopsy and needed another procedure to fix the original procedure. His urologist didn't seem to think it was anything to be upset over. The other guy had a serious infection that they couldn't seem to stop, and he was very ill and upset. Needless to say, I only spent five minutes with the urologist and politely left his office. I was very anxious and upset and did not know what to do next. It is not easy for me to think clearly enough to make critical decisions when I am very anxious.

A few days after my visit to the urologist, Nicole watched a TV segment of a urologist practicing at a well-known university hospital in Philadelphia. I finally got an appointment with the same doctor after filling out a long, involved, very detailed medical history. After meeting with the doctor, I was certain he was the urologist I needed if I needed further treatment. Further tests by my urologist confirmed it was prostate cancer. After a complete examination by my doctors, they found a cancerous tumor in my bladder.

During the winter, I had my prostate removed and another operation to remove a cancerous tumor in my bladder. It was not pleasant, but I guess everything happens for a reason, right?

Several months after two major surgeries, I was on my way to recovery. I was fortunate Nicole's health insurance covered all but a few co-pays. Excellent care at the university hospital saved my life. If my doctor had not detected the bladder tumor in time, it could have spread to my lymph nodes; I don't think I would be alive today.

You know I filled out pages of my medical history but not one question about my mental health. I listed all my meds, including psych meds, because I was afraid some of the tests or other medicine might produce severe side effects or, worse, death.

I think if the WAVES Chart was part of my pre-operation intake forms, they could identify my stress level at the time of my operations. I could have been suicidal. If I had filled out the WAVES Chart, several flags would have been listed on my WAVES Chart. The first was the lifetime stress of living with BD, then my history of alcoholism personality issues. Oh, I forgot Stu is also living with BD and a stressor in my life.

After more routine blood work, the doctor told me I needed medicine to correct a thyroid condition. Lithium was known to cause thyroid problems and kidney problems. I decided to change to another mood stabilizer. The first two meds did not help my moods. I felt I was back when I had no treatment for my BD illness; I was getting mistreatment. I had periods of hypomania followed by moody spells and bouts of anxiety attacks all my life. I almost went back on lithium, but the thought of having damage to my kidneys was unthinkable. Within one month, I had gone from feeling BD normal" to feeling and acting seriously mentally ill again. Thankfully, the third medicine stabilized my mood and anxiety levels.

## A return to nature was my way of pursuing happiness

After months of recovery, I decided to spend the time I had left on planet Earth enjoying nature. Nature I had loved since a youth on the farm. I looked at all these procedures as giving me another chance to relive the rest of my life as I was born to do, close to nature. My childhood experiences taught me living close to nature was my way of pursuing happiness or at least a little peace and tranquility. Excellent follow-up care at the university hospital assured me I was getting the best care possible and hopefully would survive at least another five years.

## I found a book that claims EO 11921 is a Blueprint for Tyranny

After one routine visit to the university hospital, I browsed book stores around the campus. I found a book in a used book store near the U of Penn Campus in Philly. The title of the book was "Government by Emergency" By Gary North." (North, 1983) The book describes a terrifying chain of events that will happen if a State of Emergency is declared in our country. The book described how the government covered up many events that will happen in a State of Emergency (SE). I call this emergency declaration a Secret State of Emergency (SSE) in our country.

The major theme book warns the powers of the Federal government will be greatly expanded in the name of national security, but very few people know anything about them. The media never seems to even mention what happens in case of a national emergency or declaring Marshal Law.

The book outlines an Executive Order (EO) Number 11921 or EO 11921 given by President Ford in 1976 along with emergency banking regulations that will be enforced after a national emergency is issued by the President of the United States or POTUS. Mr. North warns of the damage these new banking policies and regulations will have on our freedoms. By far, the most alarming revelation is the POTUS can issue an SSE with little reason or justification and does not need the approval of Congress. One chapter claims these SSE rules and regulations are a "Blueprint for Tyranny."

## I skipped the Emergency Banking Regulations No1

Mr. North's book also strongly advised reading parts of the Emergency Banking Regulations, but I was getting too upset to read any further. I was sure banking regulations would also be expanded by now to cover all types of banking regulations. I did understand we needed cash, food, and water stored in a safe place.

## Our first vacation was in our old pop-up camper

In the spring, I found an old pop-up camper that needed repairs but bought it for just a few hundred bucks; I decided to spend what little money we had on vacations and not on the old house. That was my desire. Nicole wanted to invest in new kitchens and upgrades to our turn of the century-old home. Spending money on vacations was fine with me. I hated working on our old house and looked forward to getting away to camp, far away from the car repairs and constant house maintenance.

Our house reminded me of the "White Elephant" of a house we had in New England. Well, it was really not that bad, but I needed to convince Nicole spring, summer, and fall were not made for scraping paint off the front porch. To tell you the truth, I needed to get some separation from Ryan; my relationship with Ryan, you might say, was strained at best.

Nicole did mention I spent more time and money on repairing and maintaining the camper but little time on the house. I convinced her camping would be far more enjoyable than sitting and staring at an upgraded stainless-steel kitchen appliance; besides, a new kitchen would not make her a gourmet cook. I think she did see my mood and depression were much better when I was involved in outdoor activities. Nicole was also enjoying outdoor living; she started a garden and planted plants and flowers around the house.

I was kayaking on a nearby river a few times a week. It was a great exercise and a way to escape the pressures of modern-day living with a serious mental illness. Sometimes after a heavy rain, the river would flow at several knots, and the rapids would be hard to navigate, but after a few months, I was in good psychical condition for an older guy. I would paddle up against the current for three miles up the river to a waterfall and just float back to the boat ramp.

I worked on the old pop-up camper many hours during the spring and didn't want to tell Nicole just how much repairs and upgrades were necessary to get it roadworthy. It needed tires and brakes and some interior work, but it was far better than sleeping on the hard-cold ground in a tent. The camper had no air conditioner, toilet, or even a microwave, but it was our home away from home. My motto is always frugal at any cost, but this project was getting way over any cost I could justify.

## Stu runs the sober house in Florida as a business

Dr. Freed and Stu bought a house right next to Stu's place. The halfway house was for people in AA to help people recovering from drug or alcohol abuse. He thought he could also help some of the boat people get sober. The rules were clear if you started drinking or used drugs, you had to leave the sober house. He ran the sober house like a business, but no one was responsible enough to keep people sober when Stu went up to New England for the summer.

## Stu's dog Buster dies in a tragic accident

Stu stopped in on his way up to New England. He was in a hurry as usual and said he needed to get his sailboat in the water. We could see his dog Buster was having a hard time getting up our stairs to the second floor. He also had a hard time urinating when you took him out for a walk. Stu said he is over 17 years old now was also hard of hearing. It is hard to believe Buster was over 17 years old. I always said Buster found Stu to help him shortly after he bought his house in Florida.

Stu arrived in NE, and a few weeks later, he called me and told me Buster died; he was asleep under Stu's car, and Stu backed up and ran over him. Stu was so upset. Buster was just sleeping under the car was very hard of hearing. Stu said he rushed to the hospital, but there was nothing he could do for him. Buster looked into Stu's eyes as if to say, "It's okay you took me in when I was abandoned years ago." Stu said the vet gave Buster an injection to put him to sleep, and Stu cried for days.

I often joked about how Stu couldn't find anything wrong with Buster, no matter what Buster did. Buster was what Stu needed at the time; Buster showed up at his house shortly after he moved into his house in Florida. I always thought Buster was sent to Stu to replace Aunt Maddie. Stu always took his side no matter what Buster did. Buster really did support Stu he had no money, no friends, and no job, so Stu gave him a home, and Stu got a faithful friend up until the end.

### Stu found another faithful friend Daisy
Six months after Buster died in New England, Stu decided it was time to find another friend. A neighbor had a small dog that needed a home. Stu took her in and named her Daisy. Now, this dog did not have the aggressive bulldog personality of Buster; she was very timid and quiet prim and proper like a show dog.

I questioned his decision to get another dog because a dog needs to be walked two or three times a day. It is hard to walk a dog in 98-degree weather in Florida and 15-degree weather in NE. My biggest concern is that his dog cannot be left in a car while Stu attends church, AA meetings, or even shops for food. Leaving a dog in a car in Florida is a capital crime with a minimum sentence of life hard labor in a Florida state prison. Well, I am just joking, but Florida is very tough on crimes against pets. After thinking it over, I do think a dog has always been a good companion for Stu.

### Senator Obama goes on the stump
I did not want Hillary to get the nomination for the Democratic Party. Reluctantly I changed my party affiliation to vote for Obama in the primary election. I thought perhaps our nation did need an African American that could unite the country. His message of Hope

and Change was optimistic, and I looked forward to him uniting our country, especially race relations.

All Senator Obama's speeches are carefully crafted and read from a teleprompter, but when off-script and confronted by the press, he made some very troubling comments. At one campaign stop, he told a crowd of reporters in rural PA they just cling to their "guns and religion."

Wow! This 5-second comment revealed so much to me. His off-scripted remarks started to make sense, but not in a good way. Wasn't "guns and religion" the cornerstone of our Constitution? Wasn't the 2$^{nd}$ amendment a way to protect our freedoms from tyrannical government criminals and terrorists? Isn't freedom from religion prosecution why many people left England and other countries? Doesn't the 2nd Amendment keep us safe from criminals?

## Our voyage to rustic campgrounds

In June, we camped at a rustic state campground near our home. I'm lucky Nicole is not a prima donna and is adventurous when it comes to rustic campgrounds. Some state campgrounds are very inexpensive but have very rustic facilities. I mean, some do not have flush toilets, and some remote sites have just an outhouse complete with hundreds of flies and bugs flying everywhere while you are taking a crap.

## President Obama won and made Hillary Secretary of State (SOS)

In November of 2008, Barrack Obama won the presidential election over Senator John McCain, but I felt the Republicans did not fight back in the race for White House (WH). I think the MSM was quick to claim that anyone who challenged his policies was a racist.

Shortly after President Barrack Obama became President, he made Hillary his Secretary of State (SOS). I found it interesting and troubling that he would make a political rival part of his administration. He never got along with the Clintons, but as they say, politics makes strange bedfellows.

## Will the financial meltdown trigger an SSE?

The stock market was in freefall, and the experts blamed bad housing market lending practices. Banks and lending institutions began to call in loans, and it led to a domino effect on financial markets around the world. The Obama administration decided to prop up Wall Street and the large financial institutions to prevent a 1929 type depression.

The 800-billion-dollar stimulus bill was approved, and the economy started to recover. Most of the large banks and other financial institutions recovered, but millions of working-class people lost billions of dollars in their 401K and stock portfolios.

## Our camping vacation on the Delaware River

After a few weekends of local camping, it was time to plan our long summer vacations; this trip was our maiden voyage in our new but very old pop-up camper. We tested it a few times locally in the spring and fixed some major repairs, namely the lift cable.

We arrived at the campground right along the Delaware River. The river flowed right past the campground and was a very scenic site. The river quietly flowed past our campsite.

## We booked a 13-mile kayak trip

We booked a trip for a 13-mile kayak trip down the Delaware River the following day. In the morning, the owner of the campground drove us up 13 miles upriver to a drop-off point; he placed the kayaks on the beach, gave us our paddles in and life vests, and very brief instructions. He said to watch out for the outflow from the electric generation plant in keep right of the island a few miles down the river. He said once you pass the big bridge over the Delaware River, you will see signs, and then you have reached the campground. And then he said, "Oh, if you capsize, go to shore and call us; the telephone number is on the side of the kayak."

That was it, he left, and we were on our own. Two middle-aged, well a little past mid-life people, very little experience running rapids and avoiding large rocks in the middle of a river. We never had any experience maneuvering around the "outflow" from the electric plant.

At every turn in the river, there was another panoramic view of the mountains. As we looked down the river, we could see the rapids, riffs, and boulders that we needed to navigate. After a few miles, it became a challenge, and we forgot all our cares. This is why I love nature; it takes you out away from problems, and you can concentrate on living in harmony and in the moment with nature.

In the evening, we made a campfire and enjoyed the fresh air in the natural surroundings. Now we just needed to get home safely after our most enjoyable outdoor vacation. After a few very enjoyable camping trips, we thought perhaps we could find a local campground and take all the kids camping when they got older. This trip was more than a vacation; it turned out to be a spiritual retreat for Nicole and me.

## We attended the Music Fest

Almost every summer, we attend the Music Fest in Bethlehem, Pennsylvania. We love hearing the different music groups in the open-air atmosphere of the different venues. We did hear our favorite music group play one evening. We began to follow their schedule and hear them play at venues around Philly.

### Our next camping vacation was to the Adirondack's

In the spring, we went camping several times to local campgrounds and then planned our long trip to the Adirondacks in upstate New York.

The outdoor life in New York State is awesome; they have trailheads well marked in some of the best views we have seen in our travels to date. We headed up to the Adirondacks and found a nice remote campground near Whiteface Mountain. I saw a flyer for a 13-mile kayak trip, and we signed up for the next day. We signed up without asking too many questions about the skills we needed to navigate over two very large lakes.

We rented a tandem kayak at the office and got a map of our trip. I didn't worry too much about a 13-mile trip. I have experience kayaking on the river near our house. I was not prepared to battle the entire 13 miles over two large lakes with the winds in our faces most of the trip. On a river, of course, you don't need to paddle; you can just float down with the current and enjoy the views.

We found it difficult to navigate across to the first lake but finally found the place to transfer to the next lake. It was a small series of locks where we went into a lock, and it raised our kayak up to the next lake—what a unique adventure for transporting us from one late to the other. I don't know if we would be able to carry our heavy tandem kayak over to the next lake if we did not have the lock. After paddling most of the day, we did arrive at the drop-off point 13 miles from our starting location. Weary and very tired, but again it was a unique experience of a lifetime.

### The Nicole family reunion was in WV

In the winter, our family was doing better; Ryan and Matt were doing better in school. I was still active in the BDS group. Nicole was finding work more stressful working nights.

In the spring, I went shopping for another pop-up camper because our old camper was not worth fixing up. The next day Nicole and I went to look at a small used camper, and she thought it was a good buy, and so we were the proud owners of a very small trailer for camping. After a few local trips, we were ready to plan our long vacation.

Nicole's family planned a reunion at a resort in the foothills of West Virginia. We planned to combine Nicole's family vacation with our own camping trip down to the Blue Ridge Mountains.

Ryan, Matt, and Bonnie planned to meet us at the resort. We drove down through Virginia and found a nice campground off the main highway. The next morning, we headed out to the resort, but it was very difficult to find the unmarked dirt roads going back to the resort. It was literally in the foothills of West Virginia. We finally found the resort, and it was blazing hot, and the rooms didn't have any air conditioning.

After the reunion, we moved on to another campground in Virginia. Nicole looked up some activities in the area and found an outfitter that offered a day kayak trip down the James River. The next morning, we arrived at the outfitter's shop along the James River.

We headed out down the river, and the natural surroundings were right out of an outdoor adventure documentary; the trip was very quiet and peaceful as we floated down the river and enjoyed the beautiful natural surroundings.

I don't want to glamorize everything about our camping experiences; by the time we got down to the drop-off point, the temperature was over 95 degrees°. It was probably over 100° at our campsite, and with the humidity, in our lack of good air-conditioning, it was very uncomfortable, well quite unbearable.

## We headed for the cool breezes of the Atlantic Ocean

Nicole took out a map and noticed the Outer Banks of North Carolina was less than 200 miles away. We left our campground very early in the morning to beat the heat; several hours later, we arrived at the campground on the Outer Banks. The Outer Banks did remind me of Nantucket with the wild natural beaches and sand dunes. We booked our campground site at a resort-type campground about halfway down the island. There are many small towns along the way, and some are very upscale towns like Duck, North Carolina. The beaches were beautiful, and we stayed until sunset on the beach.

Some campsites were on the Bayside, and some were on the Atlantic Oceanside. Our campsite was only yards from the beach on the Atlantic Ocean, and you could hear the waves crashing on the beach from our campsite.

It was very hot, but we could cool off by just bringing our beach chairs over the sand dunes and sitting on the beach watching the waves roll onto the shoreline.

This was one of the best but the most expensive campgrounds we have ever stayed at, but the campground had a nice pool and friendly people. After spending $150 per person at the run down, I mean rustic lodge in West Virginia, I did not complain when they quoted us $80 per night for a campsite with an ocean view.

The best part of this campground is you could just walk across the street and watch the sun go down on a deck overlooking the bay. On the days when the weather was more overcast, we would drive down the island and stop for lunch at one of the great seafood restaurants.

The sound of the surf always puts me in a tranquil mood. I felt much calmer after a few nights' stay near the ocean. We went to the beach every day and watched the waves crashing onto the beach down the shoreline. Some days we saw pods of dolphins swimming along the shoreline. Just before sunset, we would walk over to the bayside of the island to watch the sun go down. Other people also congregated on the dock to watch the sunset; it was a happening every evening.

The next day I noticed they had kayaks for rent at the office and booked a kayak for the next day. The Outer Banks really is a water sports paradise. We rented a kayak and found a nature preserve to explore. The nature preserve was natural and beautiful with all kinds of wildlife. We got a map and headed out into the marshes and small islands in the bay. We had spectacular views of the inland waterways all around the Outer Banks. Kayaking is the best way to view nature, paddling quietly and peacefully around the different tributaries of the reserve.

When we got back from our long vacation, we looked back and realized it was another great adventure camping and kayaking in the Great Outdoors.

## Fourth of July, and I'm worried about Stu

Stu's friend Lara was getting treatment in Orlando. She was very ill and dying of terminal cancer but would not give up even when her doctors told her there was nothing more they could do. Stu was afraid his old car would not make the 200 miles round trip to Orlando, but he made the trip anyway to see Lara. Lara talked Stu into bringing her back to her apartment near the ocean. They walked down along the beach like they had done many times.

Lara's family was so upset they told Stu never to visit Lara again. Lara's brother came to her apartment and brought Lara back to Orlando. Stu was very upset when he called me; I told him he did the right thing to bring her back to the Atlantic Ocean; it may be her last dying wish.

## Stu's stress level climbs even higher

Then he told me about Igor, a hopeless alcoholic and one of the homeless boat people Stu has known for 20 years. He recently got drunk; fell off the dock into a rock pile of sharp barnacles. He needed to have his foot amputated, and it spread to his leg; the doctors told him he needed to amputate his leg. The hospital put him in a nursing home, and he escaped to go back to his boat to get drunk again. Stu found him in his wheelchair at a fast-food restaurant and took him back to the nursing home. A few months later, he had his leg amputated below the knee.

Stu has helped many people with drug and alcohol problems over the years, but I can see the emotional toll it's taking on him now. I'm worried about Stu going into another severe depression. He's down in Florida trying to help Lara and has his own mental health issues to deal with every day.

Stu called me and decided to go up to New England before and leave Florida before the 4th of July. I thought with 98° heat and 98-degree humidity; everyone wants to leave Florida around the 4th of July. I notice Floridians come up north for the summer and claim Florida is not that hot in the summer. Oh, really, why do you Floridians always end up north for the 4th of July?

Stu then told me he needed to get Tom, his AA sponsor, for the last 20 years a place to stay because he was getting treatment for kidney dialysis. I was surprised Tom was still at his house. I thought he went back to New England months ago? Stu said Tom's family would not take him back, and he had no place else to go.

So now Stu is feeding and taking care of Tom as well as Lara. I thought this was not good, and I'm afraid Stu is going to slip into another massive depression. Stu never told me that Tom was staying at his house. At this point, I was very concerned Stu's stress level was getting even higher.

## Daisy gets Stu into trouble
Stu said he got a summons to appear in court, and I asked him what that was all about. He told me he went into an AA meeting and left his dog in his car in the hot summer sun with the windows cracked a little. Apparently, it's a federal offense punishable by heavy fines and possible jail time. I told Stu that doesn't surprise me; they treat dogs better than kids down in Florida.

I told him about a news clip I watched on TV about a dog that ate a baggie of heroin that was left on the floor near his food bowl. The dog's owner saw what happened and rushed the dog to a vet. The vet called a local hospital, and they gave the drug antidote Narcan to the dog. Stu was mildly amused, but I thought it was hilarious what our healthcare system does not do for the mentally ill and drug addicts.

Stu has been trying to get Narcan, the drug antidote, into the hands of all first responders in Florida for several years. Up to this point, he's having a hard time getting anyone even to acknowledge Narcan could save people's lives, but now we know for sure Narcan did save a drugged-out dog's life.

## Stu is late again
Stu said he had to get a sailboat out of the water and then head up to New England next week after the court date about the dog.

I reminded him we are going on a vacation down at the shore for a week, and if he could schedule his departure show, will we be here at home when he arrives. Now he said he would probably be at our house the day before we get back, and Ryan could help him to stay a night or two.

Nicole and I were upset that he would not leave a day or two later; we told him we had planned weeks ago for a vacation to go camping at the shore. Well, this was not a surprise to us, but we have scheduled this vacation every year for several years now and look forward to spending time camping.

It all was very complicated with Stu going to court and then driving all the way up to New England, we didn't know what his schedule would be, but we wanted to be at the shore and not waiting for Stu.

We arrived late at our campground and set up the camper. The man in the camper next to us got out to hook up the electricity and water. I noticed he had two artificial legs and had difficulty getting around. There are no mistakes in life. Here I am, self-conscious and worried about my fully functional skinny legs, and this guy has a hard time getting into and out of his travel trailer. This should be another life lesson I should be learning; I am not the only disabled guy in the world. We had a very relaxing week at the campground and ate out at local restaurants.

A few days later, Stu called and said he decided to leave early to go up to New England and stay on his sailboat and see his kids. He said he was heading out the next day. Nicole said, "I hope we are not going home early to meet Stu after we told him we wouldn't be home until Sunday. We both cherish our time together camping, traveling to different campgrounds, and having a very good time.

This is just one of many character flaws; he does whatever he wants regardless of what other people say or do. He said one time he's glad he's not tied down in a relationship with a woman. He is leaving Lara and Orlando very ill, and I don't think I could leave her so sick, but I do think Stu had to get out of Florida to keep his sanity.

Lara's family told Stu never to see Lara again. Lara does have her sister out in Orlando, but her sister is very busy, and I'm sure it's quite stressful for her family to see Lara very ill. Stu said Lara is so thin and wrinkled she looks like she could be years older, not only 55.

I shouldn't judge Stu because I don't really know his relationship with Lara at this point. I think her family does not want Stu to visit her because Lara will convince Stu to take her out of the nursing home again. Stu's risk of having a serious BD episode was increasing every day. The entire situation is so tragic. Lara is only about 55 years old, almost on hospice dying alongside people over 90.

I treasure my time camping with Nicole, and is no way I'm going back early to meet Stu; why didn't he just leave a day or two later? He said he must get to New England, but what is so important to rush up to New England I could see if he had a hot girlfriend he wanted to visit. I shouldn't judge him; he was going through a lot of stress in Florida with the heat, finding a place for Tom, and, of course, Lara's illness. Then there's the court date about leaving his dog in a hot car. They left him off with just a warning that a second offense would result in big fines.

What a stress and mess! At this point, we were all stressed out from dealing with multiple stressful situations all at the same time. This is what the WAVES Chart attempts to identify and determine the chances of a psychotic episode occurring during all this turmoil.

On Sunday, we packed up and headed out early to arrive back home at 3 PM and get dinner ready for Stu's arrival. Stu got tied up in traffic in Baltimore and arrived about 7 PM. Here we headed back early and just waited at our house for him to arrive. We invited Jane and the kids over for pizza, and then Stu started the stories of us growing up in New England. He told jokes and other stories I have heard many times; he was trying to impress Jane and the kids with these magic tricks.

Stu was the center of attention and controlled the conversation for the entire evening. I think this type of behavior is from his salesman background; he needs to impress clients in the first five minutes. Stu has his own personality and anxiety disorder to deal with, but I'm having a hard time dealing with my own mental issues and sometimes can't deal with his character flaws. I mean his narcissism.

In the morning, Stu said his dog ate part of the mattress in the downstairs bedroom. Sure enough, Daisy took a few bites out of the mattress; we are fortunate it was an older mattress. The kids wanted Stu to stay with us for a month, and I said to Nicole," That's only 29 more days". She said, "That's not even a little bit funny."

I meant that as a joke, but Nicole has enough to deal with both Ryan and me living our challenging lifestyles. I don't give her enough credit for keeping our family together.

I warned Stu he needed to be over the George Washington Bridge by 6 AM. Stu left about 10 AM, and I called him at 10 PM to see if he got to his son's place safely up in New England. He said he had a lot of traffic on the approach to the George Washington Bridge in New York; a big sign said the lower deck only had a 30-minute traffic delay, in the upper deck had a two-hour delay.

Of course, he took the lower deck but didn't realize it was only an EZ Pass Lane; he does not have an EZ Pass. At the toll booth, he removed a few cones and passed around the toll booth without even paying. I told him if the people in the two-hour-long line caught you, it would be grounds for a slow, painful death. The cops would probably see it as a mercy killing and let everyone go free.

I asked him how Lara was doing in Florida, and he said she wanted to leave the nursing home. It must be very difficult for her because she is so sick among many much older residents in the nursing home.

## More ACA health care bill details exposed

After the stock market rebounded after the real estate crisis, I expected President Obama to help solve problems in the minority and poor inner-city communities.

I was very disappointed the POTUS did not tackle poverty and the drug epidemic in the inner cities. Those families that lived in my neighborhood in Philly needed help. Better schools, jobs, and a path to homeownership would be a good start. Thousands of abandoned row houses in the city could be given to disadvantaged minority families. Instead, President Obama spent his time getting his ACA bill through Congress. He told people they could keep their doctor and save $2500 on their health care costs. The details of the massive ACA or Obama Care were not fully made available to the public to analyze.

In March of 2010, the massive ACA bill was passed by both the House and Senate in the middle of the night, with not one Republican voting for the bill. These tactics worry me greatly; not one Republican member of the House or Senate voted for the massive new bill. The Speaker of the House (SOH) declared we need to pass the bill to see what is in it.

## What about the war on drugs?

The massive 2500-page ACA bill created 125 new agencies within the government. The one thing I did not hear was a comprehensive program to help the drug addicts in our country. The ACA bill was going to provide quality healthcare for minorities and poor people. Shouldn't a comprehensive drug awareness program be a top priority for all minorities and poor people?

## Stu shuts down the sober house in Florida

Dr. Freed and Stu bought a house next to Stu's place to be a sober house for people in AA and people recovering from drug abuse. He ran the house for several years, but Stu spent every summer in NE.

Stu said he had a talk with Willy and decided to shut down the sober house. Willy told him when he went up to New England for the summer, the guys in the sober house would drink; no one was staying sober. Stu argued that he was trying to help people overcome their addiction to drugs and alcohol. Then Willy's wisdom told Stu he was doing all this for the wrong reasons. He had hoped the sober house would give him a very good income for a long time. Willy told him his real purpose in life was to help people in AA, not make money from other people's misfortunes.

Stu sold the sober house but worried about where the people would live. I think it was another project Stu started that didn't work out, and I could identify completely; I failed at completing many projects I started over the years ago and for all the wrong reasons. Many of the people at the safe house went back to live on their boats.

## Matt works his way through community college

Matt graduated from high school and decided to go to college. The cost to go to a university would be thousands of dollars per year. Living off-campus at most universities is very expensive. Some kids never graduate from college but end up with thousands of dollars in student loans.

I talked to Matt about what he wanted to study in college. He told us he wanted to be a Chemist. I must say I dismissed his desire to be a Chemist as just wishful thinking. My sarcastic attitude was like, "Really, how are you ever going to earn a degree in Chemistry?" Many kids in my class in college majored in Chemistry but never graduated with a degree in Chemistry. Anyway, Matt decided to go to a nearby community college to begin his college education. He met a nice girl named Joyce on his first day at college.

## Willy becomes very ill and dies

As time went on, Willy became very ill; he had no Medicare or Medicaid health insurance for his illness and could not be admitted to any hospital.

Willy was staying in a small apartment in the back of Stu's house. Willy had no Medicare health insurance because he could not prove he was a US citizen and resident of Mississippi. When he was 11 years old, he left Mississippi.

Stu contacted the Mississippi health and human services; they told him he could not prove Willy was a US citizen and, therefore, he could not qualify for Social Security or Medicare benefits. Stu fought the Mississippi state government to get Willy's healthcare assistance but was stonewalled at every turn.

Stu fought the bureaucracy for about a year, and after sending many letters and proving Willy had a job in Florida for over ten years, the Mississippi administration still would not give him the government benefits he deserved.

Stu finally got angry and called an administrator in Mississippi that would listen to his plea. Stu argued they don't treat their Black people very well down there at all; he claimed they should be ashamed of the way they treat poor Black people in the South.

Stu's calls may have stirred up some civil rights issues, and finally, after much more paperwork, Willy was finally qualified to get government-assisted Medicaid. However, by the time his benefits finally came through, and everything was approved, Willy was getting very ill and went on hospice care at Stu's place.

Stu said a young hospice aide, probably in her early 20s, came to his apartment. Willy could hardly speak, but he asked the girl why she came; she said: "Just to help you." Willy asked, "How can you help me?" She said: "I can sing." The young girl sang Amazing Grace without any musical instruments. After people left, Willy died alone just a few minutes later. Stu said it was the most beautiful hymn he's ever heard; he thought she was an angel sent to sing to him before he passed away. I said to Stu, "What a beautiful story; he was a very kind and spiritual man."

Stu then said, "That's not all; she came to Willy's service at the county park and sang the Lord's Prayer with her guitar. Stu said, "it was the most beautiful songs he ever heard from the young girl." I said, "Willy will be remembered as a modern-day apostle.". Here is what Stu wrote about Willy.

---

Willy Johnson
April 2, 1945, to February 17, 2011.
Always kind, gentle, and true.
Willy passed away at his home. He was lovingly known to many as the Mayor of the Blue Heron Bridge for the past 20 years. Born in Mississippi in 1945, he came to Florida in 1960 and lived in Homestead, Florida, all through his adult life. He worked at a custodian at an assisted living facility for 14 years. He will be greatly missed by many of his friends. A service will be held at the monument in the park on Sunday.

I never met Willy in person, but I always sensed he was a very spiritual man. It is no mistake. I saved his obituary from the local newspaper of Willy's death and put it in the workbook.

## A night in Tuscany was inspirational

A while ago, I had a heart attack scare and now realize I was probably stress-related. The doctor told me when I was in the hospital, I needed to take care of my diabetes because it could easily cause a heart attack or, even worse, a stroke. Winters, I planned to use music to reset my mind, as I call it. I'm still listening to music like Fleetwood Mac and some other older groups from years ago.

I recently watched a TV show promotion for a concert "A Night in Tuscany" in Italy. I turned to the channel and saw Andrea Bocelli and the Maestro walking out onto the stage. Andrea had his arm over the Maestro's arm, and I could see Andrea was blind.

I heard Andrea did lose his eyesight, but all of a sudden, it hit me, this man is blind. As he started to sing, I began to have tears in my eyes; here is a man that has overcome a severe disability and learned how to sing beautiful romantic songs on the world stage. What an inspiration for all of us. How can he possibly read music without his eyesight?

This is how our higher power works in mysterious ways; an accident took away his eyesight and gave the world a man that will inspire many of us that are physically or mentally disabled. He has been an inspiration to me because I have listened to his music for years. I even have one of his earliest CDs from the mid-70s when he didn't have a full Philharmonic Orchestra behind him.

## Stage 10 My past life returns after I awoke from amnesia

I had severe pain in one leg and went to the doctor. He thought I had a blood clot and put me on a blood thinner. I realized a blood clot could kill me in an instant, and it was time to face reality I wouldn't live forever. I decided it was time to contact old friends. Nicole thought it was a good idea; she knew some people in my past like Greg, Hayley, and my friend Maria.

Now I did not do anything illegal or criminal, but I did severely criticize and verbally abuse some people I loved and cared about years earlier. First, I tried to contact my dear friend Maria in France, but with no luck, I could not find her married name. I wanted to ask her forgiveness for not contacting her after we moved back from Florida. I wanted to thank her for being my close friend for so many years. I really did mess up after we returned from Florida. I never took the time to contact her after she sent me several postcards and letters while we were living in Florida.

I didn't have Iva's telephone number listed and thought I had memorized her number. I briefly searched the Internet but did not find Iva's number and wondered if she was still in the area. I was not trying very hard; maybe I was too afraid to call her? To tell you the truth, I did very much want to contact her to see how she was doing.

I searched the internet for Greg's name, my best friend in high school, and it came up as an address in Maine. That did not surprise me; his family had a cabin on a lake in Maine. I visited his parent's lake house when I was a kid.

I called the number, and it was like we were back in high school; we were still best friends from the past. He lived winters out in Arizona and has a summer cottage in Maine or down Maine, as they say in New England.

I heard Joe was still in Alaska but didn't want to contact him for some reason. I would need to contact his ex-wife Jody in our hometown, and she would ask too many questions. Maybe people in our hometown did know all about Stu and me both dealing with mental illness by now.

## I contacted Hayley and one of her boys

I contacted Hayley and one of the boys. Hayley lived in Minnesota, and it was 30 below as we talked. She gave me the older boy's telephone number, and I called him, and we talked for several minutes. He was building low-income housing for a charity organization and doing well; he was 39 years old.

I told Hayley I was diagnosed with bipolar several years ago; she didn't seem surprised. She didn't say anything about her mental health. She said she was embarrassed to be seen in public because she was bent over like an old lady and had plenty of wrinkles. I said I feel the same way; I have not aged gracefully either.

Her youngest boy was married but getting a divorce because his wife didn't want any kids. Hayley was very sad because she loved his wife and didn't want them to get a divorce.

I lost all contact with members of the OLS group, and I guess it is best I don't contact any of them. A few weeks later, I played more Rhythm & Blues (R&B) and some Country Western (C&W) music about sad and lonely lives and lost loves.

I had high anxiety, just thinking about contacting my 1st love Maria, but I knew I had to contact her for some reason. I did not know why because I always thought she mistreated me. Why would I want to be mistreated and rejected all over again? I was brokenhearted; I should be upset at how she mistreated me.

I told Nicole that I called Hayley Greg, and I said they were all okay. I even said to Nicole I wanted to contact Maria, but she probably wouldn't want to talk to me after Nantucket. I was vague and didn't go into details. Nicole said, "You never told me about her," and I replied, "We never talked after Nantucket." I didn't say I wanted to call Iva because she would want even more details.

## I wanted to watch less cable TV

It was a very cold day in November, and I could not take my daily walk in the park. I was slipping into my yearly case of SAD and sad because the sunset was an hour earlier. Around 5 o'clock, the sun went down, and I felt I was going down along with the sun. I needed a way to get through another winter.

After going to the Music Fest in the summer and listening to our favorite band, I wanted to listen to good music again. I decided to make some changes to my lifestyle. I wanted to listen more to music, watch less cable TV and not spend time surfing the Internet for meaningless trivia. After listening to good music at the Music Fest in the summer, I realized the music had guided me through many hardships over the years.

I relate well to music just by listening to some of the words of the songs. I think many of the songs are from deep within the soul and soothe the heart. I love blues and soul-type music and some of the songs from the disco era back in the 70s and 80s. Even Einstein said music is truth or something like that.

I went to an estate sale and bought a complete audio system for only $100. Well, it is my motto, be frugal but not cheap. The quality of the audio system was not cheap; it was state of the art, including amps, a subwoofer, and four very expensive speakers. The next day I went out to the garage and found all my old music collection. Yes, I'm still a hoarder and have kept most of the original music, even old classical LPs from college decades ago. Within an hour, I set up the system components, and the sound quality filled the room even better than in a movie theater.

The music began to make me feel sad about the past events in my life. Some music brought me back to my years spent on Nantucket and the carefree summer nights spent at beach parties. We had a terrific guitar player and sang folk songs by the bonfire at beach parties.

## All of a sudden, I was back at Maria's apartment

Thoughts of Maria flashed in my mind. I found the same powerful music the Awake spiritual growth course used during the course. The music was used at the Awake course to bring up unconscious and painful emotional memories. Reluctantly I decided to listen to several of the old CDs.

To make a long story short, a few days later, I put on one of the powerful CD's used at the Awake course, and when the first song started to play, the words "I found out what I've been missing" followed by the words "I've been looking for someone" I felt so heartbroken.

Then the song "Where do broken hearts go" began to play, and the sound of her powerful voice and the sound of the music was all around me; her voice sounded like the real emotional pain of losing a loved one.

All of a sudden, I was back at Maria's apartment over four decades ago. The truth of the words hit me so hard; it was a cold November day all those many years ago. All of a sudden, I was reliving that night. I went to Maria's apartment at 2 AM.; she was having sex with another guy. I began to break down into uncontrollable crying. The truth was coming out; I wasn't the same after that cold November night.

I composed a "Please forgive me" email. In the email I wrote, I thought we were always meant to be with each other, and I was sorry I mistreated you; you did nothing wrong it was all my fault. I did not say I was crazy, but not insane; she probably figured all that out on Nantucket.

After searching the internet, I found her married name that listed part of her email address and guessed what I thought was her actual email address. I decided to hit the send key without really thinking through the consequences. I waited ten minutes, and the email was not returned undeliverable. It was probably her email address.

The traumatic and tragic emotions of decades ago started to flood back into my mind again. It was so bizarre I had the feeling I was 22 again. I was having flashbacks of the raw emotions, feelings, and images I experienced decades ago in real-time.

## How could I ever even begin to forgive myself?

I began to sob uncontrollably; the true suppressed emotions I felt decades ago were filling my mind with the truth; I was to blame for the entire breakup; she did nothing wrong. It was all my fault, and the tears kept rolling down my face. I could not face the truth; back then, it was my mental illness, my very selfish behavior that ended our relationship forever.

Maria may have been dealing with very troubling problems of her own. She came all the way out to Nantucket, hoping I would be protective of her and treat her with kindness. The truth was causing a shock wave of emotions. I will never forgive myself for how I treated her. I am sure my crazy verbally abusive behavior was the last straw, and she found someone else that treated her with kindness and respect.

I kept on getting flashbacks of the breakup back then and what was going on in my present life. At this point, I was so upset and confused I needed to calm down separate my life into two separate periods of time.

The first period, when I was in a state of repressed memory, I call a state of amnesia. I am not a psychiatrist, and amnesia may not be the correct psychiatric term. In the second phase, after coming out of amnesia, I call my past or traumatic recollections period.

I called Stu several times, and he said I needed professional help. I did not think my psychiatrist would believe me; my thoughts were random, like I may have schizophrenia; that's one of my biggest fears, you know. Don't get me wrong; I have nothing against people with schizophrenia. Maybe I do need to get professional help, but I was certain the only way to solve my problem was to experience my raw emotions and go forward; no one else could help me relive my past emotional events in my life.

I called Stu the next day, and he said, "You should forgive yourself." I replied, "Some things in life are just not meant to be forgotten or forgiven. The most tragic part of the entire breakup, I think we loved each other."

After I hung up, I began to cry again. I am sure I forgot the most tragic event in my entire life for decades, and it did not help me. Well, maybe it did, but I was under so much stress I was afraid I would go into another state of amnesia.

You know my friend Maria and my 1$^{st}$ love Maria had the same first name, and I never connected it to my 1$^{st}$ love, Maria. That is certainly one fact that supports my claim I was in a state of amnesia; in fact, it did happen. Nicole said I always called Maria from France "My friend Maria" and not just Maria. I never mentioned Maria as my 1st love to Nicole or Iva because I was in a state of amnesia.

I lost contact with my friend Maria and never told her about my mental issues. I never mentioned my 1st love Maria to my friend Maria. I'm sure she would have understood my pain over losing my 1st love; well, I am sure she would accept my BD illness but might think my case of amnesia was a bit odd if not insane, I mean crazy.

## The AA 12 step program teaches you to make amends

I called Stu again and told him the whole story of my breakup with Maria. He said the AA 12 step program teaches you to make amends for past deeds, but only if it will not hurt your present or past relationships.

I had violated the AA rule don't ruin other people's lives by confessing past misdeeds. I thought Stu was right. I should have called my psychiatrist and told him all about the state of mind. Maybe he could help me move from my past life into my present life and help me relive my past life. I thought to myself, how can I tell anyone I was in a state of amnesia for over 45 years over a breakup with a girlfriend? It is true I awoke 45 years later, but it is true.

What a bizarre experience, but how would my visit to my psychiatrist begin and end?

My psychiatrist always asks me if I am suicidal, and I would say, "No, Dr., I don't feel suicidal, but very traumatic past events are coming up in my present life."

Dr: "Oh, really, tell me more."

Me: "I lost a girlfriend around Christmas time, and she left me for another guy."

Dr: "That's too bad; Christmas is a bad time to lose a close friend."

Dr: "Do you have a family member that can stay with you this Christmas?"

Me: "Oh no, Dr., You see, it is not this Christmas; it was a Christmas over four decades ago. Yes, it was over 45 years ago."

Me "You see, Dr. I am living between my past life and my present life. I went into a state of amnesia for over four decades. I am having memory flashbacks of events that happened over 45 years ago; I am living in both the past and present. I am confused as to what side. Am I living in my past life or the present or both?"

Dr: "Well, in that case, I'll give you a strong enough anti-psychotic to forget your past life even existed."

Me: "But Dr., that's what happened over four decades ago; I don't want to go through all that again. "

Me: "I just want to bring up my past life into my present life to help me get through a present and past crisis I experienced when I was 22.

Me: "Do you think I might, in fact, be 22 years old?"

That would end our conversation.

Well, perhaps the 22 years old again is just wishful thinking.
My psychiatrist would then have me involuntary admitted to our local psychiatric hospital. Would this be how my session would end?

I thought perhaps that's why my psychiatrist gave me anti-psychotic meds a few years ago. He probably thinks I'm schizophrenic and have been hallucinating my entire life. That's my biggest fear, you know. Of course, I meant this as a joke, but at the time, I was so overwhelmed with past and present emotions my psychiatrist might think he missed my real diagnosis completely.

A few months later, I was mentally fragile, well, almost emotionally stable but had many questions about my amnesia and my ongoing traumatic recollections of the past.

I think my traumatic recollections will be long-term, but I hope I will not experience the overwhelming feelings of grief and guilt ever again after coming out of amnesia. What a messed-up life; I had yet another mental disorder I needed to deal with, probably for the rest of my life.

By now, I have written hundreds of sheets of paper of the entire experience. I like to call this my music and journal therapy.

## Why didn't I have breakthroughs during the Awake course?

All of a sudden, I thought, why didn't I have these breakthroughs back when I was taking the Awake course? I did see many people have breakthroughs, intense emotional breakthroughs during the course. Many people found the course a very therapeutic and life-altering experience. You know, the Awake course used some of the same music I was playing to bring me out of my state of amnesia. The mind has ways to harm and protect, and I guess my memory loss of the traumatic events or amnesia did protect me from harming myself all those years.

Even at the Awake course, I did not have a breakthrough, although many people did. I thought the Awake music I was just playing may have triggered unconscious raw emotions to rise up to be conscious again. Questions began to pop up all day and night some I could not answer but only created more questions. Several well dozens of doctors and psychiatrists never brought me out of my state of amnesia.

I woke up one night and sat up in bed and thought, "I want to get her back." Of course, this is the past talking to me again regarding my tragic breakup with Maria. The raw emotions came up like I was still living in my past unstable emotional lifestyle.

Now, this was so bizarre. Was I schizophrenic? Maybe Sabrina could tell me because she had a hard time deciding if things were real or imaginary. I wish I did become friends with her. I wonder if I came out of my state of amnesia when I was 30 years old and was not treated for alcoholism, would I be able to recover my forgotten memories safely? Would I drown my sorrow with alcohol or use drugs to relieve my intense emotional pain?

If I came out to the state of amnesia before being treated for bipolar, would I'd be suicidal? Oh man, I don't need another serious mental illness to deal with it this time in my life. Why did this happen so late in life and not when I was much younger?

## I never grieved the traumatic events of my past
Here I am, 70 years old and going through many emotional breakthroughs every day now. I was aware of many of the events of the past after being treated for my bipolar illness but never came to grips with the deep emotions I had buried deep within my mind.

I never grieved the traumatic events, so I could move past them. Again, my untreated BD mind, alcoholism, personality disorders, and amnesia back then all were getting in the way of living a normal happy life, well, at least a stable bipolar normal lifestyle as I call it.

A few weeks later, I had another feeling; I lost my youth. I was afraid to get close to any woman until I met Iva. I spent four years in Seattle hanging out in sleazy bars picking up women for one-night stands. I am now feeling cheated out of an even a BD normal life after hundreds of major cycles of BD mania and depression. I need to find a positive outcome of all this confusion in my life. I believe everything happens for a reason, doesn't it? I can't seem to find a reason for living decades with a case of amnesia, not yet anyway.

I also understood why I wanted to be in open relationships with every woman I dated. After the breakup with Maria, I felt so betrayed when I found out she was having sex with another guy. I was delusional, thinking she was not dating other guys. I might have accepted it if she told me she was dating other guys; no, not really. She did nothing wrong it was not a crime not to tell someone you are dating and having sex with another guy.

The phrase "I was unworthy of her love." kept repeating in my mind again. Maria never replied to my "I am sorry" email; maybe I was not worthy of being loved by her. Then I thought, what if Iva also told me I was not worthy of being loved by her? I could not take the chance.

After the breakup with Maria, I think being open and honest with every woman I dated was very important to me. I did feel Maria was cheating on me; she did not want me; she was in a serious relationship with a guy in Boston. That is one reason I was so attracted to Iva. She told me she was not going to cheat on me after the first night we slept together. As time went on, our trust and friendship became even stronger.

### I wanted to contact Iva but didn't
Many traumatic recollections of the breakup put me into a tailspin for more than a year, and I couldn't contact anyone. About two years later, I decided it was time to contact Iva. Was this another error in

judgment? I knew Iva would understand my crisis and support me through this crisis, but I shouldn't call her. I might want to see her again, and I can't tell Nicole at this time.

Would I violate the AA rule? Don't confess your misdeeds if they might jeopardize someone's relationship? I had been through a few traumatic events in my life. I thought Iva would understand my situation better than anyone. I am sure she had horrendous and unspeakable things she witnessed during and after WW II. She often said she came to America to feel safe.

Although I never physically abused Iva, I did abandon her and wanted to apologize for not keeping in touch with her. I feel abandonment is a form of abuse; I felt abandoned and rejected all my life. I guess it's a reason I did not want to contact her all along.

I'm going to look her up again. I want to know if she is okay. I did not think she was still living in the area, but I was too busy vacationing and spending time with our family.

To be honest, I was ashamed and guilty of the way I treated Iva after I met Nicole. Maybe I would want to be with her again, and that might destroy my relationship with Nicole. Maybe Iva would not even want to talk to me, and that would be painful, but I am willing to take the chance.

After a good night's sleep, I realized I was again looking for the intimacy and affection I had craved for all my life. I am still insecure, but now I am an old and feeble older man but not an old man. I wanted her to comfort me again as she had done years ago. I feel so helpless to figure out what to do next. Maybe Iva also needs comfort and is feeling all alone now. I need to face the truth. I am a pathetic excuse for a man; my family was right. I was a sensitive and moody kid and now a moody, grumpy older man.

Perhaps I am still selfishly looking to my needs, not hers. I remember I was afraid to find her phone number a few years ago, but I was afraid to talk to her back then. Most likely, I would want to be with her again. I vowed to always be faithful to Nicole. I searched the Internet for a few minutes and found her married name and telephone number, but I did not call her; I delayed yet another task in life I promised myself I would complete.

## I needed to tell Nicole

Nicole was having a hard time at work, and I needed the right time to explain the entire amnesia story to her. She was having conflicts at work and was talking about the conflicts at work nonstop every night. Finally, her conflicts at work were resolved by management.

I decided to tell Nicole I had a very dramatic breakup with my girlfriend after college. I needed to find the right time to explain it all to her. A few weeks later, the conflict at work was resolved at work I finally talked to Nicole about my memory relapse about Maria. I said I had a traumatic breakup in college and was verbally abused on Nantucket, and I need her to forgive me. I said she never talked to me again after Nantucket. Nicole thought I was talking about my friend Maria.

I said I met her on Nantucket. Nicole said, "You never told me about her?" I said, "That's right, I had put her out of my mind until I went to call her to ask her to forgive me." I said, "I mentioned it when I was going to call some of my old friends. Remember I said Maria never talk to me again after Nantucket" Then I said, "Maria never talked to me after Nantucket because I treated her so badly, I sent an email to her to forgive me. I got very angry and jealous over her having sex with someone else. ". Nicole said that's immaturity when you're young. I said I sent her an Easter card only to see if she got my email. Nicole said that's enough; she may not want to dig up old past relationships.

As I say, my traumatic recollections of the past are an ongoing process because sometimes I have insight or sadness about something that happened decades ago. Anyway, I am glad now I discovered my amnesia before I died because it is part of my life now. Without discovering my amnesia before I died would be tragic.

During the extreme emotional stress of reliving painful distant memories, I added a hundred pages to my journal. Now I had hundreds of notes in my journal from the BDS group and my past life. Writing in my journal became a form of therapy and then became the basis of this workbook.

I would go out to the local park for an hour and write pages of notes. Every time a raw emotion came up, I would try to put it into words. My emotions were up and down after writing hundreds of pages. I was very concerned I might be having another mental breakdown. I was separating the entire bizarre experience into two separate times in my life, past, and present.

I was still having flashbacks of events that happened just before I entered the state of amnesia. I was dealing with the effects it had on me during amnesia and then after my memory retrieval. I was confused and overwhelmed, but I knew I needed to experience all these raw emotions and not go into another state of amnesia or, worse, a very bad psychotic episode ending in suicide.

Maybe I should have gone to a psychoanalyst years ago instead of group psychotherapy. I calculated if the cost of a psychoanalyst over the years would be in the tens of thousands of dollars. I self-psychoanalyzed myself with a $100 audio system and a few CDs. Now that is frugal. Of course, I am kidding; overcoming my issues is a bit more complicated than music therapy. I had to deal with my multiple character flaws, as we say.

You know, a good psychoanalyst may have discovered my case of amnesia or repressed memory when I was in my 20's. As I understand, a psychoanalyst will take the time to look for unconscious thoughts and events and dig deeper to find the root cause of trauma or mental disorders. On the other hand, I have plenty of other issues and would have taken ten years to unravel just a few of them. My psychoanalyst may have had a nervous breakdown trying to unravel all my issues.

The question still comes up, if I came out of amnesia before I was stable and under treatment for BD, would I be so unstable as to commit suicide? Would I have been under so much emotional pain I would turn to drugs? If the answer was yes, then amnesia did save my life.

For weeks I could not sleep and finally went back to my psychiatrist. I was still reliving emotional past painful memories as if they occurred yesterday. It was some form of amnesia, well, at least repressed or suppressed memories. I did not mention my sad memory recollections, but my psychiatrist did adjust my meds.

About a year later, I was emotionally stable again and wanted to get help for my anxiety and sleep problems. I did not want to bring up my case of amnesia. My psychiatrist put me on another antipsychotic med. Of course, I thought of Sabrina and the difficult life she had back when I was in group psychotherapy. I was not having hallucinations or delusions of grandeur but wondered if I would ever survive the most traumatic events of my life.

I was still reliving events that occurred decades ago. I do have personality disorders, but I want to concentrate on my case of amnesia and BD disorder for now. How many more mental disorders will I discover? Back when I was in group psychotherapy with Sabrina, I thought I had all the mental disorders in the DSM manual.

The new meds seemed to help me sleep and have better control of my anxiety issues. My life with BD, in addition to several other mental issues, was beginning to make sense and not just nonsense. I was slowly rediscovering events of my past did have a profound effect on my life.

When I was in my 20s, I would have scored the highest score on the WAVES Chart at a Stress Zone Level 7 during that time in my life. To be honest, I should have been involuntarily hospitalized after the breakup.

## I am going to turn my journal into a workbook

After reliving the traumatic events in my younger days, I started to write down all my emotions of the past and present, usually a page or two of notes every day. They were in order, but sorry to say; they were in random order. At first, most of the notes were about very traumatic events in my past. Some intense emotions I relived all over again. Some Images and intense emotions I had suppressed for decades. I thought if I was not stable and did not have a good psychiatrist, I might not have weathered the emotional storm of reliving my past. I was emerging from years of extreme stress and many dark, destructive, and tragic memories of my past life.

## My just another bipolar story

After my traumatic recollections after decades in a state of amnesia, I started to collaborate with my brother Stu in Florida about things that happened in our past. We talked almost every day for a year about our alcoholism and the many risks we took while manic and usually quite drunk. We talked about our father and the possibility he also had a mental illness and Aunt Maddie with her peculiar personality.

After a year of collaboration with my brother, we were both convinced our BD illness was the most important factor in our lives.

It explained many of the hardships and setbacks in our lives. Of course, our personality issues and alcoholism played a big part in our lives, but we constantly struggled with the unrelenting cycles of mania and depression for over 50 years before proper treatment.

It was an eye-opener to realize we survived childhood, teens, college, several relationships, career changes, and decades of alcoholism without effective medication. We often thought we were living on borrowed time. Actually, I did not think I would live past 55, which was about when our father died of a heart attack.

I did not know it at this time, but the answer is right in front of me, I needed to help other people with BD. I was talking to my brother one day on the phone, and I mentioned I had enough notes to write an entire novel. I said I must have 300 pages of notes. He said, why don't you write a book? I said I was joking; I can't write a novel; I can hardly write a proper sentence. He said, "You sound very optimistic about writing a book; you should write it before you change your mind." He knows my character flaws all right; he wants me to write the book before I change my mind. That was almost an insult, but true; I started many projects, and then I changed my mind and gave up.

## I decided a workbook may be helpful

I told Nicole, my brother, and I was going to write our entire life story about our lives with BD. She said, "Well, we don't have the money to spend on a book." I replied, "My experience with BD may be the only thing I have to offer in this lifetime." I am glad she is frugal, or we could be living in a dirt hut by now.

After reviewing the hundreds of pages of notes I had on our life history and the BDS group, I decided my observations and insights on our BD lifestyles in a workbook would be more helpful for people with BD. I began to realize our life story was just another bipolar story.

The next day I decided to write a workbook identifying our unique stressful life situations. After all the most productive periods of our lives, from 25 to mid-life, when we were both mentally very unstable.

I did not want other people to live the same life of setbacks and breakdowns, so I decided to complete The WAVES Chart; perhaps it might help people identify the stress people have at different times or stages in their lives. I had a long list of stressful situations that could apply to people with BD. Getting people with BD treatment early on became one of the primary goals of the workbook.

## *I don't think anyone will believe I had a case of amnesia*

Life is moving along, and I have decided to publish a workbook. It is now 2012, and I turned 70 years old a few days ago. Nicole and I don't celebrate our birthdays until summertime. We wait until the summer and celebrate both our birthdays at a famous seafood restaurant.

It is hard to believe I have attended Rosie's BDS group for almost 15 years now. I developed the WAVES Chart years ago, but for some reason, I cannot complete the workbook.

After I awoke from amnesia, I had a problem making the workbook believable to many readers. How am I going to handle my case of amnesia? Some psychiatrists don't even believe amnesia exists as a psychiatric disorder. Would anyone believe I was in a state of amnesia for 45 years? That is an awfully long time to be in denial and not aware I mistreated Maria in my early 20s. Perhaps I should hide my case of amnesia entirely? No, I did go into a state of amnesia, it did happen, and I was in a state of amnesia for over 45 years.

I have proof to support my claim of amnesia. First, I did not remember any events of the breakup when Stu invited us up to Nantucket. The sight of the ferry leaving the dock did not trigger any raw emotions. Also, the fact my friend Maria and my 1st love Maria had the same first name did not trigger any past memories of the breakup.

I am concerned now the workbook may be viewed as entirely a work of fiction. My story is getting longer, more complicated, and more unbelievable as time goes on. What other hidden disorders will I discover?

My story is becoming hundreds of pages longer than I expected; however, I needed to account for 20 years of bad spells after I became stable in 1992. Most likely, I will need to account for more bad spells after I just awoke from amnesia. I am afraid my just another bipolar story is turning into a psycho documentary.

## I had another case of writer's block

I continued to take notes about our lives and had several sheets of paper in my back pocket to jot down "profound" insights about my life with BD. Most notes were not profound at all but just mundane thoughts and afterthoughts I had written over the years. Many times, my afterthoughts were just crazy thoughts and were filed in the paper shredder. Sometimes I would go to the county lake in the evening on a hot day and spend a few hours walking and working on the workbook.

Two years later, I did have about two hundred pages in a very rough draft of my experiences with BD. I decided a better way to help people with BD was to complete the WAVES Workbook in paperback. I further developed a WAVES Chart that listed many life situations that cause abnormal stressors. I had over 70 life situations and events that cause stress in people with BD.

True to my BD nature, I put the project on hold again. It became clear why I was writing the workbook but had no idea how to get it published. After a year struggling with bipolar, writing the workbook, and dealing with tragic recollections, I went into a prolonged depression.

I had a bad case of writer's block and just sat in the den and listened to music. Maybe I should not have contacted people to apologize for my past misdeeds. I felt like I was in a street fight and lost several rounds to depression.

I had lost Maria, but that was over four decades ago. Would I ever feel better about myself? Somehow, I needed to pull myself up and out of despair. Nicole understood, but even her patience was in short supply. I didn't bother to get a med adjustment. Ignoring important events is a character flaw I have lived with all my life.

### I am still reluctant to go to talk therapy

I think I am reluctant to get talk therapy has something to do with growing up without a lot of confidence or physical affection when I was a kid. Another secret I did not want to disclose was the fact I was sexually abused by a teenager down the street when I was about 8. I think another big secret was discovering my breakup with Maria was hidden in a case of amnesia for over 45 years. What talk therapist is going to believe that disorder?

### It's time I contact the rest of the people on my list

It's time I contact the rest of the people on my list. I think I'm going to contact Iva and tell l her I'm sorry about the way I treated her back then. I'm going to tell her I love her and I hope she can forgive what happened in the past. I think maybe when people learn about my mental illness, they may feel relieved that they didn't have a long-term relationship with me. As a TV program about marriage stated, the first rule was, "Don't marry someone with a mental illness."

You know it's easy for "Normal" people to say, "Why does he keep going over the issues over and over again?" and "Why doesn't he just snap out of it and face the truth?" Well, I think my answer is, "My brain will not allow me to process emotions and deal with life situations like "Normal" people. The WAVES Chart attempts to point out the average everyday situations in life are much more stressful for people with BD, especially if not stable.

When I graduated from college, I wanted to get away from my abusive family. I couldn't understand my mental issues were partly to blame for my moods and bipolar lifestyle. I'm over 70 now and don't have much time left, but my mental illnesses have caused setbacks in my life. I have not realized until recently both my mental illness and physical illnesses are getting too much for me to handle. Today I started to cry, thinking my dam bipolar illness has ruined my life. At times I do resent having to live with this illness for so long.

But then Stu's words ring true, "Be thankful you have Nicole; she is the one person you don't want to lose." He is right, I do not appreciate Nicole enough, and I am getting good support and psychiatric treatment.

## I need to finally contact Iva

I went down to Philly to look at a used car and realized I was near Iva's old neighborhood. Perhaps unconsciously, I wanted to knock on her door and ask her how life was treating her. It brought back memories of staying with her and walking along the stream in Valley Green Park on the weekends. I did not even know how important she was in my life. The following evening, I got enough nerve to call her. I realized I probably should have called her a few years ago, but, as usual, I delayed getting in contact with her back then.

Within a few minutes, I found her phone number and called before I delayed any longer. A man answered the phone and asked who I was calling? I said I was an old friend of Iva and just wanted to see how she was doing. He said he was Iva's husband. He told me she died in little over a year ago and gave me a link to her obituary on a local newspaper website. I said, "She was a dear friend to me years ago, and she was a very nice and kind woman." He said, "Yes, she was," and that ended our conversation.

### Iva was gone

A few minutes later, I started to break down in tears, realizing she was gone. She was such an important part of my life. I should've contacted her years ago, and now it's too late. In the following days, I was grieving her loss, but then again, maybe this loss was also telling me I would not live forever. I need to follow my goals in this life and try to help people with mental illness before it is too late.

Helping people with BD is what my higher power, my spiritual advisor told me to do years ago, but I did not get it. Perhaps Iva's spirit is giving me a message from the other side. I do believe our spirit or soul lives on after we die.

I believe we are here to learn life lessons, and then our spirit or energy passes over to the other side upon death. Spirits on the other side can guide us. I'm feeling Iva is looking down on me and saying, "You've got to complete your workbook project.". Iva was clear about her purpose in life, to help poor people by working as a social worker.

We both had very dramatic events happen in our lives, and maybe we need to tell the world humanity will repeat the horrendous acts of the past if we don't acknowledge what's happening in the present. We never discussed the traumatic events in our lives. I was in a state of amnesia, and she would not talk about her life in war-torn Europe.

Iva showed me there is compassion and caring in the world, and she was the first woman I ever had an honest, intimate relationship with ever. My relationship with Maria was a love relationship, but we never had enough time together to form a truly intimate relationship. I always thought of Maria as my soul mate, our souls intertwined to form an unbreakable bond. I am afraid if we did, I broke that unbreakable bond on Nantucket. Looking back, I had a much closer bond with Iva, and together I think we have an important story to tell.

## I followed the link to Iva's obituary

A few days later, I followed the link to Iva's obituary in a local paper. She was returned to Eastern Europe to be with her family. That didn't surprise me because she told me several times she couldn't go back to her homeland; she implied she would be harmed in some way. Several times she said that the Russians mistreated her people before the war, and then when the Germans came, they murdered innocent men, women, and children. It is so sad she needed to pass over to get back to her homeland and be with her family.

Her funeral notice also said she was very involved with the hiking club for many years. It doesn't surprise me; many times, we would go down to a park near her apartment and walk along the path. The notice also stated she dedicated her life as a social worker for many years. She was doing social work when I met her many years ago. That did not surprise me either, she was kind, and I am sure she wanted to devote her life to helping less fortunate people. I cannot imagine the grief and sorrow her husband must be going through now.

When I was in a state of amnesia, I could not admit I loved her, and the words "I love you" could not be spoken. Maybe if I had come out of the state of amnesia back then, I would've told her I loved her every day. She also believed you could love more than one person at the same time. I mentioned if she wanted to have children only a few times, and she completely avoided my comment.

From the WW II B&W prints I witnessed when I was 12 years old, I knew she probably witnessed horrendous events before, during, and after WW II. I never questioned Iva about her life in Europe.

Now I know I had a very tragic event happen in my life, but mine was hidden in a secret world of amnesia, and maybe hers were too. My relationship with Iva was a real love relationship and not like the delusional love I had for Maria.

A few days later, I realized I always thought I was abandoned by my family, Maria, Greg, and others, but ironically, I abandoned Iva. I was a year too late to tell her I will always love her; I hope she is listening now.

## How would Iva feel about our nation now?
I wonder if I contacted her before she passed away, how she would feel about what's going on in America now. I'll bet she would feel the grave dangers to our freedom from within our own government. It's so sad she was forced to flee from her homeland at such a young age. Perhaps people being persecuted in our nation after our crisis will escape to a more tolerant and caring country. I cannot imagine the horrific events she witnessed before coming to America.

Events are now happening daily in this country that worries me greatly; our 1776 Constitutional rights are not being served to protect the average working-class citizen. Demonstrations occur daily to resist the administration, but the confusion is more propaganda to justify the overthrow of our current government.

I gave up contacting other people; thank goodness I did not uncover any other past emotional issues I had suppressed for decades. Maybe contacting people from the past was not the right thing to do in the first place. Well, discovering events from my past did cause pain in my life, that's for sure. I had issues with Maria and then more sorrow about learning about the death of Iva.

I have never cheated on Nicole. The nights I spent in honky-tonk bars taught me not to cheat behind someone's back. Half of my co-workers in Seattle, both men, and women, had serious marriage issues. Their marriages did not convince me my marriage could be a path to happiness. I learned cheating causes distrust and feelings of betrayal that can and do end relationships. That's one reason I wanted open relationships.

## Wendy was not worthy of her husband's love

For over ten years, I had been very active in the BDS group but was getting burned out because many people in the group had serious problems. Sometimes after listening to people struggle with depression, job, and relationship issues, I would come home mentally exhausted, sometimes regret I even went to the BDS group.

It was a very cold night, but I decided to go and support other people in the group. To be truthful, I also wanted to forget my grief and sorrow over the passing of Iva.

A woman named Wendy was having a difficult time. She had very low self-esteem as she talked about her childhood; she blamed herself for her difficult childhood. At one point, she bent down in her chair and then remarked, "I do not feel worthy of my husband's love." Her remarks struck a sensitive nerve. Does that mean she does not feel she is lovable? Wendy was sorry her husband loves her? Did she blame herself for a troubled childhood?

I drove home from the meeting that very cold winter night. I came home to a warm house, but I felt troubled seeing so many people struggling with BD, and there was no cure. That night I could not sleep and realized many people in the group felt like the distraught woman at the meeting; no one loved them. I also felt I was not worthy of being loved by anyone from a very young age. The phrase "I was not worthy of being loved" kept repeating in my mind. I came to the grim conclusion many people in the group were also victims of childhood abuse.

Over the years, many people in the BDS group made comments that told me they felt unworthy of being loved. Of course, many people that were divorced felt they were not loved by their ex-husbands or wives. Divorce usually leads to feelings of abandonment, and they are not lovable if your mate just walked out on you.

I was fortunate Nicole was kind and stayed with me, but I realized if I married any other woman, the chance of a divorce would be 90 percent, especially before I became stable. I am sure I would also have deep feelings of unworthiness if we ever got divorced.

Some people expressed thoughts they were somehow damaged and not worthy of love. Other people had been rejected many times by employers, friends, lovers, and even family members; others felt abandoned and worthless. Over the years, I noticed many people with BD had feelings of unworthiness; many had been emotionally, sexually, and physically abused since childhood.

After some people were diagnosed with BD, they had feelings of being somewhat inferior, damaged as I did for years. I felt there was something wrong with me for decades. Trying to find out what was wrong with me was the main reason I took the Awake course and went to group psychotherapy back in the 70s. Now I know I had a case of undiagnosed BD and amnesia, but my problems went even deeper.

## I need to accept I do have an unworthy syndrome
Sadly, I did have deep feelings of unworthiness from a very young age, after years of rejection beginning in early childhood. In addition, episodes of mania and depression caused addictions, relationship problems, and many other quality of life issues. All these negative events and situations made me feel unlovable, and for some reason, I did not deserve to lead a "Normal" life.

My deep negative feelings of unworthiness were reinforced even further after the breakup with Maria. I was in my early 20s when I went into a state of amnesia. At some level, I thought I was not worthy of Maria's love; she found someone better, maybe she did. See, that's how I felt about my life; I felt I didn't deserve love or anything better for myself.

I can look back and can partly blame my unworthy syndrome for the breakup. I understand now over the years, these feelings of not being loved have spread into other areas of my life. I don't deserve to be successful and publish a workbook.

I don't deserve to own a nice RV or have any joy in life. In other words, my unworthy syndrome has kept me trapped in my past. Emotionally I am still acting like a child. What I am saying is I cannot blame my BD or my case of amnesia for all the setbacks in my life. I need to be mindful I am living with multiple mental issues, BD, amnesia, and other issues. I was a victim of childhood abuse. My unworthy syndrome is a result of childhood abuse plus BD. I am not seeking pity or want sympathy but just want people with BD to understand they may be dealing with multiple issues in life. Again, the objective is to identify life situations that cause stress or illness and begin to accept, change or heal from them.

I don't have a cure for my unworthy syndrome, but I know now there was nothing I could do back then to fight back against my deep feelings of unworthiness. I did not have anyone to tell me they loved me and convince me I was worthy of being loved. I had no way to treat my BD. As a young child, I could not make my father reappear, or Aunt Maddie disappear.

## Stage 11 The Great Outdoors was our path to happiness

Summer arrived Jane was ready to have her fourth child. We decided to take all the kids camping to a friendly kid resort campground about an hour away from our house.

We've been to this campground just to look around, and it was a resort campground made just for kids. It had a heated swimming pool and a large kiddy pool. The activities for the kids were great; they had archery in the afternoon and some games in the evening. On rainy days they showed movies in the clubhouse. However, the best activity for all the kids at this campground, all the kids could ride their bikes all over the campground and down to the camp store without adult supervision.

The kids really did have a sense of freedom, and you could see they were happy and carefree as they rode their bikes all around the campground. It did remind me of my childhood on the farm, riding my bike up the back-dirt roads and feeling the freedom to go wherever I pleased. I was surprised all the kids loved the archery activity, and the instructor was so patient, showing them how to aim at the target on the bales of hay.

We were all very cramped in our little camper, the kids had a good time, and all behaved well. This camping trip was not as peaceful and quiet for Nicole and me but seeing the kids so happy and carefree was a very rewarding experience for both of us.

Matt visited us at the campground with his new girlfriend, Joyce. She was very friendly and got along with all the kids. I could tell Joyce was more than just a friend with benefits. They decided to stay and slept in our minivan on an air mattress. In high school, Matt broke a lot of hearts. Every time he broke up with one girl, another one popped up. I think Matt and his high school buddies went to 3 or 4 high school proms; I lost count.

## Our camping vacation South of the Border

By June, I had enough of the politics and mudslinging by all the candidates and needed a break from attending to our 105-year-old house and all our family issues. Our house was built in 1909 and about 70 years old when we bought it in the early '80s, but now our old house is showing her old age at over 105, and I am afraid I am also showing my old, I mean older age.

I had several home projects on the house lined up but decided to go camping closer to home instead. We had planned a vacation up to Arcadia National Park in Maine for a few weeks but decided to head south because June can be cold in "Down Maine," as they say.

Our destination was at a campground in Myrtle Beach, SC, for a few weeks and then visited Charleston, SC, for a week. We like to spend a few days at each stop and not rush from one campground to the next. I planned a trip around Baltimore and Washington DC. We don't like to travel on the big interstates; they don't really give a feel for the local culture. Every major exit on the Interstates has the same restaurants motel chains, and the campgrounds tend to be like one-night truck stops.

We decided to travel down the eastern shore of Maryland across the Chesapeake Bay Bridge and down through North Carolina to Charleston, South Carolina. Our first stop was at a campground along Chesapeake for two days. The next day we traveled over the Chesapeake Bay Bridge and down through the small towns in NC to a very rural campground.

We arrived at the small local campground; the people were friendly and gave us a nice site overlooking a small pond. I sensed they wanted to know more about us because we had an old camper with PA license plates.

The campground was run down, and old trailers were in disrepair. We also worried a bit if these people could damage our camper or steal our stuff. Within a few minutes, Frank, the campground "greeter," came over to introduce himself and welcome us to North Carolina. Most campgrounds have a "Greeter." Within minutes he was telling us very private information about the people in the campground and his personal struggles in life. He told us the owner got ill and couldn't keep up the campground several years ago. After our conversation, it was like we were part of the local crowd. He had no hesitation in explaining how difficult life was for the people living around the small town.

His story was not uncommon and not a surprise for us to hear, but this rural area has felt the pain of underemployment for several years. Unemployment and loss of Jobs have devastated this and many small communities we have visited over the past several years. For several years Nicole and I have camped all along the east coast. We do not stay at 5-star hotels and resorts along the major interstate highways but in very backcountry rural towns. We meet the local people at local diners, family restaurants, and shops along the way. We drive through small towns and shop at local food stores. We see many small businesses closed and the towns run down. In some places, a superstore a few miles out of town is the only employer for miles. The superstores have shut down many small families-run businesses in towns all across America. We see people driving older cars and living in very modest older houses in need of repair. I often joked we never pass a Mercedes dealer in these rural areas.

With all the hardships I saw at the campground in North Carolina, I was encouraged to see the kids were free to roam around the woods without fear. At night you could hear kids of all ages playing in the woods behind the campground. The kids would be laughing and carrying on, but we never heard fights or arguments while we camped near the small pond.

The atmosphere reminded me of the freedom I felt as a young boy growing up on the farm. I think these kids also experienced the freedom of living in a peaceful environment. I thought maybe that is why I now feel a loss of my freedoms because I felt those freedoms when just a youth. Maybe if you never experience real freedom, you cannot miss it when it is threatened to be taken away from you. The loss of feeling free is what I am experiencing now in our once great country. While the government and the MSM advance an anti-American agenda, the people in rural areas we visited still have that unique and free American spirit.

Well, we went out for breakfast the next day. Nicole left her very expensive new tablet on a chair next to our table, and as we were leaving, our waitress brought it out and gave it to Nicole. This was just one of the acts of kindness and honesty we experienced on our trip south. The next day we returned to the same restaurant and gave the waitress twenty dollars for her kindness and honesty.

As we drove out of town, we saw large solar farms with hundreds of solar panels that stretched for miles. These solar farms replaced crops, and it makes me question the government's role in advancing a green energy policy. What are the long-term consequences of all these trade and energy policies?

## We toured a working plantation in South Carolina.

Our next stop was the old southern town of Charleston, SC. We camped a few miles north of downtown and took a water taxi into the downtown area. It was quite a tourist town, the people were very gracious, and the food was great. The next day we decided to tour a working plantation just a mile away from our campground.

It was a reality check to see how slaves lived back before the Civil War. Just a few hundred yards from the main mansion were five very small brick buildings where slaves lived to work the main house. I would not call these houses simple one-room brick huts.

The tour guide explained the living conditions for families that lived in these brick huts were far better than the slaves that worked in the fields and in the brickyard. Many slaves picked cotton all day under the hot sun. Other men worked long hours in the brickyard.

The bricks were used to build lavish houses and mansions for the wealthy White landowners. These images gave me the reality of what happened back then and how slaves did build the south brick by brick. We were told some of the bricks were used to build the White House.

I came away believing all high school-age kids should tour a plantation and experience what Black people had to endure back before the Civil War and even after the war.

I remember the series Roots was a story of a Black man captured in Africa and sent to America. I don't know why the series is not shown to school-age kids across the country. It would probably put a dark shadow over how the White man treated the African Americans back in the 1700s.

## Main Street America (MSA) celebrates the 4th of July in SC

Our next stop was a very large and busy campground in Myrtle Beach, South Carolina. We arrived in the 95 plus degree heat and checked in at the office. We towed our little camper through the many rows of large and small RVs. The traffic was bumper to bumper at times, kids on bikes, kids on electric scooters, young kids hanging off the back of golf carts, or club cars, as they call them at the campground. We saw hundreds of club cars going to the pools and beaches around the campground.

This was by far the most crowded campground we ever stayed at, but everyone was courteous and friendly. Bart, the man next to our site, filled us in on the campground rules and regulations. This campground had over 1000 campsites. On an average weekend, the campground probably had over 5000 men, women, and children plus another 500 dogs and another 500 club cars.

Bart said they don't tolerate drinking to excess or drugs, and if security stops you with a drink, they take away your club car privileges. We did not see excessive drinking or drugs and not even the scent of pot in the air. The next day we went to the beach. The beaches were so crowded our umbrella would almost touch the umbrella next to us, but everyone was respectful and friendly.

The atmosphere was carefree, and young and old people acknowledged you as you traveled through the congested traffic—the campground filled to capacity as 4th July week approached. We got one of the last sites for the 4th of July weekend.

A few nights later, we walked down to the strip along the ocean. Families with kids, parents, grandparents, and even the dogs into their club cars and cruised along the strip along the ocean.

Sometimes little kids and adults would "high-five" each other as they drove by. It truly was a happening I will never forget.

Well, the 4th of July celebration at Myrtle Beach was proof of freedom, and the American spirit was still alive and well. I named these patriotic Americans Main Street Americans or (MSAs). On 4th July, we walked down onto the beach, and after dark, families lined along the beach for miles. You could see fireworks displays all along the coast.

## It was "Only an Ocean Away"

It was very hot in our little camper during the night, and I awoke before dawn. I walked over the dunes to the beach. The sun was coming up out of the ocean, it was a spiritual event I experienced several times on Nantucket, but I was too hung over after drinking all night to appreciate the spiritual nature of a sunrise. The song "Only an Ocean Away" played on my smartphone. For some reason, the words made me think about how far back in time I have lived with BD and had such a traumatic event happen to change my life forever. Looking out onto the ocean horizon triggered those tragic events in my mind all over again.

Regrets and traumatic recollections of the past came back again. Perhaps if I had avoided amnesia and had help with my BP disorder, I could have saved my relationship with Maria and not gone into a state of amnesia. Perhaps in a way, I could have easily traveled over an ocean to piece together our relationship because now I feel at it was "Only an Ocean Away" but getting back together back then was light-years away. Many times, I had a sliver of hope we could contact each other and talk about our lives, but now I know it is just an illusion I keep in my mind.

As in the past, I will recover from this latest bad spell and move on with my life, but now I am taking the time to watch the sun slowly go down over the horizon. I am grateful for the BD normal life I am living now.

The next day I had a renewed feeling the American spirit was alive and well in America, but maybe the media never reports this true expression of our freedom. I call this an original American 4$^{th}$ of July. This was the Patriotism and freedom I experienced when I was a kid.

Did I rediscover a secret and silent Main Street America (MSA) spirit that has been hidden for years? Have we been told we should not feel proud to be an American? An American Spirit that has been stifled by the radical media told us our 1776 Constitution is outdated, and we need new laws. We don't need to follow the old 1776 Constitution. Any administration that does not allow people to cherish our freedoms and honor our 1776 Constitution is anti-American. The original 1776 Constitution sets our nation apart from any other political system on the planet.

The people at the backcountry campgrounds had the same American spirit as the people at this upscale modern campground, but after years of living in a bad economy had given them a sense of hopelessness. Years of underemployment had beaten them down, but the kids continued to live a free and Patriotic life despite their hardships.

For our entire trip, we did not watch any cable TV or listen to the talk radio in our car. I began to realize the constant negative talk on both sides was affecting our beliefs regarding our 1776 Constitution. The brainwashing by the radical media was working; everyone was suspicious of everyone else. I lost my 2$^{nd}$ Amendment due to mental illness, but do I still have my 1$^{st}$ amendment rights?

## Dr. Freed died

It was around Christmas when Stu called me and said Dr. Freed died peacefully in a local hospital. Stu said he was the father he never had. I said, "I'm so sorry to hear he died I heard you say he was very sick." Stu said, "Yes, it was expected he was in contact with his wife, and she was doing okay."

He talked about how Dr. Freed took him in and treated him like a son. He provided health care medication at no cost, but most of all, he didn't expect anything in return. Stu got government benefits, medication, and treatment for years. I said, "You've known Dr. Freed a long time. It's hard to believe that it was over 20 years ago." I could tell he was in the morning because Dr. Freed was such a good and faithful friend and strong advocate for mental health care.

Stu said Dr. Freed really did care for the mentally ill he started one of the first mental health clinics in the USA. He came here from Eastern Bloc country after WW II and worked as a doctor in mental healthcare clinics around the country. He found a way to treat the mentally ill in hospitals and had 30 very mentally ill patients in one psychiatric hospital. After treatment with lithium for only 30 days, 15 were released from the hospital well enough to live on their own. He found the breakthrough medicine called lithium and was used in Europe but didn't come to wide use in America until the mid-80s.

Stu always stayed in close contact with Dr. Freed; he even took Stu out to dinner and always picked up the check. Dr. Freed did treat Stu as his son; they were both sailors and sea captains with a very strong bond. Dr. Freed also answered my prayers after we came back from Florida. I was in such a severe and prolonged depression. I thought I would never recover, but I learned lithium was a life-changing and effective med to treat my bipolar illness.

## Lara dies, Stu writes her a letter

About six months after Dr. Freed died, Stu called me and said Lara died at the nursing home in Orlando. Stu said she was strong right up until the last weeks. He said the doctors told Lara she would die years ago, but she continued to get experimental treatment through the hospital's research program. She fought a very hard fight but eventually lost, as we all do. He tried to go out and visit her in Orlando, but her family didn't want him to see her. He said the family was angry the time Stu took her out of the nursing home and brought her back to her oceanfront condo.

I said to Stu, "You were trying to help her fulfill her dying wishes even though she was very ill." He said, "I wrote a letter, put it in an envelope and dropped it into the ocean near where we walked many times in the past," I said, "That it was such a beautiful gesture. I know she will read it and appreciate what you have done for her over the years".

The next day I began to worry about Stu; he had too many losses over the last few years. Stu lost his dog up in New England, Dr. Freed, and now his girlfriend, Lara, to cancer. I'm afraid too many losses can push his bipolar stress level over the top and cause a steep downward spiral into depression or far worse. According to the WAVES Chart, Stu has too many stressful life situations occurring all at once. He needs to monitor his stress level.

## Ryan's part-time job ends

Ryan quit a part-time job with the tech company they were about to go out of business. He tried to keep the clients and start his own business but could not make it work. He found a job through a temp agency, and he seemed to be doing better in the job and liked his co-workers. His spending and behavior are not helping us around the house; he won't kick in money for a room, and he borrows money, but he never pays us back.

We have decided we need to help and support Bonnie and just tolerate Ryan's behavior. I understand many professionals will take a dim view of my attitude toward Ryan, but I believe sometimes people with emotional issues need to distance themselves from other people with emotional issues, which is my attitude now.

Right now, I am beyond helping him directly; I need to get him to help himself. Nicole said Ryan is angry because he thinks I am projecting my BD illness onto him. He may be right. I am not going to accuse Ryan of having a mental illness any longer but encourage him to be more responsible.

## *Our nation is ignoring drug-related crimes*

Reports of gun violence in Philly were aired on the nightly news for weeks. Gang violence and drive-by shootings were minimized by the Main Street Media (MSM). I suspect most of these events were drug-related, but no one seemed to be interested in stopping the drug traffic.

I rented my first-floor apt to a very kind Black woman, Violet, with a teenage daughter. Tragically, her daughter was stabbed in the back on my doorstep and died. Philly, like many East Coast inner cities, are predominately Black and Democratic strongholds. Teenage crime and drug use are hidden from the public.

Kids grow up without any male role model to guide them. In some areas, 70 percent of households do not even have a male role model in the house. Babies born to teenage kids are at risk of being dependent on the welfare state. Young kids without a high school education with a criminal record have little chance of finding a job. Many Black youths are unemployable and join gangs and use drugs to deal with hopelessness and despair just to survive. Inner-city families are destroyed by the welfare state when the government encourages teen pregnancy, and policies do not allow the father to live with their own family.

I am coming to some dire conclusions regarding the path our nation is now on; it is very disturbing to watch.

## Our next camping vacation was to the Grand Canyon of PA

For our long camping trip this summer, we plan to save some money and go to state campgrounds. We found a campground up near the New York state border; the region was promoted as the Grand Canyon of Pennsylvania.

We headed out and had some pretty steep Hills along the way and arrived in the small town of Wellsboro, Pennsylvania. We could see again the small towns were struggling to survive in a bad economy. Lots of buildings with lease signs, and we don't see many luxury cars here. I remember in the early 80s, there were millions of small businesses everywhere in Pennsylvania. I remember going to some auctions, and I saw machine tools being sold for a fraction of the cost. I remember telling Nicole then this is not right; our manufacturing jobs, along with entire factories, are being shipped overseas at an alarming rate.

We found the campground near the entrance to the Pennsylvania Gorge. It was a very peaceful campsite, and the people were friendly and helpful. The campground itself was a bit rustic with no amenities, but that is standard for state campgrounds in Pennsylvania.

We set up our camper and then went out to the Gorge to take in the view of the river. The view was picturesque and was very crowded on a summer day. From the lookout, you could see up and down the river.

We went out for dinner in the small town of Wellsboro and came back to the campground after dark. The entrance to the Gorge is only a few hundred yards from our campsite. We went around the entrance gate and went out onto the overlook of the gorge. It was a beautiful night in the view of the river below, and the stars above were a truly unique experience. These are the type of experiences we live for, the peace and quiet of the natural surroundings, and a sense of freedom living in the Great Outdoors.

Days we would drive out to the nearby towns and find hiking trails and places to stop along the way. Every night if the weather was good after the park closed, we would walk around the park gate go out to the Gorge outlook to view the stars.

## Birds live in harmony with nature

In the morning, I woke up an hour before sunrise as the birds in the forest were just waking up to sing about the beautiful morning. We were literally up in the treetops, in the canopies of the tall trees. As I listened to the sounds and smelled and the peaceful surroundings, I began to understand why I love nature. Take birds; for example, they represent the joy and happiness they bring to the world. They represent freedom as they fly around the forest with no restrictions; they all sound happy just to be alive in the forest. They keep very busy searching for food, bugs and insects, and other small grubs. They help control the insect population of the world and for the human population. The small birds also represent harmony in the world. Although there were dozens of species in our area of the forest, they all got along together. They were all in perfect harmony with each other; oh, once in a while, we would see a dispute over some food, but by in large, they lived in peace and harmony with each other.

Each species had its own habitat to live in a respected each other's area without fighting between the different species. From the time they awoke and started to sing their songs, they made the forests come alive with happy and joyous songs for everyone to hear. The whole forest of birds began to sing together like a symphony; each songbird was singing their own songs as they went about their daily chores.

## *Birds show courage in the face of grave danger*
In the late afternoon, I went for my two-mile walk. The dense forest had very tall trees. As I was walking through a dense forest, I heard a group of small birds acting very strange at the top of a very high tree. They were all different species of small birds and sounded very upset about something way up at the treetops. Due to the dense forest cover, I stood for several minutes watching the excited birds fly around this very large tree top. Then I saw a very large hawk sitting on a branch perched high out on a limb of the tree with a small bird in its talons.

Now I realized what was going on; the small birds were upset with the presence of a dangerous predator in the forest. All the small birds were trying to protect their own from this deadly predator. Many small birds of many different species were diving right at the large hawk only inches from the hawk's head. I thought, what brave and fearless little birds they were. They were all in grave danger. So, it is true; birds can face grave dangers and do come together to protect all the birds in the forest. After a while, the hawk left with the dead bird in its claws.

I thought, why don't humans show courage when faced with danger? We should come together to fight predators that might harm the human race. Unlike the bird's we humans seem to fight among ourselves and seldom live-in harmony. The birds have learned these life lessons since the beginning of time, and I'm afraid humans may never learn the simple lessons of living in harmony and protecting each other from harm.

At the end of the day, when nighttime swept through the forest, the birds started to return to their nests in the trees high above the forest floor. They all came back to roost in the tall trees, and all started to talk to each other, probably telling their experience of the day in the forest. After a few minutes, the forest was quiet; all the birds went to sleep.

Then the night sights and sounds of the forest started to wake up; the fireflies and crickets were loud but were very soothing and natural sounds of nature.

At our campsite, you could see the stars above in the moonlight and see the Milky Way spread all across the night sky like I have seen many nights at beach parties on Nantucket. Back then, I could not experience the very spiritual nature of my surroundings like I do today. The night sounds I have heard in the past, a night owl far in the distance, and sometimes we would hear a whippoorwill flying from one place or another throughout the dark forest.

Stargazing was a very common local event in northern Pennsylvania. The forests in Central Pennsylvania are ideal for stargazing. People told us stargazers gathered at the top of some mountains on clear nights far away from the city lights and spent time just watching the stars and galaxies through high-powered telescopes.

I wish we had more time to spend going to one of these stargazing events; it must be an experience of a lifetime. All in all, we had a great time in very rural Pennsylvania.

Sometimes it's hard to pack up and drive home. We couldn't go too fast with our little camper, and it took us over seven hours to get back to our house. Our trip was another spiritual retreat by getting away from the day-to-day problems at home.

As I parked the camper out back of the garage, my mood was somber as I realized nothing had changed at home. I guess we're looking forward to Nicole's retirement, so we can just pick up and go camping at any time we please. I was almost ready for a long winter. At this point, my mental and physical health problems, family issues, and the politics of our nation were very real. From late spring through late fall, I go into a state of denial and forget all these problems even exist.

We looked forward in the spring to another camping season in the Great Outdoors.

### We need to find a way to get Ryan help

After several years working for a temp agency, Ryan found a part-time job and wanted to spend more time on his music business. He found a part-time job working 20 hours a week and moved in with us. He's now working for a much smaller company and wants to stay at our house until the music business takes off.

I don't want him to stay at our house, but Nicole overrules my decision. We do love to have Bonnie visit us, and if Ryan gets an apartment, we might not see her as often. When I calmed down, I realized Ryan could move into Philly to find a low-cost apartment, and that could lead to a real disaster for us all.

I got so frustrated I just did the tasks around the house without his help. I really do want to get rid of this old house and move on to something more manageable, but Nicole now wants to wait until she retires several years from now. After several months of watching Ryan's irresponsible and moody behavior, I decided to give an ultimatum; either he gets the help, or I will move down to the spare room in the basement.

After another long episode of aggravation, I forgot about dealing with Ryan and did not move down to the basement. I needed to acknowledge I have my own issues, and Ryan's behavior triggers some character flaws of my own.

## Rosie is scheduled for a kidney transplant

Rosie told the group she was scheduled to have a kidney transplant in a few weeks. Her daughter will be the donor, and she expects to be back leading the group a few weeks after her operation. Rosie is quite a strong and determined woman, and I hope the operation goes well.

I met her daughter at a meeting one time; she's a beautiful, caring woman. She lives in New York, so that might be difficult and arranging her operation here in Philadelphia. Many times, Rosie said she would not go on kidney dialysis. She knew several people under kidney dialysis, and their quality of life was intolerable.

## Erica lost her job after 12 years

The following week I went back to the BDS group to get some help with Ryan and to vent my frustration again over what was going on at home.

A woman came to our small group, and we could tell she was in a lot of emotional pain. We see a lot of emotional pain from people in the BDS group. Her name was Erica, and she had worked for a local hospital. Her boss found out she had BD and found a way to fire her without benefits. She left her psychiatrist's orders on her desk, and somebody found out she was taking meds for a mood disorder. They started to log every detail of her work. Of course, this was a very stressful work environment, and eventually, she lost her job after 12 years as an employee at a local hospital. Erica's story is told in Chapter 5.

Basically, Erica lost her job because she has a mental disorder. Erica mentioned she did not feel worthy of having a loving husband. Her comment hit a nerve deep within my psyche because I realized sometimes, I feel I am not worthy of being loved.

You know, if I had the time for another project, I would like to set up a legal defense fund to fight against corporations that mistreat people like Erica.

### Rosie's kidney transplant was successful
Rosie's kidney transplant was successful, but after the operation, she needed to take several anti-rejection drugs and other medications. I went over to see her at her house and helped her administer doses of insulin. Apparently, it's very common for people with a kidney transplant to get diabetes automatically.

I arrived at Rosie's house, and she was sitting on the living room rug. She had 20 plus bottles of medicines all around her. I must say she's a tough and courageous woman because she never felt sorry for herself; she just did what she needed to do all these years. She has been such an inspiration, too, because she has helped all mentally ill people and their families for decades.

I showed her how to inject the insulin, and she seemed in good spirits. Her daughter came out from the operation without any complications, but they recommended she not engage in risky behavior that might damage her only kidney.

### We attended the Music Fest
We attended the Music Fest again this year, and it was very hot, but we love to sit under the trees and listen to music groups around the town. It's a great way to spend time outdoors because most of the concerts are free; you just have to walk up and find yourself a chair and enjoy the music. The Music Fest lasts ten days is a great way to get out and enjoy summer and the music at the same time.

We saw our favorite group again this year; their music is a combination of bluegrass, Country & Western. They have five great musicians. We looked up their itinerary on the internet and found out they were going to be playing in a town up north, only 20 minutes from our hometown.

## We went to Nicole's family reunion in Western Massachusetts

Nicole's family decided to have the next reunion at a resort lodge and convention center and Western Massachusetts. We decided we would not take our camper up to New England and planned a kayak trip from upstate New York down the Delaware River after the reunion.

We did the tourist stuff and took a tour of the famous artist Norman Rockwell's home in Western Massachusetts. He really was an American artist; many of his paintings are a part of Americana.

Well, after the reunion, Nicole's family when into New York City; we headed west to stay at a small Lodge in a very small town in upstate New York. They told us the lodge was right along the Delaware River.

After driving for several hours, we finally arrived at the rustic lodge. Well, it was an old rundown motel, but the rates were very, very cheap. The owners were great, and the food was well, below average. Maybe booking this dump advertised as a lodge was a little too frugal at any cost?

We settled into our new vacation lifestyle sitting in an old rocking chair outside our motel room. This is why we camp; we love the freedom of sitting outdoors in the fresh air without cars whizzing by our campground site all day and night. Well, it was certainly quite a change for us, but I think we appreciate our camping experience more than ever. These out-of-the-way places are the types of towns we visit when we go camping. In the little towns off the main interstates, we see many people struggling to make a living. I did not see a Mercedes-Benz dealership in town.

## Our kayak trip down the Delaware River

The next day we prepared for our trip down the Delaware River. We got up early and drove up the river with other people to start our trip down the river. Nicole and Bonnie stayed at the rustic rundown lodge/bar/motel and waited for us to come back down to the drop-off point.

Ryan, Matt, and I each rented our own kayak and stowed our backpacks with water bottles, snacks, and sunblock into our kayaks. Our trip would be approximately 13 miles or about seven hours on the water, depending on the water flow rate.

Our trip was fantastic; we even saw Bald Eagles along the river banks and many fish swimming upstream against the current. A few miles down the river, we encountered very large boulders that we had to navigate around and over. Running the rapids made the trip exciting, and at several spots, I thought we would capsize our kayaks, but with a little luck, we got to the halfway point on our seven-hour voyage.

Ryan and Matt were tired and severely sunburned at the halfway point in suggested we should end our trip. It was very hot, and I was concerned about heat exhaustion at that point, but I told the boys these trips build character. Besides, how would it look if we came back to the outfitters' shop in a pickup truck after only four hours? What would we tell Nicole and Bonnie if we quit halfway down the river?

After resting for an hour, we continued on and reached the drop-off point after 9 hours on the river. We finally arrived back at the lodge exhausted and sunburned after an exciting and memorable kayaking trip down the Delaware River.

## On every trip, we meet people struggling to make a living

Every trip now, we see ordinary working people struggling to make good living wages. Many people have older cars, and their houses are not kept up as you would see 20 years ago. The only sign of a good economy is along interstates, where we see franchised hotel chains, fast food restaurants, and gas stations.

I don't know how our working middle class is going to survive in this political climate. There is no talk of helping these working-class people out with better jobs. We hear there are a lot of drug problems in the small towns now; I predict drugs will eventually destroy our entire country. The small manufacturing companies are gone, with no chance of them coming back anytime soon.

It is almost Christmas, and my annual case of SAD and my sad recollections from the distant past are causing yet another bad spell. I have not had a very bad bipolar depressive episode for several years. I believe I am overwhelmed with grief and anxieties over witnessing our nation descend into chaos. Now I am afraid our nation will descend further into tyranny and then total anarchy.

## I need to be aware of my unworthy syndrome

Now I am identifying many of these feelings of sorrow and sadness to my unworthy syndrome. These feelings of unworthiness are the reason for many bad spells. I need to remember my unworthy syndrome began long before my breakup with Maria and has followed me around my entire life. Back then, I couldn't do anything about my unworthiness issues. Now I can put these unworthy feelings in the past and remind myself I deserve to be successful and live a better BD normal life.

Now I realize now these are just very old, over 70-year-old negative feelings. I need to move on and find ways to overcome my feelings of inferiority and unworthiness. I believe publishing the workbook could help me overcome some feelings of unworthiness.

## Our camping vacation to Central Pennsylvania

Well, we made it through another winter without a blinding snowstorm. It is early spring; Nicole and I are looking to get away for a few weeks in the summer. This year we are going to a campground somewhere in Central Pennsylvania.

We have planned all winter going to go out to Central Pennsylvania. I met a couple at a garage sale, and they had a lot of camping gear to sell. We struck up a conversation, and they told me about a campground in the Central of Pennsylvania that was a well-kept secret for only "campers." What they meant was ordinary people with limited funds and not RV owners with luxury class coaches. They said the campers at this campground have modest means and are old-fashioned campers. I jokingly replied, "We are not old, just older campers."

These people were real campers that didn't rely on electricity and fancy air-conditioners and large flat-screen TVs. in their 35-foot motor homes; I told him we are not really rugged campers; we haven't camped with a tent for years. I said my wife needs to have electricity to run her electronic devices. You notice I blamed Nicole for not camping like rugged tent campers. We don't want to go back to sleeping on the hard-cold ground. When I got back from the garage sale, I looked up the campground; we decided to book a campsite for two weeks.

A few weeks later, we packed up for our camping trip. The drive out the Pennsylvania Turnpike was quite difficult with our camper, and our old small SUV struggled to get up some of the mountains. We stopped several places along the way, but it was still a 6 to 8-hour drive to the campground. I have not traveled on the Pennsylvania Turnpike since I came back from LA in the 70s. Pennsylvania is a beautiful state; it has real forests and rolling hills all across the state. I remember returning from California years ago and seeing all the natural woods and dense forests for over 200 miles.

We arrived at the campground in the late afternoon and found our campsite on the top of a mountain. The view of the lake down below was spectacular. We were at eye level with the treetops in the forest. The weather was beautiful, and the people were very friendly and helpful. We did not see any very large RVs because the campsites were very small, it would be very difficult to park a large RV. Our little camper had no problem parking; we had plenty of space for our lounge chairs and the fire ring.

## Why can't we live like our feathered friends?

I awoke an hour before sunrise as the birds in the forest were waking up and singing about the beautiful morning. Birds are marvelous creatures. We literally had a bird's eye view up in the treetops in the canopies of the tall trees. As I listened to the sounds and the smells of the forest, I began to understand why I love nature. Take birds; for example, they represent the joy and happiness they bring to the world. They represent freedom as they fly around the forest with no restrictions; they all sound happy just to be alive in the forest.

They are very busy searching for food, bugs, insects, and grubs. They help control the insect population of the world and help the human population. The small birds also represent harmony in the world. Although there were dozens of species in our area of the forest, somehow, they all got along together. They sang in perfect harmony with each other; oh, once in a while, you might see the dispute over some bits of food, but by in large, they all live in peace and harmony with each other.

Each species had its own habitat to live in a respected each other's area without fighting between the different species. From the time they awoke, they made the forests come alive with happy and joyous songs for everyone to hear. The whole forest of birds began to sing together like a symphony, each playing their song as they went about their daily chores.

Why can't we humans live-in harmony like our feathered friends? Unlike the birds, we humans seem to fight among ourselves and seldom live-in harmony. Birds have learned these life lessons since the beginning of time. I'm afraid we may never learn the simple lessons of living in harmony with each other until we humans obey the fundamental rules of nature.

At the end of the day, when nighttime swept through the forest, all the birds started to return to their nests in the trees high above the forest floor. They all came back to roost in the tall trees, and all started to chat with each other, probably telling their experience of the day in the forest. After a few minutes, the forest was quiet; all the birds went to sleep, then the night sounds of the forest started to wake up. The night sounds of the forest began to come alive with the sounds and sights of fireflies, crickets, and cicadas.

You could see the stars above in the moonlight and see the Milky Way spread all across the night sky like I have seen many nights at beach parties on Nantucket. Back then, I could not appreciate the very natural beauty of my surroundings as I do today. The night sounds I have heard in the past of a night owl far in the distance, and sometimes we would hear a whippoorwill flying from one place or another throughout the forest. We arrived back home after another wonderful spiritual retreat into nature.

A few days later, I was wondering why the forests out in the middle of PA had such large tall trees. I found an article online that explained why forests had such tall trees. Apparently, the western side of a ridge in central PA gets a lot more rain as the rainstorms come across PA from the west. I then browsed further and found a website with the title "Intelligent trees." How could anyone not be interested in learning about "Intelligent trees"?

## Even the intelligent trees in the forest help each other survive

I watched the video "Intelligent trees" about how the forests protect the trees in a dense forest. The woman on the video was a forestry manager. She noticed if they planted the same species of trees, they did not prosper the same as a variety of trees in the forest. I was amazed by the findings of a relatively small team of foresters. I need to give credit to their groundbreaking; get the pun research [(Suzanne, n.d.)

The team discovered some fascinating research into how trees protect each other from harm and nurture each other. She told how the roots of all the trees intertwined with each other to help the weak and young seedlings. The research team had a diagram of how each separate tree root helped each other survive. The diagram appeared to be like a schematic of a human brain. Does that imply trees in the forest have more intelligence than most humans on the planet? I rest my case; anyway, humans need to follow nature, be kind to each other and follow the fundamental laws of nature.

## Music gave me inspiration

I continued to play music in the evening to relax and forget my problems. I put on a CD by Andrea Bocelli, and his music reminded me of the obstacles he overcame to sing arias and beautiful romantic songs in Italian. You know I don't understand one word of most songs because they're all in Italian, but some songs are so beautifully done they bring tears to my eyes. Here is a man that overcame his eyesight disability to perform on the world stage. His inspiration gave me a renewed commitment to complete the workbook.

### The Famous last words of a fool

A few days later, I began to listen to music again, to the old CDs I had collected over the years, well, decades. I found some C&W CDs were about lost love; the next song was 'Famous last words of a fool." by George Strait.

I began to get tears in my eyes even before the song began to play. Maybe I heard the song years ago in some honky-tonk bar and knew it would be extremely sad and painful. The song is about a guy telling his sweetheart he doesn't care if they break up; he would be fine without her, and then he lies and tells her he doesn't love her. She cries as she leaves.

I have not felt those emotions built up inside me for several years. It was like all the air came out of my broken heart all over again.

Like my breakup with my first love, I was a fool to tell her I didn't love her. This beautiful but sad song is the story of my breakup with Maria in a four-minute song; that sad song and others remind me what a fool I was to tell Maria I didn't love her. I came to a conclusion my sad recollections from the breakup may never end, but the episodes are less frequent and less emotional. I call these sad episodes bad spells because they trigger a series of bad emotions for several days, even weeks at a time.

### I lost my youth to amnesia

I also have a feeling I lost my youth to my amnesia and need to address that issue also. I need to understand why I came out of amnesia and why I was dealing with all these issues after my recovery from amnesia over five years ago. Actually, I am surprised I am recovering from the worst traumatic period of my life without major mental health issues, namely suicide.

I have very few negative effects from over four decades in a state of amnesia. I still feel living with the lifelong mental illness of BD has been and will be the most significant issue of all other challenges I have faced in my life.

I am also aware of my unworthy syndrome and need to keep reminding myself of the abuse that occurred in my distant past. I need to understand my negative self-image started as a child; I had no way to protect myself from abuse back then.

## Matt's college party house

Matt attended community college for two years and then transferred his credits to a local four-year college. I haven't talked a lot about Matt's life, but I understand he had a wild party house in college. I heard they made enough money to pay for the rent from cover charges at the door. I also heard some of the members of the house say Matt got aggressive when guys would show up and try to crash their house parties.

I was concerned that someone in the house might overdose on alcohol or drugs, but I guess kids need to go through that party life phase of college party life. As an afterthought, I should drive out to Matt's college and give all the students my profound words of wisdom. Then I remembered no one listened or took my advice seriously for years.

At the end of the school year, the landlord assessed the damage to the apartment and sent Matt and each student on the lease a bill for thousands of dollars to repair the damage to the party house.

We got a notice from the real estate management firm we were going to have to pay for the damages, or our credit rating would be damaged. I was so upset I contacted the realtor told him I would file a counter lawsuit if they damaged our credit rating. Matt was not on the lease, and we had no financial responsibility. This is why we would not sign a lease agreement; we would not accept any responsibility for damage or unpaid utility bills.

After a very combative year in college, Matt said that he was through with the party house scene and wanted to get an apartment with just one roommate the following semester. I was so glad he was over the college campus party lifestyle. I never told Nicole about the wild drunken party house. Matt rented an apartment with a friend in his Junior and Senior years in college and avoided the party scene.

## Matt graduated at the end of the fall semester

Matt was still dating Joyce; we thought he was in a very serious relationship. I don't pry into his personal life. Matt graduated from college at the end of the fall semester. He needed to complete some courses to graduate. Most kids who graduate with Chemical and engineering degrees need another semester or two to graduate.

It was a very cold day, but we got to the commencement ceremonies, and Joyce came with us. The commencement speaker was an alumnus of the college. He started out his speech by telling us he works in the theater industry, has a big advertising budget, and must get along with everyone.

I expected a Hollywood speech about how to make millions in a week, but his message sounded more like he had Willy's wisdom, and his message was simple and positive. He spoke about being kind to everyone, even though you may have very different values and beliefs.

He worked in the entertainment industry, and he needed to get along with many people and all different races and religions. His main theme was to find your passion in life and follow it with dignity and honesty. Treat all people with respect and put faith in God; he will guide you. He went on to say everything will fall into place, and you will be successful in life.

On the way home, I told Matt. Joyce and Ryan his message was so true it should be given to every college graduate in the country. I said, "You kids only need to follow his message to live a successful and happy life."

I was very proud of Matt; he set his sights on a degree in Chemistry and made it happen. I remember after he graduated from high school, he told me he wanted to be a Chemist. My sarcastic reply back then was like I said: "How are you ever going to earn a degree in Chemistry?"

## Matt got an important job interview

Matt has been looking for a job in his field for over six months now is getting very frustrated with finding a job in the chemical industry. Recently he went to a deli in town and saw a graduate from his college working behind the counter.

Finally, he got in contact with one is his housemates in college and had a lead to find work as a chemist. Matt and Joyce had a falling out a few months ago, and I think his frustration over finding a good job is causing a lot of stress in his personal life.

The Main Street Media (MSM) media tells everyone we must adjust to having a mediocre economy. Matt said most employers want two solid years of experience. I told him his seven-year steady work at restaurants should qualify for actual life experience.

Matt finally got a job interview with a high-profile local company, but he learned due to the tight job market, a lot of the applicants had more experience than he did.

I told him the only advice I could give him was to be truthful and not overstate his experience. I know several other people for the job will have several more years of experience in your field. I told him, "You need to convince them you have life experiences" Then I said, "Be sure you tell them you worked your way through college."

## Matt got the job

Matt came back from the job interview and told me the job interview went well. He brought up the fact he worked his way through college. He said the head of the department slapped him on the back as he walked out of the interview.

I said, "That's almost a sure sign you got the job." A few weeks later, Matt got a job offer in his field without any experience. He was hired over more qualified applicants for the job. Nicole and I were happy he landed a good job after so many years of hard work at college. After working at several restaurants' nights and weekends all through high school and college, he deserved a good-paying job. I know any company will not regret hiring Matt.

## I am proud of both Matt and Ryan

After Matt graduated from college, I was proud of both Matt and Ryan. Matt is starting his career in his chosen field. Ryan is still struggling to be more independent, but he is spending quality time with Bonnie.

I thought back to when Ryan was in high school. He was in the high school marching band. We would travel to band competitions all around southeastern PA. Some regional schools had marching bands with hundreds of students.

Matt was on the high school football team. We went to many of his football games. I remember all the proms Matt and his friends attended over the years. Time does not stand still; it is hard to believe

Matt is about 25 years old; it seems he just graduated from high school a few years ago.

## November 2015 ISIS Attacks France

I woke up one morning to the news of a terrorist attack in Paris, France, that killed 120 people, and the French President issued a national State of Emergency.

The State of Emergency in France closed down air traffic in and out of the country. The entire country was in lockdown, including all borders. I sat in the living room almost in shock and disbelief; such a minor attack, although very tragic, could shut down an entire country.

As the hours passed by and the news cycle played out, the steps taken in the name of national security were extraordinary.

I was troubled a local terrorist attack only in Paris could justify a national State of Emergency for the entire country of France. Why hasn't anyone raised red flags about the possibility of a serious event, crisis, or incident happening here in this country? Are the rules under an SSE incident in our country secret and hidden from the public?

For several weeks I had vivid dreams of people fighting people in the streets of cities across the nation. I envision cities erupting in riots and lawlessness. One night I had a vision people were attacked by terrorists but had no firearms to protect their families. I envisioned many psychiatrist offices were full of people with stress disorders, including myself.

After a few nights, the nightmares ended. I did not need to visit my psychiatrist. The national state of emergency ended in France, and Military Law ended.

## Trump declares we need to drain the swamp

After several debates, Donald Trump won the GOP nomination over 12 GOP candidates. After Trump became the GOP nominee, the liberal media exploded with vile hate messages condemning everything Trump said or did.

Trump said the swamp of political corruption needs to be drained in Washington and exposed for what they stand for, corruption and pay-to-play politics.

## The radicals need to be called out as the RADs

We are fighting for the soul of our nation. The radical Main Street Media or MSM is acting as the propaganda arm of the far-left radical Socialist Democratic Party. I think we need to call all the radicals for what they are, the Radical American Democrats or the RADs. The voices of reason are being drowned out by corrupt RAD news media. It is impossible for Trump to get his message out over the nonstop RADs blitz condemning every policy of Trump. The RAD media are only reporting the positive messages of the Hillary campaign. We have a nation divided into two separate and very different ideologies, the RADs and Main Street Americans or MSAs.

At one speech, Hillary proclaimed Trump supporters are, and I paraphrase, "Homophobes, xenophobes, and lastly, all "deplorables". Wouldn't that rhetoric be called hate speech if a Republican candidate called Hillary supporters deplorables? The great divide between the RADs and MSAs is growing further apart every day. It was a foregone conclusion Hillary would easily get the Democratic nomination for president in 2016

## We took all the kids camping

While Jane was in the hospital waiting for the delivery of her baby, we took the boys and Bonnie camping, and it was very hot. It was probably 95° at the campground; we spent most of the time at the pool waiting for Jane to deliver the baby. A few days later, a healthy boy was born, and Bonnie now had three brothers. Bonnie was hoping for a baby sister.

## Ryan is still not getting help with his issues

Ryan was still not getting help with his mental issues, and it began to wear on me, and I'm sure on Nicole as well. He had a good job and was living on his own, but he wasn't thriving and was talking about quitting his good stable job. I guess I was thinking without proper treatment; he was going to have the same life I had back with the job in the city. I was untreated at that time and wanted to leave a good stable job, but it really didn't work out as I planned.

Ryan has this mail delivered to our house, and we see the bills piling up; we see he is not responsible for paying his bills. I mentioned Rosie's BDS group several times, but he has no interest in attending or learning more about BD.

Ryan argues that I'm trying to diagnose him with the same illness that I have, so I have a hard time confronting him with my reality, he may not have BD, but he needs the help of some kind. Then again, I may be projecting my BD mental illness and other issues onto Ryan.

I may also be projecting my frustration over completing the workbook onto Ryan. Well, too much psychodrama, projections, predictions, and blaming and shaming Ryan.

I'm getting very frustrated that I've had problems of my own getting the workbook published in dealing with my own mental health and physical illness. Nicole was still working nights and had little time to devote to helping Ryan with his issues. I guess I'm just glad that I don't see a lot of drug or alcohol abuse in our family. Ryan continues to pay his child support, and we are grateful he is helping Bonnie and her brothers.

## I need to fulfill my commitment to finish the workbook

I am getting too much stress worrying about everything family, Jane's family, my and Stu's problems, and the politics of our nation. I am looking forward to the summer when I go into hibernation while camping. All my issues are piling up at the same time, and that is what put me into a state of amnesia decades ago.

I'm trying to honor my pledge to myself and now indirectly to Iva to publish the workbook. I received an email about how I could put up an internet site for under $100. I looked into it a little further and found out I could learn an Internet web application and do it myself. Here I am, almost 75. Can I learn another software program geared to many younger tech-savvy people? Then Willy's words of wisdom came back and said: "Fulfilling your purpose in life may not be easy, but it will give you peace of mind."

Ever since I found out Iva died, I realized I had to fulfill my commitment to finish the workbook. I am certain she suffered through unimaginable abuse and in war-torn post-World War II. I'm sure she was seeing the same things I am watching going on in this country right now. The RADs are now in propaganda mode and have no thoughts of honestly reporting the news.

## Willy's message and simple words of wisdom

I thought if Willy could preach his message for 20 years under the bridge to misfits, alcoholics, and the homeless, I could certainly ask my higher power to help me pursue my goals in my life. Willy was a preacher in the true sense of the word. He had his flock of homeless people, but as I understand it, he listened more than he preached to his flock. He certainly did have a profound effect on both Stu and me over the years. We often talk about his words of wisdom when we face challenging situations. Sometimes we end our conversation with "What would Willy do"? I guess it always comes down to his profound yet simple words of wisdom "Find your purpose in life through prayer to your higher power, and he will tell you what to do." I have said many times, and it's so simple it must be true.

Stu mentioned Willy once said something like, "We have everything we need on planet Earth to cure all physical and mental illnesses." I think he is right. We are not studying plants and other organisms in the ocean to cure diseases, but there is no big money to be made using natural plants and herbs from Mother Nature to cure illnesses.

A few days later, I realized again I knew this task would not be pleasant, but I am still on the right path.

## Ryan has another bad spell after an injury

Jane found a new boyfriend, and she thinks he may be the one. Don't get me wrong, I am happy for her if she can merge the two families together, but it may take a miracle.

I am not going to project my mental issues onto Ryan any longer. Stu and I had to find a way to treat our illnesses; Ryan must do the same. I told Jane the other day I was totally stressed out because he hasn't changed his behavior patterns for over 15 years now. She does not want to talk about Ryan, period.

Ryan has become more supportive of his teenage daughter. Now he is in his mid-thirties and has no plan to live on his own, He found a job as a waiter in an upscale restaurant, but I noticed their business was declining every week. He could not live on his own from wages and tips from the restaurant.

He was doing some work on the ceiling at the restaurant, fell down, and severely injured his knee. He has been on disability for several weeks, and the stress has caused another bad spell. I am afraid he might use opioid drugs in order to minimize the pain. After six weeks on disability, he has spent most days in his bedroom.

I went into several severe depressions during that time that eventually sent me to seek psychiatric help for the first time in my life. I went to several MDs back in the 70, s but no one diagnosed my BD illness. I am still upset because I have a very good psychiatrist, and Ryan could be stable in just a few weeks. I sometimes try to diagnose Ryan's problems as my own. I need to stop projecting my BD mental illness onto him.

## Is the drug epidemic going to destroy our nation?
Both Hillary and Trump had a long list of promises to the American people, but no one is talking about the drug epidemic in our country.

I learned from studying Germany during World War II; drugs were a major factor in causing atrocities against innocent civilians. Drugs could be a contributing factor to possible unrest and violence in our streets this summer. No one is talking about the drug epidemic in our country that could be a major factor that will lead to our demise and destruction.

## Trump won, and I had a dream with some disturbing visions
On election eve, the Main Street Media MSM was buzzing with projections and predictions. The election was so close not one cable network could project a winner.

I fell asleep on the couch with the TV on before a winner was announced. In my dream, it was a beautiful cool Sunday morning, and after I returned from my walk, I turned on the TV. All the cable news channels, even the shopping channels, were playing the same videos over and over. The videos had no audio, just images of attacks in 120 US cities simultaneously. The videos are the only news reported to the public every hour, day after day, 24 hrs. a day.

The entire nation is traumatized, and many people are sent to the ER by the constant images of terrorists beheading Christians as they left church services. The reports on all the cable networks had large banners across the bottom of the screen warning of many more attacks planned and to stay in your homes.

At 8 AM, I awoke in a cold sweat, and as I looked up at the TV and in big, bold letters across the screen read "Trump Wins."

After I came out of my nightmare-like state, I reasoned my disturbing dream was just a flashback to the terrorist attack in France in 2015 and hoped it was not a dream that was going to come true. The entire nation had to come to grips; Donald Trump was now the President-Elect of the United States.

## Democrats threaten to resist all of Trumps plans

Trump was sworn into office in January. After one hundred days since Trump came into office, the RAD media will not report any progress he has made. The Democrat voters are threatening to resist all of the POTUS plans, but I'm afraid it's going to get worse. The RAD politicians are now reporting Trump conspired with the Russians during the 2016 election as fact. Trump sacked the FBI director, and the press is going bananas with reports President Trump has colluded with the Russians. The RAD media sources claim they have reliable sources deep within the government.

The reason why Trump won is he has recharged that American spirit we lost over the past eight years. I remember the small towns we visited on our camping trips over the past years. People were struggling to make enough money to live on. Main Street Americans (MSAs) woke up, and the American Spirit is why Trump won.

I keep getting bits and pieces of a world we are about to enter in the future. Am I having Nostradamus-type visions of the future or just bad intermittent psychotic episodes? The first vivid dream I had was election night, but then many nights, I had more disturbing images of the future. After my nightmares, I awoke, and I was relieved it was just nightmares and not actual events in the future.

### A brilliant question goes unanswered
A guest on a conservative talk show mentioned he could not understand why the Obama Department of Justice (DOJ) did not inform the Trump campaign they may have foreign agents working for Russia attempting to infiltrate his campaign.

Wow! What a simple and, at the same time, a brilliant question. Light bulbs went off in my head; what was the reason the Obama DOJ did not warn the Trump campaign of any Russian involvement? But the brilliant question was never asked or answered by any DOJ official, so it went unanswered.

Don't get me wrong, I am not fond of President Trump's policies on the environment and other matters, but some people were whispering the word impeachment while the word coup was also heard. Some reporters claimed Trump was set up, and there was a silent coup going on in our country. At this point, all the RAD media is claiming the POTUS was in collusion with the Russians, but no one had any hard evidence.

Then I learned more about the Special Council's role in the investigation. They work in secret to find information on Trump, but

Trump doesn't have the right to defend himself against charges the Special Council finds during the investigation.

I guess the investigation is a secret trial without a jury or even a defense lawyer present, only the prosecution with no jurors and no defense. I am no lawyer, but isn't this a bit un-American? Trump could not defend himself before the election because he did not know he was under investigation or even know the allegations against him.

Then I learned the Special Council's rules to investigate Trump should only be used to investigate foreign spies and terrorists and not American citizens. I am not siding with Trump on every issue, but I think he is harassed at every step he takes. I have lived through decades of being harassed and blamed for many things over the years. I left New England after college to avoid any more mistreatment by my family. Sometimes I feel Trump is mistreated by the press, but the attacks are becoming wider and more severe. I don't blame him for lashing out to protect himself and his followers.

## I'm still working on getting the workbook published

I'm still working on getting the workbook published, but the learning curve is steeper than I thought. I haven't done real computer technical work for decades, but I haven't given up yet. I don't have the time or the money to have it professionally edited and proofread, so I decided to publish the workbook in a raw, unedited format.

I am afraid I will give up the workbook project like I have done dozens of times in the past. Before I was properly treated, I was working on three businesses, all at the same time, all of them failed.

I'm going through hundreds of pages from my journal trying to write our story in chronicle logical order, but I'm afraid it's like my thoughts are sometimes scattered and unreadable. Sometimes I forget when events have happened and call Stu, he usually remembers dates and times much better than I do. I never tell Stu the fears I have for our country or the conflict unfolding or let him read or edit the workbook.

Christmas was quiet, just our family, including our now very old cat Liberty.

## The Eagles use the "Philly Special" to win Super Bowl LII

The trash talk from the Eagles fans hit a fever pitch when the Philly fans realized we were actually going up against the New England Patriots in Super Bowl LII.

I called Stu, and he didn't seem to care about the matchup. He acted as his team had already won the Super Bowl. His phone calls were irritating and condescending because he had a superior "Sorry, but we always win" attitude.

The Eagles were obviously the underdogs, and some Eagles fans had special underdog head masks for the occasion. We had lost our starting quarterback (QB) earlier in the season and had other players sidelined. Nick Foles, the Eagles backup QB, was leading the team, and the team was a long shot at winning the Super Bowl 52, but then the Philly fans started to become confident we could win.

On February 4, 2018, the Super Bowl, the much-anticipated game of the century, began to unfold. Well, that might be a bit of an exaggeration, but the tension was high for the Eagles; the New England Patriots were expected to win big time. It was the most exciting game I have ever watched—a Patriots team led by a superstar QB Tom Brady against an unknown underdog QB. The Eagles had a backup QB with an unknown group of players. Our Eagles coach was confident his backup QB in his first Super Bowl could rise to the challenge.

As the historic game unfolded, my cautious optimism turned to confidence the Eagles could beat NE. In a 4$^{th}$ and goal play, the Eagles pulled off a once-in-a-lifetime trick play when our QB went out and effortlessly caught the football in the end zone. They called the trick play the Philly Special. At first, I didn't know how our QB ended up in the end zone until they did the instant replay.

I called Stu a few hours; maybe it was minutes after the game. I wanted to talk about NE's stunning defeat to our underdog Eagles. I don't think he was eager to talk about the Eagles' victory; he answered his phone on the tenth ring, ignored my enthusiasm, and changed the subject.

I was not going the let our win go unnoticed. He said the sportscasters were in disbelief they lost to an underdog team of marginal players. I asked him if they were going to have a sore loser, in total denial of the loss parade in Boston, and ignore their crushing defeat altogether.

I didn't hear any congratulations you won, so I chalked it up to ungrateful poor losers. I was very concerned the New England fans might need to go through many phases of grief. The Patriots fans will first be in denial, then anger, depression, and finally, acceptance. I don't think they will ever reach the acceptance phase.

The Eagles had a fantastic parade in Philly. Eagles' football was history until the fall, and I need to get through a few more months of winter until spring.

## Our family is stuck in the past

Bonnie and her brother came over this weekend and wanted to go to the movies in the afternoon. Ryan was sleeping; I told the kids to wake him up; maybe he would take them. I always want Ryan to spend more time with Bonnie, but he always has other plans. I'm getting so frustrated our family is stuck in the past and unable to move forward, including me.

I'm feeling the burden of dealing with Ryan, and my mental issues are driving me into a state of hopelessness and despair. I see no way we can help him at this point. The same situation as years ago after Bonnie was born, that's over ten years ago now. How long can I see his irresponsible behavior destroy our quality of life?

I wonder how much longer I can put up with his behavior because my moods and my health, both physically and mentally, are deteriorating quickly now. I know my physical health has seriously deteriorated over the past ten years. I remember just a few years ago camping up to the Adirondacks, kayaking 13 miles, and the next day hiking another 5 miles up into the mountains.

## I can't help my own son; maybe he just needs to help himself

I'm not blaming Ryan for all my problems right now. I just realized my health is deteriorating; I am struggling with my physical and mental health issues. My relationship with Ryan has not improved; this is at a stalemate with no one moving to make things better for us all. I think we should seek professional help even if Ryan doesn't help himself or us.

Jane is moving on with her new boyfriend and seems to be very happy. I think Ryan is feeling Jane distancing from him and is causing some abandonment issues.

Ryan has been supporting Jane and her kids for over ten years, and Ryan must feel she has abandoned him at some level. He has supported her over some serious personal issues. It is almost like they were married, and Ryan was the father of Jane's kids for several years. Here I go again, psychoanalyzing Ryan without a Ph.D.

I talk to Rosie once in a while, and she thinks we should ask Ryan to leave our house. I explain we adore our granddaughter and want her to be in our life. If Ryan moves away to an apartment in Philly, she may not want to visit us as often.

I am happy for Jane and a new love relationship. I do see she is much happier now that she found him and is moving on. She has gone through a lot for the past five years. I fear Ryan will be isolated and alone if Jane and the kids move out of the area. Bonnie is now a preteen will want to invite her own new friends over to her house wherever she lives.

As time goes on, I'm afraid Ryan will lose touch with Jane's family, and it may cause a crisis in his life. After all, Jane and her kids have been like his only family for over ten years now. He has supported Jane through many difficult life situations, including the conflict with her parents, but that's another tale to tell.

Without a Ph.D., I must stop psychoanalyzing Ryan, I have my own issues to psychoanalyze, and it will take up most if not all of my time. Maybe it is time to just let Ryan solve his problems without my advice. I often say, and it is true, nobody takes my advice anyway.

### Rosie called from the BDS group
Rosie called and wondered why I wasn't attending her BDS group. I told her I didn't want to vent my frustration about Ryan anymore. I said, "I was taking time off from a group; other people need to express themselves and start to feel better about their lives."

Sometimes when I start complaining about Ryan, I feel guilty; I drag the group down with the same old story. Nicole even said the other day she doesn't think Ryan will ever get help.

Rosie said the bipolar group attendance is lower now; she is hoping the good weather, more people will come out. Her health is good after a kidney transplant, and she is doing well with her diabetes.

Rosie is a very strong woman, and I was amazed at how fast she recovered from her kidney transplant operation without major complications. Her transplant was over five years ago, and she hasn't looked back; she continues to live a good bipolar normal lifestyle.

I should tell Rosie about the workbook, but I am afraid she will be critical and want to make too many revisions. I feel if I delay publishing any further, I will never accomplish yet another goal in life. The workbook project is my priority one, well, almost number one behind staying mentally stable, family, the old house, Ryan, Bonnie, probably many other issues.

I don't want to make a joke of all my disorders and character flaws, but I want to emphasize it does not matter how many issues I get to live with but how I manage them. The first priority I need is to make sure I stay stable and monitor my stress level.

I made a decision not to have anyone edit or proofread the workbook. There may be some or many controversial parts critical of the government. I want to take full responsibility for the contents of the workbook. I want to present my "unworthy syndrome" theory to the BDS group, but I am afraid people might think it is a dumb theory. That is my unworthy syndrome talking to me again.

## I was finally admitting I have a hoarding disorder

Summertime came, and I decided to spend less time watching cable news and more time listening to music on my high-end sound system. I took my daily 2-mile walk at the park. I took a vacation from working on the workbook.

## Camping in Amish country

Instead of working on the workbook, I decided to go on a short camping trip out to Lancaster, PA, about 70 miles from our house. This area is best known as Amish, the deeply religious people that believe in strict Christian values and the simple farming lifestyle. Years ago, we drove out on just a day trip to the outlets to get clothes for the boys. We took Bonnie to show her how the Amish people have lived for decades.

As we drove out to our campground, we passed dozens of working farms off the main road. The views were spectacular if you don't mind the scent of manure from the farm animals. Rows of crops were planted as straight as an arrow, and every inch of land had some crops growing in the fertile fields.

These people live as close to nature as anyone can get; some farms had no electric power; they didn't have a power line from the street to the farmhouse. Some say you can tell a real farmer if the barn is better maintained than the farmhouse. These folks are real farmers, and we even saw a farmer plowing his fields behind workhorses.

On Sunday, we did go down the tourist areas along the main road. You would see horses and buggies tied up to hitching posts. The horses were groomed like show horses. We took a buggy ride out through the farms; our buggy driver told us many Amish worked several jobs. Bonnie thought the buggy rides were the best; she did take some horseback riding lessons a few years ago. We toured an actual Amish farmhouse, the tour guide told us how the Amish lived off the land, and Amish customs passed down for decades.

Nicole planted a nice garden, and we had fresh vegetables to eat all summer long.

## Stage 12 My spiritual growth has taken a lifetime

On January 3, 2019, The Democrats took over control of the House of Representatives but did not provide funding for President Trump's proposed border wall. The Republicans increased their control of the Senate.

A week later, the radical House members announced they would begin the impeachment of the POTUS. The rhetoric from several of the more radical woman members of the House was outright anti-American. Calls for impeachment of the POTUS began a few days after the POTUS was even sworn into office.

I know Trump's tweets are a bit to the point, but I admire his ability to fight back against all the RAD media, politicians, Intel community, college academia elites, and we can't forget the Hollywood elite.

Nicole complains the POTUS is too direct and insults too many people to be presidential. I tell her most women do not like confrontational people, but aggressively fighting back is the only way Trump can survive in a politically charged hostile environment.

### China lands on the dark side of the moon

In a brief announcement, a report China landed a craft on the far side of the moon. The RAD or the MSA media did not go into detail. I was sure China was hiding a very important story.

Meanwhile, protests go on in Hong Kong, and their tourist trade is in trouble. All these developments are troubling because China is dictating policies that will damage our country.

The drug Fentanyl is being imported into our nation from China, and we are incapable or unwilling to stop the flow.

## The Patriots won another Super Bowl LIII

On February 3, 2019, Super Bowl LIII was hosted at Mercedes-Benz Stadium in Atlanta, Georgia. Tom Brady, the quarterback of the New England Patriots football team, won another Super Bowl championship, the most NFL world championships ever won by a single player.

I did not bother to call Stu and congratulate the Patriots on another win. The New England fans are arrogant; they just assume they will win every Super Bowl, which is quite irritating. Well, of course, Stu did call me, and I told him again he was not a Patriots fan; he just sits under a palm tree and watches the game from 1500 miles away from cold NE. He told me how many titles Tom Brady has won; I ignored his bragging rhetoric, again very annoying.

## How did China go to the dark side of the moon?

I heard a rumor China was purchasing farmland in the US. Well, now I was very curious about the timing of China's voyage to the moon. I am not a cynical person at heart, just kidding; I get very anxious when the news is not reporting important news.

While reading about the landing on the dark side of the moon, I found a documentary, "How China Got Rich." [(Wood, 2019).

I was surprised to learn just how fast China has lifted its people out of poverty to be an industrial superpower. This documentary film traces China's history from about 1980 to the present or about 40 years.

I remember back in the early 80s, and I went to auctions to buy business equipment to list on my computer magazine. I remember telling people our nation was destroying our manufacturing base by allowing companies to relocate overseas. Pennsylvania at the time had thousands of medium-size companies that manufactured parts and all types of industrial equipment. One large company had dozens of huge machine tools that sold for pennies on the dollar. I told one of the guys these companies are gone forever, and we will regret it, and he agreed.

Now I understand many of these companies did go overseas. What surprised me was how fast China educated its youth to gain economic and political power around the world. In 1980 many Chinese people that lived in rural areas were very poor and did not even own a refrigerator.

In the 80s, China educated thousands of very bright people, many here in the US. Some could argue over the past 20 years, they have caught up to us technologically, and now I understand militarily. So, while we were spending trillions of dollars fighting in wars and conflicts after 9/11 in 2001, the Chinese were educating all their youth and becoming an industrial superpower. Our government does not have a long-range plan for our future. Our infrastructure is rusting, and we are falling behind in 5G telecommunications technology.

Our politicians only spend money on short-range projects that will keep them in office. Our nation does not have long-term plans to help our grandchildren thrive. We are borrowing trillions of dollars but have no plan to pay it back. We are bankrupting our children and grandchildren.

So, I was surprised when I learned China landed a probe on the dark side of the moon, and I am concerned our security agencies are hiding the truth by omission. The truth is China is far more advanced than they report. The omission our leaders do not want the American public to know the truth.

## Senator Sanders and others announce a run for President

Three more politicians announced their candidacy for U.S. president. Senator Bernie Sanders announced his candidacy for the 2020 presidential election. Many people in the RAD press thought his ideas for our nation would be good for the country. I detect a rapid swing to the far left for the Democrats. Ten years ago, his Socialist agenda was just a fringe ideology and considered a joke.

## Our nation is bitterly divided between the RADs against the MSAs

Now I know our nation is so divided we actually have split apart into two very different nations. The Democratic Party of the 70s, 80s, and '90s has evolved into a radical anti-American group of Socialists that call themselves Democratic Socialists. I call them the Radical American Democrats or RADs and the Republicans Main Street Americans, the MSAs.

## The Special Counsel found no wrongdoing

The Special Counsel has been investigating the Trump administration since shortly after he was sworn into office over two years ago. The Special Counsel's 400-page report has been released to the public and basically cleared everyone in the President's Administration of the wrongdoing of any American.

I am upset with our Justice system; Democrats and the RAD have harassed and intimidated many people tied to the POTUS to find criminal acts. Sometimes I jokingly say to Nicole, "Have they arrested Trump yet?" Some of the RADs thought the Special Counsel's report would come with an arrest warrant attached.

A few days later, the Democrats are going deeper into Trumps' life to find something, anything to impeach the POTUS. I don't agree with some of his policies, but I admire his will to fight back against constant ridicule, harassment, hate, and false claims. His treatment by the RAD media reminds me of my constant struggle growing up with my abusive family in NE.

## A record number of 20 presidential candidates

At the end of April, former Vice President Joe Biden announced his candidacy for the 2020 presidential election, expanding the field to a record 20 candidates, the largest field of presidential candidates in U.S. history. Now about 20 Democrats are now fighting to be the Democratic nominee to battle President Trump in 2020.

Spring finally arrived, but our camping vacations don't seem as important as in past years. Nicole has retired, and her desire to get away from home is not as strong as in past years. We can't go to the expensive campground resorts.

I am approaching 80 now, and my time on this earth is slipping away, and I need to get clear on my priorities. I need to complete my goals with the precision of a Swiss watch, well, maybe a Coo Coo clock. Someone mentioned I should slow down, implying I am getting too old, but I believe I need to speed up to complete my must-do projects. I think we use camping trips as our spiritual retreat to escape from the harsh reality of our lives. While away, we ignore our family situations, but now I cannot avoid promises I made to myself any longer.

## Daisy died, and Stu had a very bad spell

In the spring, Stu stopped by on his way to New England from Florida, and we could tell his dog Daisy was very ill. Stu thought she was just getting old, but I was concerned because she could not climb the stairs up to our second floor. In the morning, she had a hard time walking and pooping on the grass. I questioned her health, but Stu told me the vet told him she has a tumor, but if she does not eat, then she may have a more serious problem. Stu left for NE the following day; he was in a hurry as usual.

Stu has had another bad spell of depression and other issues for over a year. I define a bad spell as stressful life situations and BD episodes. It was hard on me too. I called him almost every day. He was very thankful I kept in touch with him; I can tell when he is very depressed because he lacks his sense of humor. It is a horrible place to be.

A few weeks later, Stu called from NE and told us his dog Daisy died; she had inoperable cancer. He was distraught and very sad, Daisy had been at his side for years, and he fought to keep her alive. Someone told me years ago; dogs are difficult pets because they only live for about ten years, and then you need to let them go. His dog Daisy had been very ill for the past year, and I think it affected Stu more than he wanted to admit.

## Our favorite time to go camping is in the fall
In the fall, Stu said he was planning to leave for Florida in a week. Our favorite time to go camping is in the fall when the weather is warm and the nights are cool for sleeping; we look forward to camping in the Fall at the Jersey Shore. We love the fall because it usually has warm days and cool nights. The added plus, the summer crowds, leave until the following summer.

We had to cut our trip short because Stu was heading back down to Florida sooner than we thought. We don't like to rush when we camp, that is one of the reasons we love to go camping. Nicole was a bit angry; she rarely gets upset, but we do cherish our time away from home.

Nicole complained Stu could have left a few days after our vacation, but I just remarked this is Stu; I had to put up with his behavior for far too many decades. We packed up early and arrived home very early.

Stu called and said he was lost; he just went over the Tappan Zee Bridge from New York into New Jersey. He was very confused, and

I began to give him directions from our GPS. I called him a few minutes later, and he said he went back over the Tappan Zee Bridge again back toward New York. I was very concerned at this point because he had driven to Florida dozens of times.

I tried to tell him to get off the highway and ask for directions, but he just kept driving. Nicole was trying to find his location on the GPS on her tablet, but Stu could not determine if he was heading north or southeast, or west.

If he was not having such a bad spell over the past year, this would be very funny, but it was not funny at all. We did not hear from him for over 30 minutes, and then he called and told us he was on the New Jersey Turnpike and only an hour away; I was very worried he would get in an accident.

Stu finally arrived and was not making any sense at all. He was tired and in very bad shape to drive all the way to Florida. After dinner, he began talking about his summer and was looking forward to spending winter in Florida. Nicole was still upset because we could have stayed at the campground several hours longer.

I was going into my yearly case of SAD or Seasonal Affective Disorder. I have been envious of Stu's lifestyle at times in the past, but heading south for the winter has always been my dream come true.

I would kid him and say he lives like a millionaire without the hassles of being a millionaire. Think about it; he has spent his summers in cool New England and winters in warm sunny Florida now for over 25 years. Well, I am a bit envious of his lifestyle but not his difficult life with BD.

Of course, he talked about our risky adventure sailing around Nantucket. He joked about how Aunt Maddie gave him $5 every month from her pension check. I never knew that until several years ago; that was just another secret to be uncovered about our dysfunctional family. As I listened to the same old stories of our past, I began the feeling of being mistreated and abused by my family all over again.

During dinner, Stu started to talk about his divorce from Denise. He told us Denise wanted to break off their engagement and give back Maddie's engagement ring. He said Aunt Maddie was engaged to an Army soldier; he died in combat in WW I. I thought she probably had severe trauma over that tragedy.

Stu was engaged to Denise in his senior year in college. I never knew she broke off the engagement. I never even knew Aunt Maddie gave her engagement ring to Stu. Stu said that he talked Denise into marrying him. I began to feel very sad and alone again. I said to Stu, "No wonder you almost committed suicide; you lost everything and had to leave New England."

Actually, I was not too sympathetic to his story, I had lost my $1^{st}$ love forever, and I never had any time to spend with her. It's been quite some time since I awoke from amnesia, but my memory recollections are still affecting me to this day.

I said to Stu, "I don't know how you dealt with Denise living with another guy shortly after your divorce" These are the type of events of difficult life situations that may cause mentally ill people to end their lives. I was feeling the emotions I had before the tragic breakup with Maria that sent me into a state of amnesia for more than four decades. I also needed to leave New England and start my life over again.

These life-threatening events are what the WAVES Workbook is trying to measure and prevent. Stu's WAVES Chart is listed in Chapter

6. I began to feel sad all over again; I thought I had resolved all these issues over the years.

Then we started to talk about how our father died, and we didn't know about it until about a year later. I know his death had a profound effect on my life. For about a year, we didn't know he was buried in a small cemetery just above our farmhouse. These types of bizarre events in our lives a very hard to understand for normal people.

I think it is very difficult for people with mental illness to deal with tragic situations even later in life. Stu said our childhood could be called neglect. In a sense, it was, but we always had good food, a warm house to come home to. I think I suffered more from emotional abuse and abandonment issues. My anxiety turned into a case of what I call unworthy syndrome, and when combined with my other issues, life was quite challenging. I struggled in silence with feelings I was not loved after my father died.

Stu was dealing with Stu's narcissistic issues, Aunt Maddie told him he could do no wrong, and I could not do anything right. Our childhood was not a good healthy experience for either of us.

Stu said our mother told him she thought about leaving our father, but wives didn't do that back in the 1940s. This was another eye-opener I knew nothing about. Maybe our father was not the perfect father; I thought he was. My mother told us he did not drink; was there another story behind that?

Stu went on to say things that happened in our family that were hidden for decades. Stu said he learned all these details from our mother during his divorce from Denise. I think some parents think hiding painful events will protect their children, and it is the right thing to do; I don't. Stu's divorce was sad; our mother adored Denise.

Stu seemed much better in the morning; I thought if he acted the way he was yesterday, I would take him to our psychiatric hospital. The problem, Stu only had major health insurance coverage in Florida. I hoped if he got to Florida, they would straighten out his meds.

As always, he was in a hurry to get down to Florida, but I was afraid he would not make it. This is Strew when he gets in his righteous "I do things when I want to" mode without regard to other people. I was afraid his car would break down or have an accident on the way down. He was rear-ended by a tractor-trailer truck years ago on Interstate I-95, a very dangerous highway.

Nicole felt the same way; he was not in a good emotional state to drive alone all the way to Florida. It is a long 1200 mile two or three-day drive. Nicole told me not to go with him; honestly, I was afraid we might not make it without getting into an accident. Nicole said I was not in any kind of mental state to drive 1200 miles; I had to admit I was not in the best emotional health.

Stu stayed another night and seemed much better in the morning; if he acted the way he did when he arrived, I would take him to our psychiatric hospital regardless of his health care insurance.

## No one cared enough to help me
After Stu left for Florida, I started to get flashbacks of my childhood, and my emotions buried deep within me started to come up all at the same time. I started to feel again that no one ever really loved me, and then I began to see the real me, the real pain I carried deep within all my life since just as a child. From a very young age, I desperately needed my mother, father, anyone to love me and show signs of affection. Everyone abandoned me, my father, my aunt, my mother, Greg, and Maria.

I began to feel intense emotions, and then the grief hit me all at once. I was looking at the hidden me for the first time in my life. I was not sorry for myself. I just realized I was mentally ill, I had all the symptoms, but no one could see my struggle, and no one cared enough to help me. No one even asked me why I stopped dating Maria after I returned from Nantucket.

The voice inside my head said, "We don't want you anymore," played over in my mind. No one, even my family, cared about my painful and severely distorted face. I began to break down again, and for the first time in my life, in my mind's eye, I saw myself as a skinny seven-year-old little kid. I was standing all alone in the middle of a barren dirt field, no grass, no trees, just dirt as far as I could see. I felt all alone and felt no one loved me.

Then I remembered the kid Tim that lived up on the hill had a great dad that spent time with him. We would all pick strawberries in his garden, and his dad would make strawberry shortcakes for all of us. I could tell his dad loved him so much; maybe I was trying to hide how much I missed my father. I could hardly fight back the tears. Then I felt betrayed by the teenager down the street that sexually abused me.

## My life crisis started shortly after my father died

All of a sudden, I realized my life crisis started as a mentally ill and physically weak young kid and not on Nantucket, but years earlier. My crisis started shortly after my father died when I was just five years old; from then on, I felt weak, neglected, rejected, and abandoned by everyone.

After I awoke from my state of amnesia and started my recovery from amnesia, I thought my life crisis started after Maria came to visit me on Nantucket. I had to live alone with my mental illness, my mother, Aunt Maddie, Harold, my grandmother, and of course, Stu.

I felt all alone and abandoned by my own family. I also had to deal with Stu getting all the attention while I only got emotional and verbally abused for years. I cannot blame Stu; he was mistreated by getting smothered with too much attention and admiration for anything he did. We had a very unhealthy childhood. Of course, my bipolar illness was hidden from view, and all my family could see was my moody and anxious behavior.

## I felt I was being punished

For years I understood all this from an intellectual viewpoint but never experienced it emotionally as a loss that I needed to grieve and accept my difficult childhood. My childhood was lost and can never be relived over again.

I always thought I was I was a strong, healthy guy, but that was just my distorted self-image of myself. I have been physically and emotionally unhealthy since a child. I had more sickness than most kids and then had Bell's Palsy in my teens. Later in life, I had chronic sinus infections, complications from diabetes, and alcoholism.

Within days my emotional recollections of past events became less of an issue, and I thought I was finally living with the real me. I now know why I never wanted to go into talk therapy or group psychotherapy for all those years. I was afraid I would discover all these deeply painful experiences from my past.

The result of all this grief and pain further confirmed my commitment to help people with BD to get treatment early on.

## My mother told me our father died a year earlier

You know my life is a classic example of not getting help early on in life. If any child has a traumatic event in their lives, get them help as soon as possible. Both my brother and I had symptoms of mental illness from a very early age. My father's death was a turning point in my life, and I should have had grief counseling after learning our father had died a year earlier.

I remember running back into the house and asking my mother if our father did die of a heart attack. I can visualize that moment in my mind's eye like it happened yesterday. I ran back to the house, and I asked her if our father had died of a heart attack. She was at the kitchen sink and told me he did die and was buried in the small cemetery just beyond our farm—what a way for Stu and me to start our lives.

### I clung onto Maria, hoping she would fill a void
Yes, I did fall madly in love with Maria and desperately needed her affection, but I clung to Maria, hoping she would fill a void I had since a child, namely someone to love me. When I met Maria, she gave me the physical affection I had yearned for all my life. I was quite disfigured with my facial paralysis, and it was quite noticeable. She accepted me and never even mentioned my facial disfigurement.

### I was finally was grieving the loss of my childhood
I was finally grieving the loss of my childhood in the loss of having a normal and happy life. As the days went by, I felt better about myself and my childhood without a father. I never confronted the void I had without a father or even a father mentor. I think a lot of mentally ill children are mistreated and/or misunderstood by their parents, families, teachers, friends, and others. If I had been helped in any way, things would've been very different.

What a bizarre and challenging childhood, but I believe a lot of kids with a mental illness also suffer in silence. People with obvious physical illnesses are supported and, in some cases, coddled by caregivers but not so much for people with mental illness. In some cases, mentally ill kids don't have any caregivers. That is how I felt for decades.

## The consequences of living in a fatherless home

I did miss my father growing up, and I thought he was my spirit guide at times. I did put him on a pedestal and thought he would protect me from emotional and sexual abuse from my family and the teenager down the street. I believe growing up without a father was a tragic situation for me, especially since Stu was coddled by my aunt and grandmother.

If my father was alive when I was a child, my aunt and grandmother most likely would not have lived with us. Perhaps I would not have been sexually abused by the teenager down the street. I am sure we would not be allowed as teenagers to race cars around town and drink beer all night long. I understand my father did not even drink.

Recently I did find some troubling but not surprising statistics about kids growing up in fatherless families. One study from the Minnesota Psychological Association found some troubling trends. One article [(Jerrod Brown) highlighted ten adverse outcomes that may result from the absence of a father in a child's life, namely:

(1) Perceived abandonment, (2) attachment issues, (3) child abuse, (4) childhood obesity, (5) criminal justice involvement, (6) gang involvement, (7) mental health issues, (8) poor school performance, (9) poverty and homelessness; and (10) substance use.

The article goes into greater detail for each adverse outcome. I think both Stu and I struggled with at least 8 of these adverse outcomes, but fortunately, we didn't join a gang. I was never homeless, but Stu was flat broke and basically homeless in Florida after his divorce. I was never obese but developed diabetes from eating candy bars every day. Stu got a DUI, and I came close to getting one myself. Both Stu and I were on our way to becoming alcoholics by the age of 15.

Without a father, we had no discipline from about ten years old. I remember our mother tried to spank us for something; we ran outside and pretended to be hurt; we just laughed at our punishment behind her back.

I would add another adverse outcome to the adverse outcome list; many kids are dealing with cases of the unworthy syndrome. I found growing up without the love of my father was a very difficult condition for me to overcome. I am still working on it. My father died of a heart attack, so I could not physically spend time with him.

I think for many kids knowing your father is alive and well but seldom, if ever, tells his son or daughter he loves them is beyond tragic. Doesn't that send a strong message to kids "You are not worthy of my love?".

I don't want to play the child psychologist, but I would guess after the feelings of not being loved are felt by many kids for years, they either lash out, join gangs or punish themselves by committing suicide. Many kids turn to using drugs or alcohol to dull emotional pain. Of course, drug use can lead to criminal behavior or OD.

That's what happened to my next-door neighbor Blake in Philly. He went from a drug user to a drug dealer and then ended up in prison. I have a hard time shaming people that grow up without a father because I have a void in my life that I can never fill.

I have tried to be a good father to Ryan and Matt, but I know I have not spent a lot of quality time. When the boys were in their teens, they wanted to play video games instead of learning how to work on cars or computers. I did not monitor online videos they all watched, and they told me years later they watched many sexually explicit porn videos.

## Help kids with emotional issues early-on
My advice is if people see kids that are very withdrawn and moody, do not criticize or shame their behavior; many kids are suffering in silence. Maybe understand it may be a symptom of a more serious problem. Now I am not feeling sorry for myself and don't seek pity, but just facing the reality of what happened; I need to help other people deal with childhood mental issues.

## I had to face my past; I was neglected when just a child
Some people uncovered and discovered emotional breakthroughs during the Awake spiritual growth course. Some people uncovered tragic events in their lives, including sexual abuse and other regrets like abortions, divorce, and infidelity. I never discovered feelings of grieving my childhood until now. Now I had to face reality; I was abandoned and neglected when just a child. I also lost my ability to love after going into a state of amnesia.

## My spiritual growth took four decades to discover
Some people had a spiritual awakening at the Awake course, but I did not until now, some 40 years after *I took the* Awake course. I thought the Awake course would uncover all my disorders during a long weekend course, but all I learned was I was selfish and did not give back unless I got something in return.

Many people that took the Awake course did experience rapid spiritual growth during and after the course. Now I feel I am just now growing spiritually, over forty years after I completed the Awake course. I did not grow spiritually during the course, but I did meet many spiritual and kind people.

I had to admit I was getting burned out dealing with my childhood trauma, amnesia, recollections of the distant past, and BD issues.

I also was dealing with Ryan and physical illnesses over the past years. There is little left to discover, right?

### I had all symptoms of an unworthy syndrome
The emotional pain of the breakup with Maria was so traumatic I went into a state of amnesia for over 45 years. I believe I went into a state of amnesia instead of going psychotic, severely depressed, or committing suicide.

Now I understand many of my bad spells over the years can be attributed to my unworthy syndrome plus other stressful situations. I am sure some people with a good self-image and happy childhoods may think my unworthy syndrome self-diagnosis is just a little bizarre. Most kids have been told they are loved from an early age. Now I understand these negative feelings were formed when I was a very young child; I did not have a choice; no one ever said they loved me or protected me from emotional and sexual abuse.

I know I am repeating the fact no one protected me from abuse when just a child. Sometimes It is hard to admit I was a victim of childhood abuse. I need to keep reminding myself I don't need to believe I am unworthy any longer; I am not a child. I will not allow anyone to abuse me or anyone I love.

### Another member of the BD group with job issues
This discovery that I had unworthy syndrome was so dramatic I needed to tell people. I wanted to find someone that could understand my sad but real message of never feeling loved. I wanted to explain my case of unworthy syndrome to the BDS group.

The following week I went to the BDS group to talk about my childhood and the feelings of neglect from a very young age. I had to admit I do selfishly use the group at times to vent my frustration over Ryan and get a little sympathy. The group leader, Rosie, always asks if anyone has a pressing issue; they want to share before the session begins.

I just sat there embarrassed that I was an older guy grieving over my difficult childhood, but I knew the group would be supportive. How could I tell the group I recently discovered I was not worthy of being loved for over 70 years? Would the group think I was too old to make such a bizarre statement? What if the group all agreed, I was not worthy of being loved? Now that would not be a joke. The group would certainly understand my feelings of being neglected; many members I know in the group have experienced similar feelings of rejection at some point in their lives.

## I struggled for decades with dual disorders

I wanted to see if anyone in the group thought they might also have a case of the unworthy syndrome. If they did agree, then those people not only struggled with BD from birth but, in addition, were victims of childhood abuse. We had to live with two or dual conditions for the rest of our lives, not only BD but also the shame of abuse, which was quite challenging.

Well, time was up, and the meeting ended; I did not get a chance to introduce and explain my theory, my newfound unworthy syndrome, to the BDS group.

## How do I cope with an unworthy syndrome?

Well, now that I have self-diagnosed myself with another new disorder, how do I cope with it? How do I convince myself I am worthy of being loved? I know I am capable of loving someone else.

Of course, I don't believe my unworthy disorder or syndrome is not listed in the DSM manual; I just think it is an accurate description of my unconscious frame of mind from about the age of 5, shortly after my father suddenly died of a heart attack.

When feelings of abandonment mixed with anxiety come over me, I need to keep reminding myself my unworthy syndrome began long before my breakup with Maria. Maria was not responsible for my case of amnesia either. Anything could have triggered a case of amnesia. These negative feelings have followed me around my entire life. I need to keep reminding myself I couldn't do anything about my unworthiness issues when I was a child. Now I can leave these negative feelings in the past and keep reminding myself; I do deserve to be successful and lead a happy life.

## I wanted to introduce my unworthy syndrome again to the BDS group

A few months later, I went to the BDS group to introduce and explain my unworthy syndrome again. As usual, several other people in the group had serious issues that night. I did not bring up my issues in the group; several other people needed support and reassurance they would get better. Many people come to the group with a dismal attitude they will never get better.

A young woman named Sherry had a common issue of finding another job after being fired for BD behavior. Sherry blamed herself and wondered if she could ever find another job. She did not know if her former employer would even give her a job reference. It sounded like she might also have a case of unworthy syndrome. These types of job-related stresses and negative feelings of self-worth are very common for people with BD. I think many people with BD feel they do not deserve to have a good-paying job because of their BD illness. If Sherry had been abused and neglected from a very young age, she could have a case of the unworthy syndrome.

I praised her for getting help from her psychiatrist as well as the support group. I told her she was not alone; most people with BD have a difficult time getting and keeping jobs. She was surprised when all the members of the group agreed. I remember the first meeting I attended; I was also surprised many members of the group also had difficulty with normal everyday tasks, like job issues.

The WAVES Chart lists several stressors related to job issues. That is one role I have in the group. I have become an advocate for people to get treatment early on. I explain the very difficult life both my brother and I had until midlife before getting treatment.

I make clear to the group I have several very tragic real-life experiences to prove my point. I also point out both my brother and I had a traumatic childhood and wished someone could have helped us. I'm sure some younger people think I am older, but I hope not an old guy with an outdated message of how to live with BD. Nevertheless, I still preach to people with mental issues to get help early on.

So, the meeting ended, I did not get a chance again to introduce and explain my unworthy syndrome again to the BDS group.

## I met Owen at sunset, a man with Cerebral Palsy

It was time to take my two-mile run around the county lake. Well, my run was more of a very slow nature walk than a run. I didn't get up to the county lake because it is about a one-hour drive from our house, but it was a nice clear warm day to take a ride and to see the sunset overlooking the lake.

As I was walking along a path around the lake, I noticed a man sitting on a bench watching the sunset go down. I stopped to watch the sunset on a nearby park bench. He was talking to a woman. I noticed he could hardly talk and was severely disabled as he sat crouched over on the park bench.

After watching the sun go down over the lake, the woman left, and I walked over and struck up a conversation with him. I asked him why he was so disabled and if he was okay. I think he was a little surprised I asked him such a personal question. He told me he was born with an incurable disease called Cerebral Palsy and was told he would not live to be forty years old. He then told me he was 59 and was grateful for every day he lived because he did not know if he would live to enjoy another sunset.

I got tears in my eyes as he spoke about his extremely difficult life. I could hardly understand him, but I knew what he was saying was truly meaningful, and then I asked him his name and if he needed any help. He said his name was Owen and was having a rough time.

He began to ask me about my life and was genuinely happy for me as I told him my wife Nicole and I kayak on the lake and camp up in the mountains. I realized Owen was a truly unique and extraordinary man. Here he was not only accepting his disability but also embracing his tragic situation. He knew he would probably die with his illness but was not letting it destroy his very limited quality of life.

He was an inspiration for me to accept the realities of my mental illness, along with other issues, and be more appreciative of what I have in this life. I need to be more truthful and accepting of my illness and not be a victim of having a mental disability.

After a few minutes, he returned to his old van using his walker and struggled to get up into the driver's seat of his old van. He did not ask for help or sympathy. I wrote down my name and telephone number on a piece of paper and told him to call me if he needed anything.

On the hour-long drive home, I felt sorry for Owen living with so much pain and suffering. I wish I could help him live without pain, but all I can do is offer to help him. It is not fair; I could not understand why he was living with such a devastating illness all his life. Why am I dealing with all these issues so late in life? I hope I can resolve some of them before it's too late.

Today babies born with birth defects like Owens's may not even be born. Today some people see Owen as a burden on society. I know it is not right to think that way. Then I thought if they could detect babies in the womb had BD before birth, would either Stu or I have been born? I was getting depressed just thinking about it; maybe I am a burden on our family and on society. Maybe these emotions are just another bad spell.

## Another bad spell
August came, and I had another bad spell; house and car repairs kept me busy for a few weeks. Our shed was still leaning over, and I had no idea how to fix it. The weather was hot and humid, so we decided to go camping at the Jersey Shore for five nights. The campground we stay at is always booked every weekend, so we booked from Sunday night through to Friday. Early Sunday morning, we got caught in heavy traffic. The weather was very hot, and I guess everyone in Philly headed for the shore at the same time. After a few hours later in heavy traffic, we arrived at the campground and set up camp. After we set up the camper, we headed straight for the cool breezes of the Atlantic Ocean. We set up our beach chairs close to the water to get the cool breezes off the ocean.

## I decided to publish the workbook again after meeting Jack
My workbook project had been on hold for several years while Nicole and I spent time enjoying the great outdoors, but then a significant event happened to validate the commitment I made almost ten years ago to complete the workbook project.

Last summer at our neighbor's shore house, I met a young guy Jack about Matt's age, and he was in a very serious relationship with a young woman named JoJo. They seemed to be a perfect couple. They started a scuba business in Florida. Last year I felt she was a free spirit. She wasn't concerned about a lot of material things in life.

This year I saw Jack in the kitchen, and he looked very stressed and worn out. Jack excused himself and left to go down to the beach. Jack was with a young woman; she told us about the tragedy he suffered about two months after we met last summer. They were both in a serious boating accident, and she was killed right beside him. He was seriously injured and needed to go through several operations and physical rehabilitation.

To make a long story short, he was under a psychiatrist's care for BD but was not getting better. Of course, I was concerned his traumatic event could result in a serious psychotic breakdown.

Jack's story reminded me of the traumatic events that happened in my life when I was about his age. I may have overreacted in my effort to encourage him to get help, but I did see the workbook could be a valuable tool or aid in evaluating if someone was at risk of a BD psychotic episode. Jack and JoJo's story is told in Chapter 4.

I called my brother and told him I was finally going to finish the book. He said, "Didn't I tell you to finish the book years ago?" I hesitated for a minute and spoke. "You said to write the book before I changed my mind, but I never changed my mind." He said, "I guess you are right technically, so now what are you telling me it will be another five years?"

I changed the subject to talk about our weather up north. After I hung up maybe, his criticism would be the inspiration I needed to complete the book project. I didn't dare tell him it was closer to ten years ago when I started to write a long 300-page novel about just another bipolar story.

I guess he was right. I did change my mind and decided a workbook instead of a very long novel might be a better way to help people with or without BD. He lost interest in working on our "Just another bipolar story" long novel, as I called it years ago, and probably thought I would never publish it anyway.

Anyway, he did not know I was writing a workbook on the stresses people with BD cope with every day. I did not mention the workbook because I gave up on telling our life stories. I did not want to be honest and tell him our lives are "Just another bipolar story." Like millions of other stories. I did not want to talk about my problems; he had enough of his own to deal with.

I resented his criticism for my chronic delays over completing the book. He has several major character flaws I could mention, like mood swings, hoarding, a history of alcoholism, and plenty of personality issues. Then I realized I was also talking about myself. I have the same character flaws. As you know, we call our mental issues character flaws. Sometimes we need to joke about our less than perfect BD normal lives.

I could have brought up his chronic delay in releasing his "drug-free video" project he has been working on for at least five years, maybe even longer. He has been working on a video to encourage young kids not to even start to use drugs or alcohol. He has been rewriting the script for several years.

I know firsthand the feelings of failure when you have a project started when manic and then cannot complete it when depressed. I should call him and shame him for delaying his pet project. Well,

I do encourage him to keep working on his drug-free project, although, like me, he delays projects when he has a bad spell.

I have experienced this feeling for the hundredth or maybe a thousand times in my life. You know Stu and I have lived a total of over 25,000 days so far. If every bad spell lasted 25 days, that would be 1000 bad spells over our lifetime. No wonder people with BD live an average of 9 years less than the "Normal" people. A thousand bad spells over our lifetime might illustrate how difficult life can be with BD. Jack's story is told in Chapter 4.

### Stu is having another bad spell but finds Pebbles

Stu arrived in Florida a few months ago but is having another BD episode aggravating depression mixed with anxiety and everything else. I can tell because he doesn't have a sense of humor. I remember he had had another downward cycle again after his dog Daisy died.

We tried to tell Stu he should not get another dog after Daisy got so ill and died, but he argued a dog is his only support at times. I thought back in my single days, maybe a dog or cat would be a good idea because I was desperately depressed felt all alone and isolated most of the time.

He found another dog and named her Pebbles, but I don't think she had a rough personality like Buster or the show dog beauty of Daisy. Pebbles was quiet and well-behaved when he met her, but after he brought her home, her personality changed; she barked at strangers and at big dogs. One day she got out of Stu's yard and ran away. He found her tired and hungry about three miles away.

I told Stu Pebbles acts more like his past relationships with his women friends, quiet at first but then demanding and prone to running away. Well, Stu did not think that was funny at all.

I got him a support dog tag from a website on the internet. The support dog tag gave Stu a way to take Pebbles to stores, restaurants, and other events. The most beneficial outcome was he didn't need to leave Pebbles alone in his car at AA meetings. Stu even got a letter from his psychiatrist that allowed his dog to fly free on any airline. Now many people have a dim view of emotional support dogs, but I do believe in Stu's case; his dogs have provided him valuable emotional support.

The WAVES Chart has an entry for the loss of a pet, and I think Stu's relationship with his dog is more than just a common pet. It seems Stu goes into a BD bad spell when his dogs get very ill. Now it is not a psychotic episode but probably sort of a prolonged period of grieving the loss of his pet. Well, I probably should not be guessing Stu's psychodynamic dog disorder at this time.

My brother and I thought we had a unique and extraordinary life story to tell, but it is a story that could be told by millions of people living with BD. Our story was extraordinary only to my brother and me; it is really just another bipolar story.

We all thought Stu would recover in Florida when he got back to his AA group and the warm weather. I am still envious of his millionaire lifestyle on his frugal $10 a day budget.

I was very concerned at this point. I called him every day and could tell he was not getting better. I was afraid they were going to take him to a medical or psychiatric hospital and then to a nursing home to be rehabilitated or locked up. Mistreatment of some people with BD is a reality, and Stu was acting like he was on drugs and psychotic and not capable of taking care of himself.

A few days later, he landed up in a hospital in Florida after his neighbor found him incoherent and very ill in his house. He called me from the hospital, and he still sounded like he was on drugs. I thought he was having hallucinations because his words were garbled, and so I called his son Wes.

Wes was aware of the situation and flew down to Florida, boarded up his house, took Stu out of the hospital, and flew him back to NE. Now I can't say enough about Wes; he is working 60-hour weeks and weekends at times and still has time to help Stu; now that's a great son.

It took several months to get Stu stable again. What happened, his clinic in Florida doubled his lithium dose, and that made him very unstable. He was also dehydrated and lost 20 lbs. He said people thought he looked great. He said he didn't feel great at all. Normal people may say, "You look so physically healthy you cannot possibly feel ill.". These types of comments show people do not get it when it comes to mental illness. A few months later, he was in recovery and very thankful his son rescued him from nearly being admitted into a nursing home forever.

Stu slowly recovered at his son's place in NE. I could tell he was getting better because he complained about the bitterly cold weather in NE and wanted to fly back to Florida. I called him every evening to see how he was doing but still no sense of humor. He appreciated my support, and I was sorry I could not help him.

From my experience, it is not good to tell people with BD; they should not feel this way or that way because they cannot. I did not want to mention the drug-free video project that could make him even more depressed and hopeless.

A few weeks later, I could tell he was feeling a bit better. He takes his meds but is not taking care of himself. I don't even want to mention the workbook; it may not improve his mood. I was so helpless to help him. Wes has supported him for years, but all this is hard on Wes's family. I think it is very difficult for Stu and me to live life with mental and physical illness as we get older. It is hard enough for ordinary people to deal with physical illness in old age.

## Owen should be an inspiration to us all
On a bright summer day went up to the county lake to kayak, collect my thoughts and reset my mind, as I call it. It is a long one-hour drive up to the county lake, but I have not seen Owen for over a year. I was sure he would be at the lake to watch the sunset.

It was a very hot day, and I decided to kayak up at the county lake. When I paddled out in the middle of the lake, I watched as a very dark cloud was overhead, and I had no time to paddle back to shore. I did not hear thunder, and then it suddenly started to rain so hard I could not see the shoreline.

In the middle of the downpour, I watched very large drops of rain falling in slow motion, and as they bounced off the water, they looked like teardrops bouncing back up out of the water in slow motion. Within a few minutes, the sun came out, and I paddled back to the dock. The experience was truly spiritual, as if the heavy raindrops shaped like teardrops were meant to teach me something I had learned and then forgotten a long time ago.

I was surprised my kayak did not sink and only had a few inches of water. I tipped over the kayak on the bank, quickly dried off in the hot sun, and decided to stay for the sunset.

I went over to the picnic area to see if Owen was still watching the sunset. Owen was sitting in the front seat of his old van, waiting for the sun to go down. I noticed he still had a following; several people came up to talk to him before the sun went down. As I crossed over a small bridge to the parking lot, I bumped into a woman leaving Owen's van and mentioned how Owen was such an inspiration to me. She seemed surprised and said she had the same experience after she got to know him. She said his health was very poor, he couldn't even get out of his van to watch the sunset from his park bench, but he had a good view of the sunset from his old van.

I went over to talk to him and saw his physical health was indeed failing. He didn't get out of his van and watched the sunset from the front seat of his old van. I could see his overall health was very poor, but his positive outlook on life was always ever-present. He did not complain or seek pity, and I marveled at his will to live with such a disabling illness.

He was always kind to everyone and never complained about his quality of life; although he accepted, he did have a terminal illness. He admitted living with Cerebral Palsy was very painful, he told me so, but I could tell he also lives by Willy's 4 rules to live by.

I admire him for getting to the lake and watching the sunset; it is a very spiritual thing to do when he is in so much pain. I now realize why Owen's message was so important to me. He is a very spiritual man and courageous to get out to see the sunset almost every night. He was teaching me to accept my illness, learn to be kind, and understand life, for some people will have pain.

When I first met him, he said he was thankful for being able to see the sunsets because he didn't know if it might be his last. Did I need any more compelling proof he is an extraordinary and a very spiritual man? On the way home, it occurred to me I may not have much longer to live myself. I have a history of cancer, blood clots, diabetes, and various mental illnesses. I need to show gratitude for the meds that have kept me stable and the support I have from my family. I also need to have gratitude for many people that have helped me, doctors, surgeons, psychiatrists, people in the BD group, and of course, my wife.

I thought that's one reason why I am here on earth to experience BD and find meaning but always live Willy's 4 rules to live by. I am here to help other people while still struggling with other issues. I guess that is the challenge, live with setbacks but learn to be kind to everyone.

I need to be grateful; because both Owen and Sabrina are living with illnesses that don't even have any cure.

I am not truly a spiritual being yet, but I can say I have grown spiritually, but it's taken over 75 years. Spiritual growth is what I have been pursuing for all these years, but I needed to overcome many obstacles in my way. Well, I am on the right path to complete the workbook; hopefully, it will help people, and I am at Willy's rule Number 3 to be kind to everyone. No, that is not true; I am still on Rule Number 1, learning to be kind.

Also, I need to remind myself I went into amnesia for over four decades and don't want to repeat that forgettable period in my life. I will forget all the advances I have made so far and don't need to start all over again. Well, I hope that is only a joke?

## Stu's humor returns in Florida

After Stu spent several winter months at his son's house in NE, he wanted to go back to his place in Florida. His son Wes straightened out his meds and nutrition issues. Wes probably thought it was past his time for him to go to Florida or anyplace soon. Stu is a little bit narcissistic and forgot to take his dog for a walk in the 15-degree mornings. Of course, after a few poops on his son's rug, Wes probably thought he was staying a little too long and eager to see him go back to Florida. As a joke, I asked Stu, "Did Wes leave your duffle bag on the front porch?"

I did not want to talk about my problems; he had enough of his own to deal with in NE. We didn't see Stu this spring because he flew directly to Florida from NE.

A few weeks after he returned to Florida, his personality came back; he was the Stu of the past, well, the Stu of the BD normal past. His son Wes gave him an automated voice system to monitor his meds and nutrition every hour of the day. He gets an automated woman's voice that reminds him all day long to take his meds and what to eat. He complains her voice is worse than a controlling nagging wife. I tell him it's better than going back to doing hard time prison life in the bitterly cold weather of NE. That usually keeps him quiet for a few days.

Stu even started to talk about promoting his video on the dangers of using drugs. Years ago, he created a short play and then a video to convince kids not to start to use drugs. He even mentioned it could end up on Broadway. Well, that is a joke, but it shows he is on his path to fulfilling his commitment to helping people with drug and alcohol issues. His program is all about teaching young kids not to start using drugs and alcohol.

As I say, I can tell if Stu is getting better if his sense of humor returns. Within a month, he decided to sell his little place in Florida. Both his son and I have been trying to get Stu to sell his place in Florida for a few years. His neighborhood was getting overrun with people on drugs just a few blocks away. One day there was a gunfight just blocks away from his house. Of course, I often told him of my bad experiences of living in the inner city for ten years; I did not recognize at the time how stressful my life was after the drug dealers took over our block. The WAVES Chart has an entry for living in dangerous areas.

He put a for sale sign in the front yard of his house, and within a few days, he had several people make offers on his house. The real estate market is hot in Florida, and investors are buying up houses in any condition in his area. Stu quickly found a low-cost condo in a 55 plus community in Florida.

He sold his house within a week and is looking for a low-cost 55 plus condo. I am so relieved to see him living a stable, BD normal lifestyle again. For the past several years, life has been difficult for Stu's son. It is very stressful for me to see his stressors accumulating up to the point he was heading into the emergency level stress zones. At one point, he went from stable to unstable after his doses of lithium were doubled, and his psychiatrist added several other meds. This caused his stable lifestyle to become unstable within days.

The stress on me was also very upsetting. I know how quickly he could go from unstable to suicidal. The WAVES Chart has an entry for this life stressor going from stable to unstable by taking toxic meds. Chapter 6 tells Stu's story and lists the situations that put him at the highest stress level of 7.

I told Stu we might not have survived to be older without supporting each other throughout life. He agreed many times we were the only ones that understood and supported each other. I often mention if he didn't find Dr. Freed in Florida, we might still be dealing with undiagnosed BD for the rest of our lives. We both agree if we did not get the help, we would not live much beyond midlife.

My hope is people will give the WAVES Workbook to other people, both mentally disabled and normal people. I think of the WAVES Chart as a learning aid for all people to learn more about BD.

## Lessons from a Native Indian storyteller

From living on the farm, I did see nature as a higher power as a spiritual religion based on the fundamental laws of nature. I traveled across the country three times but never felt sad about how the Native Indian nations were decimated by the White man. Back then, I was just racing from one place to another.

I found a video by Little Hawk, a Native American Storyteller [(Hawk) a YouTube video. I hope I am not offending the Native Indian peoples by attempting to interpret their beliefs. This Native American story needs to be told by an actual Native Indian storyteller. I hope everyone can find the video and listen to him speak in his own words.

Little Hawk, the storyteller, talked about the natural cycle of life and death. Little Hawk is an older man, probably about my age, and as he told his story, I listened very closely to every word he said. He was talking the truth about what is happening today in our nation.

He said, and I paraphrase, "America is dying from within because they forgot the instructions on how to live on earth." He spoke about how time evolves a then renews all over again. He thinks the time has come for renewal in America.

His wise and thoughtful words could be interpreted to be negative and very disturbing to many people, but I believe his prophecy is what America is going through right now. Cleansing and renewal is a natural cycle where everything may need to be destroyed only to be renewed again.

I have used his words and Native Indian wisdom as a basis for my beliefs about the fate of our nation. Hopefully, his wise predictions of our nation's future can be told in the future and throughout time. It is hard for me to put his thoughts into words. As you can tell, it's hard enough for me to put any thoughts into words. I encourage people to find his video and hear him speak in his own words.

## I have not been a strong climate change advocate
I have been a strong advocate for the mentally ill to get help early on, but I have not been active enough to protect our environment. Humans are destroying our planet. Our oceans are a dumping ground for trillions of tons of trash. I read yesterday the planet has over 5 trillion; that's not a billion pieces of plastic trash. That is a staggering amount of plastic, and plastic will not degrade like glass. We are strip-mining our precious earth to harvest a few ounces of precious metals, gold, and other minerals.

## I need to acknowledge climate change is real
I have been critical of the RADs climate change policies for a long time. I read that Maine has banned Styrofoam containers. I said years ago; plastic containers should be replaced by glass. Glass is basically sand and recyclable. The reality is clear; our planet is being destroyed acre by acre. I am afraid it is actually happening around the world. Climate change may be the only RAD policy I support. The POTUS disputes climate change is real. The wildfires in CA are a sign we are not following the rules of nature. Remember, someone once said, "Mother Nature makes the rules, and humans only need to follow them."

## Deforestation is real, even at the park
I see the destruction of the planet on a small scale near the pond, where I walk almost every day. About three years ago, the hillside near the pond had tall trees on a hill above a small pond. The rainwater flowed down the hill onto the small pond. The pond was teeming with wildlife, much like around our small farm in NE. Around the pond were cat-in-nine-tales with red-wing blackbirds, frogs, and other wildlife.

Just a few months ago, a developer cleared the entire hillside of trees. The developer destroyed the natural habitat and turned the small pond into a water catch basin. The entire natural habitat around the pond was bull dosed over, and the developers turned the pond into a concrete catch basin. Almost all the trees except three large fir trees were cut down on the hillside, and a few small trees were planted around the catch basin.

For over three years, the developer built over 25 homes on the land above the hillside. A sign entering the development stated a community of 25 custom homes starting at $500,000.

I am still upset because the developer did not need to cut down almost all the trees on the hillside or destroy the wildlife habitat around the little pond. I am sure it was more profitable to build custom houses without any trees.

Over the years, I have been in denial of the damage humans have caused to our environment. I claim to be such a lover of nature but have failed to speak out about how climate change affects our entire planet. I do believe our manmade pollution of the sky, earth, and the oceans have resulted in a climate change disaster we might not be able to reverse.

I remember a statement Einstein made, it read.

"Look deep into nature, and then you will understand everything better." Albert Einstein.

I believe Einstein is right; we do not understand nature because we do not follow the fundamental laws of nature. We are not treating and protecting Mother Earth as sacred and spiritual. We are polluting the oceans with plastic. The deforestation of the trees in the Amazon is happening at an alarming rate. We are strip-mining the land for a few thousand ounces of gold. We cannot even protect our fellow humans or show them kindness and respect.

## So why am I here on planet Earth?
So, I had to ask myself, why am I here? Did I find my purpose in this life? It became clear to me I needed to tell my story because I had the right knowledge and experience to complete the workbook.

I am here to experience a mental illness called bipolar disorder. I have studied mental illness from books and manuals and even attended a psychotherapy group with a woman, Sabrina, that has schizophrenia.

I have attended the BDS group for years to learn about mental illness and help myself and other people cope with BD. I learned to ask for and get support from many members of the BD group. I became an advocate for people with BD to get treatment early on. I also have a brother for support and advice from a very young age.

So, I am here on earth to experience BD and use my knowledge and experience to help other people. Like Owen, my life will not be without hardships, setbacks, and pain, but I should still live by Willy's 4 rules to live by. I still think my unworthy syndrome is one reason I have a difficult time accepting I will be successful in any project I undertake.

## I need to give myself credit
It is hard to believe it has been over 40 years since I took the Awake course. Many people in the course did grow spiritually, but now I realize I had several obstacles to overcome to get to a place where I am enlightened or more spiritual, you might say.

Now I understand I could not grow spiritually, until I discovered and dealt with several obstacles in my path, namely my BD, unworthy syndrome, amnesia, and alcoholism. I keep forgetting my hoarding disorder.

I need to give myself credit for handling all these complex and difficult issues, but it has taken me almost 80 years. I also need to show gratitude for the people that have helped me achieve my goals and supported me through many setbacks.

I believe we are sent to planet Earth to learn from our experiences and overcome obstacles during our visit. We all need to practice Willy's 4 rules to live by. His wisdom is so simple it must be true. I don't expect to love everyone but to show kindness and respect for all races, religions, and lifestyles. So, Willy was right; showing kindness toward everyone is the answer for the human race to survive and thrive. Humans need to reject a war and conflict mentality.

So, it has taken me almost 80 years to become more spiritually aware. Can I call myself a truly spiritual being? No, I am still learning; I like to think I am in the process of becoming a spiritual being. Becoming spiritual will take a paradigm shift in consciousness; I am not there yet. I have found my purpose and following a path to accomplish one goal in life. One goal, of course, is to help people with BD lead more productive, safe, and happy lives early on in life.

I don't expect many people with BD will discover, at 70 years old, they have been in a state of amnesia for over 45 years. Perhaps my story will encourage people that think they may have emotional issues to seek help early on in life.

I hope if people do discover they are living with unworthiness issues, they can find ways to overcome feelings of unworthiness. I personally need to keep reminding myself I deserve to be loved and be successful in life. I am not a child any longer and can make decisions to improve my self-worth and avoid any form of abuse.

I hope publishing this workbook is one way I am fulfilling a promise I made a decade ago to help people with BD to get help early on in life. Yes, I am finally giving myself credit for overcoming several difficult obstacles in my life. I am also within days of completing a major Outstanding Accomplishment, publishing The Bipolar WAVES Workbook.

The workbook is almost published. I just need to add these last stages of my life living with BD and the concerns I have for our nation's future.

## No extended camping trips are planned this summer

We didn't have any long vacation planned for this summer; we realized we would be camping at very rustic but inexpensive campgrounds. The state campgrounds are the only ones we can afford it right now. We have been out a few nights at the shore and to the state campgrounds in the mountains. We are fortunate and grateful to have time to spend in the Great Outdoors.

In the late fall, I decided to sell our kayaks; the last time I went kayaking, I had a difficult time sliding the kayak onto the roof of our small SUV. After selling the last kayak, I was thankful Nicole, and I was able to enjoy kayaking on lakes and the bays from the Adirondacks of NY State to the Outer Banks of NC.

I am thankful Nicole encouraged me to kayak up at the county lake many times while she was sleeping in order to work the night shift. She was aware kayaking was my spiritual retreat away from my BD normal life.

## The summer of dealing with my hoarding disorder

I rushed to complete my projects on our old house before winter. I had the chimney fixed and got another dumpster to fill to the top with my stuff. Yes, I am finally dealing with my hoarding disorder after picking up stuff off the street on trash day for years. I was attempting to be frugal at any cost, but now it is costing us $1 for each item I toss in the dumpster. I am feeling good about throwing out stuff I don't need; it is a form of therapy; they took up space in my mind. Maybe I am growing spiritually after all, but I still don't know what to do with our old shed; it is still leaning over and is now taking up space in my mind.

## The Navy confirmed UFO videos are real

In September 2019, a news article popped up on my tablet. It read "Navy Confirms UFO Videos Are Real. ". [(navy-confirms-ufo-videos-real, n.d.), The nightly RAD and MSA media did not have any breaking news reports that the Navy confirmed. UFOs are real. I needed to find the truth, very challenging in today's toxic news environment. I navigated over to the HISTORY website and found it was true.

## Navy wants us to refer to UFOs as UAPs'

According to the Navy, we now know UFOs are real. The Navy wants us to refer to UFOs as "Unidentified Aerial Phenomena," or UAPs, a more formal term for UFOs that don't have all the little-green men with overnight bags. I have always known UFOs are real, but this revelation is the last piece of the puzzle. I think it is interesting the national news is not reporting any updates to the most important admission you could say since man invented the wheel.

## Bob Lazar claims UFO's and ET's do exist

Now that we have the proof of real UFOs, then the possibility of extraterrestrial (ETs) beings becomes very real. A man named Bob Lazar [(Lazar, n.d.) claims he witnessed nine interstellar spacecraft, which were housed near area 51. He claims he was part of the reverse engineering program for over ten years. He also claimed he was briefed and worked on alien technology in the mid-70s.; a conflict occurred between the UFO group and the kids, as they called the ET's, which resulted in the death of over forty personnel. As I understand it, the aliens abandoned the site leaving behind nine spacecraft and a promise to return. Wow! Am I hearing the ET's promise to return, but for what, revenge? Am I getting any closer to answering why are ETs are here?

Bob Lazar also made a very revealing statement on his website, and I quote,

"The fact remains that there is a small autonomous group within the American government that is making decisions about what you and I are allowed to know about extraterrestrial life and humanity's interaction with it." Bob Lazar.

From his statement, I could speculate about two things. First, UFOs and ETs do exist. Secondly, our government is hiding secrets about extra-terrestrial life and why ETs are here. For years I just assumed ETs do exist and are here, but I want to know why they are here.

I will call the small autonomous group the covert UFO group. Is that what Ike was warning our nation about, a small UFO group and the MIC are becoming too powerful?

## Ben Rich of Skunk Works said we have spaceships

Ben Rich of Skunk Works made a statement about a secret that could benefit humanity. He said, and I paraphrase,

"We already have means to travel among the stars, but this technology is locked in a Black Box, and it would take an act of God to ever get them out to benefit humanity."

Any secret that could enable the human race to live on the planet in harmony with nature should be called a super-secret. The super-secret may disclose the mysteries of the universe or harness enough energy in a drop of rain to power the entire planet with free electricity. Ben said we already have a spaceship to go to the stars.

Other comments Ben made before he passed away in 1995 was interesting, and I paraphrase again;

Someone asked Ben, "How does the propulsion system work?"

Ben replied, "Let me ask you, how does ESP work?"

The man replied, "All points in time and space are connected" Ben then said, "That's how it is done."

Does that mean the super-secret is all about developing our 6th sense to gain advanced knowledge? As I understand ESP or psychic abilities, it is about using our other senses to gain information. Several visual guidance processes at the Awake course were designed to tap into that ESP universal knowledge. I did not understand ESP. All these psychic abilities or ESP stuff does not make any sense but is just more nonsense right now.

## Why don't we use super-secret technology to benefit all mankind?

Ben Rich's statement makes it clear for some reason, someone or some group, I will call the covert UFO group, does not want advanced technology to benefit humanity. Who or what could that possibly be?

Some people said Tesla had inventions that could provide enough energy to power the entire planet with free electricity. Could the covert UFO groups and the MIC have acquired Tesla's and other advanced technology from ETs to provide power and other resources free to everyone on the planet?

I believe we are close to a full disclosure event that will prove extraterrestrials exist and why they are here, I hope I am still here on the planet to see it happen.

How could any small covert UFO group or any individual deny the world free energy and hide super secrets that could benefit all mankind? Another afterthought, which corporations or people would not profit if the planet had free energy? We'll let's see, the MIC, including the oil, gas, auto industry, and the utility corporations around the globe, would not profit from free energy. Now that possibility makes me quite upset; why don't all the covert groups want to help all mankind?

## Has our nation been mistreating aliens for 75 years?

I found some information that may explain why the covert UFO group does not want to disclose anything about extraterrestrials or why they are here. The Navy did disclose UFOs do exist. For years I always thought after the first atomic bomb went off in the desert in the '40s set off an intergalactic alarm across the universe. So, I guess the reason aliens are here has something to do with nuclear weapons.

I watched the film [(Long, Alien Crash Retrieval, 2016) that showed after a UFO crashed in 1941, 6 years before Roswell, a military recovery team rushed to the scene of the UFO crash. Small alien beings were found dead at the crash site. A clergyman was summoned to give the alien beings their last rights. People were threatened with severe punishment for releasing any information about the UFO or the alien beings.

Total secrecy (cover-up) was also the case with the famous Roswell UFO crash. Then the most troubling accusations came out; over the years, our military may have intentionally shot down some UFOs, and some aliens died; others were captured after several UFOs crashed across the US. Later on, special recovery teams were sent to collect downed UFOs and aliens from around the world.

Bob Lazar and others claimed the military reverse-engineered alien technology for our own technological advancement.

Let me try to process all that troubling information about our relationship with ETs. A special team collects crashed UFOs. Our small UFO group has been capturing, harming, and possibly killing aliens from other planets to advance our nation's technology. I read back in the 50s, ETs wanted the superpowers to eliminate all nuclear weapons on the planet. Our nation, along with other superpowers, did not agree to eliminate all nuclear weapons on the planet. I understand extraterrestrials are closely watching nuclear installations around the globe.

What does that say about our small UFO covert groups within our own military-industrial establishment? I guess you could argue our military did not want to fall behind in the nuclear arms race during the Cold War with Russia. Another UFO expert thought full disclosure would cause panic, civil unrest, and destabilize world economies.

If we did intentionally shoot down, kill and harm aliens, any hostile action could put our entire nation at grave risk of retaliation by the aliens. Bob Lazar also claimed we have a small UFO group that controls what the public is allowed to know about extraterrestrial life. The UFO puzzle is missing a few pieces. Why won't the small UFO group just release the truth about UFOs and ETs?

I believe our military should not harm any species in the universe unless we are attacked or harmed by ETs. I am no expert on UFOs, but I cannot find any proof aliens are hostile; aliens have not invaded planet Earth yet.

I do think human abductions by aliens have occurred, and aliens are possibly creating human hybrids. I also think hybridization is a natural evolution of all the species in the universe. Of course, my views are just my opinions on the status of our relationship with extraterrestrials.

## Will anyone help the mentally ill?

I don't want to give the impression I understand physical or psychic energy or other psychic phenomena, but I think ETs will have a powerful voice in the future of the human race on or off planet Earth.

If the covert UFO groups are mistreating alien beings, what are the chances covert groups will help and protect the mentally ill or disabled?

I guess we will need to use ESP or other psychic methods to help all the mentally ill, but how do we learn how to do that? I did not learn how to use my Extra Sensory Perception (ESP) at the Awake course, but some people did. I remember the guy that used remote viewing to see his relatives at an outdoor gathering 3000 miles away in Italy.

## I dropped my interest in UFOs

My quest to find out why extraterrestrials are here was interrupted by more political drama. The Speaker of the House (SOH) announced the start of a formal impeachment inquiry against President Trump. It did not surprise me because the Special Councils' report did not convict the POTUS of collusion with Russia. It was predictable they would start yet another investigation after the Special Council's report exonerated the POTUS.

I dropped my interest in finding out why UFOs are here. My time was consumed by the nonstop impeachment hearings of Trump.

We had a great Thanksgiving dinner this year. I have delayed publishing the workbook again until after the holidays.

## Stage 13 The pandemic is here

This Christmas has been a very stressful time for me. The very unseasonal cold weather reminds me of the bitterly cold weather in New England. I will admit I am envious of Stu living like a millionaire in warm sunny Florida. Here he has a condo in Florida and a place in New England in the summer. Perhaps next year, Stu will summer on Nantucket and live on a yacht to be closer to his yacht club millionaires.

Our family is not doing well. Ryan is on disability, and I am having another bad spell, as I call it. I am still stable on effective meds and living a BD normal life but need to accept this is not a "Normal" life and never will be.

I want to plan a short vacation in February down to South Carolina, but we don't have a reliable tow vehicle to make the round trip. I need to look forward to something besides another 100 days and nights of winter.

In an attempt to boost my mood, I went shopping for a used tow vehicle, but I had sticker shock after inspecting a used older model pickup truck. I overheard a salesman telling a couple they could not qualify to get financing on an older used truck I was looking just a few minutes earlier in the used car lot.

I did not want to have a salesman tell me I would not qualify for even an old truck unless we put 100% cash down. I am truly grateful we have enjoyed camping up and down the East Coast for over ten years.

I need to blame myself for not making enough money to even buy a decent RV that can travel further than 100 miles.

Nicole is scheduled to work on New Year's Eve again this year. After Nicole retired, she thought they would not want her to work, but they did call almost every week. Now she can pick when she wants to work. I need to acknowledge Nicole has been our caregiver for years now. She has supported both Ryan and me ever since we moved back from Florida over 25 years ago.

I think to live a good BD normal lifestyle, most people with BD need a caregiver, someone to guide and support us without judging or criticizing our odd behavior. My brother has his son Wes for support, and both Ryan and I have Nicole.

On a positive note, I am not having any more intense traumatic recollections of the past after emerging from a state of amnesia years ago. Years ago, I would dwell on the highly emotional recollections that would take me back to the heartbreak over my first love, especially around Christmas time.

Now I recognize it is about my unworthy syndrome more than the traumatic breakup. I have more sad recollections now about the events I experienced before I even met Maria. My childhood abuse and the traumatic loss of my father did cause my unworthy syndrome. I am trying to put sad recollections in the past and move on. I don't want to contact Maria any longer. Nicole was right; Maria may not want to bring up old forgotten memories.

Sometimes a bad spell could last for months, especially if I was severely depressed and had a severe case of SAD. I am beginning to think these bad spells are one reason I feel so stuck in the past. I not only do not feel loved, but I don't feel I am worthy of being successful or being happy. The negative feelings spread into other areas of life. I am getting closer to publishing the workbook, hoping it will boost my confidence and self-worth issues.

### The House impeaches the POTUS

I cannot keep up with the political turmoil in our nation. A transcript was released to the press about a conversation Trump had with the new President of Ukraine. Within weeks of hearing the secret testimony of the whistleblower and other people picked by the impeachment committee, the House hastily voted to impeach President Trump just days before Christmas. Instead of sending the articles of impeachment to the Senate for a trial, the SOH decided to wait until January 7, 2020.

### Is China covering up a possible pandemic?

The news came out that China has a possible coronavirus pandemic. A coronavirus had broken out in one province, and people were ordered to wear face masks. China announced 7000 people were diagnosed, and over 100 died from the virus.

As always, I filter all news through my scattered mind until I become even more confused by the reports. Then the news reported voice-activated drones were hovering overhead, telling the Chinese people to wear their face masks. Entire cities were on lockdown and under quarantine. People from the quarantined provinces were told to stay inside their houses, and only one person per household was permitted to go out and get food and household supplies.

China has blocked its citizens from using the internet for several years, and now they are openly reporting a potential virus attack that could spread into a worldwide pandemic. This disclosure could possibly be the beginning of a global humanitarian disaster.

Reports of entire hospitals in China are being used just to house coronavirus victims—videos of dead people lying on the floor in hospitals. I am fearful China may not be reporting the full extent of the potential pandemic outbreak to the world. I am also very afraid that the actual threats to the human populations of China may be far more serious than what is reported by the Chinese news media.

Even more disturbing reports show health care workers dressed in full hazmat protection-type gear taking the temperatures of people in public, very surreal.

Our Center for Disease Control (CDC) seems to be preparing for a potential pandemic. The POTUS has ordered people that return from China to land in only seven airports in our nation, and travelers were held under quarantine for 14 days.

One undercover reporter found out Chinese doctors wanted to warn the world two months earlier of a possible pandemic but were silenced by the CCP. If China can cover up a potential or real pandemic, then what else are they not telling the world? A cruise ship has been quarantined near Japan. One man said he must stay in his interior cabin with no windows 24/7.

I am having a difficult time processing what is going on in our nation, but the reports from China seem surreal. The daily broadcasts from China are right out of a 1950's B&W horror movie.

## The COVID-19 pandemic is here

On January 21, 2020, the first case of the COVID-19 coronavirus in the United States was confirmed by the Centers for Disease Control and Prevention (CDC).

On January 31, President Trump imposed travel restrictions preventing foreign nationals from entering the U.S. if they visited China within the previous two weeks. Predictable outrage from RAD media, claiming Trump is, of course, a racist.

### Super Bowl LIV 54 SF49 errs and Kansas City Chiefs
Super Bowl 54 was scheduled for February 2, 2020. The Philadelphia Eagles or New England Patriots did not make it to the Super Bowl, and the game was not that exciting anyway. We wanted the Chiefs to win because the Chiefs coach was a former Eagles coach and a good guy; the Chiefs won Super Bowl 54.

### The Senate impeachment trial ended in an acquittal
The impeachment trial did not remove President Trump from office. The Senate acquitted Trump of all charges on February 5, 2020.

The media was airing nonstop coverage of the possible pandemic. I was a bit irritated Congress was spending so much time and effort to impeach Trump while the real threat was from the pandemic and China.

### Biden wins Super Tuesday
On March 3, In the Super Tuesday contest, Biden came out on top. Super Tuesday is when one-third of the delegates are up for grabs.

As I watched as Biden gave his victory speech, I noticed he had trouble even reading the teleprompter, and I thought he had a speech impediment or maybe a bit of a memory issue. Someone mentioned said he had issues with stuttering when a kid. I felt sorry for what he will go, though, for the rest of his life. All these candidates are about the same age as me. Bernie had a heart attack, and Biden seems to have memory issues.

### The WHO declared COVID-19 a worldwide pandemic
On March 11, 2020, the World Health Organization (WHO) declared the coronavirus a worldwide pandemic. They said the virus spread to 114 countries. The mortality rate was estimated at 2 % on January 29, 2020. The mortality rate could be over 3 percent. The

rising estimates caused panic, and everyone was braced for a massive worldwide loss of life.

I told Nicole we might need to get an emergency plan together. We ordered 50 face masks online but then found out they were not effective because they would not cover the entire face.

I talked Nicole into buying enough food and water for at least two weeks. In the afternoon, I went to our warehouse dry goods store, and the parking lot was full; even carts were in short supply. The store was so crowded people could not go down the aisles. Most people had carts filled with everything, including piles of diapers and bathroom tissue.

After watching many survival stories, I learned water, food, shelter, and fire are essential for long-term survival. People cannot live after a week without water and about 3 to 4 weeks without food. I am afraid this is the calm before the storm.

## I needed to delay publishing the workbook again

I should have published the workbook months ago, but now I need to deal with the unique stress of the pandemic. I waited too long again. My priorities need to be reevaluated; the virus is a real threat to most older people, including me.

On March 12th, the POTUS added some new policies regarding the coronavirus virus they named (COVID-19). Today he stopped all travel from Europe for 30 days. Of course, the RAD media criticized this ban and emphasized that healthcare workers needed masks and test kits.

## The POTUS declares a National Emergency

It was Friday the 13th of March, 2020, when I returned from my walk in the park and heard the President address the nation. When

I heard the two alarming words "National Emergency," my heart sank" after he said those are very big words.

The President talked about how private industry has come to aid to help the (COVID-19) task force. Companies like the two biggest labs were going to streamline (COVID-19) testing. Even several large superstores were going to allow testing in their parking lots. He described how the government was going to partner with the private sector to speed up testing and provide testing and masks and other support for the (COVID-19). He did not mention the CDC.

One of the best plans was to use teleconferencing to have doctors communicate and diagnose people suspected of having the (COVID-19) online. The biggest search engine website even offered to create a new website to allow people to determine their chance of having the virus (COVID-19).

Weeks ago, experts not from the government told the (COVID-19) task force thousands of people could not show up at the emergency rooms of hospitals around the country. People criticized Trump for everything, but I think he is getting a handle on the (COVID-19) disaster. I do think that not providing masks and hazmat-type suits and gowns have allowed the (COVID-19) to spread very fast.

Some people think Friday the 13th brings bad luck, but I believe this will be the worst bad luck Friday the 13th in the history of our nation.

Today they closed all the state liquor stores in PA. I hope they have thought that action through; some people need their beer and sports games. Oh, and they closed down all sports bars. I was one of those people years ago that sat at a bar for hours. Now I just shame people with addictions to sports and booze. Sorry, just trying to find a little humor to help my schizoid affective anxiety, my worst fear. What will happen when people have neither booze nor sports? If our cell phone service goes down, we are all in trouble. What about people on meth and opioids? Our lives could be very stressful from now on. The only positive thing is we will still have a source of food, and our kids are safe for now.

I spoke to Matt yesterday, and he still plans to rent an apartment in a marginal part of Philly; I told him about the 1977 blackout in NYC. Just a few blocks of NYC had a power blackout and ended in anarchy in the streets in a matter of hours. The power was restored in about 24 hours, law and order were restored, but it was a wake-up call. Matt ignored my concerns and plans to live in Philly; no one ever takes my advice, including myself.

## Most schools in the country are closed

Most of the schools in the nation are closed until further notice. I was very upset because I think kids get support and comfort by being with other kids. Bonnie and her friends were very pleased with the decision. Sadly, we think Bonnie should not visit us until more is known about the virus.

On March 16, most schools in the country are closed across the nation. The Dow Jones jumped up by over 2,100 points, or 11.3 percent—its biggest one-day percentage gain since 1933.

On March 31, 2020, the Dow recorded the worst quarter in US history with a 23.3% drop. Our nation seems to be on an economic rollercoaster.

## It is time for old people to sacrifice

Our brave young soldiers fought in WW II to protect our nation from an evil dictator. Many men and women made the ultimate sacrifice and lost their lives in dreadful and violent battles.

I say, now we should let young people go back to work under some restrictions. Many reasonable precautions can be used to keep old people safe. Most old people do not work and could shelter in place. Watching millions of healthy young people and kids isolated behind closed walls is not the solution to our problems; it is a problem. As the days pass by, the pandemic is quickly dragging down our economy and our chances for recovery from the world's worst financial collapse in history.

I only speak for myself when I say I am willing to risk contracting COVID-19 to allow my family and loved ones to live a better life in the future. I have been fortunate to have time to enjoy the freedoms under the 1776 Constitution and the Great Outdoors all my life. I am almost 80 now and in poor health, so how much longer do I have to live anyway?

As in wartime, it is time to talk about sacrificing some of our older citizens in order to save our nation from total collapse. Emergency care workers battling COVID-19 are now the soldiers on the front line fighting for our survival. They bravely go into a coronavirus war zone every day.

### Stu is in lockdown in Florida
Stu is having a difficult time in Florida; the strict lockdowns are very difficult for his well-being. He is a very social guy, and he is locked up in his condo. Even the community pool is closed until further notice. He scheduled an AA meeting outside with thirty people all wearing masks, and the police came and broke up the meeting 20 minutes after the meeting began.

### Stu Meets Alice
Stu said he met a woman named Alice at the AA meeting, and he said she was very friendly, almost too friendly. Stu said she called

him three or four times a day, and he did not know how to tell her to stop calling him. The next day Alice told him she needed to go with her father to get her monthly injection. I asked Stu, "Why does she need an injection?" I was afraid Alice might be hiding some sort of fatal illness. That was the case for Lara; she did not disclose her she had an incurable form of cancer for months.

Stu said, "Alice was very vague and did not tell me why she needed a monthly injection" Stu then said, "Alice is about 60 years old and says she wants to marry me. Wes is working day and night to protect old people at the nursing home. He is not afraid of contracting the virus."

I did not know what to tell Stu; Alice seems to have some sort of health issues, and Wes is at risk of COVID-19. Stu relies on Wes for support. The pandemic is the biggest stressor for Stu right now.

## Can Ryan and I both shelter in place?

I am also having a difficult time with the pandemic. I thought I could spend all my time on the workbook, but I am more concerned about contracting and dying of COVID-19. The workbook is not my top priority in the middle of the pandemic. I am caught in quicksand I cannot move forward to complete anything.

Ryan is also having a difficult time with the pandemic, as well as Nicole and me, of course. Ryan is still in denial of his personal issues and comes up with some bizarre thoughts and actions. The other night he wanted to move into our camper in the backyard of our house at 10 pm in total darkness. Our camper has a cover and no heat or electricity. Then he wanted to sleep in his car out back and needed a long extension cord to reach his car in the back of our house.

Here I am out in the garage looking for an extra-long extension cord at 10:30 at night in a cold garage. I found the extension cord but could not find Ryan; he drove off in his car. He returned a few hours and decided to stay in his room. That was enough for me; I needed to separate quickly from his bizarre demands and behavior.

Over the years, Ryan has burned his bridges; so, to speak, it will be hard for him to get help now because many psychiatrists will not treat him without a one-on-one session. He does not have any health insurance in case he needs to be admitted to a hospital. This is my worst fear; he does not have a psychiatrist or anyone to treat his issues. Actually, I don't think anyone is being admitted to any emergency room; everyone is afraid of a COVID-19 outbreak. Most hospitals are afraid of people with the COVID-19 virus. I have given up at this point.

I have threatened to move downstairs until he can bear some responsibility for his life and our wellbeing. Nicole is at her breaking point with dealing with two mentally challenged adults. It is time for me to shelter in place downstairs and keep the little sanity I have remaining to deal with this pandemic crisis.

### The pandemic is causing enormous stress

I needed to score my WAVES Stress Zone level again to evaluate if I am accumulating too much stress with the pandemic, Ryan, and "discussions" with Nicole about our 110-year-old house and Ryan's issues. I was very upset we lost thousands of dollars in the value of our old house in just a few weeks. I should not complain because millions of people are losing their homes, jobs, and their quality of life.

I scored these new stressful situations using the WAVES Chart in Appendix A. I added up these stresses of the coronavirus and old issues dealing with Ryan and our old house. I added the loss in the value of our old house as the stress of a big financial loss. Any hope of selling a 110-year-old house is slim to none by now. I also added 50 points to my WAVES Chart for the stress of the pandemic.

My stress level now is a concern but not an emergency situation requiring hospitalization, but I need to use caution to avoid a possible psychotic episode.

I cannot blame Ryan for all our problems; we are all under enormous stress. I immediately understood the unique situation and decided to let him stay with us until the shock of this pandemic settled down. He could suddenly leave and rent a rundown apartment in a less than desirable part of Philly. I know he might be taking advantage of the situation, but he might move out and never talk to us again.

I don't think I can keep accusing Ryan of ignoring his emotional issues, he is not doing anything illegal, and in fact, he is supporting Bonnie under extraordinary situations.

I need to monitor my stress levels during this pandemic. I have My WAVES Chart listed in more detail in Chapter 9.

## Is online Tele Help therapy the wave of the future?
We had a family meeting that night. We came to an agreement he could stay with us under two conditions. First, he must get a healthcare plan with mental illness coverage. The second condition, he must find a talk therapist soon, preferably a good psychiatrist or psychologist. He agreed, and we hugged to seal the deal. I told Ryan I loved him.

After we reached our agreement, he said he was ready to sign a rent agreement over the weekend. He said he was talking to Bonnie from his car window at her place every day.

The angry, hostile unsympathetic hypertension was immediately lifted. I felt we might come out of this crisis without someone, including me having a total breakdown or even worse.

These are extremely troubling times for everyone, especially challenging for people with mental illness, including myself, of course. So, the WAVES Chart attempts to look at stress coming from external factors and internal family situations.

The day after our agreement was signed, Nicole searched the internet for healthcare plans. The basic insurance plan cost was over $400 a month with an $8000 deductible. Just one year of coverage would be about $5000. He shopped around for just a mental health professional and found most good psychiatrists charge $100 to $150 per visit. Our small town has mostly middle-class families, but we live in a very wealthy county in PA.

Ryan did not want to call my psychiatrist, but he did call a family doctor he had a few visits with a few years ago. I understand she has not returned his call after almost a week now. He thought many good psychiatrists in our upscale towns do not need to accept people with private healthcare coverage, only cash or check, not even a credit card.

## Is Tele Help the future way to deliver mental healthcare?

Ryan found an online website that provides online therapy via email, text messaging, and some virtual online, virtual face-to-face therapy for about $200 to $400 per month. This option I will call Tele Help is a wave of the future.

Due to the coronavirus, I am sure many healthcare professionals do not want face-to-face meetings in their offices at this time. The more I thought about this new virtual online therapy, the more I am convinced virtual online therapy is the answer to delivering both mental and physical healthcare to millions of people. These online virtual mental treatment methods could also use face-to-face video conferencing to even deliver group psychotherapy sessions to people thousands of miles apart.

I told Ryan I was proud of him; he has found a way to help himself over these very troubling times. I see Tele Help online therapy could even be used for virtual BDS group meetings. It could be very much like Rosie's support groups, but online.

That reminds me to return Rosie's call before the pandemic hit months ago. I did not want to call her and talk for the n$^{th}$ time about my frustration over Ryan's lack of responsibility any longer.

I called Stu and told him I was going to buy Ryan a cheap $20 one-way airline ticket to Florida and have him stay at his condo for a few months, maybe until the 4$^{th}$ of July.

Stu did not appreciate my humor; he was also stressed about; his son. Wes is caring for seven residents of his nursing home with the COVID-19 virus in NE. Wes made the decision to allow the healthy nursing staff to take care of the other 100 plus residents. Talk about leadership and risking your own health and welfare to help others less fortunate. Wes has already rescued Stu once after he became very ill in Florida. Back then, Wes flew down to Florida, shuttered up his cottage, took him out of the hospital, and flew him back to NE.

Stu told me the police broke up his AA meeting again because they had 30 people at an AA meeting and not the ten people required by the safe distancing rules. Oh, and they were all outside practicing safe distancing rules. And they say I am crazy, but these politically-driven authoritarian orders are insane and a clear and present danger to our freedoms.

## I did not want Stu to reject Alice

I asked Stu about Alice, and he told me he needed to tell her to stop calling him. Stu said she has bizarre behavior and still calls him several times a day. She tells him she wants to get married every time she calls. Stu tells her he does not want to get married to anyone.

He said he learned Alice was in a mental hospital for a month. I said it sounds like she has a very serious mental illness. That ended our conversation.

After our conversation, I began to feel very sad, here Alice is practically begging Stu not to reject her. In my opinion, I fear Alice is living with the most serious mental illness, schizophrenia, and has been rejected by hundreds of people, maybe most people over her 60 years on this planet. I often complain about how stressful life can be with BD, but Alice is living alone in a world I cannot even imagine it exists. I found an article online about treatments for schizophrenia. Sometimes psychiatrists do recommend monthly injections instead of daily meds.

I felt so sad and did not want Stu to reject Alice. Doesn't her wish to be married only say, "Please, someone love me"? I thought of Sabrina, the woman with schizophrenia, and how I was so afraid to become her friend. I also rejected Sabrina because her thoughts were scattered and bizarre.

I called Stu back the following day and told him, "Alice is probably suffering from schizophrenia. She has had a very difficult life; her family has shunned her, and she is just asking for someone to love her. Isn't that what everyone with a mental illness wants? Remember you were shunned by your family before and after you moved to Florida."

Stu said, "I still can't take her bizarre behavior.". Then I asked him, "What would Willy say? He would say, be kind to everyone." That ended our conversation.

After our call ended, the words "She just wants to be loved." kept repeating in my mind. This is like the same phrase I have heard in the BDS group many times.

A few days later, I called Stu again and asked him, "Could you just give Alice some hope. Maybe offer to take her for a walk, even order takeout from a fast-food restaurant and go to a park. Anything to show someone cares about her. Just a little kindness could go a long way to make her feel better.".

Stu called me the next day and did plan to order takeout for her birthday. I told Stu, "That is all you can do is offer to help her. I know we all have problems of our own, like the pandemic to deal with on a daily basis."

I guess I am super sensitive to any form of rejection, especially when I see someone that is all alone and just asking to be loved. Willy was right; just a little kindness can go a long way to make some people feel much better.

## Is China covering up the source of the pandemic?
Reports China did not allow domestic flights within China after the virus spread in Wuhan, China, but did allow international flights to fly to hundreds of countries around the world.

In my humble opinion, this could be considered using a virus as a bioweapon to destroy the economies and people's freedom around the world, including our own. Further reports, they are secretly testing nuclear devices. A press release by China claimed they had no cases of the coronavirus that day. Could that be pure propaganda?

## Has China become the world superpower?
I understand our nation has lost over 6 trillion dollars of wealth since the pandemic started at the beginning of 2020. Some economists

claim China has surpassed us as the world economic power in just a few months. No surprise, according to the film How China Got Rich [(Wood, 2019), we shipped our factories overseas decades ago. Now I am very concerned we will ship our farmland overseas; I hope I am just kidding.

## Joe Biden disappears from view

Joe Biden, the Democratic nominee, has not had an open press conference for weeks. Speculation, the DNC and RAD politicians do not want him to answer questions because his answers are rambling and incoherent.

I don't want to pile on Joe because I believe he has some more serious cognitive issues than just a speech impediment. His mind does not seem to follow a train of thought. Now I cannot criticize his lack of mental alertness because I suffer from similar issues.

I think it is a sad situation when the RADs are propping him up and encouraging him not to be in the spotlight. He does not act as the leader of the free world, although I don't know if we are free any longer.

## Operation Warp Speed to develop a COVID-19 vaccine

On May 15, the Trump administration formally announced Operation Warp Speed for accelerating the development of a COVID-19 vaccine. Several other projects were unveiled to develop antiviral therapeutic medicines. As predicted, the RAD press downplayed the announcement as just improbable and based on showmanship.

## As the COVID-19 death toll approaches 100,000

The RAD state-run cable propaganda network CNN still displays the number of deaths in our nation. As the death toll reaches over 100,000, I am sure the RAD media will politicize the deaths as Trumps' failure to govern. It seems every day the RAD cable networks eagerly watch the death count climb above 100,000 and then will blame Trump.

To be fair, I want to see the number of deaths from drugs, the flu, overdoses (ODs), alcoholism, and suicide listed under the number of deaths by the coronavirus. For example, if the COVID-19 took 500,000 lives in 2020, the statistics might look like this on December 31st of 2020.

Coronavirus est. 2020 ..........500,000
Influenza Flu (2018-19)..........61,000
Drug overdoses (OD)...............67,000
Suicide .....................................50,000
Alcohol ....................................88,000
Diabetes ..................................83,000
Cancer ...................................600,000
Auto deaths.............................35,000

These numbers are rough estimates, but we are not taking into account other causes of death and quality of life issues into consideration, issues like homelessness, poverty, depression, anxiety, and mental illnesses like bipolar.

The RAD media relentlessly puts out the narrative the number of cases of COVID-19 will increase dramatically if masks, social distancing, and other stay-at-home rules are not enforced. Of course, increases in the number of cases will increase as more people get tested positive for the virus. I also claim that hospitalization rates and deaths will not increase enough to shut down the economy forever.

## Let's put this COVID-19 pandemic in perspective

So, let's put this COVID-19 pandemic in perspective. We may hit a total of 500,000 total deaths in 2020 and, let's say, another 2.7

million deaths from other sources. Really this COVID thing is tearing apart our entire nation into irrational fear and crippling lockdowns. Estimates of about 50 percent of COVID-19 deaths will be people over 75. Maybe 250,000 people would have died of natural causes anyway within a few years. I don't want to minimize the loss of life by COVID-19 but let's step back and view this pandemic from 30,000 feet and not from some WH COVID-19 briefing by lifetime bureaucrats.

I predict the pandemic will be over after an effective vaccine is approved. The point I am trying to make is this, the deaths and suffering from OD, alcoholism, and suicide will rise significantly in 2020 and then continue to rise every year thereafter.

People are going to die. I have said I would take the risk of contracting COVID-19 if it could help younger people stay in school and families live productive, happy, and prosperous lives. I think many old people are basically selfish and want to live a lavish lifestyle while working middle-class Americans struggle with the pandemic, job losses, and paying off their mortgages.

## Allowing drugs to freely enter our nation was the next mistake

I think it is a mistake to lock down the nation due to the pandemic, but other mistakes go unnoticed. Allowing the drug cartels to import and distribute drugs freely inside our country is a huge mistake. As the Drug Inc [(Inc, Drugs) documentaries reveal, tons of drugs have been smuggled into our country from Colombian and Mexican cartels in the 70s and 80, s.

One episode exposed the corruption around Miami. Tons not kilos of drugs were imported, and millions of dollars in cash were laundered and used to build high-rise buildings and other legit businesses. Could China be using the same business model today? Is

China using drug money to build factories and high-rise buildings around the world?

## An unarmed African American killed by a White officer

On May 25th, a bystander in Minneapolis took a video of a police officer holding down an unarmed African American George Floyd suspect by kneeling on his neck; he died. The protestors demanded the other officers on the scene be arrested immediately and held in jail. The community protesters led to rioting and looting.

From what I saw on the video was a criminal act, pure and simple. The authorities waited until enough evidence was collected before an arrest was made on formal charges. For several nights the protests became more violent, and looting spread across the city. Basically, the mayor said they could not arrest people because they were outnumbered. The next night a curfew went into effect at 8 pm, but the police did not enforce the curfew and arrest people.

On the day of George Floyd's memorial service, millions of people in hundreds of cities around the world peacefully demonstrated in honor of his untimely death.

Peaceful demonstrations were held in many cities across the nation and overseas, but some protesters rioted and looted after dark. I believe George Floyd's tragic murder is much worse than the Rodney King beating back in the 90s. The police were exonerated back then of all charges. I think this time, the police will be held accountable for George Floyd's tragic death.

## Stu is still in lockdown in Florida

Stu is getting condo fever in Florida. The management of the condo is harassing people that do not follow their strict COVID-19 guidelines. After protests by the condo owners, the pool at his condo community is open but under the strict mask and distancing rules. A woman used an "unauthorized" lounge chair, whatever that is at the pool, and violated some arbitrary pool rule.

The woman that used the "unauthorized" lounge chair was banned from the pool. What is happening to normal rational people? I believe very sadistic people are coming out of the closet and using the pandemic as a way to overstep their authority. They are on a power trip by ordering arbitrary rules and regulations that make no sense but a ton of nonsense.

## Is Ryan becoming more responsible?

The day-to-day challenges of dealing with the pandemic are causing fear and anxiety across the nation. We decided Bonnie was not a threat to spread COVID-19. Ryan was talking to Bonnie from his car window. We do see a risk of us contracting the virus from Bonnie, but I think the benefits outweigh the risks. We want her to stay with us but go back and stay with her mom Jane at any time. Bonnie is handling the pandemic very well. She can text her friends and does not whine and complain about the lockdowns. We are very proud of her, and I am sure she will be a kind and caring adult.

I think the pandemic has made us all more aware of the important things in our lives. Ryan is spending more quality time with Bonnie, but he does not want us to ask him about personal issues. We respect his wishes and assume he is getting some help from online Tele Help talk therapy. Bonnie is going to school online; personally, I think it is a total waste of time for most students.

I am thankful Ryan has shown much more responsibility and is taking good care of Bonnie. We have dinner together once or twice a week, something we never did a year ago before the pandemic.

Maybe he is using Tele Help to help him get some direction in his life. We don't pry into his personal matters anymore.

The problem, I think I am a trained professional, but I do not want to become a nagging parent and pseudo-life coach. No one ever takes my advice anyway. I should worry about my own problems before I over psychoanalyze other people's issues.

The pandemic did cause some major challenges, but it also made us value our family and friends more. The pandemic has brought us together, and we realize our lives are far better than many people in our nation and around the globe. Many families are dealing with job losses and the loss of loved ones dying of COVID-19.

Although tempting, I made the decision not to project my BD mental illness onto Ryan. Throughout this workbook, I have been very careful not to diagnose anyone with BD; I will leave that to the mental health professionals.

On July 14, Pharmaceutical Company Moderna announced that its vaccine would begin the final phase of testing, with approximately 30,000 human volunteers.

## *I need to reevaluate spending time on the workbook*
Before the pandemic arrived here from China, I was just days, well, weeks away from publishing the workbook.

Now I am reevaluating the risks vs. the rewards. I told Nicole I could be dead in 5 days if I contract COVID-19. My age and preexisting health conditions make me at a very high risk of dying of COVID-19. I am not afraid of dying but worry what a mess I would be leaving Nicole. I don't have any life insurance, and she would need to sell our house during the pandemic. Ironically that is how my father left our mother, no life insurance, and a farm in need of major repairs.

## Biden picks the former SF prosecutor for VP

Nicole found me on the front porch to tell me the news; Senator Kamala Harris is Biden's pick for VP. I told Nicole months ago the DNC would pick a Chicago insider to be his VP running mate. Joe Biden has not held a major press conference in weeks and gives very bizarre brief interviews from his basement bunker. One reporter asked if he was going to take a cognitive mental test. His reply and I paraphrase, "Hey man, why would I ever do that? Let the people decide."

I am not going to criticize or mock former VP Biden because I do believe the DNC campaign power brokers are shamelessly using and abusing Biden to accomplish their radical agenda. They do not show any human traits of compassion to help him. I am surprised Joe's wife does not stand up and stop the power brokers from propping him up and letting social media and others treat him like a piñata at a kid's birthday party. It is hard for me to watch because, over the years, I have watched people with mental issues in the BDS group being abused by their families, employers, and coworkers without a shred of kindness or compassion.

One reporter claimed former VP Biden has pre-dementia. I am not saying Biden is struggling with dementia, but it is obvious he lacks the concentration and ability to handle the highly stressful job as POTUS.

## Talk show guest warns the 2020 election results could be contested

A guest on a conservative talk show made very interesting but very disturbing remarks about a possible contested 2020 election. He warned the 2020 election results could be contested because mail-in ballots have been mailed out to millions of voters across the nation. As I understand it, the ballots will be mailed to all registered voters, but in some states, voters can also vote in person. Other news outlets reported mail-in ballots would be sent to "everybody," but in some states, registered voters have moved out of the state. Mail-in ballots could be left on the doorsteps of vacated houses. Trump has similar concerns, but the RAD press dismissed his comments, as you guessed it, as racist.

The Attorney General (AG) Barr does not voice his opinions very often, so I listened very intently to his concern the election could be contested after the 2020 election.

## Mail-in voting is the final piece of the puzzle
The next day I was certain mail-in voting is the final piece of the puzzle the RADs need to win the 2020 election. I claim the election will be contested in order to generate more confusion and distrust of the outcome of the election. I understand the rules for mail-in voting are different in many states; however if voter ID is not required on mail-in ballots, the RADs may win.

## US Postal Service (USPS) cannot process mail-in ballots
It was revealed today in a 20-second news clip the US Postal Service (USPS) told the administration they might not be able to process all the mail-in ballots before the election. Critics of mail-in voting talk about ballot harvesting, where a block captain collects ballots from around the neighborhood. I don't see any chance of voter fraud, do you? Could ballot harvesters collect blank ballots left at the doorsteps of vacant houses? Could they be filled out by "guessing" the intent of the former occupant?

After hearing many concerns, the Republicans and the POTUS have about the 2020 election; I was convinced the 2020 election would be contested in November 2020, only a few weeks away.

I predict the Democrats will win the popular vote in most states solely based on mail-in ballots. The results of the Election College might not be decided until the Supreme Court hears the case. In my opinion, the chance of mail-in ballots being counted accurately without voter ID is a recipe for disaster for the integrity of the voter system.

### Where is Operation Drug Speed?

We have a health crisis far more fatal than the coronavirus because we are not looking for a cure for addictions. Operation Warp Speed is on track to deliver three COVID-19 vaccines but no Operation Drug Speed to end drug use and addictions.

The POTUS came out to announce two COVID vaccines were going to be released soon, with a third on the way. Treatment for millions of high-risk health care workers and older at-risk people could begin by mid-December. I felt the tone of Trumps' voice was somber; he will not get credit for developing vaccines in record time.

It was only back on May 15, 2020, when the POTUS announced Operation Warp Speed, he hoped the medical industry would develop two vaccines by mid-December of the same year. That is less than nine months from start to distribution.

I think it takes a very spiteful RAD person not to give the POTUS some credit amid the economic, political division, civil unrest, negative press, and the pandemic. The DOW is expected to close at over 30,000 soon, and I am quite sure the promise of 3 vaccines is fueling the optimism. I still don't see a stimulus bill come out of the House to help small businesses.

### Hope for a vaccine by the end of 2020

Pharmaceutical company Moderna announced that its vaccine would begin the final phase of testing with approximately 30,000 human volunteers. Trump announced his Operation Warp Speed back in May, and hopefully, a vaccine will be approved before the end of 2020. The WH COVID 19 Taskforce seems to be very critical and questions if any vaccine will be ready before the end of 2020.

## Young people are beginning to revolt
The so-called experts claim a vaccine is still one year to 18 months away. Young people are beginning to revolt and are gathering at beaches and pools without masks and do not obey the masks or safe distancing rules.

A report came out cloth masks do not prevent the spread of the virus. The RADs continue to shame anyone with a different opinion.

Scientists and mathematicians from Stanford did a study, I believe, in June 2020 and found the actual risk of dying from COVID-19 was very low for people under 65. If only older people are at a high risk of COVID-19, then older people could shelter in place and allow kids to return to school. Most adults could return to work under some conditions.

Now, I am quite upset because I am falling victim to the RADs nonstop propaganda trap. Keep the public confused, afraid, and watching the death count rise on most of the RADs state-sponsored cable news networks.

## I need to get away from my prison cell, far away
Lockdowns, lockups, the pandemic, mask mandates, riots, police killing unarmed citizens, defunding the police movements, our 110-year-old house, and the fate of our nation is making my stress level continue to rise; Oh, I just remembered I need to fix our shed, it is slowly tipping over.

Then I need to obsess over the chaos and conflict around the world that is not reported in the press. That's right; I have high anxiety over the news the media does not report around the world.

I call this condition truth by omission. The truth, the WH coronavirus team, is not telling the public the truth. The omission, the WH coronavirus team, does not want to tell the public the truth. No wonder I am stressing over world news that never gets reported by our RAD or the MSA press.

I need to find a way to reduce my stress and anxiety soon. The summer has been very hot and humid but is coming to an end. Like many high-risk people with diabetes and other health issues, I needed to stay in our house all summer. I had the feeling the lockdown mandate is actually a lockup order in my own home.

Now it is late summer, and at times I felt I was under house arrest since March 2020. I would stay at home and think of all the home projects I should be doing but didn't. I did not work on the workbook. The shed is still leaning over, and I have no idea how to upright it; that's the story of my life; I cannot make anything stand upright.

I am having a difficult time completing the workbook. I thought I would have all the time in the world to complete the workbook, but I can't seem to put events into the right order but will not give up. I hope my thoughts are not too scattered and random for other people to understand or follow.

I did not even take the risk of going to an RV dealer to find a better camper. I would get an hour of freedom in my peaceful prison yard, the park with the pond, and then back to my holding cell in our house. I desperately needed to find a way to escape my four-wall prison cell and get more than one hour outdoors in the prison yard at the park, so to speak. I need to show my appreciation to be able to walk at the park; some parks and playgrounds are closed due to COVID-19.

The sun was rising above trees in our front yard. It was 5:30 AM when I went on the NJ camping website and found only one campsite that was not reserved for the following week. Nicole was not awake, and I booked the site within a minute.

After Nicole had her coffee, I told her the good news. Nicole was not a happy camper. She worried about the virus and the challenging time without electricity or air conditioning in our small camper. I told her the vacation was for my mental health; I needed to go on another spiritual retreat down to the Atlantic Ocean. Thankfully Nicole agreed I needed to get away from our old house and Ryan for a few days.

We packed up the camper and left my prison cell at home behind. Upon crossing the NJ state line, a big electronic billboard read, "Call 511 to determine your quarantine status". Nicole quickly looked up our status on her cell phone. NJ now has 31 states on the 14-day quarantine list, but thankfully PA was not on the list. I couldn't even escape the 24/7 nonstop COVID-19 harassment for the two-hour drive.

Can you imagine the hassle of calling in for our out-of-state quarantine instructions? I made a comment to Nicole, "I'm sure we would need to fill out contact tracing forms back to our forefathers and eventually stay quarantined for 14 years, not 14 days."

It was very hot when we arrived at the campground, but it was a spiritual oasis for me to finally get away from house arrest for a few days.

It was very hot and humid in the camper without air conditioning; we decided to go to the beach until sunset. The beach cooled down late afternoon, and it was my ideal temperature, 74 degrees with a gentle breeze, no more than three knots, maybe four coming in off the ocean. Usually, at the end of the summer, the weather is cool with less humidity.

We went to the beach again the next day, and the surf was very rough; I mean, huge cascading waves were crashing on the beach, but overall, the beach weather was perfect.

I decided to go swimming in the very rough surf to get cooled off, but the first wave knocked me down. I tried to get up, but another even stronger huge cascading wave hit me from behind, knocked me down, and dragged me further out to sea on my back. I was being battered by the relentless pounding surf; the strong undertow was pulling me out to sea with the tide. I could not stand up.

Four young bystanders, without masks, mind you, took pity on my pathetic situation and helped me stand up, and then they called for the lifeguards to help me. I told the lifeguard I was ok as I staggered up the beach with a lifeguard behind me. Nicole assured the lifeguards I was ok.

It was a humiliating experience because I needed to admit I was a feeble, not just older but much older man now that couldn't stand on my own two feet in very rough surf. I have enough trouble enough getting down the stairs at home. Nicole was more worried about contracting the virus from my reckless unmasked rescue team than my fragile psychological and emotional wellbeing.

Later on, Nicole quietly reminded me the surf and undertow were not that strong, and many young kids were riding the waves on boogie boards. So, the surf did not have huge cascading waves. Yet another humiliating moment I needed to admit to myself; I was not only getting older but much weaker.

After that embarrassing debacle, I decided to go for a walk alone up the beach. After walking for about a mile on a crowded beach, I only found a total of six people with masks on. I found it very refreshing to see kids playing in the surf and families without masks enjoying the beach and the beautiful weather. It almost felt like the virus never happened. My fragile mind finally started to emerge from months of nonstop RAD and MSA indoctrination into the post-COVID-19, social distancing, and mask-wearing nightmare. I also forgot to open my laptop to work on the workbook.

Without air-conditioning, in our small camper, we spent most of the day on the beach, sometimes until sunset. We ordered out and avoided contact with public bathrooms and other people. I convinced Nicole our risk of getting the virus was very low, but she became obsessed with masks, social distancing, and hand sanitizer.

Nicole was very concerned people were not socially distancing on the beach. We had a few "discussions" about where to spread out our blanket. I told her I would get a tape measure from my toolbox and measure exactly six feet to the next family's beach blanket. That threat seemed to calm her COVID-19 obsessive-compulsive behavior. A few days later, the sun and the sound of the waves put us in a tranquil state of mind.

I was so thankful we had the time at the shore but realized most people were struggling with the economic and psychological effects of the pandemic. We called for takeout at the Italian restaurant in a small town a few miles from the campground.

Last summer, without the pandemic issue, the restaurant was always busy and usually had several families eating in the large dining room. This year the large dining room was dark, and I sensed the staff was struggling just to survive; of course, not one waitress in the dining room and a skeleton crew working behind the takeout counter. I know most waiters and waitresses make most of their money on tips. I thanked them all for the good food and friendly service and left a good tip. They all expressed gratitude for my kind words of support.

On the way back to the campground, I felt the painful reality the pandemic was devastating our economy as well as our American spirit. Unless you are completely delusional, you cannot escape the devastating financial, spiritual, and emotional toll of the virus. The financial toll of the virus alone is felt everywhere and has gripped our nation and the entire world.

## What! Abductions and off-planet metal implants

In the morning the weather was perfect but very hot. We went to the beach early, and the surf was very rough. I enjoy watching the surf but did not want to risk another humiliating experience of being tossed around in the surf again.

We took out some seafood for dinner again and went back to the campground around 9 pm. I usually go to sleep before midnight, but for some reason, I had some floating anxiety and couldn't sleep. I decided to watch one more video about UFOs on my tablet. I am quite sure ETs will not let the planet Earth be destroyed by nuclear bombs, but I was determined to know the actual reason why they are here.

I found one video called Patient Seventeen [(Patient Seventeen ) or P17 for short. He was a middle-aged man; P17 found a foreign object in his leg. He went to a UFO scientist, a man named Doctor Rodger Leir. P17 had some strange paranormal experiences when he was younger and claimed years before he was visited by alien beings.

P17 was very upset ETs could break into his home uninvited and mess with his privacy. He said he would kill them all if they returned.

He was a Christian man and did not want to believe the object could possibly be made by from ETs from another galaxy.

An X-ray did show P17 did have a small metallic-like object embedded in his leg below the knee. A few days later, the doctor proceeded to cut into P17 leg to remove the object. Well, as soon as the doctor cut into P17's leg and pulled out a small metal object, I had a flashback. I remembered I had an object embedded in my groin. The object was not in my groin at the present time, but it was there in the past. The object embedded in my groin was the size of a tip of a pencil. The object was hard, I could squeeze it very hard, and it was not painful.

I remember I did not think it was a problem because it did not grow any larger and did not get swollen or infected. The area around my object did not get red, swollen, or infected. I have had many nails in my hands, legs, and my feet on the farm and camping. I usually just cut them out with a sterilized razor blade before they get infected.

When the object was in my groin area was actually in my scrotum, it was not a nail, that's for sure. Then I began to speculate, was the object an implant from an ET? Who or what removed the object? Who removed the object became more an issue than who implanted the object? I just assumed an Extraterrestrials (ET) embedded the object. Could a metal object just disappear from inside my body? If it was implanted by an ET did, they remove it and then programmed my mind to forget the entire incident?

Speaking about forgetting, what if I went into a state of amnesia after an abduction? If I was abducted by ETs, I could be hiding another traumatic incident. Well, I am going to forget the possibility I am in yet another state of amnesia over an alien abduction. That does not make any sense either but more nonsense.

The possibility of having an ET implant a chip in my groin did not upset me, but for some reason, I needed to know who removed it. That is my crazy curiosity in psychic phenomena talking to me.

If a doctor removed a foreign object, I would want to know if it was from another galaxy. If I could determine who removed the object, I could ask them to tell me the origin and if it was off-planet.

I would not be upset if I had an encounter with an alien now because I understand they do not harm humans. Sometimes ETs just probe humans to study human reproduction. On a second afterthought, I am not open to being probed by little grey aliens. Don't get me wrong; I don't have anything against any species from other galaxies; I don't want to be called an intergalactic extraterrestrial racist.

Now it was 2 am, and I was wide awake trying to figure out who and when removed the object. The only logical explanation was my surgeon or the ETs. I had two operations years ago; the first was for the removal of a cancerous tumor from my bladder. The second operation was about a month later I had my entire cancerous prostate removed by the same surgeon. I was heavily sedated for several hours during and after both operations, so I would not feel any pain in my groin if the doctor surgically removed an object.

Maybe I should call my surgeon and ask him if he removed any off-planet object? Would he think I was crazy? My chart has "History of bipolar" listed as a medical condition in bold letters at the top of my chart. My nurse did not log off the computer with my medical record chart, and I could read the first page of my medical records. The first page looked like the Table of Contents of a medical dictionary; I was sure my mental health records were not private any longer.

That's another issue; no one asked me about my BD before or after my operations. Getting back to the metal object, I am sure my surgeon would ask me, "Why do you need to know about a foreign object?" I would reply, "Well, doctor, it could be more than just an object; it might be a real foreign implant by ETs from another galaxy."

Does it even matter if the object was fabricated by a species from another galaxy or universe? Yes, I think it would; I would probably have a note attached in big, bold letters at the top of my medical chart. "NOTE: This patient thinks he may have had an off-planet metal object implanted in his scrotum."

Unfortunately, Dr. Leir passed away before the test results came back. Well, getting back to P17 again, the results came back from the lab, and it confirmed the object was fabricated from 36 elements. The lab noted most metals have only 4 or 5 elements. The doctor's research team came to the conclusion; the object was made by intelligent beings, not from planet Earth.

It was now well past 3 am; the sun would soon rise above the horizon; then I remembered we needed to check out of our campsite in the morning; I needed to get some sleep.

I heard the first songbird of the day, which means planet Earth will survive for another day. I was having vivid visions of our future as I drifted into a restless trance-like state of semi-consciousness.

## Stage 14 The Teardrops attempt to speak out

In my visions, the 2020 elections were over, and protests were held in all the major cities across the country. The swearing-in ceremony for the new POTUS was just hours away, and what looked like military-style police in riot gear lined the streets of the cities to keep order. I started to get severe chest pains and fell off my old recliner onto the floor.

Nicole recognized it was a heart attack and called 911. The EMTs arrived in what seemed like hours but were actually just a few minutes. On the way to the hospital, the EMTs were in constant contact with the emergency room and authorized the use of the shock paddles to restart my heart. We arrived at the emergency room, and then I heard the emergency room doctor say, "He is having a massive heart attack and needs to go into surgery as soon as possible, or he will not make it." I felt the shock paddles being administered to my chest several times in hopes of starting my heart. All of a sudden, I heard a steady flat tone on a heart monitor.

As I drifted into an out-of-body state, I did not know if I was dead or alive. I was experiencing an out-of-the-body dreamlike state and was floating above the operating table, looking down at the operating room. I saw the medical staff prepping me for the operation, shaving my chest, and putting IV tubes in my arms.

Then I floated over to the waiting room, where I saw Nicole sitting in the waiting room. Someone in the waiting room switched between TV channels; they all showed the same video of people protesting in the streets.

All major networks, sports cable, and even shopping channels all played the same video. All the men and woman reporters all seemed to dress alike in custom uniforms. The men had tailored suits that appeared to be bulletproof vests, and the women all had the same pantsuits

Then the news switched to show people protesting in the streets. Again, the same video was simultaneously played on all the TV channels. This new video showed throngs of people protesting in the streets and demanded the POTUS to do something about the so-called terror attacks. The video had no audio-only closed caption across the bottom of the screen with the words, "Citizen's demand action by the POTUS."

I am always suspecting the worst, and I wondered if the closed caption message was true. Were the people really demanding action from the POTUS to declare a national emergency? The SSE actions are so harmful to our freedoms people should be taking to the streets in massive protests across the country not to enact Marshal Law. Maybe that is why the video does not have audio and just a closed caption. Without the audio, no one could tell what the protestors were saying or even what language they were speaking.

## Protesters demand action–emergency is declared

As time went on, the news switched between the terror attacks and people protesting for the POTUS to do something. The public only sees a panel of 10 men and women on national cable TV, but they are all saying exactly the same thing. All the cable network contributors were suffering from Stockholm Syndrome anyway. I can see the nation watching and waiting for another announcement.

## Teardrops try to speak out

The TV cable network news feed is interrupted, and something that looks like a live Teardrop appears on the TV. The Black & White (B&W) TV transmission begins to cut in and out, and the voice becomes garbled. The voice says, "We are the Teardrops; we are here to protect the...." The transmission is interrupted, and people with mirror helmets covering their faces are scrambling to gain control of the press conference. The Teardrops are shaped like Teardrops and made of crystal-clear blue ice, almost translucent. The panel of 10 cable network contributors has magically disappeared from the stage.

Finally, the person in charge of the meeting steps up to the podium. He is dressed in wrap around one-way mirror helmet, completely covering his head. This person is wearing a silver jumpsuit with gloves to match.

The spokesperson has what looks like a patch of a globe on the left arm. As the spokesperson turns toward the camera, I see the patch is blue and represents the Blue Planet. The first words are, "I am here to protect the globe from all enemies, both foreign and domestic, and from outer space."

The next spokesman steps up to the podium and has in big letters CCCC on going down his right arm. His first words are, "As you know by now, we lost 120 fellow citizens in a terrorist attack on our nation last week. We must protect all our citizens from further attacks and keep the rule of order to assure the country is safe and secure.

The POTUS had no choice but to evoke the 1976 Executive Order (EO} number 11921 and subsequent additions and revisions to protect the country from all our enemies at home, abroad, and especially from outer space. This EO and emergency banking regulations will go into effect immediately. Everyone will need to follow the New Rules of Order or NROs. The new Central Command and Control Commission or CCCC will take over and enforce the NRO policies until the State of Emergency (SOE) can be lifted by the POTUS". Then he says, "The CCCC is here to protect you, the brave citizens of our nation." My heart skipped a beat; whenever any official claims they are here to protect you, they really mean to protect themselves.

Another member of the CCCC steps forward and states, "France found it necessary to enact a state of emergency or SE after being attacked in 2015. As in France, the State of Emergency (SOE) will be lifted as soon as the country is secure. The president and the former members of Congress will be protected by the CCCC at a secret location. We will protect our citizens from enemies from within and from outer space.

After the speech, another official spokesman for the CCCC briefly outlines the New Rules of Order or NROs procedures and protocols that must be followed by everyone.

Wait a minute; he said, "former members of Congress"; I don't think he misspoke, but I cannot speak out; these officials are in charge.

No one's ever heard of the CCCC. We don't even know the background of these so-called officials of the CCCC. The CCCC officials are lined up and are all wearing special face guards and custom silver jumpsuits with CCCC patches on their right arms and chests. I don't see any reference to our American flag on the stage, but I see several flags on the stage with CCCC embossed in large letters. The plain silver jumpsuits have familiar letters down one arm of every CCCC official, but I cannot read them.

I suppose this is to show the CCCC is now in control and convince the public they are protecting the public from terrorists, but I am afraid the real reason is to protect the officials from the law-abiding citizens of the country.

What are these NRO policies and directives after an SSE? We have never been briefed on why and when the event justifies the nation going into an SSE. I notice he does not call these emergency regulations, but only New Rules of Order or NRO's we all must follow.

Almost everyone except me is relieved the POTUS has finally ordered someone to act to prevent bloodshed and prevent more terror attacks. What the public does not know is we just gave up our freedoms under the 1776 Constitution to an unknown CCCC agency after only 120 deaths. However, it's justified because France also issued a National Emergency after only 120 people died. Oh, and another point, why does the first spokesman have a globe patch representing the Blue Planet and not an American flag? Am I the only one that sees every new announcement brings us closer to tyranny?

Sadly, everyone is in for a very rude awaking as to the scope and power an EO gave up to the CCCC under the NRO policies and bank regulations. As I understand President Ford's EO 11921 of 1976, even the POTUS loses the ability to govern the country. Only new security agencies we know nothing about will control every aspect of our lives.

Actually, 99.99 percent of the population doesn't even know we are in an SSE. The public is told the CCCC will enforce the NRO policies until we can return the country to normal. No mention of any laws under the 1776 Constitution; everyone must follow the NRO's issued by the CCCC. The public will often be told that NROs must be enforced to keep order.

## Teardrops do not exist

The state-run CCCC Truth Agency spokesperson is asked about the Teardrops but is told the CCCC Headquarters or HQ will handle all questions regarding the Teardrops. People begin to panic and prepare for a possible invasion by the Teardrops, but within hours the Vast Information Conglomerate (VIC) denies the Teardrops even exist.

As usual, the public believes the misinformation. I want to speak out and say, "People, please wake up the Teardrops were live on the TV."

The Truth Agency claims it was just a clip from an old B&W alien space invasion movie from the 50s. They claim the silver UFOs are real but are just our nation's advanced antigravity secret spy drones. The spokesperson assures the public is no proof of little shiny Teardrop invaders from outer space. Then she raises her voice and shouts into the camera, "Teardrops do not exist."

## The super-secret is out, free power for the entire planet

Oh, really, didn't the entire nation just watch a Teardrop speak live on TV, and now the Truth Agency is trying to cover up the truth in plain sight?

Then an HQ staff member claims the silver UFOs are real, and an attack could be imminent, but don't worry, just one advanced super-secret antigravity Own Flying Objects or OFOs has unlimited free energy that could power the entire planet. She is abruptly escorted off the stage.

I cannot believe it, the CCCC admits they can power planet Earth with just one OFO, but people are so confused they cannot grasp reality. Even the CCCC spokespersons who think they are spreading lies are actually telling us the truth by mistake.

Another CCCC spokesman then admits they acquired the super-secrets from ETs in 1944 that could help mankind were stolen by the CCCC. Then she said she misspoke and denied any super secrets even existed.

I remember a Frenchmen named Voltaire said something like absurdity breeds atrocities. I don't have any time for this nonsense, but another quote comes to mind from Voltaire "Common sense is not so common." I better not quote Voltaire aloud; I could become a victim of the atrocities.

Talk about misinformation; the public is told ETs don't exist, but now they might be a threat to our nation. Of course, this is a proven tactic; lie and create so much confusion people will eventually believe anything they are told. Someone misspoke, and the truth finally comes out, covert groups within the CCCC do have super-secrets to help all mankind, and they were locked up in a Black Box until five minutes ago.

I guess all the misinformation and absurd thoughts are working; I am totally confused; don't we know ETs are not a threat to humans? Then I understand the covert group is creating another narrative; our nation needs more bombs and more dark money from our treasury to start another war.

## The CCCC will enforce the NROs

Yet another official states, "There is absolutely no need to worry; the CCCC will provide all the logistics and services necessary to enforce all the NRO's." We are here to help you, the common people.

My anxiety began to skyrocket; whenever any official says they are here to help, it usually means a disaster ahead. Now, these NROs have been in effect for two days before the attacks were aired on national TV. But did the attacks even occur? Any threat, real or imaginary, could force our nation into declaring a national emergency.

I try to login onto social media, but most sites are blocked, and the reason is always to protect the public. Then another official from HQ states, "Under NRO, the CCCC will have the authority to impose other rules and regulations to keep order."

A respected investigative reporter asked one of the CCCC officials exactly where the public could find the emergency regulations and NROs; she is quickly escorted out of the conference room and into a waiting CCCC van. She was one of the best investigative reporters in the drug wars.

Then another official announcement; four NRO's will go into effect immediately to keep the order. The four NROs are quickly disclosed to press reporters.

Rule number one restricts bank withdrawals, NRO number two restricts firearms, NRO number three does not restrict immigration, and number four deals with the pandemic problem.

## The Heath Care Rationing Act (HCRA)

CCCC officials announce the new Heath Care Rationing Agency (HCRA) will help all people live much longer lives. The new sweeping policies are announced in a long 60-second clip and not the usual 30-second news clip.

The CCCC cannot get the raw chemicals from the Far East to make any medicines any longer. This cannot be true; the Free Drug Agency is acquiring billions of raw chemicals to produce trillions of Grams of meth, Fentanyl, and other illegal drugs. I don't believe they cannot even manufacture birth control pills?

I'm very upset; what's next, food and medication rationing? Then I found out my psychiatric meds went up 1000 percent. I need my meds. I have been stable for over 25 years now on just two medications.

Without proper meds, people with illnesses will die by the millions. Is this what the Health Care Rationing Agency (HCRA) is designed to accomplish? Could this agency deny care to the old, disabled, and mentally ill?

A few days later, the CCCC announced death taxes would rise to 50 percent. Well, now that is probably just a mistake; someone misspoke, right? Are they planning for old people will die, and the CCCC will collect 50 percent of their wealth in death taxes? I thought Socialism was going would be fair and equal for everyone? Then they imply CCCC officials will be first in line for organ donations. The CCCC claims they need 10,000 new agencies to handle the rapid growth of the government benefits.

Wait a minute, are you telling me old people are dying, and the CCCC is profiting by collecting a 50 percent death tax. Wouldn't this NRO be a convenient conflict of interest? The CCCC is using death taxes to fund its 10,000 plus agencies while denying life-saving medical care to the old and the mentally ill.

I see cargo container ships full of masks, drums of chemicals, medical equipment, and huge piles of solar panels arriving at ports all along the East and West coasts. Actually, the containers are chemicals used to make more meth, Fentanyl, and other designer drugs.

I see a few people are wearing masks; they have TR247 in large white letters across the front. I thought the pandemic was over years ago. No one complains or protests; they seem to be content, or are they all under some type of mind control?

## What about our former security agencies?

The next 30-second news clip announces more sweeping changes. All the former local and city police force units are to be sent to guard Mt Rushmore in the foothills of SD.

Well, that's a bit overkill; there must be a million police officers; I wonder who will replace our local and city law enforcement? The CCCC then announces crime is out of control; firearms must be confiscated from all registered gun owners.

Hold on, let me process this new policy. Does that mean only criminals and gangs will have firearms? Of course, crime is going to skyrocket all the former local law enforcement are out guarding Mount Rushmore.

I don't dare ask any questions, but why are millions of police protecting granite portraits of former presidents and other patriotic Americans? Now that is insane, but I can't voice any opposition or even question any NRO. I know I would be quickly escorted away into a waiting CCCC van.

Let me process these new policies; only armed gangs and criminals will be left to "protect" the people in towns and large cities. How is that going to work? Private citizens will not have firearms to protect their families and friends.

Now I am confused; there is no mention of any 3 letter security agencies, only the CCCC. In the next brief announcement, all three-letter national security agencies will be combined to form the National Strike Force or NSF. Furthermore, all branches of the former military will be folded into the new Oversees Strike Force or OSF.

Wow! I can't believe the CCCC has complete and total control of our lives and all branches of government, including the military, within hours of the emergency declaration.

I am baffled; who will protect all the citizens in the cities and towns across the nation? I am afraid the answer is no one, the "defund the police" movement worked. Now only gangs and criminals have firearms and are in total control of all our cities and towns. Law-abiding citizens do not have any firearms to protect themselves. I thought all the radical ideas to confiscate firearms would never work. I was wrong; the radicals are executing their Socialist agenda with surgical precision.

That reminds me of my procedure, I feel some pain on my right side, but the procedure seems to be taking hours.

Why that is preposterous, but I cannot criticize the CCCC. Another afterthought, without police, won't women be at risk of sexual abuse and White men be targeted as being racist and expendable?

The CCCC officials cite the 1976 EO 11921 whenever a controversial policy is brought up. Everyone must follow NROs we know nothing about.

## Citizens are in denial of the real dangers of the NROs

As I look down on the waiting room, the calendar on the wall turns to the year 2028, and I hope to see an end to these disturbing events. I am witnessing firsthand the heartache, pain, and enormous stress.

Well, what happened to the 2024 election year election? I hoped we would have Patriot elected president that would restore our nation back to 1776 Constitutional laws. No mention of any elections in the future.

I see people in shock with no emotion of what is happening in the world around them. The TV showed violence against the citizens of the country, men, women, and children being murdered in the streets across the nation. People in the waiting room are fixated on their tablets and cell phones. Some people are wearing masks with TR247 in large white letters. The video shows people attacked as they leave their churches and synagogues.

Have people been so brainwashed to ignore the violence and bloodshed they don't show any human emotions? The people must be in shock and cannot even help one another.

## Blame MSA that capitalism does not work

Everyone thinks they will be spared if they just follow the NROs, but these are hollow promises and are used to keep total control of the public. The CCCC begins to espouse true Socialist policies and act more like the RAD radical socialist Democrats (RAD) before the 2020 election. The promise everyone will get everything for free keeps the public calm as they wait for true equality. The Propaganda Agency proclaims the middle class will be the beneficiaries of the new NRO's, and the rich billionaires must pay their fair share.

## The middle class is drained of assets

Now the CCCC is successfully draining the wealth of old citizens by collecting a new 99 percent wealth tax, but with most old people dying, new ways are needed to fund the CCCC. I can't question the high 50 percent death tax rate or the 99 percent wealth tax, but I still think it is a conflict of interest. By rationing care to old people, old people are dying at an alarming rate. Was this the sole intention of the HCRA from the start, to eliminate the old by literally taxing them to death?

The CCCC emergency bank regulations order cash can be only be dispensed at certain times and places and are all controlled by a CCCC bank teller from a central location. All banks are closed across the country, caused by, of course, the pandemic. Now the CCCC is withdrawing funds directly from mainly from the working class.

I should have read those Emergency Banking Regulations back when I found that book in the used book store. The book described the new rules under an emergency as a "Blueprint for tyranny."

## The CCCC, NSF, and OSF control the world economy

Under the CCCC, all rules break down drugs, corruption, and greed are the only real rules of disorder left around the world. The regime started to restrict bank withdrawals even from the NSF and OSF members and imposed harsh penalties for citizens selling stock or bonds without paying excessive fees and penalties to the Revenue Agency. The middle-class population of the world is methodically being drained of all assets, including cash, stocks, bonds, homes, and even their solar-powered golf carts.

Most people still alive are suffering from severe grief and have severe symptoms of bizarre and psychotic behavior. People wander the streets in shock with no signs of joy or happiness. The pursuit of happiness is gone. No one feels safe; most people find drugs the only way to cope.

## The new CCCC Social engineering programs
Not only are radical economic policies destroying our nation, but new social programs are also ordered to assure the regime will stay in power for 1000 years. Women of childbearing age must register for the mandatory CCCC Birthing Agency selection program. Abortions are declared illegal and necessary to ensure the population level is stable. Newborns selected will be sent directly to a community agency to learn the NROs taught by certified CCCC instructors. Mothers will be returned to work under the CCCC only hours after giving birth.

Wow! The CCCC has a program to indoctrinate our kids not only from kindergarten but from the moment of conception. I don't want to know about the newborns not selected?

This social change is certainly a radical departure from the woman's right to choose policies of just a few years ago. Kids are being inoculated and indoctrinated from birth and not from daycare. Oh no, I just had another afterthought; I hope this program is not somehow tied into the Health Care Rationing (HCRA) reforms. Could newborn baby parts be used to keep CCCC members alive with new or better body parts? Well, now that is a barbaric and a crazy afterthought, or is it?

## Is the CCCC trading our natural resources for masks?
How will the CCCC continue to stay in power with all the chaos in the streets? Why isn't there an American-style revolution?

In order to keep the public from taking to the streets, the CCCC trades all the mineral and agricultural resources of North America to a foreign government for only 500,000 TR247 masks.

I think to myself, won't most all the people in our nation starve to death without agriculture and the logistics to get food to the people? I cannot question any policy of the CCCC.

Sure enough, after our nation descends further into darkness, a more intelligent and focused nation swoops in and claims they now own all our natural resources in exchange for only 500,000 TR247 masks.

How could that be, the CCCC spokeswomen claims it was a good business decision, and the sale will benefit the entire nation. She emphasizes for it to work, everyone needs to wear TR247 masks day and night. I noticed many people did wear the TR247 masks but thought they were just for people who could not believe the pandemic was over years ago.

I don't understand the mask mandates; I thought the pandemic was over years ago. Finally, a brave whistleblower exposes the details of the trade. The TR247 masks are laced with a Time Release (TR) mix of meth and Fentanyl and designed to work 24 hours, 7 days a week. The scandal spreads like wildfires, but the HQ spokeswomen cannot be found.

The details of the historic trade deal are released by another whistleblower. The trade includes all our nation's raw minerals, vast reserves of natural gas, oil wells, and refineries. *The* pipelines will carry oil and gas products to the west coast to be exported overseas. Cattle farms, grasslands, farmlands, wheat, soybeans, and cornfields stretch for a thousand miles in every direction will be farmed by the new owners.

I always knew foreign entities had their eye on our vast natural resources for centuries. They knew the North American continent had enough natural resources to feed billions of people and power millions of factories.

People do not realize our nation's natural resources have been stolen by a foreign entity. The CCCC spokesperson cannot even be found.

## What happened to the person in the wrap-around mirrored helmet?

I think it's about time we find the person responsible for all the economic and personal suffering in the world. Something, no, everything does not make any sense, just more nonsense. What happened to the person that holds the super secrets to help mankind? Remember the person in the wrap-around mirrored helmet with a Blue Planet patch on his arm; I call the globalist. Come to think about it, we have not seen the top commander of the CCCC or even know his name.

That begs another question where is the HQ even located? The CCCC HQ is silent now, but years ago, they announced a new NRO every 5 minutes over the loudspeakers.

We are then told the OSF has now conquered and occupied all countries around the globe but ignores the threat from the other two superpowers.

By now, planet Earth has lost several billion people to the ravages of war and many more by starvation and disease. All this is very confusing even for my scattered mind; I still cannot process what is happening; the cities are "guarded" by criminals and gangs. The local police were all sent to guard Mount Rushmore?

I thought the pandemic was over years ago, and we don't need any more mask mandates. Now we learn our vast natural resources have been traded for only 500,000 TR247 face masks laced with meth and Fentanyl. Now everyone is demanding mask mandates. Everyone clings to their TR247 masks and waits for the bloodshed to end, but sadly it does not end.

Yes, it does all make sense to my scrambled mind but utter nonsense to any other rational being. Speaking of beings, could the person with the Blue Planet patch be secretly in control of the entire planet by now? That would be a global conspiracy of epic proportions. Maybe this person is the leader of the global elite trying to take over the entire planet? I cannot even think of conspiracy theories; the thought police could read my mind if I get too close to a cell tower.

My cell phone vibrates; it shows my GPS coordinates with the caption "afterthoughts detected." Oh no, they know about my crazy thoughts; I always thought I could hide my afterthoughts. Advanced surveillance technology is being used to track my location and afterthoughts.

A thought pops into my mind "The VIC is tracking everyone on planet Earth" I think to myself, "Who is VIC? I don't know anyone named VIC." My mind answers, "Doesn't everyone know VIC means the global Vast Information Conglomerate (VIC)."

Now they are also using telepathy to communicate with me; I cannot even have my own thoughts or afterthoughts. My afterthoughts are permanently erased from my memory.

The VIC is the top secret-secret global information network used by the global elite. So, the globalist is using the VIC and telepathy to control the entire planet. So, whoever controls the VIC, controls the

Planet Earth. Oh no, now they know I know the globalist is the only diabolical evil person responsible for the destruction of mankind.

## The CCCC HQ takes no responsibility

Millions of people want to protest outside of the CCCC HQ. The problem, no one knows the location of CCCC HQ. A brief announcement over a loudspeaker claims all information on any top CCCC official is top secret and cannot be disclosed to the public.

I think to myself, years went by, and the public still does not know the names of the small covert group of people in charge of our lives. A rumor circulates the person with the Blue Planet patch on the arm; the globalist is to blame for the total destruction of planet Earth. The CCCC claims laws under the SSE prohibit disclosure of the names of any CCCC official.

A brief announcement states under the 1976 EO, no one can learn his name or even if he is human. They always refer back to that decades-old 1976 EO, don't they?

## Is the POTUS going to restore the nation to the 1776 Constitution?

The underground anti-CCCC resistance Intel reports show Congress safely in bunkers and waiting for the SSE to be lifted by the POTUS. They all appear to be busy filling out hundreds of forms and regulations and passing legislation to help the middle class.

I am sorry, I don't believe a single word; Congress hasn't passed meaningful legislation to help the working class for decades. The POTUS cannot be found, and only the POTUS can restore the nation back to the 1776 Constitution.

I notice a very high fence around the compound; one member looks straight into the camera. I notice he blinks three times, followed by a blink and another three blinks. Oh no, that is the universal SOS distress signal. Congress is not being protected; they are being imprisoned behind a tall metal wall.

Come to think about it, where are all the panels of cable network contributors? Now I know all those cable network contributors were just used as collaborators for the CCCC. They did blindly promote the radical's agenda and are now all expendable. After the SSE was declared, all the cable news contributors were just considered collateral damage.

## Will we ever return to the 1776 Constitution?
Well, I wanted to believe our nation would return to the 1776 Constitution, but sadly, I know it will not. Now I know our nation is a war, but I still need to follow my goal to help people with BD get treatment early on. Sometimes I think to myself, why am I spending my time on my workbook if our nation descends into darkness and despair for most all RAD and MSA Americans.

Now I realize the workbook is one goal I must complete, although I know it will not be a pleasant task ahead. How am I going to finish the workbook in the middle of WW III? Yes, I should be able to use WW III as an excuse not to publish the workbook. Things are getting more bizarre every minute; maybe I am schizophrenic after all, not that there is anything wrong with being schizophrenic.

## The person with the Blue Planet patch has orchestrated WW III
By now, I am not the only one with crazy afterthoughts; the person with the Blue Planet patch, the globalist, is responsible for all the destruction around the globe.

In order to distract the millions of protesters, the globalist convinces CCCC HQ they can take back all our natural resources. The

CCCC can win WW III by a surprise nuclear attack simultaneously on both superpowers. The OSF launches all of our nuclear warheads on both superpowers, but they are all intercepted by silver mirror ball-shaped lightning bolts. The lightning bolts instantly destroy all the nuclear missiles before they can land or detonate in space. The OSF sends out all their Own Flying Objects (OFO), but their control installations are disabled by satellites from outer space, and they all crash on the ground on impact.

Now it is clear to everyone the man with the Blue Planet patch has skillfully orchestrated WW III, the war that will bring humanity to the edge of extinction.

### China disables all solar panels in the entire world

As agreed, back in 2020, an attack on one superpower is an attack on the other superpowers. From the manned space station hundreds of miles above North America, an anti-terrorism unit disables all solar panels in North America and around the world. The superpowers have been watching the OSF as a threat for years. The policy of having one nation the sole manufacturer of solar panels and smartphones is now destroying the entire power grid of the entire world in just seconds.

You see, kill switches were embedded into every solar panel and cell phone to allow shutdown on command. Even the solar panels on the roofs of billions of club carts are instantly disabled across North America and the rest of the world.

### I found a glass bottle with a scroll in it

I needed to take a break from all the turmoil in the world. I decided to go down to the ocean to reflect on the meaning of life again. The sound of the ocean waves always soothes my soul, and I can reset my scrambled thoughts and ignore those confusing afterthoughts. I desperately need to reset my mind back to be BD normal again.

I stood with my feet in the water and watched huge cascading waves crash onto the beach, and then I noticed a large glass bottle floating in the ocean. A wave gently placed the bottle at my feet. I uncorked the bottle and unrolled the scroll, and was titled "The true story of the human race."

It read:

With all the power out around the globe, the Teardrops have decided to contact all the humans left on planet Earth by using ancient glass bottles.

## Only indigenous tribes have survived WW III

Without any electric or solar power left in the entire world, only people in the most remote regions of the planet are still alive but are living without electricity. All of these people rejected the modern technology of the modern world and chose to live close to nature. Many of these tribes had no contact with the outside world for decades. They cured all illnesses, including all viruses, man-made pandemics with roots, herbs, and medicines made from wild mushrooms.

With the world in ruin and communications destroyed, only the indigenous tribes that followed the fundamental rules of nature have survived the devastation. The Blue Planet has been returned back to Mother Nature.

## The true story of the human race on the Blue Planet

It is time to tell the true story of the origins of the human race.

Once upon a time, about 10,000 years ago, a race lived on the planet light-years away from planet Earth. The far distant planet was inhabited by a race that did not live with peace and harmony. Their planet was close to destruction from years of wars. The caring, kind, and honest citizens were forced to leave the chaos to find another planet. They wanted to start over and live with other caring and compassionate citizens of the universe.

A fleet of intergalactic spaceships headed out over the vast expanses of the universe to find a peaceful planet to live and thrive.

On the way to another galaxy, millions of light-years away, some of the kids on the mother ship wanted to stop and swim in the vast oceans on the Blue Planet. Stories of blue sky and oceans with miles of sandy beaches had the kids excited for several thousand years. One of the kids telepathically found an interstellar 3D travel brochure about the Blue Planet. The kids then began to complain and ask the crew, "Are we there yet?" After traveling trillions of miles with kids constantly asking, "Are we there yet?" the crew members were finally fed up with the unruly kid's behavior. All the kids wanted to do was swim in the oceans of the Blue Planet. After years of the kids, grandkids, and great-grandkids whining, arguing, and pleading to stop at the Blue Planet, the Commander of the flagship finally gave in".

After the spaceship landed, all the unruly kids just took off in all directions without their parents' permission. A few days later, the unruly kids still did not return to the mother spaceship. After waiting another few days, the Commander decided to continue on the voyage to their travel destination without the kids. Now it is not known if the Commander and all the parents intentionally left the disruptive and incorrigible kids on the Blue Planet, but most parents with annoying hyperactive kids probably know the answer to that question.

The spaceship Commander promised to return periodically to see the progress of the kids. No mention if the parents ever returned to pick up their own kids. Over the years, the Teardrops did come back to find the status of the human race on the Blue Planet. They quickly left without seeing any improvement for thousands of years.

Around 1944 a nuclear bomb was detected on planet Earth. An intergalactic alarm sent many ETs from around the universe to investigate. A few years later, over 500 atomic bombs were detected around the globe. The conclusion, the kids dropped off 10,000 ago evolved into irresponsible adults capable of destroying themselves but could also destroy all living things on the Blue Planet. Now the planet has over 5 billion descendants from just a few incorrigible kids.

The Teardrops are only here to protect the Blue Planet. Every human was given the gift of free will but did not use it to create peace and harmony on the Blue Planet.

Some humans have the knowledge to reach a higher level of consciousness but are held back from teaching the super-secret. The super-secret is to learn to be kind and be kind to everyone in the universe.

The leaders of the superpowers only represent a small insignificant number of people on the planet but want to decide the destiny of billions. They do not want the masses to use their gift of free will and learn universal knowledge of love and kindness. They want to use fear and violence to attain and keep political and economic power. Most people on the planet want to live in peace and harmony. It is time for the human race to become true citizens of the universe."

It was signed

The Friends of the Blue Planet.

## That story explains a lot about the human race
I quickly rolled up the scrolls, placed them in the bottle, put on the cork, and dropped it back into the ocean.

Well, I thought that's quite a "Once upon a time story" it was literally out of this world. I usually don't like stories that begin with "Once upon a time," so cliché. That explains a lot about the human race, doesn't it? So, the human race on planet Earth is a product of the evolution of a few annoying kids. They were accidentally left but most likely not accidentally dropped off on the Blue Planet some 10,000 years ago? No wonder the true story of the human race has been kept a super-secret for 10,000 years. I can be seriously confused at times, but that story does make perfect sense.

### I had some intergalactic afterthoughts
I know what to do next; we need to update that 10,000year-old 3D travel brochure and attract kids from all over the universe. Those kids watched a 10,000-year-old travel brochure; we need to update it to 5D with all the new Blue Planet travel destinations, theme parks, island resorts, cruise ships to the Mediterranean, and winter ski resorts in the Alps. Kids from across the universe will arrive by the billions.

We need to prepare for our intergalactic guests. First, we will need an intergalactic reservation system to book all the arrivals and departures. The Blue Planet will be the travel destination for the entire universe, but what happens if we overbook? Well, we may need to limit reservations to only our Milky Way galaxy, but then we could be called out as intergalactic racists.

On the second afterthought, the 10,000-year-old 3 D travel brochure may have already attracted billions of kids throughout the universe, and now they are all adults. Could 5 billion unruly kids have been dropped off on the Blue Planet in just the past few centuries and are now all be irresponsible adults?

They claim the Milky Way has over 300 billion stars, so it is possible alien civilizations across our galaxy could have sent 5 billion unruly kids to our planet. No wonder the human race is so dysfunctional; we now have 5 billion humans with questionable genes.

Have interstellar spaceships intentionally dropped off their problem kids for the past 10000 years? Are other alien civilizations across the galaxy still dropping off only their unruly kids?

Now, this is insane; I need to forget about the intergalactic reservation systems; we have enough dysfunctional adult humans on the planet from our own Milky Way galaxy.

Now I know why ETs are trying to hybridize the human race, what a challenge. Now I also know why adults from planet Earth have a reputation of being violent misfits of our galaxy; I hope not the entire universe. I need to go for my morning walk.

What am I thinking? I can't start another project; I can't even complete the workbook; my afterthoughts keep sending me in crazy directions, now I am planning to design some intergalactic spaceship reservation system? I don't want to mention my crazy thoughts to anyone; now I know my afterthoughts are just more crazy thoughts.

## Einstein Understood nature

As I began my morning walk along a path next to a stream, I watched a beautiful sunrise and birds chirping and the trees blowing in the cool morning breeze. I remembered back when I noticed how all species of birds lived in harmony with nature when we camped years ago in the forests of PA.

As I walked through a Healing Garden, I came upon a waterfall. The words are written on the wall behind the waterfall read:

"Look deep into nature, and then you will understand everything better." Albert Einstein.

I learned this truth as a young boy living on a small farm. We had all we needed to live a productive and happy life. With fertile land to grow crops and a few farm animals to provide basic food, we had all we needed to live in harmony with nature.

Now less than 100 million humans are living in small villages across North America. This was about the population of the Native Indians of North America before Columbus arrived over 500 years ago. The Native Indian storyteller was right; we all needed to follow the fundamental rules of nature, or mankind will not endure.

### I walked along a stream below a waterfall

As I walked further along the path below the waterfall, I saw crops of wheat growing in the fields and farm animals grazing in lush meadows. Wildflowers and plants are growing everywhere. Mother Earth has been returned back to nature. There are no rich or poor any longer, and everyone is valued for what they can contribute to their community. Women are equal to men, and children are cherished and not abandoned as it was during WW III.

I see a world without organized religion, just the spirituality of nature, as the driving life force of all life across the globe. Children of all different races and species are taught to reach a higher level of consciousness and become true citizens of the universe.

I envision the hybrid race living on food primarily from only natural whole grains and plants and herbs and seafood. I see physical illnesses cured with natural plans and herbs. I see all mental illnesses cured by spiritual healers and not toxic chemicals.

### A wise and noble elder appears before us

I walked out of the Healing Garden and down a path toward the shore. I was suddenly suspended out over the ocean. A weathered and wise elder dressed with a headband appears before us. We are all suspended over the ocean, looking toward him on the shore. The wise elder is on the shore is speaking to all of us. A gentle cool breeze is blowing in from the ocean. He begins to speak to all of us, to all the billions of humans that have passed over to the other side.

He begins by saying, "It is apparent your hate, greed, and selfish inhuman behavior toward each other have brought the entire human race to the brink of extinction. The universe gave humans a gift of free will, but a small covert group of selfish humans has misused and abused the precious gift of free will. The Teardrops have saved the natural recourses on Blue Planet. Our people have lived beside the Teardrops for tens of thousands of years and learned from them the laws of the universe. We have been taught how to live in peace and harmony with nature here on the Blue Planet."

He goes on, "We believe everything is spiritual, has a spirit; rocks, trees, lakes, and streams all have a reason to exist, but humans needed to follow the fundamental rules of the Blue Planet. Humans had their own rules to follow, to behave like humans, not like predators' in the wild. Humans needed to demonstrate human qualities of caring, compassion, love, and kindness toward each other.

The evil being with the Blue Planet patch has completed his diabolical mission on the Blue Planet; now, the planet has less than a billion inhabitants. This diabolical evil being has singularly orchestrated WW III and will go on to destroy all life on other planets unless they learn the laws of the universe.

## Super secrets could give free resources to everyone on the planet

The small groups that destroyed the human race have escaped to the dark side of the moon. These small covert groups have taken super secrets that could benefit all mankind, and they have used them to only benefit themselves and the CCCC.

Yes, super secrets could have provided mankind free energy, clean water, and healthy food to everyone on planet Earth. The small covert groups will eventually repeat the same crimes against humanity on another planet in another galaxy. They will not be allowed back to visit the Blue Planet until they become true citizens of the universe.

Humans were given the gift of free will. Some humans allowed small covert groups of people to commit crimes against humanity. They sought absolute power by using war and conflict instead of teaching all people to reach a higher level of consciousness. The hybrids are now in control of the Blue Planet.

## The Blue Planet is not ours; we are just visitors

He went on to explain Teardrop's role in the universe. "Teardrops have co-existed peacefully on this Blue Planet for thousands of years alongside the indigenous peoples until the threat of nuclear war became a reality in WW II.

The Teardrops were attempting to tell your leaders for over 70 years they came here to protect the Blue Planet from destruction from nuclear warheads. The Teardrops did not protect the human race from self-destruction. The Teardrops want to keep the planet's oceans as a safe harbor for all extraterrestrials to visit from other planets in the universe.

Our peoples see the spirituality and beauty of the Blue Planet as sacred; we want the peaceful citizens of any galaxy in the universe to enjoy and not destroy the Blue Planet. Humans have followed small covert groups that profit from war and conflict. The covert groups have not allowed humans to learn the spirituality of nature or the laws of the universe. The hybridization of all the species in the universe is one of natural evolution.

Hybrids have taken over the planet and will follow the fundamental laws of nature but also teach children to expand mind and body

Philip Van Ostrander

consciousness. The Blue Planet is not ours; we are just visitors. Learning true love and kindness is a gift from above and is the only way to become a true citizen of the universe.

## I asked the nurse, "Is our nation at war?"

As I came out of the effects of anesthesia, I asked the nurse, "Is our nation at war?' She said, "No, I don't think so, but your vital signs showed major brain activity during the entire 12-hour operation, and then she asked, "Did you feel any pain?" I said, "No, I could not feel any physical pain except lower right-side discomfort but the emotional pain was very disturbing to me. Some images were quite real. I was having dire forewarnings of the future for the world and not a dream at all". Well, she said, "Your right kidney was removed without any complications." I said, "There must be some mistake. I was having a heart attack and did not need a kidney transplant; my doctor said I have the kidneys of a 20-year-old".

Then she said, "The new Health Care Rationing Agency (HCRA) requires all matching organs be harvested if a match for CCCC officials. The HCRA needed your healthy right kidney. The HCRA has chosen you to be the first organ donor for a very important Hollywood director." Well, I thought the HCRA did promise they would prolong people's lives, but they did not mention they would harvest other peoples' organs to do it. Quite barbaric, but I cannot complain; it was not my brain they harvested this time.

I said, "I signed up to be an organ donor after my death and not during an emergency heart procedure." Well, she said, "The NRO policies went into effect during your operation," I asked, "Does NRO stand for New Rules of Order"? Then she said, "Oh yes, and the CCCC will take over all operations and logistics to keep the country safe from all foreign and domestic enemies. They will provide everyone with goods and services."

## The Bipolar WAVES Workbook

I did not bother to ask what the CCCC stood for. She said the officials would have complete command and control of all security functions of the old government

I did feel pain and see the surgeon put something in a stainless-steel kidney-shaped pan. Is this what the new Health Care Rationing Agency (HCRA) program is all about, to detect and harvest people's healthy organs and "donate" them to officials on demand? Then she showed me a clipboard with "Donor Number 1" in big letters. She said, "You must feel very proud you "donated" your kidney to a famous director of war films?"

I wondered, was this director kept alive to produce the propaganda films aired during the staged terrorist attack? I better not say that video was very poor quality, like an old B&W movie from the '50s.

I could not tell her the horrific images I watched unfold, or they could wheel me into the psychiatric ward. That's why I need to hide my mental illness diagnosis, but of course, the HCRA has all my records in detail. They knew I had the kidneys of a 20-year-old guy. I just need to keep my-crazy thoughts to myself, but my manifest dreams showed the challenges the mentally ill will need to face in the coming years ahead.

I hesitated; I wanted to ask her if the surgeon had removed a metal object embedded in my scrotum that was implanted by ETs from another galaxy. I am glad I hesitated to ask; I would probably be sent immediately to the nearest psychiatric ward to "donate" my brain to science.

She went on, "The entire country let out a sigh of relief; the CCCC will rage war against all enemies of the CCCC; we just need to follow all the New Rules of Order (NRO)."

# Stage 15 Wake up! Your nation is at war

I heard Nicole say, "We need to pack up soon and leave before checkout time." I mumbled something about I could not get to sleep until dawn. She let me snooze for a few more minutes.

I like to get a good night's rest before we travel. Packing up the camper to travel is a bit of a hassle; it may have something to do with going back home and facing the same issues again.

I had my three cups of coffee to satisfy my caffeine addiction., Oh no, I almost forgot I do have another addiction, an addiction to caffeine ever since I worked on Nantucket.

Nicole kept reminding me we needed to be out of the campground before checkout time. She stowed away most of the things in the morning while I was sleeping. After my fifth cup of coffee, we broke down the tents, stored the rest of the camping gear, and we hooked up the trailer to our SUV. The park ranger drove by our campsite just as we pulled out. I was drinking coffee all the way back home to keep me awake.

Well, it was still 2020, and the world did not come to an end during our camping trip. This camping trip was not as relaxing as other camping trips in the past. One change I would make for our next trip is to leave my tablet and laptop behind, as well as my cell phone. Sometimes my cell phone is nothing but an electronic version of handcuffs.

The next day I was exhausted as I unpacked and stored our camping gear. I needed to mow the lawn and attend to the chores around the house. Our shed was still leaning over; I still have no idea how to fix it, which is symbolic of my life right now.

## Yet another stressful situation

During our vacation at the Jersey Shore, I did not worry about Ryan; his mood seemed good before we left. He watched Bonnie during our vacation, and they seemed to get along just fine. One night before we went on vacation, we watched an outdoor survival adventure series together and planned to watch another episode when we got back from the shore.

I promised myself I was not going to stress out about Ryan; he is an adult. A neighbor came over and told us his inspection sticker on his car expired two weeks ago. I went down and knocked on his door, opened it just a few inches, and told him his car needed to be inspected; he just said he wanted to be left alone.

He could get a very expensive fine if he got stopped by the cops. If his sticker was only expired for a few days, the cops might not write him a ticket, but after several weeks, that's just irresponsible.

His sudden change in mood troubled me greatly; he was fine before we left to go on vacation, and now, I want to call 911 for an intervention. Nicole does not see the risk of him isolating himself; I do. From my experience, several things worry me, he is not stable, he will not answer simple questions, and he is isolating himself from reality—for example, the penalties of not getting his car inspected.

I could ask for involuntary emergency intervention, but he is smart enough to spend the required number of hours under observation and then will check himself out of the hospital.

He does not appear to be under the influence of drugs, but Stu claims Ryan has been smoking pot for years. I am worried about that, too, because drug dealers are lacing pot with a mix of meth and Fentanyl. Tomorrow I am going to get a Narcan kit. Right now, I am deathly afraid he will have a serious psychotic break with reality, and that could lead to suicide.

I am very concerned because I know people with BD can decide in an instant to end their own life. I think if I was "Normal," I would not take his behavior as extremely troublesome. I might just say leave him alone he will be ok; he is just going through some personal stuff.

## I was probably acting irresponsibly from Ryan's point of view

We still don't have a medical diagnosis for Ryan's issues; maybe he is just working on his personal problems. We should not compare Ryan to Matt; they each have challenges to overcome in life, as do all of us. I need to realize I was acting like an idiot before we went to the shore on our risky COVID-19 vacation. Without a vaccine, I was probably acting irresponsible and stupid from Ryan's point of view.

I should be working on completing the workbook. I will feel the workbook is a success if it helps some people understand many "Normal" everyday stressful life situations can accumulate and cause someone with BD to quickly lose all sense of reality. Too often, the result ends in a psychotic episode. Sadly, sometimes the solution is to take your own life.

So, for several years I have been an optimist, Ryan was getting some form of help. Now I need to stress over something I have no control over. I need to step back and try to let Ryan find help. I am so upset because I feel helpless and hopeless. We just got back from our camping trip, and the worry begins all over again.

## The common Robin has a great work ethic

As usual, I went to the park around sunset for my walk. After my walk, I sat down on a bench to watch the sunset and noticed a common Robin still foraging for a few bits of food. I thought this little bird had been busy nonstop all summer long removing earthworms, insects, and grubs. Sometimes they work from 5 am to 9 pm, which is a 16-hour day: What a work ethic, no naps, lunch breaks, or work protests. Humans, on the other hand, only work from 9 am to 5, have long lunch breaks, paid vacations, holidays, and complain all day from 9 to 5 about how hard they work. Perhaps the common Robin is not so common after all.

Well, the sun went down, and I went home still concerned about the state of our nation and the world. Birds really are marvelous creatures, and they are also intelligent; as the winter approaches, they head south for the winter. I wonder if that little Robin is giving me a sign; head south this winter.

## Iva calmly said, "Wake up! Your nation is at war."
The night after we returned from the shore, I had another manifest, which is another real-life dream. Iva stood in front of me and calmly said, "Wake up! Your nation is at war."

I sat straight up in bed. Iva's message was right in front of me all along. Of course, we are at war, and it has been hidden in plain sight all along. I needed to resolve so many personal problems, BD, diabetes, and my case of amnesia before I could fully understand the future of our nation. I have had months of bad spells over the years, and they consume many days and nights. Perhaps Iva unconsciously knew the fate of our nation back then but could not tell anyone of the dangers we will all now face.

I noticed Iva said your nation because her nation or homeland in Eastern Europe was completely destroyed during WW II. How tragic she needed to die to return to her homeland.

I believe both of us had very traumatic events happen in our past for sure; perhaps she also had a case of amnesia during WW II and is now telling me to prepare for WW III.

She never spoke of the horrors of war, but she had to see the genocide of her people and the total destruction of her homeland. She often said the Russians treated them like dirt, and then when the Germans invaded their homeland, they murdered innocent men, women, and children.

Wake up! That's what she is attempting to warn me; we are not safe. That's why she came to this country at eight years old to feel safe, and now she is now warning me of what horrendous things that happened in her homeland will be happening here in our homeland. Is it a stretch of the imagination to think she passed on a few years ago to avoid witnessing another genocide here, like what happened in Germany during WW II? Is this the reason she did not want to have children?

I know all these thoughts to "Normal" people may sound insane; I like the word crazy, but is it? You know people at the Awake course had similar revelations about events that happened in the past and will happen in the future. Is it crazy to think Iva's spirit is encouraging me to write all my dire predictions as the final stage of the workbook?

The visions I had that night at the Jersey Shore told of the dire consequences of blindly following evil people with evil intentions. Most people in my vision were addicted to drugs. My visions ended with the human race close to extinction and hybrids taking control of the planet.

In my vision, I asked the nurse if our nation was at war. Now Iva is warning me from the other side to Wake up; our nation is at war.

## Our nation is divided between the RADs vs. the MSAs

Now I know our nation is so divided we actually have split apart into two very different nations. The Democrat Party of the 70s, 80s and

'90s has evolved into a radical anti-American group of Socialists that call themselves Democratic Socialists. I call them the Radical-American Democrats or RADs and the Main Street pro-Americans, the MSAs.

## Has China now become the global superpower?

The pandemic that arrived here in March of 2020 had a devastating effect on our economy. The stock market has lost trillions of dollars in value. I understand many experts claim our nation has lost over 6 trillion dollars of wealth after the pandemic hit in March 2020. Does that mean China has caught up to us economically after the pandemic hit just a few months ago?

I remember when China sent a probe to the dark side of the moon just a few months ago. The national cable news network's spent weeks on the impeachment trial of Trump. Our cable networks barely covered the story of China's voyage to the dark side of the moon. What else is our media not telling the public?

In March 2020, we locked down schools and went to online education. Our nation has handled the pandemic poorly; we have locked down businesses and stopped educating our youth.

I believe we should protect the old people and let the young people work and kids go back to school. Most of our old people are not working and can shelter in place. Back in the 80s, we made the tragic blunder of shipping our factories and skills overseas. The decision to lock down our entire nation may be another tragic blunder we will regret.

Now our media cable channels are spending all day and all night talking about the number of deaths by COVD-19. Our national news coverage should be covering the number of deaths caused by drugs and crime.

## Documentaries exposé the drug culture in our nation
The most disturbing news seldom reported, drug cartels are importing tons of toxic drugs.

As someone who has believed in the power of nature for all my life, I have watched a [Nat Geo (Geo) series of outdoor life around the world. I marveled at how the camera crews could get close enough to film nature close up and in spectacular color. Lately, I have noticed Nat Geo has documented other very important events going on around the world.

There is a documentary series Drugs Inc on the Nat-Geo channel that exposes the drug culture in our nation and around the world. Every episode focuses on one city in the country. Many episodes follow the flow of drugs from the manufacturer overseas and Mexico to the user in our country. In every city, they show how drugs are destroying our nation from within by drugs, crime, and corruption. Drug-related crimes go unreported or minimized by the radical city administrations.

The most alarming revelation is many of the chemicals to make Fentanyl, meth, and many other drugs are imported from overseas.

## Iva's Wake up warning is coming true
The events in our nation, even after Iva passed on, have been very disturbing; the war between the RADs and the MSAs is raging on right now. So far, the radical left ideology is winning the war. Our nation's future parallels that of Germany in the 30' is breathtakingly similar. We now have three highly industrialized superpowers, all fighting to attain absolute power in the world. Our nation is in conflict with two superpowers, China and Russia.

During WW II, Japan and Germany formed a pack. When we declared war on Japan after Pearl Harbor, Germany declared war on America. Could China form a similar pact with Russia?

During WW II, our nation was at war with two superpowers, Japan and Germany. As in Germany before and during WW II, our nation has an out-of-control drug epidemic. The corrupt media does not want the public to know about 100,000 people die of an overdose of illegal and legal drugs every year. The media continues to persuade the public the pandemic is the most destructive force since the flu in 1918, over 100 years ago.

Germany indoctrinated young children in youth camps to obey and hate so-called inferior races. The Nazis convinced their citizens to hate the Jews and inferior people, including the disabled and mentally ill. At Nazis rallies, Hitler blamed the Jews for Germany's problems. The solution, the Holocaust, the Jews needed to be eliminated to solve the social and economic ills of Germany.

Will the propaganda of the left persuade radical Democrats that White people are all racists? Will they claim our 1776 Constitution must be eliminated in order to accomplish true racial, social, and economic justice?

We are not following the 1776 Constitution; I think I know what comes next. In Germany in the '30s, the Nazis' rise to power used violence, propaganda, and intimidation to terrorize the people. The German people were taught to believe the Aryan race was the superior race.

The Jews, the physically and mentally disabled, were inferior human beings. The genocide of Jews and others was the result of drugs, hate, and racist propaganda aimed toward its own people. See any similarities, I do?

Our nation is being controlled by a rapidly growing number group of radicals using social media to stifle free speech and limit our rights. We no longer follow the 1776 Constitution.

So, in my opinion, the hate and rage against the White race in our nation strongly parallel the treatment of the Jews and other physically and mentally disabled people in Nazis Germany in the 30s.

In my visions I had that night at the shore predicted a three-way conflict between the three superpowers would end in WW III. WW III eliminated billions of people from the face of the earth. Only the humans that live without modern technology did survive.

After WW III is over, ETs will return to teach the kind and caring people the laws of the universe. The same advanced technology used for weapons of war before WW III will be used to help all mankind on the planet after WW III. Will all my visions come true? I don't know, but I do think Iva's wake-up warning is coming true right now.

## I feel fortunate to be born an American.

Yes, I am very fortunate to be born an American, but I know as it stands now everyone will not have the freedoms I had as a teenager growing up in America. Peaceful people cannot fight against the superpowers; they don't own weapons of war. Peaceful people of the planet need to cause a major shift in people's beliefs and behavior, and it needs to happen very soon. Americans generally take for granted our civil liberties will be protected by the 1776 Constitution, but we are drifting away from the 1776 Constitution and denying rights to many citizens.

## We may need to start a legal defense fund

Looking to the future, I would like to start a legal defense fund for people with mental illnesses. Most of us don't have the money to retain lawyers and paralegals to help us fight for our rights under the Americans with Disabilities Act.

I believe people with mental issues should band together and fight for their rights under the law before it is too late. Some laws are written to protect people with mental illness under the American Disabilities Act. The disabled could retain a team of lawyers that could defend people with mental illness.

The right to own firearms has been taken away from people with a history of mental illness. I do not think mentally ill people should own firearms. So how do we protect ourselves in our homes and in the street? Every American has the right to feel safe in our homes, on the job, and on the street.

I know I do not have the funds to defend myself in a court of law for alleged crimes or misdemeanors. I propose mentally ill people start a legal defense fund. If 100,000 people with mental health issues could spend $100 each, that would be 10 million dollars. The fund would be used to protect our right to feel safe in our own homes.

Feeling safe was the reason Iva came to America. She left her homeland after the war because she did not feel safe. Now I know how Iva felt during and after WW II; she needed to find a country she could feel safe from harm and prosecution.

### Some people with BD are ashamed to accept help

We need to find a way to help and protect people with mental illness. Sometimes people in the BDS group are reluctant to accept help from the government. I feel people with mental illness should accept help from any legal source. The aid includes social aid programs, welfare, SSI, veteran benefits, food stamps, and other resources. Our nation spends billions on programs that do not benefit our own citizens. Many programs are simply wasteful spending.

I think anyone with mental illness should apply for as many benefits as they can while they are stable and in good physical health. The time may come when many people with BD will have difficulty even filing for benefits. Many times, when mentally ill people reach despair, they find it difficult or impossible to navigate the many social aid systems. I compare filing for government benefits can be very stressful and time-consuming, maybe even more stressful than applying for and getting a job.

## People with BD will need to accept ETs do exist

I know it may sound a little bit crazy to think about aliens from other galaxies, but I believe a full disclosure event will happen very soon. Credible UFOs were filmed by the military back in 2004. Whistleblowers and others in the UFO community have been exposing more details about what our government knows about UFOs. In 2020 several other film clips were released showing UFOs traveling at speeds much faster than hypersonic. I believe people with mental illness and others will need to accept ETs do exist and eventually could help the human race.

I think ETs are here to protect the planet from destruction from nuclear bombs and radiation. In my crazy, I mean humble opinion, I believe our nation has kept many secrets about UFOs and ETs from the public for over seven decades.

## I am not encouraging violent protests or riots

I am just a messenger and not a political revolutionary. I am encouraging a peaceful spiritual revolution and not a violent political revolution.

I need to apologize; the theme of my workbook is so dire about our nation's future, but that is one goal of the workbook. I am just a messenger of what I believe is my truth. My truth is our nation is at war on many fronts. We are following a very similar path of Germany before, during, and after WW II.

I continue to get messages from Iva's spirit after she did warn me our nation is at war. I have no reason not to believe her warnings will not come true; we have a war raging between two very different ideologies in our nation, pro-American and Anti-American. However, our nation is also at war with many hostile nations and terrorist groups around the world.

Again, I am not encouraging violent protests to achieve our goals of living in peace and harmony. Mentally ill people cannot protect themselves with firearms. War and conflict will not help the human race survive and thrive; humans need a radical or paradigm shift in consciousness.

## How to cause a global paradigm shift in consciousness?

I watched the film Superhuman [(Cory, 2020) the other night about the power of the human mind and consciousness. The film showed several kids could read a book while totally blindfolded. Several other psychic demonstrations told me our minds could switch between disbelief to belief in an instant and accept the impossible. Some people claim to see is believing, but after watching kids read a book blindfolded, I had to acknowledge I watched some type of psychic phenomena. I need to question what I can see with my eyes blindfolded or not blindfolded.

I also had watched someone use their psychic abilities when I was on the farm. After the water douser located a source of water with just two sticks, I did not question how he did it. Now I know the man used his psychic abilities or higher consciousness to find water hundreds of feet below ground. I guess it is all about believing we can experience things beyond our five senses using what I will call ESP. I am convinced we all have the ability to reach a higher state of consciousness. We just need skilled instructors to teach and guide us.

This award-winning film gave me some optimism; if enough peace-loving humans could collectively come together through meditation, prayer, and positive intention, it could cause a paradigm shift in people's beliefs and behavior. Millions, maybe billions of people could instantly gain the universal knowledge of love and caring and reject a war and conflict mentality.

You know I do not believe in organized religion, but I do think prayer, meditation, and kindness can change people's beliefs and behavior. To battle evil forces in the world, we may also need to look for supernatural solutions to prevent a human catastrophe.

## A paradigm shift could change the world

This Superhuman film was so eye-opening to me; just a few years ago, I could not see any way peaceful people could win a war against the mighty superpowers on the planet. The superpowers have mighty weapons of war and the Vast Information Conglomerate (VIC) to shut down any dissent.

I think a global movement based on teaching ESP and consciousness should be offered worldwide in person or online. The course could be called "Paradigm: The power of consciousness" and be offered in person in over 100 countries and 47 different languages. The course would be designed after the Awake spiritual growth course I attended back in the mid-70s.

I remember the remote viewing processes and other demonstrations of psychic abilities during the Awake course had a profound influence on my spiritual growth, although I did not realize it at the time.

## A global Paradigm movement

I believe billions of people in the world want to reject a war and conflict mentality but have been taught or more likely indoctrinated by small, powerful covert groups. These groups convince people to use hate and violence as the only way to solve social and economic problems. They use propaganda, fear, and the VIC to gain and hold onto power.

Is this just another one of my crazy afterthoughts? Not at all; the planet has many very knowledgeable and spiritual people. Gifted instructors could teach all humans they do have superhuman powers, powers that can turn the planet into a kinder and more peaceful world.

I don't claim to be a gifted psychic, but after I watched the film Superhuman a few times, I had a profound shift in my thoughts. I had a much more positive outlook on the future of the human race here on planet Earth.

We have gifted parapsychologists and spiritual leaders that could lead a super-powerful global Paradigm movement. I also believe it could also help people with addictions, BD, and other mental illnesses. The Paradigm movement would not be based on any organized religion but just changing the world by the power of thought and consciousness.

I believe the near extinction of the human race will happen unless there is a paradigm shift away from the war and conflict mentality of the many groups currently in power. That includes both RADs and MSAs in our nation. Iva is right; our nation is at war; we are all in danger on several levels.

After I watched the film Alien Crash Retrieval [(Long M. J., 2016), I learned our covert UFO groups did not protect alien beings from other worlds. The film claimed our covert UFO groups have been shooting down UFOs, killing and perhaps holding some alien's captive. So, our covert UFO groups may have mistreated or disrespected some aliens for over 70 years.

## Were our intentions noble and just after WW II?

Bob Lazar claims our nation has a small UFO group of people in charge of our nation's fate. I think our nation's current military forces are led by relatively a few small covert groups.

I believe our nation's purpose and intentions were noble up until WW II. Were our intentions noble and just after WW II? Our involvement in Korea, Vietnam in the 60s, and then the Middle East wars after 9/11 have both ended in failure. We are technically still at war with North Korea. We have troops still stationed in South Korea. Wars and conflicts have cost the American taxpayers trillions of dollars.

## I hope people with BD will be ready to accept ETs.

Well, now I am sure ETs are here and watching us, but many humans are in total denial ETs even exist. Most humans do not understand aliens may have been mistreated for over 70 years, perhaps longer. So, a movement should begin to free all innocent humans and alien prisoners on the planet.

I know for some people, this may sound insane, but we need a global shift in consciousness to think on an intergalactic scale. A major shift in consciousness will eventually happen anyway after a full disclosure event by ETs happens, and I predict very soon. However, I can only see a full disclosure event happening when the world becomes more peaceful and caring.

The Teardrops in my vision represent all species of ETs, and we need to acknowledge their existence on planet Earth. Peace-loving people need to wake up and focus their intention on being kind to all beings, including ETs and all life forms in the universe. Planet Earth needs to embrace all forms of beings in the universe. I only hope people with BD will be ready to accept a new reality.

It is apparent from what Ben Rich stated back in 1995 the covert UFO groups have no intention of helping mankind. Here it is about 25 years after Ben Rich passed on, and I do not see anyone unlock the-super secrets in the Black Box that would help all mankind. However, Ben did imply using ESP, or I assume other psychic powers can overcome our physical and mental limitations.

## Noble and just Intention is everything
I believe ETs did assist in helping our nation become independent during the Revolutionary War. Our intention was noble; our Founding Fathers wrote the 1776 Constitution to protect all people in our nation. Why would ETs help our nation now? Our nation is at war within our own borders, Middle East, Far East, Iran, terrorists, and others.

Was Iva telling me we also are at war with ETs? No, not violent combat with ETs, but I claim ETs are not helping our nation any longer. Can anyone argue ETs cannot help or harm the human race? Wake up! If ETs can shut down our nuclear weapon facilities, why couldn't they help any nuclear superpower they choose to win a war?

Are ETs warning all the superpowers they are heading down the wrong path? That is what happened in my visions, but ETs protected the planet from nuclear destruction but not the human race.

What is the reason our covert UFO groups are covering up our relationship with ETs? Is this my truth by omission theory? The truth is UFOs and ETs are real and have helped our nation win WW II. The omission, ETs have been betrayed and mistreated for over 70 years by the covert UFO groups. After WW II, our UFO groups had evil intentions, and ETs will no longer help our nation.

Our nation has not won a major war since WW II. Our reputation in the world as a beacon of freedom and justice is evaporating before our very eyes.

According to my visions at the shore, the superpowers attempted to eliminate the human race entirely by nuclear weapons. Will the evil intentions of all the superpowers and other groups end in WW III?

Not one superpower is offering a peaceful solution to the chaos and violence in the world.

## Are ETs protecting or harming our nation?

I watched an episode of Ancient Aliens titled "Aliens and the Presidents." [(Ancient Aliens: Aliens and the Presidents, 2020)].

The film followed many US presidents that had some contact with UFOs and ETs. George Washington had some sort of positive encounter with ETs. He had some kind of premonition he would win the Revolutionary War. Perhaps alien beings did help our country gain independence during the Revolutionary War.

Of course, Abraham Lincoln fought to free the slaves in the Civil War in 1865. I also think ETs helped end the Civil War. Freeing the slaves was a noble and just cause. Several battles were won by overcoming some very difficult obstacles, almost impossible odds without some sort of divine intervention. President Lincoln warned our nation could only perish if we did not obey the laws of the land. He thought we could only be defeated from within if we did not follow the laws of our nation.

President Truman had UFOs fly over Washington, DC in 1952 not once but twice within two weeks. Of course, President Truman ordered the atomic bomb dropped on Japan twice. Were ETs warning

President Truman they had UFOs ready to eliminate any nuclear threat?

I think ETs did help us win WW II. Some say President Eisenhower (Ike) also had contact with ETs. A rumor spread. Ike had a meeting with ETs and made an agreement with ETs. The agreement was ETs could study humans, and we would get to access their advanced technology. According to Bob Lazar and Ben Rich, we did get advanced technology from ETs. Did the agreement also state we would never use nuclear weapons again?

I remember as Ike was leaving the White House in 1961, he warned our nation that what he called the Military-Industrial Complex (MIC) could become so powerful and be a risk to our country. Now six decades later, I am beginning to understand Ike's warning. Was Ike telling us the small covert UFO groups were already gaining too much power back in 1961?

President Ronald Regan also had a keen interest in UFOS and ETs. He witnessed a UFO following his plane at 30,000 feet. At a UN conference, he said something like 'If we were invaded by aliens, would the world come together?"

President Carter also witnessed a UFO. So, I think up until we got involved in the Korean, Vietnam, and Middle East wars, ETs may have helped us use their advanced technology to win wars.

## The ultimate battle between good vs. evil intentions

I do believe there will be fierce resistance by many evil forces and the superpowers in the world to continue down a path of war and conflict. A Paradigm peaceful movement may set up the ultimate battle between good vs. evil intentions of people in the world. Focusing on good intention is everything, but we need to learn how to use our psychic powers. I know there are billions of peace-loving people on the planet; they all need to focus their intention to help all mankind, including ETs.

The visions I had that night at the Jersey Shore told of the dire consequences of blindly following evil people with evil intentions. Most people in my vision were addicted to drugs. My visions ended with the human race close to extinction and hybrids taking control of the planet.

Sadly, our nation was attacked on 9/11, 2001, almost 20 years ago, the loss of about 3000 innocent lives was tragic, but I fear the next attack in our homeland will end with millions of innocent people dead; I fear multiple terrorist attacks on our innocent citizens may be from within our own nation. The attack on the Twin Towers on 9/11/ 2001 started wars and conflicts in the Middle East that are still being fought today in the year 2020 in Afghanistan.

## The human race has a choice, peace or perish

What I am saying is if covert groups with evil intentions continue to use propaganda, fear, and intimidation, then we are all doomed to perish. Peaceful people need to rise up and cause a paradigm shift in the thought and behavior toward all living things, including ETs.

So, peace-loving people with good intentions need first to become conscious or aware of who or what has evil intentions. Peace-loving people need to also become aware ETs do exist, and they can help us if we have good and noble intentions. I believe ETs did help several US presidents win wars. I believe our nation did have good and noble intentions until after WW II.

If humans can cause a paradigm movement with peaceful and good intentions, then I believe full disclosure by aliens will happen. Billions of people will then survive. After full disclosure, aliens will unlock that Black Box with the super secrets. Again, I say good and noble intentions are necessary to win any battle. I also believe good intentions are necessary for ETs to help us solve other problems.

Regardless of the path humans take, planet Earth will be returned back to Mother Nature. If our nation does not have peaceful intentions, I fear our nation will perish. The way I see it, our nation has a choice, peace or perish.

## One of Einstein's quotes seems appropriate now
Iva's warning keeps repeating in my mind. I know our nation is at war, but I feel paralyzed to do anything about it.

A few years ago, I watched the HISTORY channel to learn about Einstein's theory of relativity, but I never could understand his theory of bending of time and space. I thought I would understand the cosmos and contribute to all humanity in my lifetime, but little time is left. Well, that is meant as a delusional BD joke, but at the end, before the credits rolled, they put up some of Einstein's famous quotes, and I wrote down several of them in my journal. My journal now has well over 500 pages, just a symptom of my hoarding disorder. The workbook needs to account for almost 80 years of my life with BD. I am done with the workbook; I am going to retire my journal to the garage with my other stuff. Sorry, I am getting distracted with my many afterthoughts again. Anyway, I looked through my journal one last time and found one of Einstein's quotes it read,

"The world will not be destroyed by those who do evil, but by those who watch them without doing anything."

Einstein's quote was hard for me to understand at first because I think we need to first identify exactly who or what is evil. Our nation does not quite yet understand the dire consequence of not even identifying evil. That is, first, we need to identify evil before we can fight evil. Unfortunately, I do not think kind and peaceful people in our nation identify evil. Many kind and peaceful people do not or cannot accept we are not safe; we are at war.

Einstein's quote was very important for me to understand because he did identify the Nazis as evil and did something about it. Many German citizens during WW II did not see the Nazis as evil. He fled to America to be safe and avoid persecution by the Nazis. Do I need to point out Iva also came to the same conclusion about evil?

## Those horrific B&W pictures of the Holocaust were real

You know, I think the Jews learned a valuable but very hard lesson during WW II. Jews will never again be at the mercy of another evil dictator. I don't pretend to know the politics or the history of the Jewish people, but I do know genocide and crimes against humanity did happen about 75 years ago all across Europe. I saw with my own eyes those horrific B&W pictures of the Holocaust when I was only 12 years old. I still have a picture in my mind of a SS officer standing on the backs of hundreds of bodies in a long trench. The SS officer was shooting people in the back with a pistol.

Before and during WW II, the Jews in many Eastern European countries had no way to fight back against the Nazis regime. Now I am sure the Jewish people will never allow themselves to be slaughtered again in the streets without a fierce fight. The Jews will always have weapons of war to fight threats from any adversary.

I heard someone argue years ago Israel should never have been allowed to become an independent state. I ask you, where did you expect the Jews to go after WW II? I understand Jews were not welcome back in Europe after the war. Many of the homes of the Jews were occupied by the survivors of WW II.

From my perspective, the most outrageous abuse of power during WW II was the Nazis systematically exterminating and terrorizing the Jews, the disabled, and the mentally ill. The disabled and mentally ill were used for experimentation and torture. Some mentally ill people were used to test the limits of human endurance. Some prisoners were given performance-enhancing drugs like meth and forced to walk with heavy backpacks until they collapsed on the ground. Yes, I am very concerned the same cruel and sadistic behavior could happen right here in our nation. I argue what happened in Germany could be repeated here in our nation.

## Iva's spirit is telling me we are not safe any longer

Iva often mentioned she felt safe in America. I believe her spirit is telling me we are not safe any longer in America. I have admitted our nation has made many blunders or mistakes since Columbus arrived in North America, but I believe small covert groups have started and continued conflicts to accumulate wealth and power.

You know Iva and I were born about a year apart during WW II. When I was eight years old, I was out riding my old bike up the dirt road behind our farm. At the same time, Iva was living in war-torn Eastern Europe after WW II getting ready to come to America around 1950. Iva would never talk about her experiences before coming to America, but I had to assume she endured some horrific and unspeakable experiences. I am certain her experiences were unspeakable because she could never speak about her past life in worn-torn Eastern Europe.

## Iva has a message for all Americans

Our nation has never watched as armored tanks rolled through our cities, small towns, and villages. We never watched heavily armed troops occupy the streets of our cities and kill innocent men, women, and children. We have never watched in horror as churches burned down with innocent old men, women, and children being burned alive while locked inside. We have never heard innocent men, women, and children screaming in pain, but maybe Iva did.

So, Iva, my 2nd love, was right when she warned me, "Wake up, your nation is at war." and now I need to "Wake up and publish The Bipolar WAVES Workbook."

## The End of My Bipolar Story

CHAPTER 3

# How to Use the WAVES Chart

If you skipped over my very long bipolar story in Chapter 2, I need to go over a few important periods of my life that deal with my BD lifestyle. That is my very different life with BD before and after I was diagnosed and treated with lithium at mid-life.

The year 2020 has been a very exhausting, challenging, and stressful year for everyone, including our family. The pandemic with lockdowns, stay-at-home orders, homeschooling, business bankruptcies, and the personal risk of contracting the virus has caused my anxiety to rise to dangerous levels. I am afraid the added stress of having BD may put me at a critical stress level. I needed to know if I was at risk of a mental breakdown or at risk of a physical breakdown, including the chance of suicide.

I have come to the conclusion many of these life situations can cause extreme emotional stress and, if not treated early on, may lead to extreme psychotic episodes or even suicide. Emotional stress and the consequences of BD illness can also lead to physical illnesses.

## My BD Stress, abuse, rejection, abandonment issues
I claim many people with BD may have many mental, psychological, and physical illnesses in addition to BD. Constant emotional and physical abuse, harassment, ridicule, and the shame of having a

mental illness over time can result in serious lifelong consequences. Struggling with a mental illness for a lifetime can wear the strongest person down and cause other serious issues like anxiety, addictions, job, relationship, and marriage problems.

## *I am not worthy of being loved*
After attending the Bipolar Disorder Support (BDS) group for several years, I came to the conclusion "I was not worthy of being loved" since a young boy growing up on our farm. I accepted on an emotional level I was a victim of childhood abuse. Living with both BD and childhood abuse, I developed what I call an unworthy syndrome. The unworthy syndrome is not listed in the DSM [(American Psychiatric Association, 1987 manual. I think it defines a condition I had lived with after my father died when I was about five years old.

This deep-seated semi-conscious belief kept repeating in my scattered BD mind for my entire life. Every new situation accumulated until my stress level was so high I had many mental breakdowns I call bad spells. For over 75 years, I have had many bad manic and depressive BD episodes. Now I feel I understand my feelings of unworthiness hold the key to unlocking some of my troubled and challenging times in life.

My breakup with my 1st love in my early 20s reinforced those feelings of unworthiness, and I went into a state of amnesia. My finding I always felt unworthy explained many setbacks and challenges. I struggled with rejection issues since a young boy living on a farm.

The WAVES Chart lists many of these stressors in life that eventually lead to feelings of loneliness, despair, anger, rage, and unworthiness. In my case, my abuse led to a case of amnesia, alcoholism, anxiety, and other mental issues. I was incapable of loving and being loved by anyone, including myself. I don't think I even dealt with the sexual abuse issues until just recently.

Now I know many "Normal" people cope with similar situations, but people with BD often have issues with rejection, harassment, abandonment, other negative factors, relationship issues, job and marriage problems for years. Many of these problems are directly related to a diagnosis of BD. I also claim these life situations can lead to feelings of becoming victims of our mental illness.

After I received effective treatment for my BD, I was stable and what I call BD normal, but after 40 years of living with many stressful situations, I still felt I was not worthy of being loved.

The realization I have been living with the belief I was not worthy of being loved has given me a more positive outlook on life. I think many times when I had a BD episode about my 1$^{st}$ love or felt rejected; it triggered the feelings; I was unworthy. Now I identify and confront these very destructive feelings as a condition I need to challenge and overcome. I call this condition my unworthy syndrome.

## I claim many people with BD have a unique condition

I claim many people with BD struggle with a condition I call unworthy syndrome. What I am trying to say is some people with BD suffer from more than just a BD mental illness but, in addition, a unique condition I call unworthy syndrome. After attending the BDS group for over 20 years, I noticed some people, including myself, had an added unique condition I named an unworthy syndrome.

I found many people have very disturbing and hurtful beliefs about people with BD. I remember when the host on a TV show told the audience, "Don't marry someone with a mental illness." Comments like that can cause harmful and hurtful beliefs of unworthiness.

Other beliefs and feelings become ingrained in people's minds at a very young age. Feeling I am too broken to be lovable. My husband does not want me anymore. I guess I am not worthy of anyone's love, I was married three times, but they all left me. I will never get better. I am worthless; I am broke and don't have a home anymore. I was fired because I have a mental illness.

Would anyone be fired because they had MS?

All these false and negative experiences turn into deep-seated beliefs over the years and create a very difficult condition to overcome.

I have an unworthy syndrome. I have not completely overcome this condition, but now I understand these feelings were created when I could not fight back. I was a victim of childhood abuse and had no control over my environment. I was not diagnosed with BD and had no treatment for episodes of mania or depression. After my father passed away, I did not have grief counseling or support. I was mentally ill and abused, very difficult if not impossible obstacles to overcome without help.

Now I can say I deserve to be loved, have a good home, and live with dignity, but I also need to be responsible. I need to stay mentally stable, stay sober and be kind and generous to the people around me; however, I am having issues with the generous part.

## What I learned from living in Philly for ten years

I bought a row house in a marginal part of Philly in the late 70s. I learned many minorities in our neighborhood in Philly struggled to live a normal life. Poverty, drugs, and racial bias did occur in our neighborhood. The result was people turned to dealing and using drugs to dull the pain. I had a drug dealer living next door for ten years. I believe many mentally ill, the homeless, and people with drug and alcohol addictions also struggle with what I call an unworthy syndrome.

Someone once said anger relieves emotional pain. I think this statement is true; anger and violence can relieve but not resolve emotional and physical pain. Physical, sexual, and emotional abuse can lead to drug addiction, alcoholism, depression, homelessness, and other issues, including suicide. Some poor people, I assume, are struggling with mental health issues as well. I am sure many of these people are never diagnosed or treated for any mental illnesses.

Today in many parts of our nation, especially the inner cities, we are witnessing the results of the unworthy syndrome. Many young and older adults are dealing with feelings of racism and inequity. I would say very few Black kids, if any, had a father figure or even a mentor involved with the kids in my neighborhood in Philly.

I also grew up without a father or a mentor. I replaced my father with older friends that had serious issues with alcohol, including me. That path did not help me overcome the feeling of poor self-worth. Teens today are at far greater risk; they need to navigate peer pressure not to use or sell drugs.

Many teens replace the guidance of a father by joining gangs. The result of no discipline is a lifetime of criminal behavior. I argue our unrest and conflict across our nation is a direct result of many kids and adults with an unworthy syndrome.

I contend an unworthy syndrome is a very difficult condition to overcome or manage. The new socialist agenda wants to break up the family unit. This model will cause further conflicts between both young and old minorities and White people alike. I don't pretend to know how to treat an unworthy syndrome or the unrest in many inner cities. I don't think breaking up the family unit will help our nation heal when young people grow up without a family unit intact.

## Several studies about kids growing up in fatherless homes

Recently I watched a film named Irreplaceable. [(Sisarich) This film sites some very disturbing statistics about kids growing up in fatherless homes. For example, more than 80 percent of all children who show behavior disorders come from fatherless homes. How many of these kids are struggling with BD?

## Are people living with mental illness victims?

I believe if someone will not or has never been diagnosed with BD eventually, they do become victims of their mental illness. I think it is interesting to refer to someone who has a heart attack as a victim and someone with a mental illness as their mental illness or being bipolar. People may say Betty is a heart attack victim. You would not say Betty is a heart attack, yet people might say Betty is bipolar. I must say I sometimes refer to people as their mental illness. I should say Betty has an illness called bipolar disorder. Sometimes, I'm afraid our mental illness does define us. There is no reason to be a victim of your BD illness any longer; you can get stable on proper medications, gain more control over your life, and stop being victimized by your mental illness.

So, without proper treatment, we become victims because we have no control over our mental state.

## Are we victims, or are we survivors?

Owen, a man I met with Cerebral Palsy, was very physically disabled; he was an inspiration to me because he was dealing with his disability with dignity and honesty. He was sincerely appreciative of his life and was truthful about his health condition but did not seek pity or sympathy. He understood living a good life was not a given, and he was determined to make every day count. He did not consider himself a victim, although he was severely disabled with Cerebral Palsy. I consider Owen a survivor because he accepted his illness as part of his life and did not see himself as a victim.

He did not demand extraordinary treatment and did not expect handouts from other people. He was proud, and he was not burdening other people with his illness. He leads a very simple lifestyle; he told me he lived alone and had a part-time caregiver that only shopped for him and took him to his doctor appointments. I guess the lesson is not how long we live but how we live our lives. Some people live as victims and others as survivors.

I believe Owen's unique character traits allowed him to beat the odds and live 20 years longer than most people with Cerebral Palsy, but more importantly, he lived his life as a survivor.

I had to ask myself if I was a victim or survivor of BD. My brother and I are over 75 years old. The life expectancy in the US is about 76 years old [(OECD, n.d.). The statistics (stats) for people with BD have a life span of 9 years less than "Normal" people. That means statistically; we would not live past 67 years old. I believe if my brother and I did not get treatment with Lithium at midlife, our lives would have ended prematurely, even years before the age of 67. I also believe treatment allowed both my brother and me to beat the statistics and survive to lead more productive and longer BD normal lives. We did our best with the challenges we faced in our lives.

I believe we are living as survivors because we understand living with BD is how we are born to live. I'm not saying sometimes we didn't feel sorry for our situation and needed a little sympathy, but we came to terms with our illness and did not want to be victims.

I am not saying longevity alone is a measure of a meaningful life. Living life as a survivor can lead to a more productive and longer BD normal life. With effective meds and a good support system, we are now over 75 years old. I attribute our survival to be directly related to getting treatment. As I say, without treatment, many people with BD see themselves as victims. Therefore, I think you could call us survivors and not victims of our BD illness.

## Are people with bipolar responsible for their behavior?

Spouses and family members often blame people with BD for irresponsible and abusive behavior, but are they at fault?

No, but maybe mentally ill people are responsible, but at the same time, I say they are not totally at fault until they become stable. I believe someone with BD cannot become stable without proper medications or other therapy. Someone unstable cannot be entirely responsible for their actions, especially if they are on toxic or harmful medications.

I believe once someone is stable, they need to become more responsible for their behavior and begin to realize the BD illness was the cause of many abusive and destructive events in their lives. Yes, people with BD are responsible for bizarre behavior, but they have little or no control over their behavior if not properly medicated for their illness.

Is someone responsible for drunken behavior when drunk? Yes, but they have an illness and have no control over their behavior when drunk but need to be held accountable after treatment. That is one of the AA 12 step rules that make amends to people you may have abused or mistreated after you become sober or are in recovery.

I also think people struggling with BD need to be more appreciative of people around them to put up with their abusive and bizarre behavior before and after treatment. Living with someone with a mental illness is difficult, and loved ones often get little or no credit for their support.

I met a woman at our BDS group who had a daughter with lifelong physical illness and a son with BD. She told me it was far more challenging and time-consuming to deal with her BD son.

## The disparity in treatment between physical and mental illness

The unfair treatment of people with BD brings me to the disparity in treatment between physical and mental illness. I want to vent my frustration about medical treatment for the mentally ill, but I am getting too distracted, so I will stick to working on the WAVES Workbook. I will not get into all those disparity issues; I want to have people use the WAVES Chart to identify stresses in their lives. That is one purpose of the WAVES Workbook, to learn about the abnormal stresses in the life of someone with BD.

Sorry, I need to give just one example of the disparity between mental and physical emergency treatment. I had severe chest pains very early one morning and called my primary care physician's office. The doctor on call told me to go directly to the emergency room at the nearest hospital.

I was immediately taken into an assessment room, given an EKG, and hooked up to five different monitors. They took a sample of my blood, and it showed I did not have a heart attack, but to be sure, they wanted to admit me overnight to observe any changes. I was hooked up to several monitors all night long. In the morning, the head of the cardiac department came into my room with several resident doctors and asked me several questions. At this point, I wanted to leave, but the doctor wanted me to have a heart stress test the next day. I stayed another night under observation. I scheduled a stress test the following day, and the results showed my heart was in good condition.

Would I have had the same comprehensive emergency treatment if I had a psychotic manic or depressed episode? I do not believe I would get equal treatment unless I went to an excellent psychiatric hospital. I think the doctors at a local hospital might have released me sooner or perhaps not even have referred me to a competent psychiatrist.

We are very fortunate to have a first-class psychiatric hospital near us. We have encouraged people in the BD group to take advantage of their excellent care and follow-up policies.

However, the chance of getting first-class mental care in many rural areas of the country is problematic for many people with serious mental illnesses. Several people have come to the BDS group from other parts of the country; they tell us they did not have a good mental hospital within hundreds of miles from their rural hometowns.

Sorry, I did need to vent my frustration again over the disparity in the health care system.

## The need for interventions

We have people attending the BDS group from all walks of life, Black, White, Hispanic, Indian people from India, Asian, and other ethnic groups. I understand there is no group more at risk of BD than another group.

Sometimes we recommend to people in the BD group if their mental state is not improving in, say in two or three months, get a second opinion. If your stress level is in the emergency zones, we strongly recommend going straight to the nearest hospital.

One night a guy by the name of Keith was so depressed at the bipolar group meeting one of the members took him directly to the psychiatric hospital right from the BDS meeting. He recovered after two weeks and was stable on only two meds. This guy made it through a life-threatening depression because we identified he was on the verge of suicide and drove him to our excellent psychiatric hospital.

Keith came back to the group to thank us for bringing him directly to the hospital that night. We are very fortunate we have a first-class psychiatric hospital in the area. We strongly recommended he should get a second opinion.

## We need to thank all our caregivers, past and present

The focus of The Bipolar WAVES Workbook is on people with BD. I also think we need to show an exceptional level of gratitude toward loved ones and others that have put up with us throughout our lives.

As someone with a serious mental illness, I need to give thanks to people who have helped me during the turbulent and chaotic times in my life. Caregivers include people that have tirelessly supported me over the years, but it also includes people I feel that may have harmed me over the years.

Sometimes it is hard for us to see how our illness affects the people around us. At times, our caregivers and family members may need to separate from our abnormal, abusive, and bizarre behavior, but we need to be thankful for the times they have helped us during our struggles and setbacks. Perhaps instead of focusing on how people treat us, we need to understand better how we treat other people, especially if we are unstable.

One thing I learned from writing this workbook is living with BD is a challenging and complicated illness that touches us as well as the other people around us either directly or indirectly.

When stable, I think it is therapeutic to view our past behavior from our caregivers' perspective; this includes spouses, co-workers, BDS group members, therapists, psychiatrists, teachers, family members, lovers, and friends.

Throughout this workbook, I have documented the vast difference between being stable with proper meds and support and being unstable on no meds or ineffective meds and no help. When people with BD are stable on meds, their perspective on life is insightful, and they become more aware of how they view themselves and other people. Sometimes the people we think have mistreated us have been our best advocates and caregivers.

These are the benefits of getting help early on and starting to heal the scars of the many setbacks over a lifetime. I always looked at my life as two separate lives, before and after treatment.

## *I need to show my gratitude*

I do not give enough credit to the people that have supported me. I am grateful for many people that have made and kept me stable and supported me for over 75 years now. Even with their support, life was sometimes difficult, but without their support, life could have been intolerable. I have listed several people who have helped me throughout my life on the acknowledgments page of this workbook.

A few very special people should be acknowledged again here.

I am grateful for my mother's courage and support throughout our childhood. I am sure our mother was ready to abandon us after many years of dealing with our bad, destructive, and risky behavior.

I am grateful for my brother's support throughout my entire lifetime; without his diagnosis and treatment for BD, I may have never been diagnosed correctly for my BD illness.

Finally, I am grateful for my wife's support throughout our entire marriage. Her kindness and caring have carried us through some very turbulent and challenging times. I do not show my wife the gratitude I have for all she has done for our family, especially my son and me.

## Our family could be more supportive of my wife's situation

I feel caregivers bear the burden of our actions or non-actions and must put up with our behavior in silence. I say silent because members of our family and others do not discuss or support my wife. Nicole is supporting two adults with mental issues. Perhaps I should be more confrontational with her family; after all, she has supported us for over 30 years. I feel it is not my place to stir up a conflict between her family and our family. My wife has enough to deal with in our home life.

I notice, at family gatherings, some people do not ask my wife how she is coping with two adults with issues. At times, I feel some family members live in a bubble where our mental issues are not allowed to get in or out of the bubble, as I call it. Many times, I get the impression they do not want to discuss or even acknowledge my mental illness. They do not want to mention any bad news that may upset a positive outlook in all phases of their lives.

Often family members have empathy for someone with a physical disability or illness but avoid talking about the challenges we face with mental illness. Unless someone asks me how I am coping with BD, I do not mention all the challenges our family faces with mental illness.

Sorry for my rant; at times, I do think members of our family could be more supportive of my wife's situation.

## What does a diagnosis of bipolar mean for our future?

A diagnosis of BD can be devastating for some people because I believe it does limit your opportunities in life. Many careers do not allow people with any form of mental illness to work at many jobs, especially security, law enforcement, and transportation.

I met a woman at the BD group, and she was devastated by her daughter's BD diagnosis because she hoped she would be a successful professional. It is so sad because, realistically, our illness does limit some opportunities in life, but I think her mother was underestimating her daughter's chance for success. If she manages her illness and gets support, she could be successful, but she will not be an astronaut.

I have learned over the years; I need to stay stable and minimize my stress levels to live a better life. Sometimes I do need to cancel or not start some risky and possible harmful projects. I try to be aware of my stress zone limits and avoid going into higher stress zones. I need to know my limits and not risk a breakdown by taking on too much responsibility at one time. I need to accept I will not be able to pursue many projects "Normal" people may tackle and accomplish the same tasks with minimal effort.

I have witnessed other "Normal" people with similar backgrounds lead very successful lives. Many have good pensions, high-paying jobs, and second homes. After I became stable, I needed to be realistic and accept my limitations with my illness. Like Owen, I need to accept my illness and not become a victim of my illness. Owen is the man I met at a lake with Cerebral Palsy. Identifying your stress levels and triggers is what the WAVES Workbook is trying to accomplish for people with BD.

## Importance of the BDS group

I have referenced how important becoming active in our local BDS group was to leading my BD normal lifestyle. I could not have written this workbook without the insights and knowledge I learned after attending the first BDS group meeting over 15 years ago.

I am not in a position to suggest some breakthrough therapy that would cure people with mental illness. I do have a few ideas that may help people cope with a diagnosis of mental illness before the age of 50 years old.

## Importance of my Journal

The bipolar group leader is a good writer and encouraged people to keep a diary; she wrote several articles about the BDS group in the local papers. She also wrote several books. I talked to several women who also found it therapeutic to keep a diary to examine thoughts and emotions and detect a pattern. For example, someone may have a BD episode after spending time with an abusive relative. I had been keeping a journal for several years after reliving that very traumatic time in my life.

As I attended the BD group, I began to observe and keep notes on the many and various personal problems most people were facing in their lives. Many people, like me, were living chaotic lives dealing with family and job situations. As time went by, I realized many people were from dysfunctional homes, and many family members also had severe mental or emotional issues.

Now looking back, I could not have written this book without my journal. Reading the pages of my journal from years ago helped me understand and heal from some very traumatic experiences.

I am not saying everyone should keep a journal; I am just saying for me, keeping an active daily journal has helped me organize my chaotic and scattered life.

## Community Help and Healing (H&H) programs

The state of our mental health system is in chaos. Recently some tragic events have happened to innocent citizens of our country by mentally ill people. We need to find a way to help people with mental illness and emotional issues at a young age.

I believe a network of support groups should be available in every town in our country. Perhaps a help program could be modeled after the Alcohol Anonymous (AA) program. Anyone with or without emotional issues would be able to attend meetings anonymously, without judgment, or need to give names or personal information. With substance abuse climbing at an alarming rate in this country, we need a way to bring this problem out in the open. I do think many people with drug or alcohol addiction are also struggling with some form of mental illness.

Some people argue against a support group for the mentally ill. They argue that mentally ill people will not attend a help group. Some mentally ill people are in denial of their illness, but I say many alcoholics and drug abusers are also in denial of having substance abuse issues. After fellow alcoholics and drug users meet, they begin to get treatment by helping each other. These programs could also help other people with no mental illness understand the struggles people with mental illness live with every day.

Years ago, I was in denial of having a serious mental illness. Years later, after I attended the first BDS group meeting, I realized a support group was where I belonged to get relief from years of turmoil and rejection. I believe once someone gets involved and feel better about themselves, they will continue to stay in contact with like-minded people. Furthermore, when people with mental issues observe other people getting stable, they are more receptive to taking psychiatric meds and getting therapy.

I found our support group to be non-judgmental and supportive. Maybe these group meetings should not be called a mental illness support group due to the stigma it implies.

Perhaps the self-help group could be called a "Help & Healing" (H&H) club.

## Tele Help the coronavirus and other crisis situations

After the coronavirus attacked our nation, we needed a way to help people recover emotionally from the shock of the virus. Maybe Tele Help is one way to help people of all ages in crisis. I define Tele Help or Telemedicine as any online system to provide physical or mental support via the internet by using professional health care professionals. This type of help could reach all people in our nation, from inner cities to the most remote regions of our nation. We have the technology to treat people in their homes or apartments. We need to be careful the government does not use the technology to diagnose people with a serious mental illness without a one-on-one meeting with a certified mental health professional.

## Should medical records be sent to government officials?

Recently some people in our government called for medical records to be sent to government officials.

Perhaps, but a word of caution is in order; anyone "diagnosed" with a mental illness stays with them for a lifetime. Unfortunately, once diagnosed, the person is never declared cured of a mental illness. A wrong diagnosis of having a mental illness stays with a person their entire life and could be disastrous for anyone wrongly misdiagnosed as being mentally ill.

The definition of mental illness could apply to someone that has infrequent mild panic attacks. After referring to the DSM [(American Psychiatric Association, 1987), I have concluded the majority of people have some form of mental issues. The broad definition of mental illness could apply to the majority of people living today. Misdiagnosis could pave the way for the government to take away the 2nd amendment rights of the majority of citizens of our country.

I agree most mentally ill people should not be allowed to own firearms, but who decides the definition of mental illness? The definition of mental illness could include gambling, hoarding, learning, personality disorders, and other disorders, as defined in the DSM. How about someone in a state of amnesia? Couldn't some clerk declare I have a case of amnesia? How could I prove I did not? I am joking, but you can see how these definitions and diagnoses can get very subjective and harmful.

I want to use the Cautionary Statement from the DSM IV-TR (Text Revision) manual.

"The proper use of these criteria requires specialized clinical training that provides both a body of knowledge and clinical skills."

Do we want a government clerk in one of the 125 health care agencies without clinical training declaring millions of "Normal" citizens mentally ill?

I agree most people with BD never lead "Normal" lives and should not have access to firearms. The majority of people with BD should not be tracked and harassed by some government agency if they have no history of violence. Again, who decides the definition of being mentally ill? Should all people with a drug addiction be tracked and monitored by some government agency? Again, who decides the definition of a mental disorder or a drug addict? Could a false diagnosis be used to harm or prevent someone from getting a job, a political position, a medical or security position?

This harmful policy could deter people from seeking treatment and cause harm to both the individual and family members. I hope no one will be without effective mental health care for over 50 years, as my brother and me.

The Goldwater rule was adopted years ago after about 1000 health care professionals diagnosed Barry Goldwater with a mental illness without a one-on-one meeting. His political career was ruined, and he even won a lawsuit to collect damages.

## The four examples of how to use the WAVES Chart

I want The Bipolar WAVES Stress Chart to act as a learning tool for "Normal" people and help people with BD. I want to show what constant lifetime stresses people have with BD before and after effective treatment. I want to use some actual life situations of people to chart and score the stresses on people with BD. I have included four examples of how to use the WAVES Chart in the following four chapters.

In Chapter 4, Jack lost his soul mate JoJo in a tragic accident. This true story is an example of how relationships can produce abnormal stresses on someone without proper treatment after going through tragic life-changing events. Meeting Jack and JoJo was no mistake; their story made finishing my workbook project crystal clear.

Chapter 5 is about Erica, who lost her job. This is a true story of how careers and job-related stresses on people with BD can cause extreme stress, even when stable and have good family support. Many people with BD have similar very stressful experiences during and after losing a job. For many people with BD, job-related issues can be repeated several times during their lifetime.

Chapter 6 This is a true story of my brother Stu who, after 50 years of untreated BD, loses almost everything, including his own life, to suicide. It is a story of how extremely difficult life can get if not diagnosed and treated early on for BD. His story is about how challenging life can get when a job, marriage, family obligations, alcoholism, and struggling with BD build up to create an extreme medical emergency. His story is also about overcoming many obstacles before realizing his mission in life is to help other people with drug and alcohol issues.

Chapter 7 Henry's story is about a typical young guy who has never been diagnosed with BD but is struggling with starting a family, job, financial issues, and alcoholism all at the same time. Henry's story is a typical case of someone with unstable and undiagnosed BD taking on too many responsibilities all at the same time. Taking on too much stress is a very common theme of many people in the BD group before being diagnosed with BD. Henry's story is very similar to my story, except I was not diagnosed or treated until midlife.

In Chapter 8, I want people with BD to "Find your Bipolar Stress Zone," and that is one goal of the Bipolar WAVES Workbook.

In Chapter 9, I score my Bipolar Stress Zone using The Bipolar WAVES Workbook Stress Chart.

Refer to Appendix A, The WAVES Chart, to find a list of all the life situations I have identified as relevant. Of course, this list can be expanded to include other unique situations, conditions, and events that may be relevant to people with BD. The pandemic is an example of a situation that is not listed in the WAVES Chart. The stress points will be different for everyone dealing with the pandemic.

CHAPTER 4

# The tragic story of Jack and JoJo

FOR THE PAST SEVERAL YEARS, our neighbor has invited us to their beach house for a few days. Last year I met a young couple, the guy was here from France, and his name was Jacques, but people called him Jack. His girlfriend's nickname was JoJo. JoJo was a vibrant young woman in her early twenties who was very dedicated to helping kids. You could see they had a close relationship. The couple started a scuba diving business in Florida to help disadvantaged youth. Last year I felt JoJo had a free spirit way about her; she was not concerned about any material things in life and was very happy with her mission in life to help kids. Jack didn't say much but had a charming French accent. They led quite the bohemian lifestyle; they drove an old car and rode their bikes everywhere.

This year I saw Jack in the kitchen of our neighbor's shore house, and I noticed he was with another girl and seemed very stressed and worn out. We all noticed Jack seemed solemn and withdrawn as he headed down to the beach before the thunderstorms came through the area. I wondered if he broke up with JoJo.

After Jack left, his friend told us about the tragedy that happened about two months after we met last summer at the shore. Jack's friend told us she was just a friend of Jack and was with him to provide support from his tragic loss. Jack and JoJo had a serious boating accident in Florida, and she died right beside him after the boat capsized, she drowned, but he escaped. He was seriously injured and needed to go through several operations and extensive physical rehabilitation. His friend told us he had been in chronic pain since the accident.

Later that day, I met Jack down at the beach and asked how things were going for him, and he said he was practically living out of his car. He said he was living with JoJo's parents. I replied, "Did you find someone to continue your scuba diving school?" He replied, "No, I am not over the loss of JoJo almost a year ago now." All of a sudden, I had to ask myself, "Why was I so insensitive? Of course, she was very important to him?" Then he said, "She was going to be with me my entire life.".

What an insensitive thing I said about his tragedy; I suddenly realized JoJo was his soul mate and just not a girlfriend and business partner. I said, "I guess she was your soul mate?" and he nodded, yes?" I said, "How do you deal with such a tragic loss?" and he replied, "Not too well at all; they say I have a minor case of bipolar." I said, "I also have bipolar, and it's tough to handle average life situations." Jack excused himself to go up to the house and get ready to go grocery shopping.

All of a sudden, the events of my past started to flood my mind. Jack lost his soul mate, was injured in a horrific boating accident, and now he tells me he may be bipolar. I thought he might be a grave risk for suicide like I had been decades ago in my early 20s over a traumatic breakup with my 1st love.

Why didn't I see they were soul mates when I met them last summer at the shore house? That is what I sometimes do; say inappropriate things to people without being respectful of their feelings.

Then I realized I needed to tell him I am very concerned about his wellbeing before he goes out to the store because we may leave to go home before he gets back.

I went up to the house and found him in the kitchen, ready to go to get groceries for dinner. I said to Jack, "I need to talk to you because I have bipolar, and I lost my first love when I was about your age." I asked him if it was okay to ask him a few questions if he didn't mind. He acted very defensively, but I needed to know his emotional state. Here it was almost a year after JoJo's tragic death, and he was still in crisis.

I finally asked him if he thought of harming himself. I knew it was a very awkward question because several people came into the kitchen for lunch. He replied, "Yes, sometimes I want to forget the whole thing and be with her." Then he said, "The accident keeps repeating, and I can't get it out of my head." This statement was very alarming; that is what happened to me after the loss of my 1st love. I could not get the tragic events of the breakup out of my head, and I went into a state of amnesia for over four decades.

Jack's friend was sitting listening to our conversation, and several more neighbors were coming in and out of the kitchen to get drinks and snacks.

I was more concerned for his safety and asked him, "Do you mind if I asked you if you're under professional care?" He said, "Yes, I am, but my psychiatrist tends to talk more about his problems than what I have been going through lately, and he put me on three different medications that are not helping me."

At this point, I am extremely concerned about his well-being because he lost his soul mate; he has physical injuries and is in severe emotional and physical pain. Also, he probably is not getting proper psychiatric treatment with his meds.

I said, "Jack, you need a good psychiatrist. I will give you my psychiatrist's name and phone number." I went on to say, "Some doctors do not want to deal with serious mental problems."

Jack and his friend went out to his car to go to the store. I followed him out and said, "Jack, I'm very concerned about your wellbeing; you can call me anytime, and please let me know how you are doing." I told him about our BDS group that usually meets two times a month and provides excellent support. I gave Jack and his friend my psychiatrist's name and number and went back into the house.

I should have asked him for his email to follow up, but I did not want to alarm him and meddle any further into his personal life. I did not want him to ignore my plea for him to find a good psychiatrist. Maybe he did think I was a crazy BD older man and had too many of my own mental health issues to be advising him.

I don't know if it was my personality disorder or my BD disorder talking, but I tend to say and do inappropriate things sometimes. Maybe I did exhibit crazy behavior in front of our neighbors, but that is what I do at times.

He had an extremely stressful year, with the tragic loss of his soul mate plus physical injury. His comment, "He wants to forget the whole thing and be with her," was very troubling because this is the same type of situation that put me into a severe stress type disorder, and then I ended up forgetting the event with a case of amnesia.

On the way home, I told Nicole I was sorry; now, all the neighbors know I have a serious mental illness. Nicole said, "I am sure the neighbors already know you have a mental illness because you emotional and physical pain. Also, he probably is not getting proper psychiatric treatment with his meds.

I said, "Jack, you need a good psychiatrist. I will give you my psychiatrist's name and phone number." I went on to say, "Some doctors do not want to deal with serious mental problems."

Jack and his friend went out to his car to go to the store. I followed him out and said, "Jack, I'm very concerned about your wellbeing; you can call me anytime, and please let me know how you are doing." I told him about our BDS group that usually meets two times a month and provides excellent support. I gave Jack and his friend my psychiatrist's name and number and went back into the house.

I should have asked him for his email to follow up, but I did not want to alarm him and meddle any further into his personal life. I did not want him to ignore my plea for him to find a good psychiatrist. Maybe he did think I was a crazy BD older man and had too many of my own mental health issues to be advising him.

I don't know if it was my personality disorder or my BD disorder talking, but I tend to say and do inappropriate things sometimes. Maybe I did exhibit crazy behavior in front of our neighbors, but that is what I do at times.

He had an extremely stressful year, with the tragic loss of his soul mate plus physical injury. His comment, "He wants to forget the whole thing and be with her," was very troubling because this is the same type of situation that put me into a severe stress type disorder, and then I ended up forgetting the event with a case of amnesia.

On the way home, I told Nicole I was sorry; now, all the neighbors know I have a serious mental illness. Nicole said, "I am sure the neighbors already know you have a mental illness because you

Then I realized I needed to tell him I am very concerned about his wellbeing before he goes out to the store because we may leave to go home before he gets back.

I went up to the house and found him in the kitchen, ready to go to get groceries for dinner. I said to Jack, "I need to talk to you because I have bipolar, and I lost my first love when I was about your age." I asked him if it was okay to ask him a few questions if he didn't mind. He acted very defensively, but I needed to know his emotional state. Here it was almost a year after JoJo's tragic death, and he was still in crisis.

I finally asked him if he thought of harming himself. I knew it was a very awkward question because several people came into the kitchen for lunch. He replied, "Yes, sometimes I want to forget the whole thing and be with her." Then he said, "The accident keeps repeating, and I can't get it out of my head." This statement was very alarming; that is what happened to me after the loss of my 1st love. I could not get the tragic events of the breakup out of my head, and I went into a state of amnesia for over four decades.

Jack's friend was sitting listening to our conversation, and several more neighbors were coming in and out of the kitchen to get drinks and snacks.

I was more concerned for his safety and asked him, "Do you mind if I asked you if you're under professional care?" He said, "Yes, I am, but my psychiatrist tends to talk more about his problems than what I have been going through lately, and he put me on three different medications that are not helping me."

At this point, I am extremely concerned about his well-being because he lost his soul mate; he has physical injuries and is in severe haven't worked for years, and your physical health seems fine." Then Nicole said, "Jack has loving friends and family, don't get too involved in his life." I said, "You don't know what is going on in his head; he may decide to "be with her."

Then I said, "I have been studying how life situations affect people with bipolar, and he probably has a very high-Stress Level Score. I would not even consider him stable after hearing how insensitive his psychiatrist is to his very tragic situation".

Nicole tried to reassure me Jack was ok, but I was sure his stress level was in the Emergency Zone.

I said, "I'm sorry. I hope I didn't shame or embarrass Jack in front of the entire neighborhood at the shore house." My wife said, "You acted insane at the shore house." I replied, "I prefer the term "maybe crazy" to insane if you don't mind."

Maybe I did overreact when he looked and acted as if he was still in a state of shock for what happened about a year ago." Without proper treatment, I was in a very unstable state of mind after I broke up with my first love and was emotionally extremely unstable. I calculated my stress level in the Extreme Zone at that time in my life.

On the drive back home, I was thinking to myself; perhaps this is a sign telling me to publish the workbook. Maybe I was acting like an amateur psychiatrist.

Well, we got back to our house. I got our camper ready to leave for a campground in the mountains, but I thought of Jack still back at the shore and his well-being. The next day I called Rosie, the leader of our BDS group, and told her Jack might come to the group for the next meeting to look out for him. I did want him to make it through this tragedy and go on to lead a "Normal" life, but it may be more of a BD normal lifestyle. I think all the red flags I saw flying in a full gale, not one of them was coming down.

## Mistreatment vs. Effective Treatment
The WAVES Chart for people with BD has two different BD lifestyles, stable and unstable.

In Jack's case, he said he is under psychiatric care, but his doctor did not seem to be treating him effectively even though he diagnosed him with bipolar. Jack told me he was taking three meds, but they did not seem to be helping him and could be harming him. I don't know what his psychiatrist meant by "He thought Jack had a minor case of bipolar" either. I am not a psychiatrist, but I never heard of such a vague diagnosis. Anyway, I assumed he was not stable after almost a year of treatment. I do not know how long he was under his care; I just assumed he found his psychiatrist after the accident, but his quality of life did not seem to improve under his psychiatrist's care.

Jack mentioned he was taking several psychiatric meds. Now I do not pretend to be a psychiatrist, but I do not think the meds he was taking were not proven mood stabilizers, but I could be wrong. I guess it does not matter because his quality of life was not better. As I have said before, it does not matter the class or dose of medicine if it helps you get a better quality of life. I'm afraid Jack may have been getting mistreatment instead of effective treatment.

## Jacks' Unstable Bipolar lifestyle
I took out the WAVES Chart and scored Jack's stress level in the Emergency Zone, Level 6. In this zone, he needs immediate medical attention. Refer to Jack's Unstable Stress Chart 1a,

My contention is he is at a far higher risk of having a severe mental breakdown when he is not getting proper mental health care, including talk therapy.

To calculate Jack's Stress Level Score (SLS), refer to the WAVES Chart for people with BD In Appendix A. I found and checked off all the life situations that applied to Jack for the past year. I totaled up all the points on sections 1,2, 3, and 4 of the WAVES Chart. I transferred the points from COL-B (unstable) to COL C, and then I added up all the stress points in COL C to get his SLS.

Most life situations scored on Jack's chart are self-explanatory, but some may need further clarification. Refer to Appendix A for a more detailed description of many of the life situations relevant to Jack's case. Jacks' story is an example of someone at risk of a severe mental breakdown or far worse. Jack's stress score is in Stress Chart 1a.

According to Jack's Unstable Stress Chart 1a, he had too many highly stressful events that occurred within a year without proper treatment to be stable. I assumed he was not getting effective medications because he was not stable. Actually, from the meds he was taking, I think he was getting mistreatment for his mental disorder. Harmful or toxic meds will add 84 points to his SLS score. He told me he was still having chronic pain after several operations caused by the boating accident and that alone scored 66 points.

Although he was not married to JoJo, emotionally, I felt he was married to her. He had a very close, loving, and business relationship with JoJo. The death of JoJo was a major stressor and added another 132 points to his total score. They shared a close professional lifestyle. He lost his income as well as his wife, and that scored 60 points. Jack also had lifestyle changes in his life when he moved in with JoJo's parents, and that adds another 36 points. Jack was almost homeless, but JoJo's parents were supportive, so I did not score any points. Jack also had changes in lifestyle and sleeping habits. It was apparent Jack's life was complicated even if he did not have BD. He was 3000 miles away from his family in

## Jack's Unstable BP WAVES Stress Chart

*Find your Bipolar Stress Zone*
Taken from The Bipolar WAVES Workbook
Copyright © 2021 by Philip Van Ostrander

| Bipolar Lifestyle | COL-C |
|---|---|
| **Unstable BP Lifestyle      COL B** | **130** |
| **Other Mental Disorders** | |
| Personality, Stress, Anxiety - Untreated | 54 |
| **Physical Illnesses** | |
| Long-term e.g. Cancer /Chronic pain | 66 |
| **Career and Jobs** | |
| Financial burdens- Can't find work- | 60 |
| **Marriage & Family** | |
| Death of a spouse (Suicide OD, accident} | 132 |
| **Personal Situations** | |
| Change stable/no meds to toxic meds | 84 |
| Changes in activities, sleeping, eating | 36 |
| Major changes--moving/retirement | 54 |
| | |
| **Stress Level Score (SLS)=Sum C** | **616** |
| | |
| **Emergency-Zone Level 6     600 --->699** | **616** |

Jack's WAVES Chart 1a

**Stress Chart 1a Jack's Unstable WAVES Stress Chart**

France and living with JoJo's family. I am sure both JoJo's parents were also grieving her death, and he may have felt abandoned.

WAVES Bipolar Stress Chart 1a lists the events happening at the time we met at the shore house. According to his unstable WAVES Chart 1a, he had an SLS score above 600 points, which puts him in the Emergency Zone Level 6.

Refer to Appendix A for an explanation of the Emergency Zone Level 6.

It is no surprise he was in the Emergency Zone; most "Normal" people with no history of mental illness could develop a severe stress disorder after such a tragic accident. Again, my claim is people have much more stress for the same life situations if they have BD.

When I met Jack, he seemed he had a "Normal" reaction to the tragic loss of JoJo. As he began to share his diagnosis of BD and his emotional state, I began to add up all the very stressful life situations he was facing, and then I began to be very concerned for his wellbeing. Determining risk is what the WAVES Stress Chart is designed to do, check off all the stressful conditions in his life and sum up his total points. The total then determines the level of risk he has for a BD episode or even the chance of suicide.

## Jack's life after effective treatment

About a year after I talked to Jack at the shore house, I was walking uptown with our granddaughter Bonnie to get an ice cream cone when I saw Jack riding his bike down the street, and I flagged him down.

He told me he was doing okay, and he was over the worst tragedy of his life, the tragic death of JoJo. I was so happy for him; he looked so happy and relaxed. He said he had a part-time job at scuba diving school and was looking for a full-time job. Well, that was certainly music to my ears. I honestly thought we might lose him; he was so devastated by the loss of JoJo.

He told me he went to my psychiatrist, but they did not have good chemistry. I guess I understood that my psychiatrist; is more of a pharmacology-type psychiatrist and not that warm and fuzzy country doctor type. Jack is now back to being that down-to-earth free-spirited young man with the charming French accent.

I introduced our granddaughter to him, and we continued on our way to get an ice cream cone. My granddaughter asked me about Jack, and I told her he was in a serious boating accident and was very stressed out the last time I saw him. I said, "Did you know stressed spelled backward spells desserts?" and she replied, "It seems everything you say spells desserts." Maybe that is why I think about ice cream cake every time I feel stressed out." I am sure Jacks' BD normal lifestyle will not be all ice cream and cake, but it is far better than an unstable BD lifestyle.

I could tell Jack was stable, and I did not want to intrude in his personal life with more personal questions. I do think using the WAVES Chart gave me a snapshot of the enormous stress he was under back then.

After I realized he was unstable and at risk of a possible suicide, I did become a little too personal and maybe a little "crazy" during my conversation with him at the shore house.

The WAVES Stress Chart 1b is Jack's stable BD normal lifestyle after treatment.

*The Bipolar WAVES Workbook*

# Jack's Stable BP WAVES Stress Chart

*Find your Bipolar Stress Zone*
Taken from The Bipolar WAVES Workbook
Copyright © 2021 by Philip Van Ostrander

| Bipolar Lifestyle | COL-C |
|---|---|
| **Stable BP Normal Lifestyle  COL A** | 65 |
| **Other Mental Disorders** | |
| Personality, Stress, Anxiety - Treated | 25 |
| **Physical Illnesses** | |
| Long-term e.g. Cancer /Chronic pain | 55 |
| **Career and Jobs** | |
| Financial burdens- Can't find work- | 50 |
| Filling out job applications | 30 |
| Job interviews- gaps in job history | 30 |
| Starting a new job or career | 45 |
| **Personal Situations** | |
| Changes in activities, sleeping, eating | 30 |
| Major changes--moving/retirement | 45 |
| | |
| **Stress Level Score (SLS)=Sum C** | 375 |
| | |
| **X-Caution-Zone Level 3     300 --->399** | |

Jack's WAVES Chart 1b

Stress Chart 1b Jack's Stable Bipolar WAVES Stress Chart

In Jack's stable Stress Chart 1b, Jack is getting good meds and treatment, and that lowers his Lifetime Bipolar Stress Level (LBSL) to 65 from 130. He has less stress from chronic pain; I am assuming his loss of income was still a factor because he is still living with JoJo's parents. Jack has come to terms with the death of JoJo; he is not suicidal over her loss, so I did not score JoJo's death. Jack's life is less stressful because he is stable and getting good support. His stress level has gone from Emergency Zone Level 6 before treatment to X-Caution Zone Level 3 after treatment.

Jack is looking for a job, so he will have a financial burden of no income. He will have other challenges of someone with BD, like filling out job applications, interviews, and starting a new job or career. All these everyday tasks are difficult for someone stable but can be extremely stressful if unstable. Notice all the career and job situations alone add up to over 150 points. These accumulative BD stress factors occur when life's stressors build up and are not resolved normally.

Now, of course, all these stress points are subjective and will vary from person to person. The general idea of the WAVES Stress Chart is to identify all your life situations and then score each situation to get your SLS score. You can then find what WAVES stress zone according to your SLS score. From your Zone level, you can evaluate how much stress you have and then work to lower or eliminate stressors in your life. Sometimes you may need a psychiatric intervention in a hospital if your life has too much stress.

The best way for Jack was to lower his overall score was to get treatment and become stable. His treatment has lowered his Lifetime (LBSL) from 130 to 65 and lowered all other scores.

Refer to Appendix A for an explanation of the X-Caution Zone Level 3.

Jack and JoJo's story was one of those life events where I got a renewed commitment to publishing the Bipolar WAVES Workbook. The rough draft of the WAVES Chart has been in my journal notes for several years. Jack's tragic story was the motivation or trigger I needed to complete this WAVES Workbook project.

Of course, not all the assumptions and situations may apply in Jack's case, but I hope you get the idea; people with BD need to look at many unique BD life situations to find their Stress Zone.

## What if Jack has an addiction to painkillers?

Sometimes it is interesting to do a "what if" scenario. Even if Jack is stable and is taking his meds, other life situations could put Jack back in the emergency zone. What if Jack became addicted to his painkillers for his chronic pain caused by his accident and then was not being treated effectively for his addiction? What if he was buying illegal painkillers on the street?

What if JoJo's father became ill and Jack could not stay at their house? What if Jack lost the support from JoJo's family due to his addiction to illegal painkillers? Then he might become homeless and need to stay with his friend. He might feel abandoned by everyone because his family was back in France. These lifestyle changes can be devastating for someone struggling with BD and drug addiction issues. His addiction to legal and illegal painkillers may also cause toxic side effects and interfere with his psychiatric meds.

I am quite sure he would feel abandoned by JoJo's family and his soul mate. The feeling of abandonment would easily add even more points to his SLS score. He might be at risk of a complete mental breakdown.

Jack's WAVES Stress Chart might look like Stress Chart 1c

## Jack's Stable BP WAVES Stress Chart

*Find your Bipolar Stress Zone*
Taken from The Bipolar WAVES Workbook
Copyright © 2021 by Philip Van Ostrander

| Bipolar Lifestyle | COL-C |
|---|---|
| **Stable BP Normal Lifestyle  COL A** | 65 |
| **Other Mental Disorders** | |
| Personality, Stress, Anxiety - Treated | 25 |
| **Physical Illnesses** | |
| Long-term e.g. Cancer /Chronic pain | 55 |
| **Addictions** | |
| Alcohol and/or Drug No treatment | 60 |
| **Career and Jobs** | |
| Financial burdens- Can't find work- | 50 |
| Filling out job applications | 30 |
| Job interviews- gaps in job history | 30 |
| Starting a new job or career | 45 |
| **Marriage & Family** | |
| Loss of family support rejected shunned | 55 |
| Family member illness | 50 |
| **Personal Situations** | |
| Homeless Lost Home/Room/Apt | 50 |
| Changes in activities, sleeping, eating | 30 |
| Major changes--moving/retirement | 45 |
| | |
| **Stress Level Score (SLS)=Sum C** | 590 |
| | |
| **X-Danger-Zone Level 5       500 --->599** | 590 |

Jack's WAVES Chart 1c

Stress Chart 1c Jack's stable BD normal lifestyle but has an addiction to painkillers.

By adding these destructive behaviors to his life, he would be in the X-Danger Zone Level 5 with a score of well over 500 points. Just one more stressor will put him back in the Emergency Zone Level 6 again.

I think you can see these types of situations can quickly add points to Jack's SLS score and put his stress level into the X-Danger Zone even if he is stable on his meds.

Even if he gets treatment for his stress and BD, his addiction to painkillers added new stressors, including homeless and loss of family support. With an addiction to painkillers, I assume his chances to get and keep a job will become much more difficult for Jack.

So, by adding addiction to his lifestyle, he has added several more stressful situations to his BD normal lifestyle. Notice the unintentional consequences of starting just the harmful addiction to painkillers can have a domino effect and trigger many other adverse conditions in Jack's life.

Notice his lifestyle is now affecting many areas of his life. He needs to deal with his BD, physical illnesses, and career issues. He may have conflicts with JoJo's family and personal living conditions. Although Jack has received treatment for his BD, he will need to become clean on his addiction to drugs to have a better quality of life and lower his risk of having another serious BD episode

CHAPTER 5

# Erika's Career and Job Story

ERICA'S STORY IS ABOUT A woman that lost her job at a general hospital.

## Erica is stable but has lost her Job

Erica came to the BDS group and told us she got fired from her job at a local general hospital. We could all see the emotional pain and stress she was experiencing at the support group.

Erica was about 45 years old; I should never guess a woman's age had worked at the hospital as a patient coordinator for over 12 years and had an excellent employment record.

She left a note from her psychiatrist with a list of her meds on her desk, and someone told her supervisor. After the hospital administration assumed she was BD from her list of meds, they began to track and document every little mistake she made for several months. She was fired with no notice. She did not even have a meeting with the administration or get a warning about poor job performance. How humiliating to be fired for trivial reasons after over ten years on the job.

I think we can conclude Erica had a good case of discrimination because of her mental disability called BD. There are laws, the

American with Disabilities Act (ADA), that protects workers with disabilities, but many people with mental illness are often pushed out the back door of many corporations.

In Erika's case, she was harassed and humiliated by management and fired because of her BD disability.

We asked her to get an attorney to fight the hospital for the unjust treatment of a disabled person. She said an attorney told her it would be a waste of time and money because they followed her around for several months to document every mistake to justify firing her. We have heard many stories of the unjust firing of people with BD, but it was truly heartbreaking to see her so distraught and ashamed of her tragic situation.

We asked her if there was anything the group could do to help her. She said she just needed to vent her frustration at the group session; the hospital would not help her. She told us her supervisor would not even give her a referral to help her find another job.

Erika's situation was sad; she has been a physically healthy woman on stable meds for years. She had a good work history and is now out looking for a job at 45 years old.

I could be a little less understanding if she was unstable, refused treatment, and had some irresponsible behavior to harm a coworker, but all she did was leave a doctor's note on her desk. If she was not stable, we would recommend she get a good psychiatrist or get a second opinion.

What cruel and unjust punishment because she committed no crime; she was being punished for having a mental illness. Would they mistreat someone with MS the same way as Erica? Of course not; they might end up with a big lawsuit.

## Erica's Stable BP WAVES Stress Chart

*Find your Bipolar Stress Zone*
Taken from The Bipolar WAVES Workbook
Copyright © 2021 by Philip Van Ostrander

| Bipolar Lifestyle | COL-C |
|---|---|
| **Stable BP Normal Lifestyle  COL A** | **65** |
| **Career and Jobs** | |
| Fired because you have Bipolar Disorder | 60 |
| Threat of being fired for BP behavior | 40 |
| Financial burdens- Can't find work- | 50 |
| Filling out job applications | 30 |
| Job interviews- gaps in job history | 30 |
| Conflict / harassed by co-workers | 50 |
| Starting a new job or career | 45 |
| **Personal Situations** | |
| Changes in activities, sleeping, eating | 30 |
| **Stress Level Score (SLS)=Sum C** | **400** |
| **Danger-Zone Level 4      400 --->499** | **400** |

Erica's WAVES Chart 2a

Stress Chart 2a Erica with her stable Stress Chart but lost her job

So, if you tally up the points for Erica, her stress chart looks like Stress Chart 2a.

It is very fortunate Erica is mentally stable and has a good psychiatrist.

Of course, the bullying and the threat of being fired also added points to her score, but I assumed she has no addictions or other mental disorders in her life. It is fortunate Erica has a husband that fully supports her mental condition, but she did mention the loss of her income would be a burden on the entire family, so I added points to her chart.

After she got fired, another set of new stressors began to enter her life. She was under pressure to find a new job or career. Filling out job applications and job interviews is very stressful for most people with BD. She mentioned she was not sleeping or eating regularly; I added points to her score. Not being able to get sleep on a regular schedule is a red flag for me to seek help very soon. All these life events occurred within a year of being fired on the job for having a BD illness.

## The accumulative BD stress factors

Many life situations are common to all people, like finding a job, but I claim these same life situations are unique for people with BD because we also need to deal with our BD illness.

All these job-related BD stress factors add up to cause a high level of stress, as illustrated in Erica's WAVES Chart 2a. She endured many of these job-related stresses even before being fired without even a meeting with the hospital administration. I'm afraid this type of bad treatment is common for people struggling with mental illness. The additive BD stress factors for her job-related situations alone scored about 300 points. Erica needs to face many of these job-related tasks plus other conditions like a major depression all within a year. All these tasks can become overwhelming if she cannot find work.

Refer to Appendix A for an explanation of the Danger Zone.

I am hopeful Erica can weather her storm and lead a good stable BD normal life. Erica's unfortunate job loss is an example of someone stable on meds but is having many everyday BD stressors due to career and Job loss situations.

## What if Erica became unstable on toxic meds?

In WAVES Chart 2a, Erica is under excellent mental care with a good psychiatrist, and of course, she has the BD group for support. However, what if she made a few unfortunate mistakes that made her unstable?

What if she stopped taking her good meds and went to a new psychiatrist that mistreated her with toxic meds? What if then she lost support from her husband and family. What if then she became verbally abusive toward her family members and children? These situations do occur for mentally unstable people not on any medication or taking toxic meds. We have seen cases in the group where, after being fired on their job, their entire life and families then start to break apart and spin out of control.

Abnormal stress can also occur if she is living with other family members with mental issues.

In this "what if" example, Erica goes to a new psychiatrist that puts her on a toxic med that causes her to become even more unstable than no meds at all. Because she is now unstable on toxic meds, you need to use COL B on the WAVES Stress Chart to score Erica's SLS points. Note that the consequences of going from stable meds to toxic meds resulted in the loss of family support and conflicts with her spouse. Just these three life changes will add over 200 points to her score.

It will be challenging for Erica to handle several job-related tasks and deal with conflicts with her family issues. Most likely, she also is going into a cycle of depression over all the turmoil in her life. Many times, people in these situations hit a wall and go into the Emergency Zone. They end up not being well enough to even find a job.

Erika s Bipolar WAVES Chart may look like Example 2b.

Now you can see becoming unstable by taking toxic meds may result in several additional stressful life situations. Now her Lifetime (LBSL) from BD is 130 from 65.

Now she has all the job-related stresses of finding a job or new career.

Let's assume she begins to have arguments with her husband over her irresponsible behavior. Quickly stopping her meds can lead to bizarre BD behavior and a loss of family support. Stressful life situations do occur, but staying on stable meds is very important.

Now, these changes have put her in the Emergency Zone Level 6. She should be rushed to a trauma unit of a psychiatric hospital and begin to be stable again. Note just a few more stresses in her life may put her in the X-Emergency Zone; then, she probably should be involuntarily admitted to a trauma unit of a psychiatric hospital.

*The Bipolar WAVES Workbook*

# Erica's Unstable BP WAVES Stress Chart

*Find your Bipolar Stress Zone*
Taken from The Bipolar WAVES Workbook
Copyright © 2021 by Philip Van Ostrander

| Bipolar Lifestyle | COL-C |
|---|---|
| **Unstable BP Lifestyle      COL B** | 130 |
| **Career and Jobs** | |
| Fired because you have Bipolar Disorder | 72 |
| Threat of being fired for BP behavior | 48 |
| Financial burdens- Can't find work- | 60 |
| Filling out job applications | 36 |
| Job interviews- gaps in job history | 36 |
| Starting a new job or career | 54 |
| **Marriage & Family** | |
| Conflicts with spouse over lifestyle | 60 |
| Loss of family support rejected shunned | 66 |
| **Personal Situations** | |
| Change stable/no meds to toxic meds | 84 |
| Changes in activities, sleeping, eating | 36 |
| | |
| **Stress Level Score (SLS)=Sum C** | 682 |
| | |
| **Emergency-Zone Level 6     600 --->699** | 682 |

Erica's WAVES Chart 2b

*Stress Chart 2b Erica her stable to unstable Stress Chart*

Nevertheless, I hope you can see why the divorce rate is so high for someone with BD. Erica's story is an example of someone going from a stable BD normal lifestyle to a very unstable BD lifestyle.

Many people with BD begin in an unstable condition and then become stable on good meds and psychiatric care. In this "What if" scenario, within a year, she has gone from the more stable Danger Zone to the very unstable Emergency Zone. Level 6.

Refer to Appendix A for an explanation of the Emergency Zone.

Sometimes if a BD group member has a dangerously high life-threatening situation, we take them to our local psychiatric hospital right from the group session.

## CHAPTER 6
# My brother Stu's Story

THIS STORY IS ABOUT STU, my brother's life before and after he got treatment for BD. Life was a series of setbacks and disappointments for him and his family. He had several bouts of severe depression, followed by manic spending sprees on new projects.

Stu was married, had two young children, and was living in New England at the time. He had a good-paying job with benefits but never got effective treatment for BD.

### Stu's unstable bipolar lifestyle
He went to several psychiatrists and medical doctors for depression. The doctors put him on anti-depressants and some other meds that were toxic. His meds were harming him. Of course, he was drinking heavily, and that added more stress to his life and probably interfered with his medications.

As a last resort to help with his devastating depression, they recommended ECT. His depression got so bad he was involuntarily admitted to a mental hospital. After talking to several people in the hospital, they recommended ECT as his last resort to help him out of his life-threading depression. While waiting in the hall in a wheelchair, he noticed one woman in a wheelchair repeating the days of the week over and over. He got out of the wheelchair, left the hospital in his hospital gown, and ran out into the street. The staff brought him back into the hospital. When questioned, he told the doctor everyone looked like a zombie, and he refused ECT treatment.

After he got a DUI after a late-night drinking party with his drinking buddies, he was court-ordered to go to AA for several months and lost his driver's license. At AA, he met several people that helped him get sober. His wife needed to take him to his sales appointments after he lost his driver's license. At this point, his wife was ready to file for divorce. Well, you can see why the divorce rates are so high if one spouse has a mental illness like BD.

His boss was harassing him because he was not making his sales quota, but they were also cutting his sales territory. It was clear he was being tracked and monitored at his job. He told me he would sneak into the back door of his pharmacy so no one would see him pick up his meds. He left a good-paying job before he got fired for poor performance. These serious setbacks were caused by his drinking, prolonged deep depressions, and episodes of manic spending, but the underlying cause was his BD illness.

He left the big corporation and started a real estate venture with a business partner. The real estate market collapsed, and he lost all his property and his family home to the bank. His marriage was falling apart due to his alcoholism and reckless spending. After almost ending up in bankruptcy court, his wife filed for divorce; then, he spiraled into a very severe and prolonged depression. He could not find a good-paying job and became suicidal and homeless, living with our mother in her small cottage.

Stu should have been rushed by helicopter to a trauma emergency room of the nearest psychiatric hospital. It's no surprise he decided to commit suicide with a stress level in the X-Emergency Zone level 7 with a score of over 800 points.

He was planning his suicide but could not decide on what method to use. Just before the final act, he prayed to his higher power to save him. He made an agreement with his higher power if he spared his life, he would help people with drug and alcohol addictions.

Stu felt he was saved from suicide by his agreement with his higher power, but his physical, emotional, and mental health outlook was dismal. After several months, he got his driver's license back and decided to leave NE. Stu's world was crashing in on him from all sides.

After recovering from near suicide, he decided to leave New England (NE) and move to Florida and start a new life. We score Stu's WAVES Chart after arriving in Florida.

Stu's unstable WAVES Stress Chart looked like Stress Chart 3a.

A detailed description of my brother's chart tells a story of extreme stress in his life before he was stabilized on lithium. Before he became sober, his alcoholism was producing a lot of stress for him and his family. About the only thing Stu had going for him when he arrived in Florida was his sobriety. If he was still drinking and living around active drug users and alcoholics, I think his life would have ended in tragedy.

He lost all his family's support due to his reckless business ventures, bizarre abusive behavior, and alcoholism. He left New England (NE) in a beat-up old van towing an old beat-up pop-up camper. In Florida, he found an encampment with most people down on their luck, including Stu. I cannot call this place a campground; it was more like a tent city, an encampment. The daily fees were very low, but most people were drug addicts, and many were hopeless drunks, but Stu had made a commitment to his

## Stu's Unstable BP WAVES Stress Chart

Find your Bipolar Stress Zone
Taken from The Bipolar WAVES Workbook
Copyright © 2021 by Philip Van Ostrander

| Bipolar Lifestyle | COL-C |
|---|---|
| Unstable BP Lifestyle      COL B | 130 |
| **Other Mental Disorders** | |
| Personality, Stress, Anxiety - Untreated | 54 |
| **Physical Illnesses** | |
| Long-term e.g. Cancer /Chronic pain | 66 |
| **Addictions** | |
| Alcohol and/or Drug Clean and Sober | 30 |
| **Career and Jobs** | |
| Financial burdens- Can't find work- | 60 |
| **Marriage & Family** | |
| Divorce | 102 |
| Conflicts with spouse over lifestyle | 60 |
| Loss of family support rejected shunned | 66 |
| **Personal Situations** | |
| Homeless Lost Home/Room/Apt | 60 |
| No Psychiatric care insurance | 48 |
| Changes in activities, sleeping, eating | 36 |
| Major changes--moving/retirement | 54 |
| Living - High Crime /violence | 42 |
| **Stress Level Score (SLS)=Sum C** | **808** |
| X-Emergency-Zone Level 7 700 Plus | 808 |

Stu's WAVES Chart 3a

Stress Chart 3a Stu's very unstable
WAVES Stress Chart

higher power to help all people with drug and alcohol addictions. It is fortunate he had become sober after his DUI because Stu told me some people were drinking and using drugs from sunrise to sunset. Oh, and the others were drinking and using drugs most of the night.

He had a heart attack five years before his divorce, so I did include it in his chart because his heart disease was a long-term physical illness. He also had medical bills after his heart attack but had no money to repay the hospital. Stu was in the highest X-Emergency Zone Level 7 with an SLS score of over 800. He was also dealing with other untreated personality and mental anxiety disorders.

My brother and his wife were arguing over finances even after separation. I also believe the medication he was taking was harming him, and he would be better off not taking them at all. That is what happened; he stopped taking all psychiatric meds after trying them for just a short period. At times, the psychiatrist would tell him he needed to take the new med for a month to be useful, but his psychiatrist failed to disclose the harmful toxic side effects that made him even more mentally unstable.

After moving to Florida, he had several personal situations that added points to his SLS score. He was basically homeless, moving, living in a high-crime area, had no insurance, and had trouble sleeping.

These are the accumulative BD stress factors I claim to put people with BD in extremely high emergency stress zones. From the WAVES Chart 3a, his personal life situations alone totaled about 200 points.

He decided to go back up to New England and sail his sailboat back to Florida solo. I thought at the time sailing solo 1500 miles was another suicide attempt. After several weeks and more than a few risky misadventures, he arrived in Florida and lived on his sailboat.

He decided to start a sailing school in Florida and live on his sailboat, but his sailboat was up in NE. He went up to NE and loaded his sailing gear into a huge trailer. On his way back to Florida from NE with a trailer full of boat gear, he was rear-ended by a tractor-trailer. He settled with the trucking company for $15,000 and bought a very small cottage.

## Stu's very unstable lifestyle after moving to Florida

So, I scored Stu's WAVES Chart before and after he moved to Florida. He had an addiction to alcohol but was active in AA. He had financial burdens, conflicts with his x wife, loss of family support, no psychiatric care, living in a high crime area, and the stress of moving 1500 miles from his family, and I probably missed a few other stressors.

## Stu becomes stable after meeting Dr. Freed

In Florida, he was still severely depressed and looking to find a low-cost family country doctor for his depression. He did not have medical insurance and was flat broke. He found an old-time country doctor that helped the very poor for free. When she learned he was sober and helping other alcoholics; she helped him get healthcare for free at a county clinic.

Stu decided to offer sunset cruises to groups to offset his sailing school business. On one sunset cruise, he met a fellow sailor that was also a psychiatrist. The doctor's name was Dr. Freed; he offered to treat Stu's mental illness free of charge. They became friends, and he treated Stu with lithium; just a few weeks later, he became stable after 50 years of struggling with BD.

Of course, I was also diagnosed and treated with lithium. At first, I refused to believe Stu was stable with only one dose of lithium a day. Stu had been treated for depression at some of the best hospitals in NE, and they even recommended ECT as a last resort.

After a few months, I also became stable after 50 years of struggling with BD.

## Stu's Stable bipolar normal lifestyle
Dr. Freed also referred him to the county medical assistance program to help very low-income county residents. Dr. Freed diagnosed his mental illness in just one visit as BD and put him on lithium. Here Stu has gone from a very upscale yacht club lifestyle In New England to on government assistance in less than two years.

## Stu's chart one year after treatment with lithium
I will chart the stresses in Stu's life a year after treatment with lithium. Refer to the WAVES Stress Chart Stress in Appendix A. Because he was stable on meds, I am now using Col A on the WAVES Stress Chart to calculate his total SLS.

The life situations that apply to Stu after treatment are scored in Stress Chart 3b Stu's stable chart now looks like Stress Chart 3b.

So, after 50 years, Stu was effectively treated by Dr. Freed for his bipolar illness with lithium.

Stu's base stress level (LBSL) is now lowered to 65 because he was diagnosed and effectively treated by Dr. Freed for his bipolar illness with lithium. This means he was BD normal, as I call it. Stu was now stable, but he still had many other life situations that caused stresses unique to his BD normal lifestyle.

## Stu's Stable BP WAVES Stress Chart

*Find your Bipolar Stress Zone*
Taken from The Bipolar WAVES Workbook
Copyright © 2021 by Philip Van Ostrander

| Bipolar Lifestyle | COL-C |
|---|---|
| **Stable BP Normal Lifestyle COL A** | 65 |
| **Other Mental Disorders** | |
| Personality, Stress, Anxiety - Treated | 25 |
| **Physical Illnesses** | |
| Long-term e.g. Cancer /Chronic pain | 55 |
| **Addictions** | |
| Alcohol and/or Drug Clean and Sober | 25 |
| **Career and Jobs** | |
| Financial burdens- Can't find work- | 50 |
| Starting a new job or career | 45 |
| **Relationships & Dating** | |
| Dating - fear of making mistakes | 30 |
| Dating anxiety telling date about BP | 30 |
| **Marriage & Family** | |
| Loss of family support rejected shunned | 55 |
| **Personal Situations** | |
| Changes in activities, sleeping, eating | 30 |
| Major changes--moving/retirement | 45 |
| | |
| **Stress Level Score (SLS)=Sum C** | 455 |
| | |
| **Danger-Zone Level 4       400 --->499** | 455 |

Stu's WAVES Chart 3b

Stress Chart 3b Stu's Stable Stress Chart

He still has personality and anxiety disorders but is being treated with therapy, so that added more points to his SLS score. He is getting psychiatric and limited health care through the county health care system.

Stu has a history of alcohol addiction, but he is now sober and active in AA, which lowered his point score but added several points to his SLS score.

Stu was finally coming out of a fog of living without proper treatment for 50 years. By starting his sailing school, he avoided filling out forms and job stressful interviews. He avoided several other very stressful job-related tasks common to many people with BD illness.

Even at his new place, he was living around prostitutes, drug dealers, and criminals; he calls them the boat people at the marina.

His hardships were hard for me to understand because his family had no empathy for his mental illness. Stu's oldest son talked with him but provided very little financial support at first.

We could not give him any financial aid because we had a huge mortgage on an old house with high repair costs. At this point, we were living on just one income. I was so depressed I could not even apply for a job.

He obviously could not pay the court-ordered alimony payments of $1600 a month. His divorce was settled, so that stressor was sadly resolved as well as constant conflicts with his former wife.

I do not think Stu realized how difficult it would be to help down and out alcoholics and drug users, but he joined AA and became very active in the AA program. He was fulfilling his commitment to helping people with addictions. He even started a sober house to help people on drugs and alcohol.

I told him at one point I thought his higher power was taking advantage of him; he hesitated and then just laughed at my comment. He said, "We did our share of drinking, and now we are paying the price for our misdeeds." I always thought I had more insight than Stu in real-life matters, but Stu was now getting it and climbing out of a very deep and dark hole after he had reached rock bottom.

Stu met a nice woman at AA, and he became friends with her, and eventually, he did disclose his BD illness. Of course, the stress and anxiety of telling your date you have a mental disorder adds even more points to your SLS score.

Stu is now in the Danger Zone Level 4 with an SLS over 400 and must not add any more points to his stressful lifestyle.

I think Stu's chart is generally a good snapshot of his BD lifestyle a year after becoming stable. Within a year, Stu went from the X-Emergency Zone Level 7 to the Danger Zone Level 4, but he is not anywhere near the safer Caution Zone. He lost family support, but his oldest son is helping him get back on his feet, and it could mean getting better family support in the future. His son has praised his sobriety and Stu's commitment to helping other alcoholics.

As time went on, he worked out an agreement with his x-wife not to pay 1600 dollars a month. If his x wife did drag him into court, I would need to get involved and educate her on the risks of depression, causing suicide. At times I did want to confront his family and tell them they were abandoning someone with a severe mental disability. Stu's oldest son told his family Stu was on government assistance in Florida, flat broke but was sober and under psychiatric care for BD.

Was Stu's family coming to terms with his mental illness? I thought the court order his x wife was placing on Stu was gruel and unjust punishment when he was so down and out. I guess she finally realized it was not in her best interest to drag him into court over a judgment he could not pay. From my experience, it is not uncommon for "Normal" family members; to punish someone with mental illness due to bizarre or abusive behavior.

He still has a long-term illness to care for his heart condition, but he is getting treatment from a heart specialist.

## Our illness is no joke for our family, friends, and loved ones

Throughout the WAVES Workbook, I have given examples from the perspective of someone with BD, but we need to recognize our illness creates enormous stresses on families, friends, and loved ones.

Maybe I should add points for "abandonment" to Stu's unstable SLS score after he arrived in Florida. The only support was from his faithful friend Buster his dog. That is a joke, but sometimes we need to laugh at our misdeeds. Stu says laughter is the only thing that keeps us out of a psych ward. It is true we often laugh at our strange and bizarre BD behavior, but it is no joke for our family, friends, and loved ones.

## Stu reduces several of his stressful situations

Now Stu was finding a way to reduce his stress by eliminating several of his stressful life situations. He found a compassionate psychiatrist to treat his BD illness, started a sailing school, and removed the financial burden of a court order. He also started a relationship and became active in AA to help other people cope with addictions.

When Stu decided to move to Florida, I never realized Stu was under so much stress until I scored his WAVES Chart. When Stu arrived in Florida, every part of his life was in turmoil. He was at the most psychological and emotional stress anyone could endure; he should have been involuntary committed to a mental hospital.

Looking back, I believe Stu showed remarkable strength to get past this phase of his life. He often says he had his spiritual guide to thank for surviving the most challenging period of his life. Personally, I think it was his dog Buster, the only one that stood by his side all those early years.

I guess he is right about his spirit guide; he moved 1500 miles to Florida to find a compassionate psychiatrist who diagnosed and treated his mental illness correctly during his first visit. He also found non-judgmental, compassionate support from his faithful friend Buster.

So even becoming stable on meds does not solve all your stressors in life. Stu needs to be very careful because just a few more stressors could put him back in the highest X-Emergency Zone.

I believe Stu's chaotic life and destructive behavior were the results of not being diagnosed and treated earlier for his BD and anxiety issues. Stu was married right out of college and, within six years, had the responsibility of starting a stressful sales career, family, and marriage obligations, plus the burdens of struggling with his undiagnosed BD. By the time he received treatment at the age of 50, he had accumulated hundreds of stress points as scored in his WAVES Stress Chart 3a.

The WAVES Stress Chart 3a shows why Stu needed to be stable much sooner. He struggled 20 years with family, career, and alcoholism before getting any relief from his BD lifestyle. At 50 years old, he had so many stressors in his life that he could not eliminate. If he had been stable earlier, say at 30 years old, he might have saved his marriage by getting sober and eliminating many stressors in his life, like his highly stressful sales job.

So again, the most important key factor in living with BD is to become stable at a very young age before your life becomes unmanageable.

## Could Stu's stress return to the X-Emergency Zone Level 7?

It was a fortunate set of circumstances that led to both my brother and me being diagnosed correctly and getting effective medications. After Stu had recovered from 50 years of living with untreated BD, I also became stable on lithium. Lithium was a miracle medicine for both Stu and me to become mentally stable.

Who could have thought Stu would meet a psychiatrist and a fellow sailor on a sunset cruise. Stu had gone to several highly respected doctors up north that did not help him.

Stu said his agreement with his higher power to become and remain sober was a start to healing. I mentioned several times his sobriety and helping other people become sober was what saved him from suicide, and he agreed. Getting sober was undoubtedly a good step toward a better life, but Stu still had the problems of his BD illness to manage.

## Let's assume Stu started drinking again

In this "What if" scenario, the unintended consequences of starting to drink again will lead to many more stressors in Stu's life.

What if Stu started drinking again and could not continue his sailing school. The people at the marina were harassing and threatening him for coming to the marina drunk and then found out he was mentally ill with BD. In Stu's Stable Stress Chart 3b, he was stable and in the Danger Zone of stress level 4.

Let's assume after his sailing business failed, he had to face the consequences of finding work all over again. All the everyday job tasks come up if you have a diagnosis of BD, filling out applications, Job interviews without references, gaps in your job history are not easy to hide from a potential employer. For practical purposes, you must lie and cover up your diagnosis of having any mental illness.

In Stu's case, perhaps he would hang around the boat people and be around alcoholics and drug users. He would be living in a crime-ridden area again; more points added to his total score.

With a long history of alcoholism, the encampment is not an ideal living situation.; it must be a challenge to invite your lady friend from AA to have dinner with you at the encampment.

What if Stu broke up with the woman he met at AA after she learned he had BD, and he started to drink very heavily again. His alcoholism would be affecting his social life. He would not be attending AA meetings, and although he was still stable on meds, his drunken behavior would be affecting his quality of life on several levels.

The newly updated chart is updated to reflect Stu's decision to drink again and is scored in Stress Chart 3c

## Stu's Stable BP WAVES Stress Chart

*Find your Bipolar Stress Zone*
Taken from The Bipolar WAVES Workbook
Copyright © 2021 by Philip Van Ostrander

| Bipolar Lifestyle | COL-C |
|---|---|
| **Stable BP Normal Lifestyle  COL A** | 65 |
| **Other Mental Disorders** | |
| Personality, Stress, Anxiety - Treated | 25 |
| **Physical Illnesses** | |
| Long-term e.g. Cancer /Chronic pain | 55 |
| **Addictions** | |
| Alcohol and/or Drug No treatment | 60 |
| **Career and Jobs** | |
| Fired because you have Bipolar Disorder | 60 |
| Threat of being fired for BP behavior | 40 |
| Financial burdens- Can't find work- | 50 |
| Filling out job applications | 30 |
| Job interviews- gaps in job history | 30 |
| Conflict / harassed by co-workers | 50 |
| **Relationships & Dating** | |
| Breakup after learning about your BP | 50 |
| **Marriage & Family** | |
| Loss of family support rejected shunned | 55 |
| **Personal Situations** | |
| Homeless Lost Home/Room/Apt | 50 |
| No Psychiatric care insurance | 40 |
| Death of a pet | 50 |
| Changes in activities, sleeping, eating | 30 |
| Major changes--moving/retirement | 45 |
| Living - High Crime /violence | 35 |
| **Stress Level Score (SLS)=Sum C** | 820 |
| **X-Emergency-Zone Level 7  700 --->999** | 820 |

Stu's WAVES Chart 3c

Stress Chart 3c Stu returns to the X-Emergency Zone Level 7

As you can see, his untreated alcoholism has spread to have more harmful effects on his relationships, business, living, and other quality of life issues. What if he could not find work without a job reference and became severely depressed again? These situations can and do happen to people with mental illness.

Stu was now again in the X-Emergency Zone Level 7 with an SLS of over 800 and at risk of having a psychotic episode. Even if he continues to be stable by taking my meds as prescribed by his psychiatrist, drinking again could cause his level of stress into the X-Emergency Zone Level 7 again. This possible real-life example illustrates just how several mistakes can escalate to cause enormous burdens on the individual and the entire family.

Stu is still mentally stable by taking effective meds, but his decision to drink again could have grave life-threatening consequences. I have included his long-term illness with his heart condition, but of course, he will be under enormous stress that could lead to a massive heart attack. The stats support the claim people with BD have a shorter life span of about 9 years.

Also, if his faithful friend Buster suddenly died from a blood infection, it would add several points to his chart. I cannot emphasize enough how this affects people when they lose a pet. That is why I scored high points for this tragic event. In some cases, the death of a pet can be like losing a family member. Stu told me Buster was his only family support during those dark days after he arrived in Florida.

Stu's life is now back in the highest X Emergency Zone Level 7 caused by his drinking and could cause him to have an auto accident or another DUI. He will then need an emergency trauma intervention in a psychiatric hospital to protect him and other people's lives.

After a stay in a psychiatric hospital, he will face even more challenges to become sober and get treatment for his addiction to alcohol.

So, this "What If" scenario illustrates just being stable on good psychiatric meds is not the only factor to live a better quality with BD; you need to lower, avoid and/or eliminate other stressful conditions. He could decide to get sober and start looking for another job, but he has made a bad situation far worse by starting to drink again.

I do believe job situations are challenging for anyone with a mental illness but extremely challenging for someone when unstable. Unpredictable cycles of mania and depression suggest to co-workers and employers you have a mental illness. Often bizarre behavior must be reported to management for review.

Also, by drinking again, he has less of a chance to get support from his family, who currently have supported his sobriety. The only family member in contact with Stu is his oldest son. He could lose his son's support and make his life even more complicated for himself and everyone.

As you can see from the WAVES Stress chart 3c, just a few additional mistakes will put Stu back into the X-Emergency Zone again at over 800 points. Of course, this is what he is trying to avoid at all costs, but unexpected events do happen to all of us, and sometimes they do have tragic consequences.

Again, I claim all this stress is caused by the accumulative BD stress factors in his life. Each new event and task could increase the stress enough to create a domino effect for Stu.

I do not want to preach or judge anyone with a serious mental health issue because, like a heart attack victim, death is only a heartbeat away. Likewise, someone with BD is only a psychotic episode away from life-threatening events in there our own lives.

Yes, theoretically, it could happen; Stu could return to the highest X Emergency Zone level 7 again even if he is mentally stable and on effective medications.

CHAPTER 7

# Henry's Marriage and Job Story

HENRY'S LIFE IS BASED ON the typical lifestyle of many people with BD. They grow up with just a few moderate stresses in their lives like college and starting a career, but after they are married, have children, mortgages, in-laws, these new responsibilities cause severe stress. The burden of having a serious mental illness and the duties of a family causes turmoil ending in divorce or separation.

According to the article "Managing Bipolar Disorder" in Psychology Today [(Managing Bipolar Disorder, 2003), an estimated 90 percent of marriages end in divorce. Isn't this a sad statistic, 90 percent of marriages end in divorcé if one spouse has BD. I do not have any statistics, but I could speculate if the other spouse is not stable, the divorce rate is even higher than 90 percent.

If you look at this statistic from the perspective of the person who is struggling with BD, they have only a 10 percent chance of their marriage lasting a lifetime. The Bipolar WAVES Stress Chart lists many life situations under Marriage & Family that may lead to divorce or separation.

The WAVES Chart lists several marriage and family situations that can apply to someone struggling with BD and illustrates how complex family situations may get.

## Henry's unstable lifestyle before treatment
Henry's story of living with marriage and job-related issues is typical for many married couples.

Henry is a guy that has never had a diagnosis of BD. Henry grew up in a middle-class neighborhood and went to a local college. At college, he liked to party, and he had some issues with drinking and ended up with a DUI. He has always been moody and, at times, reckless and anxious but considers himself a "Normal" guy with no mental health issues. After college, he found a good steady job with an average starting salary. He is paying off his college loans and is living a so-called "Normal" lifestyle, but he is living with a hidden case of BD.

He dated his childhood sweetheart, and they started to plan their life together by saving for a large house in the suburbs. They had a beautiful wedding, and then they purchased their expensive dream home in the suburbs. She has a good-paying job, and they settled down to married life. After three months, his wife got pregnant and had to leave her well-paying job due to medical issues with her pregnancy.

Henrys unstable BD lifestyle score is in WAVES Stress Chart 4a.

Because Henry is not on effective medications, his lifetime LBSL is 130. If you refer to the WAVES Stress Chart in Appendix A, Henry is in the Emergency Zone Level 6.

Note only two disorders BD LBSL (130) and his addiction to alcohol (72) alone account for over 200 points. I believe the stress points are generally accurate, although I have not done a scientific study. These points are subjective, depending on the person scoring the chart. I wanted to make the WAVES Chart subjective for anyone

*The Bipolar WAVES Workbook*

## Henry's Unstable BP WAVES Stress Chart

*Find your Bipolar Stress Zone*
Taken from The Bipolar WAVES Workbook
Copyright © 2021 by Philip Van Ostrander

| Unstable BP Lifestyle       COL B | 130 |
|---|---|
| **Addictions** | |
| Alcohol and/or Drug No treatment | 72 |
| **Career and Jobs** | |
| Conflict / harassed by co-workers | 60 |
| **Marriage & Family** | |
| Marriage | 78 |
| Conflicts with spouse over lifestyle | 60 |
| Wife Pregnant | 54 |
| Loss of family support rejected shunned | 66 |
| **Personal Situations** | |
| Large Dept Mortgage /College Loans | 42 |
| Changes in activities, sleeping, eating | 36 |
| Major changes--moving/retirement | 54 |
| | |
| **Stress Level Score (SLS)=Sum C** | 652 |
| | |
| **Emergency-Zone Level 6     600 --->699** | 652 |

Henry's Unstable WAVES Chart 4a

*Stress Chart 4a Henry's Unstable Bipolar WAVES Chart*

scoring the points on the WAVES Chart. That means if someone thinks a situation is different, they can lower or increase the points on the WAVES Chart.

The financial stresses of married life are beginning to take their toll on Henry's so-called "Normal" married lifestyle. Henry's steady but low-paying job will not cover expenses after his wife leaves her well-paying job.

Let's assume the loss of income from his wife's well-paying job is a financial burden, and he needs to get a promotion at his job. The new job has more responsibility, has longer hours, and is now in conflict with his boss and coworkers because he cannot complete his work on time.

Henry is beginning to lose family support due to his "irresponsible" and erratic behavior, but he has no control over his life. He cycles from mania and depression and cannot control his anger and abusive behavior.

After a few months at the new job, Henry begins to drink heavily after work and often comes home late. Now he has lost his family's support because of his drinking, erratic, and angry behavior. Because of all this, he is suffering from a case of severe anxiety. Now within a year of getting married, Henry is dealing with several major lifestyle issues. Now, he has a serious drinking problem, marriage issues, job and family conflicts, mortgages, college loans, and other life challenges common to "Normal" married life.

Now all these life situations put his total stress score (SLS) into the Emergency Zone of well over 600 points.

From the WAVES Stress Chart, you can see how and why the stresses on Henry's marriage can and do end in divorce. Without being properly medicated for his BD and treated for alcoholism, he is at a much higher risk of a mental breakdown. Without proper medication, he is too unstable to handle all the responsibilities of marriage, plus a stressful job. The accumulative BD stress factors are at work, pushing Henry's BD stress level to the limits.

Now a "Normal" person might have similar marriage and lifestyle issues but may handle each situation with much less stress than Henry. If Henry were "Normal" we would use the Holmes and Rahe Life Stress Scale in Appendix B.

Appendix B will give an example of Henry's chart with no history of mental illnesses.

## Let's assume Henry sought treatment and is now stable

Henry started to drink heavily and was arrested for DUI. The court ordered him to get treatment for his alcoholism. After several months of sobriety, he became severely depressed over his life in general. He stopped drinking but became so depressed he went to his primary care physician, and she referred him to a good psychiatrist. His psychiatrist correctly diagnosed and treated Henry for his BD, anxiety, and alcoholism.

Henrys stable BD normal lifestyle score is in WAVES Stress Chart 4b.

In Henry's case, he is fortunate to find a competent psychiatrist to treat his alcoholism, but more important is his stress living with BD. His psychiatrist realized Henry was drinking to medicate his BD, but Henry's underlying diagnosis was BD and was making his life unbearable.

Now Henry's life situations are similar, but he has received excellent treatment and now has family support. His family now has a better understanding of Henry's problems and is less critical of his past abusive behavior. He still has his issues with alcohol but is getting treatment in AA and has significantly less stress in his life. He is taking his meds and being more responsible at his job and family life.

Henry still has most of the stressful life situations of marriage like mortgage, moving, and a pregnant wife, but his life stress score has dropped from 130 to 65. He has less stress in his life due to proper treatment and has fewer fits of anger and moody behavior.

Most of Henry's life situations have fewer stress points, and now Henry's Bipolar WAVES Chart looks like Stress Chart 4b.

Now the major differences between stable and unstable lifestyles are Henry's Lifetime LBLS score is 65 instead of 130; he is now getting family support and fewer conflicts at work. His treatment for his addiction to alcohol is now 25 points. I do believe heavy drinking or drug use is much harder on the family and friends. If drugs and alcohol are used to self-medicate his BD illness, any chance of having a better quality of life is slim.

Henry's BD normal lifestyle now is still stressful, and according to the chart, he is at risk of physical illness, but I do think most people with Bipolar have Stress Scores above 300 and are at risk of a physical illness most of their lives.

Again, I can cite a study by [(National Institute of Mental Health, n.d.) that says people with BD live an average of 9 years less than "Normal" people. That supports my claim BD has more life stresses than most "Normal" people, but I claim people with BD that are not on effective medication are at a far greater risk of being both physically and mentally ill for the same life situations.

## Henry's Stable BP WAVES Stress Chart

Find your Bipolar Stress Zone
Taken from The Bipolar WAVES Workbook
Copyright © 2021 by Philip Van Ostrander

| | |
|---|---|
| **Stable BP Normal Lifestyle  COL A** | 65 |
| **Other Mental Disorders** | |
| Personality, Stress, Anxiety - Treated | 25 |
| **Addictions** | |
| Alcohol and/or Drug Clean and Sober | 25 |
| **Career and Jobs** | |
| Changes -promotions/demotions | 40 |
| **Marriage & Family** | |
| Marriage | 65 |
| Wife Pregnant | 45 |
| **Personal Situations** | |
| Large Dept Mortgage /College Loans | 35 |
| Changes in activities, sleeping, eating | 30 |
| Major changes--moving/retirement | 45 |
| **Stress Level Score (SLS)=Sum C** | 375 |
| **X-Caution-Zone Level 3     300 --->399** | 375 |

Henry's Stable WAVES Chart 4b

Stress Chart 4b Henry's Bipolar WAVES
Stress Chart when Stable.

Most "Normal" people have bad days but usually only last for a few weeks. I think most people with BD have hundreds of bad days, but I probably had had one thousand or more very bad days before I was 50 years old. I claim many bad cycles are why people with BD live about 9 years less than other people. I call these long-prolonged "bad spells," an assortment of physical, mental, and cycles of BD.

I hope that the WAVES Stress Chart will help people understand the unique psychiatric stress on people with a lifetime mental illness live, especially people with BD mental illness.

Of course, every person's chart may be different and vary from person to person, but hopefully, the WAVES Stress Chart provides a reference point to examine and determine the total stress over a given period of one year or more.

Again, the most crucial factor in using the WAVES Stress Chart is first determining if a person is stable or unstable.

CHAPTER 8

# *Find your Bipolar Stress Zone*

THE SUBTITLE OF THE BIPOLAR WAVES Workbook is "Find your Bipolar Stress Zone." In this workbook, I have listed four examples of finding other people's Stress Zone Levels; now, it's time to find your own Bipolar WAVES Stress Zone.

I think we can agree a diagnosis of BD is a difficult illness to accept, understand and manage. Due to the nature of BD, finding your WAVES Stress Level in this workbook will require a little work.

To find your own Bipolar Stress Zone level, you will need to answer a few questions. Refer to The WAVES Chart in Appendix A.

Are you living in a stable BD Normal lifestyle or an Unstable BD lifestyle? Check only one.

| |
|---|
| _____ Stable on effective meds  Use COL-A |
| _____ Unstable No meds or ineffective meds Use COL-B |

### What is your Stress Level Score (SLS)?
According to The WAVES Chart in Appendix A, what are your stressful life situations over the past year or more?

After adding up all your stress points in COL-C of Sections 1, 2, 3, and 4, what is your Stress Level Score (SLS)?

**Your SLS score = _____**

What is your Stress Level Score (SLS)?

## The Bipolar WAVES Stress Chart
### The 7 WAVES Bipolar Stress Zone Levels

*Find your Bipolar Stress Zone*
Taken from The Bipolar WAVES Workbook
Copyright © 2018 by Philip Van Ostrander

| The 7 WAVES Bipolar Stress Zone Levels | Col C |
|---|---|
| **X-Emergency-Zone Level 7     700 --->999** <br> Extremely high risk of a psychotic episode <br> Air lift to a hospital trauma center | \_\_\_ |
| **Emergency-Zone Level 6     600 --->699** <br> Emergency at risk of a Psychotic Episode <br> Rush to a hospital trauma center | \_\_\_ |
| **X-Danger-Zone Level 5     500 --->599** <br> Possible Psychotic Episode Extreme Danger <br> Go to a Hospital | \_\_\_ |
| **Danger-Zone Level 4     400 --->499** <br> In Danger of a Psychotic Episode <br> Go to a Hospital | \_\_\_ |
| **X-Caution-Zone Level 3     300 --->399** <br> Use Extreme Caution -Possible Psychotic <br> Episode Contact your Psychiatrist | \_\_\_ |
| **Caution-Zone Level 2     150 --->299** <br> Moderate risk of a Psychotic Episode <br> Contact your Psychiatrist | \_\_\_ |
| **Safe-Zone Level 1     65--->149** <br> Low risk of a psychiatric Episode <br> Contact your Psychiatrist | \_\_\_ |

The 7 WAVES Bipolar Stress Zone Levels

**The 7 WAVES Bipolar Stress Zone Levels Chart**

## How may future events affect your quality of life?
It may be beneficial to see how not adding future events or situations may affect your quality of life, for example, not changing jobs.

What Zone Level will you be in if you add major lifestyle changes or dangerous projects to your life, for example, getting married or a DUI?

> **If you are planning to add new events/projects what will be your future Stress Zone?**
>
> _____

## What if you eliminate some stressful situations or events?
What Zone Level will you be in if you eliminate or get treatment for some stressful situations or conditions in your life, for example, seek treatment for alcoholism and become sober or get clean for an addiction to drugs?

> **If you can eliminate events/conditions what will be your future Stress Zone?**
>
> _____

What are your risks of a serious psychiatric episode at this new Stress Zone level?

## If you are unstable, how can you become stable?
As I have stated many times, the best way to lower your overall stress level is to get psychiatric help from a competent psychiatrist. If you feel you need help, go to the nearest emergency room of any

hospital or call 911. They will evaluate your condition and refer you to a mental health hospital or clinic. There is no reason to be a victim of your BD illness any longer; you can get stabilized on proper medications, gain more control over your life, and stop being a victim of your mental illness.

You are not your mental illness; you have a disability called BD. You are capable of accomplishments regardless of your mental illness. You may have many skills and gifts to share with the world. Get and stay stable and share your skills and accomplishments with other people. Give yourself credit for identifying and managing your BD.

Remember, "Stressed spelled backward spells desserts." That is the goal of the WAVES Workbook to help you turn your stressed BD life into a sweet, stable BD normal life filled with many desserts.

Let us hope you are stable, stay stable, and stay in the Caution Zone

CHAPTER 9
# My WAVES Chart

THIS WORKBOOK HAS COVERED SOME troubling and challenging events in my life, BD, alcoholism, emotional and sexual abuse, wars, rejection even living with a case of amnesia for over 45 years.

As they say, all these events have made me who I am today. I do believe living with BD has been the most challenging and destructive force in my life, especially before I was treated with lithium at the age of 50. After I was in treatment, my life and our family issues improved over time.

Now I need to give myself credit for overcoming several difficult obstacles in my life, but I also need to acknowledge many people helped me along the way.

If you skipped my long bipolar story in Chapter 2, I want to summarize what I learned about BD and the people that have helped me for almost 80 years now. I need to make an apology because I will need to cover some of the same events described in my story in Chapter 2.

## What I learned from my childhood

My brother Stu and I were brought up on a small farm in the early '40s in New England (NE) until we were about 12 years old. I was about five years old when our father died of a heart attack.

After our father died, our home life became very stressful for our entire family, especially for me. After my father died, we took in our grandmother and her sister we called our Aunt Maddie.

Both my brother and I had symptoms and behavior patterns of bipolar disorder (BD) at a very young age. Without a father, I became moodier and more prone to have fits of anger. I was constantly being harassed and shamed for my behavior; I could not change without some professional help. No one protected me from criticism, especially my Aunt Maddie.

After my father died, I developed what I call an unworthy syndrome. This condition was brought on by years of emotional abuse by everyone in our family and struggling with an undiagnosed case of BD. I also was sexually abused when I was about 8. I was the victim of childhood abuse and had untreated BD. I have a name for these two conditions, my unworthy syndrome.

We moved uptown from the farm when I was 12 years old. Shortly after we moved uptown from the farm, I saw hundreds of Black and White (B&W) pictures of the Holocaust in a small print shop in town. These horrific pictures of piles of dead bodies have stuck with me my entire life. I had a recurrent nightmare of one picture of a German SS soldier. He was standing on the backs of men, women, and children as they lie face down in a long trench. He was shooting them in the back with a pistol.

I learned crimes against humanity do happen in times of war. Those pictures had a profound impact on my views of our nation fighting in wars and conflicts around the globe after WW II.

## A breakup with my 1st love and then a case of amnesia

I met a young woman named Maria I call my 1st love. We met on Nantucket when I was about 17, and I fell madly in love with her.

Maria and I drifted apart for several years, but I always loved her. I invited Maria to visit me on Nantucket before I entered my senior year in college. After I discovered she was having sex with another guy, I told my 1st love, "I don't love you.". After the tragic event on Nantucket, we broke up during my senior year in college. I was so distraught I went into a state of amnesia for over 45 years.

I was dealing with too many issues all at once—the stress of college, my unworthy syndrome, alcoholism, to name a few. As a result, I could not handle the pain of the breakup with Maria and went into a state of amnesia for over 45 years.

I think of my case of amnesia as having two stages, the time I spent in amnesia and then what I call the recollections phase after I awoke from amnesia when I was about 70 years old.

## Was amnesia a blessing or a curse?
Sometimes questions pop up. What would happen if I never went into amnesia? I don't want to say the effects of my amnesia are over. Sometimes I do think of how my life could have been very different if I didn't go into a state of amnesia. I now believe my case of amnesia was a blessing and not a curse. I could have ended up in a psychiatric ward for years, or I could have ended my own life. Of course, my amnesia influenced my relationships with women.

Maybe if I could resolve my traumatic case of amnesia when I was in my 20's, I could have recovered from my amnesia in my 30's instead of much later in life at 70. These what-ifs are why I became an advocate for people with BD to get treatment early on.

My hope is the workbook will help people identify and resolve emotional and BD issues much earlier in life. I don't expect all people to uncover major dark secrets hidden years ago but perhaps get insights into how BD has limited their opportunities, especially if not stable. People may learn being unstable does destroy relationships and cause irresponsible and reckless behavior.

Again, I see many struggles and setbacks I have had in my life go back to the fact I was never treated effectively for BD until midlife. I was also a victim of childhood abuse and, in combination with my BD illness, caused what I call an unworthy syndrome. My recollections after recovery from amnesia are ongoing and most likely to be an issue for the rest of my life.

Maybe one reason I had a case of amnesia was to encourage people to get help early for any mental issues. I am kidding, but amnesia was certainly a traumatic event in my life but not as traumatic as struggling with BD all my life. Amnesia is certainly a dramatic example to illustrate for people to get help early on for any physical or mental illness.

I read somewhere some psychiatrists don't believe people can live in a state of amnesia; well, maybe my amnesia is not the accurate DSM [(American Psychiatric Association, 1987) definition, but I definitely had some sort of repressed memory loss after the breakup, and then I had traumatic recollections of the breakup with my 1st love over four decades later.

## I have a different perspective on my breakup

I have one regret; I wish I did contact and talk to Maria years ago. Now I feel I may have traumatized her with my anger and selfish behavior. I recently looked at our breakup from her perspective. Maria came all the way out to Nantucket and wanted to be with me. After a few days, I was physically sick and angry when I found out she was dating and having sex with some guy in Boston. I had bizarre behavior at the time; I was so abusive and very unkind to someone I claimed I loved. Ironically, I may have ridiculed and probably traumatized her as my family did to me.

I realize now whenever I had those feelings of not being loved or rejected, I lashed out and fought back against my deep feelings of unworthiness. Of course, my anger only produced more ridicule and conflict. Maria was not going to be abused by a crazy guy and ended our relationship. I don't want to admit it, but I do think Maria made the right decision at the time. I had so many unresolved issues to deal with at the time in my life.

What could I do or say now to make her feel better if she was traumatized by my behavior? I don't think my "I am sorry" email was enough to apologize for my abusive behavior. I want to personally talk to Maria, explain my mental state at the time of the breakup, and ask her forgiveness.

I guess I better let it go before I make another mistake in judgment and do something else entirely inappropriate. I guess I am still selfishly trying to make myself feel better about the most tragic event in my entire life.

Before I awoke from amnesia years ago, I would not have scored amnesia as a stress factor. Of course, I did not know I had the hidden stress of amnesia for over 45 years.

## What I learned from my brother Stu

My brother Stu and I was born about a year apart and shared something in common; we were diagnosed with BD but not until about mid-life or 50 years old. My brother Stu and I have had our differences over the years. We have very different personalities; he is outgoing, and I am more of an introvert. I think we both had unique and challenging lives before we were diagnosed with BD. At times we did not communicate for months, especially when we were both depressed, but we did support each other throughout our lives.

After college, I found a job with a military draft deferment in Seattle. Those horrific pictures of the Holocaust convinced me more crimes against humanity were being committed in the Vietnam War on both sides of the war.

When the job ended in Seattle, I found another job in New Jersey. Within a year, the plant closed, and I moved to Philly and collected unemployment benefits for several months. After several jobs and trips to many doctors, I was told by one doctor my physical health was excellent and referred me to a psychiatrist. My psychiatrist recommended group psychotherapy.

Group psychotherapy did not help me. I took a vacation to Europe and returned in a hypomanic state of mind. Then I made a hasty decision to move to LA. After my senseless hypo manic trip to LA in the mid-70s, I did not know at the time why I came back to Philly. It is not an accident. I came back to Philly, met a woman named Iva, and took a spiritual growth course called Awake.

## What I learned from Iva, my 2nd love

I met a woman named Iva shortly after I came back from LA in the mid-70s. Iva came to America from Eastern Europe after WW II when she was 8 years old. She would never talk about her life in war-torn Europe after or during WW II.

Before I met Iva, my life was a series of failed relationships, meaningless open relationships, risky behavior, and failed business ventures for years until I met Iva. Iva showed me I could have an intimate relationship with a woman and learn to trust someone for the first time in my life. She taught me to slow down and not strive for financial gain and status.

We were attracted to each other right from the start. We went from Hello to let's have an open relationship, and it worked for several years. Due to my amnesia, I was still in denial of how important she was in my life.

Now I know why I thought she was so special; I was falling in love with her from the first night we were together. No wonder I forgot her name; unconsciously, I probably thought I was going to be brokenhearted all over again, but she was so honest and caring I trusted her not to reject me. I deeply regret I abandoned Iva after I met Nicole.

## I learned Willy's four rules to live by

Stu had a Black African American friend named Willy from rural Mississippi. He was a very tall Black man with a checkered past but found his purpose in life was to help poor and disadvantaged people. Willy often said you only need to follow 4 rules to live by in life. Learn to be kind, be kind, be kind to everyone, and don't expect everyone to be kind to you. Stu and I often refer to these 4 rules of wisdom; I say these 4 rules are so simple they must be true.

## What I learned from the Awake spiritual growth course

After I met Iva, I attended the Awake course on spiritual growth. I did not know it at the time, but I did learn valuable lessons from the people at the sessions and people I met during the course. The Awake course taught me to be more generous and less frugal, but not cheap for sure. I did learn I was selfish and did not give back without expecting something in return.

The course taught me there are beautiful and kind people in this world and to be grateful for what life has given me. Another message was also important for me, giving back without expecting something in return.

At the time, I was very disappointed with the Awake spiritual growth course because I did not find my purpose in life, and the course did not tell me what was wrong with me.

I would not be diagnosed and treated for BD for another 15 years at 50 years old. I did not understand at the time the consequences of being emotionally and sexually abused in my childhood until decades later. I also did not understand my childhood abuse created deep feelings of unworthiness. I have a name for these deep feelings of unworthiness, my unworthy syndrome.

## Life lessons from my wife

I met my wife over 35 years ago, around the time I took the Awake course. At the time, I joked I met several women but couldn't find a loving, kind, and caring woman until I met her. Well, I was right; she has stood by me through turmoil and many setbacks. She does live by Willy's 4 rules. She is kind, generous, and giving to everyone and does not expect kindness in return. I am very grateful to have her in my life.

I seldom mention my wife in the workbook, but she has been behind the scenes supporting, helping, caring, working, and yes, sometimes praying to help our family and others.

I know it is not easy to deal with two emotionally challenged adults. I am sure her mission in life is not pleasant, but she never complains or seeks pity or sympathy for herself. The only major issue we still have is our "discussions" about selling our now 110-year-old house. My life lesson is to love and respect her selfless devotion to our family.

## Lessons from the BDS group

After I was diagnosed and treated in 1992 for BD, I was 50 years old, or at mid-life, I began to read and study about the illness. I became active in a BDS group about five years after I began treatment with lithium.

Our BDS group taught me valuable life lessons to be kind and have empathy for all people with mental illness. The group also taught me to ask for support from the group; the lessons and observations I learned were the basis of the workbook. I learned people with BD struggle with unique challenges most "Normal" people never experience.

I want to make a point I don't see myself as a therapist but as a member of our BDS group. I feel I have observed and learned from the struggles of many people in the group, including myself. I learned people with BD can help each other live better lives.

Having BD is a challenging illness for most people with BD. The BD group support was far more beneficial than the psychotherapy group sessions I attended with people years ago. My hope is support groups like Rosie's bipolar disorder support (BDS) group will be available in every city and town in this nation.

## I have lived with a condition I call an unworthy syndrome

The second obstacle, I am still dealing with childhood abuse. After years of emotional abuse, beginning after my father died, I developed what I call an unworthy syndrome. Managing my unworthy disorder is a work in progress. When I have bad spells many times, it goes back to the traumatic memories of the breakup with my first love Maria but also back to my abusive childhood.

After attending the BDS group for several years, I noticed many people also struggled with a condition I call an unworthy syndrome. This is a feeling of not being loved; it usually starts from a very young age. So, I claim people that are victims of childhood abuse and have BD can have a unique condition I call an unworthy syndrome.

I claim dealing with BD and unworthy syndrome can be very difficult for many people. I believe I did develop a case of unworthiness from a very young age, and it has been a very challenging condition to overcome. I had deep feelings something was wrong with me from a very young age. I believe I have been struggling with more than two conditions for almost 80 years now.

## Lessons from living in Philly for ten years

In the late 70s, I bought a row house in a marginal area of Philly. Unfortunately, our neighborhood had a drug dealer living right next door.

I did learn valuable lessons from living in the inner city of Philly. I learned the government did not make the lives of poor people better.

I believe many people in our neighborhood, including me, did live in fatherless households. Most kids did not have a father to guide and discipline them. Without education and discipline, many kids found gangs and crime to ease their pain of abuse and abandonment. Someone once said anger and emotional pain leads to anger and violence. I think abandonment issues force kids to join gangs for a sense of belonging. Sometimes when kids join gangs, it can lead to violence and crime.

I think that is what is going on in many cities across the nation. I think many people with the unworthy syndrome either lash out in anger or internalize the pain and become depressed and suicidal; many kids turn to drugs and alcohol.

That is just my unprofessional psychological assessment of what happened in my neighborhood in Philly over 35 years ago. I understand from news reports that drugs and crime are still going on in many parts of Philly.

### Our spiritual retreat into Mother Nature.
I had two major operations several years ago. My wife Nicole and I decided to return to our childhood roots and escape the demands of modern life. We bought an older camper and began camping along the East Coast. We spent spring, summers, and fall traveling to campgrounds from the Adirondacks down to Charleston, SC.

### Managing my BD illness, bad spells, and the pandemic
I have managed to live with BD for almost 80 years. I am managing my BD disorder and monitoring any stressful events or situations that could put my stress level higher. I use the WAVES Chart to manage my stress level regularly. Now I can identify new stressors that are not on the WAVES Chart like the pandemic. Today millions of people with mental illnesses are dealing with the added stress of the pandemic.

The third challenge I am managing is my case of amnesia. I am still recovering from over 45 years in a state of amnesia. After I awoke from a state of amnesia when I was 70 years old, I was emotionally very fragile. I needed to manage extreme stress over the breakup with my 1st love, even though it happened over 45 years prior. Sometimes it is hard to believe I was in a state of amnesia for over 45 years.

I did not score any stress points for my sad recollections on my WAVES Chart now because I don't have severe episodes of sadness and grief any longer over the breakup with Maria. I am still dealing with my childhood abuse issues after decades in a state of amnesia. So, I did score the stress of being a victim of childhood abuse. My WAVES Chart is listed below.

## My Stable BP WAVES Stress Chart

Find your Bipolar Stress Zone
Taken from The Bipolar WAVES Workbook
Copyright © 2021 by Philip Van Ostrander

| | |
|---|---|
| **Stable BP Normal Lifestyle  COL A** | **65** |
| **Other Mental Disorders** | |
| Personality, Stress, Anxiety - Treated | 25 |
| **Physical Illnesses** | |
| Long-term e.g. Cancer /Chronic pain | 55 |
| **Addictions** | |
| Alcohol and/or Drug Clean and Sober | 25 |
| **Marriage & Family** | |
| Conflicts with spouse over lifestyle | 50 |
| **Personal Situations** | |
| Victim of childhood abuse Unworthy | 50 |
| Outstanding Achievement -Phd | 50 |
| Major changes--moving/retirement | 45 |
| | |
| **Stress Level Score (SLS)=Sum C** | **365** |

X-Caution-Zone Level 3    300 --->399

**My WAVES Chart**

*My Stress Chart 5a My stable BD WAVES Stress Chart*

From my WAVES Stress Chart 5a, I have identified my life's situations and then totaled up the points to get my SLS score. I determined from the WAVES Chart my SLS score was 365 and in the X Caution Zone Level 3. I can then decide which life conditions I can change and decide how to change them. Some conditions cannot be changed, for example, my history of alcoholism and the lifetime stress of living with BD, but I need to be aware of these conditions.

I still need to list the stress of managing my addiction to alcohol. Thankfully I have been sober now for over 25 years, but I still must monitor this condition closely. I need to thank Nicole because she does not need to drink to excess. I can never forget alcoholism was a very destructive force in my life for decades. The AA 12 step program wisely warns I need to treat my sobriety one day at a time. Stu sometimes says, "Alcoholism is curable; you just must never drink again."

## I need to account for my unworthy syndrome

I do need to account for the stress of my unworthy syndrome. I scored 50 points for being a victim of childhood abuse or for my unworthy syndrome. I know to some people I am too old to have stress over abuse in my childhood, over 70 years ago now, but to me, it is still a real issue.

Another stressor in my life is our "discussions" over lifestyle. I want to move to a condominium or an apartment, and my wife wants to stay in our 110-year-old house. Our house was only 70 years old when we purchased it in the early 80s. Now 40 years later, our old house is 110 years old. I am ready to sell the lawnmower, snow shovels, all the tools and spend our winters in Florida. Our conversations are not constant conflicts yet, but we do need to work on a solution soon. Although not constant, I did score this stressor as constant conflict with a spouse.

Like many older people, we have many more health costs now with dental, eye care, medications, and other long-term health care issues. My meds and doctor visits are very costly, but I would not score them as a financial burden.

Another factor is our retirement; it has made us more financially responsible and hesitant to get into debt over things we do not need but want. We are under moderate financial stress due to the high cost of repairs to our 110-year-old house. Our chimney fell in during the winter; the repair costs will be very expensive.

When I hear the hardships and the struggles of many people in the BDS group endure, I come home appreciative and thankful for my relatively stable lifestyle.

I also need to add the stress for writing and publishing this workbook. After hours, well years of writing and rewriting, publishing this workbook, I scored it as an Outstanding Achievement. Now many people would not consider writing a workbook outstanding, but with my history of delaying some, maybe most projects for more than ten years, it has been an exceptional personal accomplishment.

Of course, I also have the added stress of supporting my brother, who also has bipolar. Sometimes I do not realize how stressful it is to deal with him even though he has been stable for years. He is older now and somewhat forgetful. I often worry about him due to the unpredictable nature of our BD illnesses.

Years ago, I did account for the stress of almost daily contact with my brother as if he was living with us with his BD mental illness. Sometimes I tell Nicole he is coming to visit for the entire summer. She usually says, "Two is enough," referring to both our son and myself.

I don't know how I could live a semi-BD normal life without Nicole. I guess I will not score any points on Stu's stressor; he has been stable for several years. Notice if my brother Stu came to live with us, it would add another 45 points to my SLS score. That would increase my stress level to at least Zone Level 4, but I need to also add points for situations and events not found on the WAVES Chart.

## The stress of the pandemic needs to be added to my WAVES Chart

The WAVES Chart does not take into account unique or unusual events like the coronavirus. The pandemic has affected most people around the world. I subjectively scored the pandemic as 50 stress points. The stress caused by the pandemic is subjective and will vary greatly between people.

Of course, if you or a family member has COVID-19, the points assigned to that tragic illness could easily reach Stress level 7, the highest risk of a psychotic episode or suicide. After adding 50 points for the pandemic to my stress chart, my new score is 365 plus 50 for a new total of 415. So, the added stress of the pandemic has increased my stress level into the Danger Zone Level 4.

## Some ways that helped me cope with BD

I want to list some things that helped me cope with the challenges I have faced for almost 80 years.

1. My first priority was to find a good psychiatrist. After 50 years without treatment, I found a good psychiatrist. Actually, Stu found a psychiatrist first that treated him with lithium. I was very fortunate Stu met a good psychiatrist by the name of Dr. Freed. He diagnosed Stu with bipolar and treated him with lithium.

I found a psychiatrist in PA that also put me on the same dose of lithium. After a few months, my psychiatrist suddenly moved his practice to a town 30 minutes away from our house. Shortly after he moved his practice, I ran into some anxiety issues. He did not return my repeated calls; I found a new and better psychiatrist.

Many new people came to Rosie's support group very fragile and depressed. Many had psychiatrists that were incompetent and mistreated patients instead of treating them. Some psychiatrists were not even prescribing their patients a proven mood stabilizer.

If my psychiatrist does not keep me stable, I will ask people to help me find a competent psychiatrist. I will ask Rosie to find a psychiatrist on her good doc list. If I can't find a psychiatrist on Rosie's good doc list, I will start my search on the WebMD website. I think the WebMD website is a good place to begin a search. My psychiatrist has overall good and fair reviews on WebMD. If a psychiatrist does not have good reviews, I may seek another psychiatrist.

I also encourage people to also find a good talk therapist, although I did not take my own advice. Nicole encouraged me years ago that I needed to talk to a therapist, someone with an objective viewpoint. I should have taken her advice.

I now know I was hiding several secrets. I did not want to confront my sexual abuse, sexual identity, and the traumatic breakup with my 1st love Maria. My hidden pain of the breakup with my 1st love was hidden in a case of amnesia for over 45 years.

2. My second priority was to get help early on. I did try to get help early on several times. Before Stu and I were diagnosed correctly with bipolar, I went to several psychiatrists, and some put me on only anti-depressants. I also attended group psychotherapy in the 70s. I still did not get effective treatment for my BD disorder there either.

I also attempted to self-diagnose my mental illness. That was a mistake; I thought I had many mental illnesses. So, finding a competent psychiatrist and getting effective treatment early on is critical. This is one of the primary goals of the workbook.

In my case, delaying treatment resulted in many personal, professional, and business hardships. Marriage, relationships, job issues, and many other situations only got more stressful as they accumulated or built up over the years.

3. I monitor my mental and physical health by using the WAVES Chart and asking friends or loved ones to monitor my moods. I give my wife the authority and permission to tell me when I need help. I want Nicole to admit me to a hospital if necessary. Although I have not taken my own advice, it might be a good idea to have a written agreement on paper. I will write and sign a letter before I end up with a psychotic or suicidal episode.

4. I am working on improving my physical appearance. For years I have not cared about my physical appearance. At times I had enough of a struggle to get to the next day; I needed to work on my appearance and self-image.

As I approach 80, I am very weak and fragile, but I still need to take better care of myself. The pandemic has made keeping up with my personal health a chore. Sometimes I would skip taking a shower and stay awake until 4 am surfing the internet.

Changes in sleep patterns can be a red flag for me to get help soon. I had an online Tele Med session with my psychiatrist about my sleep patterns, but he did not adjust or add meds. I will take my number one advice and find a new psychiatrist if I become unstable.

I am aware of the risks of COVID-19. For now, during the pandemic, the risk of going to a barbershop, dentist, or my urologist in the middle of the pandemic is far too great.

5. In keeping with my hoarding disorder, I continue to keep a journal. I have kept hundreds of pages of notes from years ago. Sometimes I add notes to my journal; I find it therapeutic. At other times I review my journal and my WAVES Chart to find conditions or events I need to avoid or modify.

I would encourage people with BD to keep some type of journal or just a brief status of their mental and physical health.

I am going to discard 35 years of stuff. I am going to fix our old shed; it continues to lean over to the right. Someone thought if I waited until it leaned over to the left, it could eventually stand upright again without doing anything. Great afterthought; I will delay fixing our leaning shed a few more years and hope it will stand upright again. I am still in denial about my hoarding disorder.

6. I joined a bipolar disorder support (BDS) group years ago. With the pandemic, only online meetings may be allowed in your state. People can now form an online support group from anywhere in the world. I could not have published this workbook without the observations and insights I observed and discovered in the BDS group.

7. I use nature as my spiritual retreat. One of the most beneficial habits I do almost every day for my wellbeing is to use nature as my spiritual retreat. Every day, weather permitting, I walk about two miles. I found walking in a park without traffic or background noise helps me sleep better at night. After the background noise fades into the distance, I just listen to the sounds of nature, the birds, and sometimes the wind through the tall trees.

Nicole sometimes asks me, "Are you going for your walk?" She does notice when I am anxious, and I need to reset my mind by walking out in nature.

Someone at the BDS group had a very old and wise psychiatrist. He wrote on his prescription pad something like, "Go for a 30-minute walk every day". At one point in time, I thought about changing my psychiatrist because he was a very spiritual doctor, but he was not taking on any new patients. Of course, he was on Rosie's "Good doc" list. Unfortunately, he passed away a few years ago; we need more very spiritual psychiatrists like him.

8. I am going to find more spirituality in my life by joining an online meditation group. I believe meditation apps or online videos can help all people reach a higher level of awareness and spirituality. The courses can help people young and old manage their spiritual and physical wellbeing.

I wish I had found meditation as a way to cope with my stress issues decades ago. I relate well to music and now use healing sounds late at night to calm my scattered mind. I am going to continue to practice meditation to help me sleep and deal with my anxiety issues.

I am finding before I go to sleep, I listen to meditation with ancient healing sounds. The sounds help me escape from the modern and chaotic world. I imagine I am living in ancient times, no cars, planes, cell phones, or centralized governments, quite relaxing.

I need to thank a very spiritual woman, Skyler, I met at the park. She told me about the excellent meditation app I use on my cell phone. We need more people with her kind and caring attitude in the world.

I am going to focus on bringing more people into my life. I know some people do love me. I just need to believe I am worthy of being loved, and then I can overcome some negative energy my unworthy syndrome gives off.

I will continue to learn more about the power of the mind, meditation, consciousness, and other physic phenomena.

9. I continue to use all types of music as a way to grow spiritually. As you know by now, I do not believe in organized religion, but I do think most organized religions believe in a higher power. I do believe hymns, prayer, and other rituals can bring people closer to a universal truth of love. I use all kinds of music and nature sounds to help me focus and help reset my mind.

10. I am going to manage my unworthy syndrome. I will begin to heal from a lifetime of not feeling loved. My family accused me of being moody and sensitive most of my childhood into my teens. In my early 20's, I lashed out at my 1st love, and that ended our relationship forever. I am not cured of my BD disorder or my unworthiness issues; I just need to be aware and manage my feelings of negative self-worth.

I understand people with a good self-image and a "Normal" childhood may think my unworthy syndrome is just a little strange, but that is ok. I have been fighting feelings of unworthiness since a young kid. Now I understand these negative feelings were formed when I was a very young child; I did not have a choice; no one said they loved me or protected me from emotional or sexual abuse. Now I can look back and see all that is in the past.

To overcome some of the feelings of unworthiness I had as a child, I needed to understand back then; I could not fight my deep feelings of unworthiness; however, now I can.

My deep negative feelings of unworthiness were reinforced after the breakup with Maria. I was only about 22 at the time when I went into a state of amnesia. Now I look back and can partly blame my unworthy disorder. I understand now these feelings of not being loved over the years have spread into other areas of my life. The false belief I do not deserve to be successful or have any joy in my life.

In other words, my unworthy disorder has kept me trapped in my past. I don't have a cure for my unworthiness issues; I just know there was nothing I could do when I was a child to overcome my feelings of unworthiness. I could not make my father reappear, or my abusive Aunt Maddie disappear.

I scored 50 points for victims of childhood abuse on my WAVES Chart. Some people might want to score many more points, especially if they were badly physically or sexually abused as a child.

I continue to use the internet and online recourses to find information on mental illness. I found the official DSM [(American Psychiatric Association, 1987) a bit overwhelming to understand. After reading the DSM years ago, I began to think I had all the psychiatric disorders listed in the manual. Self-diagnosis did not work for me. After I was diagnosed correctly, I read many books and articles on BD.

12. I will show more gratitude for the things I have in life. I am grateful I have lived in a nation that has kept me free and safe from the tyranny of war until several years ago. I am grateful to my wife for being such a kind and loving partner. Of course, I need to thank my brother for his help and support for over 75 years. We went through some very difficult times, especially before mid-life.

13. I plan to contact national focus groups that help mentally ill people of all religion's races and sexual preferences. Disabled people

have a right to feel safe in their homes. Long term, I will contact national mental health agencies to lobby Congress to protect all our civil rights. This includes the NAMI and others.

14. I plan to speak out against the mistreatment of people with pro-American and conservative views.

I was a passive onlooker during the Vietnam War. I plan to speak up at protests around our area. I plan to talk to mentally ill people and voice my concerns about the future of our nation.

15. I plan on following new developments in UFOs, ETs, and alien abductions. I guess many people with BD may think my interest in ETs is a bit strange, maybe even insane. I think a full disclosure event is inevitable, and the consequences will be profound for people with mental illness.

Humans will need to accept and communicate with beings from another world. I believe our acceptance and respect for all beings in the universe will help humans and help all mankind. Recognition and respect for all ETs in the universe will be a true test of human's ability to accept different lifestyles.

If humans can show compassion for other species in the universe, we may find ETs can teach us advanced spiritual knowledge.

We may find ETs may even have cures for all physical and mental illnesses. People may even be able to time travel. I want to go back and be 22 years old again before I had a case of amnesia, just kidding.

16. I keep a list of emergency mental health resources on our bulletin board in the kitchen. I have the contact info to reach the Suicide Prevention national hotline. I have the phone number of

our outstanding local psychiatric hospital. I have the phone number of my psychiatrist. I have Rosie's cell number; she has a wealth of information recourses on mental illness. Of course, a 911 emergency call will put anyone in crisis in contact with mental health and other recourses. I did get a Narcan kit an anti-drug overdose (OD) kit.

17 I keep a timeline of my life. I got the idea somewhere to write a timeline of my life from birth to the present. I got out a lined blank page of my journal and wrote down a separate line for every year I have lived on planet Earth, almost 80 years. I folded the pages lengthwise.

It was a few pages long, and I listed the years from my birth in the early '40s to the year 2020, and besides each year, I wrote my age at the time. Next to my age, I wrote major events that occurred in that year, the positive events on the right side of the page and the negative events on the left side of the page.

For example, in 1992, I was 50 and diagnosed and was properly treated for BD. I put that event on the positive or right side of the page. I was surprised to learn Stu, and I spent 2/3 of our lives without proper treatment for BD.

I also noticed I had known Rosie from the BDS group for almost 20 years that was on the positive side. Several other important negative events I noticed, like seeing those B&W WW II pictures at only 12 years old age that was in the negative column.

I listed when I went into amnesia and when I awoke from amnesia. As I looked at my long 80-year history, it became clear both Stu and I need to reach our goals soon. The point I am trying to make is my life is coming to an end, and I need to accomplish my goals before I am too ill to complete them.

Now I listed all my bad events on the left side of the page and pleasant events on the right. I then folded the paper in half and focused on seeing only the good events on the right sides of the pages.

Many years were not filled with good experiences, especially before I met Iva. The bad list, as I call it, demonstrated how many years I struggled with untreated BD with very little joy in my life until around the time I met Iva and took the Awake spiritual growth course in the mid-'70s.

The left or negative side of the pages also showed me how many years of my life were spent having bad spells. During many bad spells, I was incapable of completing most tasks.

The good list continued after I met Iva, attended the Awake course, and then my marriage to Nicole, the birth of Ryan and Matt. Then I had memorable camping and kayaking trips in the Great Outdoors up to today. Of course, the birth of our granddaughter Bonnie was a very positive event in our lives.

After I got treatment, I could list something positive for every year after 1992. Getting sober in 1992 and tent camping trips with the family and Nicole were the most memorable. Also, our family trip to the Southwest was a very positive experience.

I guess bringing up negative events in my life before 1980 is not helping my mental health. I need to continue to complete the workbook but need to limit emphasizing those years in my life. Unfortunately, I cannot erase the first 50 years of my life.

## We may need to start a legal defense fund

Looking forward to the future, I would like to start a legal defense fund for people with mental illnesses. Most of us don't have the money to retain lawyers and paralegals to help us fight for our rights under the Americans for Disabilities Act.

I know I do not have the funds to defend myself in a court of law for alleged crimes or misdemeanors. I propose mentally ill people start a legal defense fund. If 100,000 people with mental health issues or advocates for mental health could spend $100 each, that would be a 10-million-dollar legal defense fund.

The fund would be used to protect our right to feel safe in our own homes. A legal defense fund could also protect mentally ill people from losing their jobs solely based on their mental illness.

Remember Erica's story in Chapter 5? She was fired because her employer discovered she had a BD. I think a few carefully worded letters from a good attorney to the hospital administration could have saved her job. Perhaps she could get a different job within the hospital. I am sure a good attorney could get her unemployment benefits and a job reference from their HR department.

## *I need to find some positive things about my life.*
I don't think I left out any critical situations or events in my life. I should score points for my hoarding disorder, but I am in total denial of that disorder and just hide my stuff in our garage and in the back of my mind.

I am making it a priority to find more positive things about my life. Telling my BD story has taken an emotional toll on my life. Once the workbook is published, I will have a sense of accomplishment. I hope the workbook will help people cope with BD better. Some people might also identify with my unworthy syndrome and find ways to heal from years of feeling unworthy in addition to the shame of BD.

## Can anyone use The Bipolar WAVES Chart?

I want to make it crystal clear the WAVES Chart should not be used as a way to diagnose someone with BD. This workbook should only be used to determine the stress level of someone diagnosed with BD. This workbook is designed to be a "check the box" mental and physical evaluation of someone with BD throughout a year or more.

Once someone is diagnosed with BD, anyone can use the WAVES Chart to determine the stress level. The interviewer may need to ask some very personal questions to get a realistic picture of the person's BD lifestyle. First, you want to determine if someone is stable or unstable. If you cannot determine their BD lifestyle is stable, use the unstable column on the WAVES Chart.

I don't expect all people to fully understand these unique BD conditions if they don't experience and live with BD. I am not critical of those people because I can't expect them to fully understand the abnormal conditions people with BD live with on a day-to-day basis. Remember, "Normal" people will never experience life with a mental illness.

The WAVES workbook attempts to predict a crisis by evaluating many unique life situations and living conditions. Hopefully, the WAVES Workbook will also help ordinary people" see" our invisible mental disability and learn more about BD. Perhaps after scoring points on WAVES Chart, people will then acknowledge the many stressful situations we face throughout our entire life. Maybe, just maybe, some people will help us without being judgmental.

Being nonjudgmental is why BDS groups are so important because we all experience the same illness. We can help each other thru the tragedy and triumphs of life without being judgmental.

The WAVES Workbook Stress Chart is designed to be filled out by anyone by simply going through the four sections of the WAVES Chart and scoring each life situation that may apply to the person with BD.

Anyone with or without BD can add up points on the chart to arrive at your WAVES Stress Zone level. Sometimes the person with BD may be in denial of a particular life situation. For example, someone with BD may deny living with a brother-in-law is causing extreme conflicts and stress, but the reality, the entire family is living very chaotic lives. The person interviewing can then decide to score the event or condition higher, lower, or not at all.

Yes, I do believe the WAVES Workbook can help anyone learn about the BD lifestyle and determine the stress zone level of someone with BD.

## The goal is to "Find your Bipolar Stress Zone."

My hope is people with BD will use the Bipolar WAVES Workbook to identify and better understand the many unique situations we face with a diagnosis of BD. The WAVES Chart may even help people with BD in denial of the illness or unstable people identify and understand the stresses in their daily lives better.

Perhaps people with BD and others will better understand and learn how many unique situations can accumulate or build-up to cause psychotic episodes or, even worse, suicide or the risk of suicide.

So, again the primary goal of the Bipolar WAVES Workbook is for people with BD to "Find your Bipolar Stress Zone."

# Appendices

## Appendix A The Bipolar WAVES Stress Chart

Because the Bipolar WAVES Stress Chart has over 70 life situations, I divided it into five sections as follows.

Section 1 The WAVES Stress Chart—Lifestyles Disorders, Illnesses, and Addictions.

Section 2 The WAVES Stress Chart—Careers, Jobs, and Relationships.

Section 3 The WAVES Stress Chart—Marriage and Family.

Section 4 The WAVES Stress Chart—Personal Situations.

Section 5 The WAVES Stress Chart—The 7 WAVES Stress Zones. Level 7 is the highest zone and represents Extreme (X) Emergency treatment. Extreme levels begin with X.

# The Bipolar WAVES Stress Chart
**Mental-&-Physical Illnesses-Addictions**

*Find your Bipolar Stress Zone*
Taken from The Bipolar WAVES Workbook
Copyright © 2021 by Philip Van Ostrander

| Life Situations/Conditions | STABLE | UNSTABLE | POINTS |
|---|---|---|---|
| **Bipolar Lifestyle** | | | |
| Lifetime Bipolar Stress Level (LBSL) | | | |
| Stable BP Normal Lifestyle  COL A | 65 | | |
| Unstable BP Lifestyle  COL B | | 130 | |
| | | | |
| **Other Mental Disorders** | A | B | C |
| Personality, Stress, Anxiety - Untreated | 45 | 54 | ____ |
| Personality, Stress, Anxiety - Treated | 25 | 30 | ____ |
| **Physical Illnesses** | | 0 | ____ |
| Terminal e.g. late stage cancer /HIV | 65 | 78 | ____ |
| Long-term e.g. Cancer /Chronic pain | 55 | 66 | ____ |
| Short term e.g. broken leg | 30 | 36 | ____ |
| **Addictions** | | | |
| Alcohol and/or Drug No treatment | 60 | 72 | ____ |
| Alcohol and/or Drug Clean and Sober | 25 | 30 | ____ |

Section 1  Mental-&-Physical Illnesses-Addictions

Section 1 WAVES Chart—Lifestyles Disorders, Illnesses, Addictions

# The Bipolar WAVES Stress Chart
## Career and Jobs- Relationships & Dating

*Find your Bipolar Stress Zone*
Taken from The Bipolar WAVES Workbook
Copyright © 2021 by Philip Van Ostrander

| Career and Jobs | A | B | C |
|---|---|---|---|
| Fired because you have Bipolar Disorder | 60 | 72 | |
| Finding employment after stay in | 35 | 42 | |
| Threat of being fired for BP behavior | 40 | 48 | |
| Financial burdens- Can't find work- | 50 | 60 | |
| Filling out job applications | 30 | 36 | |
| Job interviews- gaps in job history | 30 | 36 | |
| Returning to job after stay in hospital | 50 | 60 | |
| Conflict / harassed by co-workers | 50 | 60 | |
| Layoff | 40 | 48 | |
| Starting a new job or career | 45 | 54 | |
| Changes -promotions/demotions | 40 | 48 | |
| **Relationships & Dating** | | | |
| Dating - fear of making mistakes | 30 | 36 | |
| Dating anxiety telling date about BP | 30 | 36 | |
| Dating someone with BP mental illness | 40 | 48 | |
| Breakup after learning about your BP | 50 | 60 | |
| Breakup after long term relationship | 65 | 78 | |
| Psychiatric Hospital stay while dating | 50 | 60 | |
| Death (Suicide) of a close friend | 60 | 72 | |
| Loss friends - shunned, shamed | 50 | 60 | |

Section 2 Career and Jobs- Relationships & Dating

Section 2 WAVES Chart—Careers, Jobs, and Relationships

# The Bipolar WAVES Stress Chart
## Marriage & Family

*Find your Bipolar Stress Zone*
Taken from The Bipolar WAVES Workbook
Copyright © 2021 by Philip Van Ostrander

| Marriage & Family | A | B | C |
|---|---|---|---|
| Death of a spouse (Suicide, OD, accident} | 110 | 132 | ____ |
| Divorce | 85 | 102 | ____ |
| Marriage | 65 | 78 | ____ |
| Separations, affairs, desertion | 70 | 84 | ____ |
| Conflicts with spouse over lifestyle | 50 | 60 | ____ |
| Spouse with BP Unstable | 50 | 60 | ____ |
| Spouse with BP Stable | 35 | 42 | ____ |
| Wife Pregnant | 45 | 54 | ____ |
| Wife Pregnant with BP Unstable | 50 | 60 | ____ |
| Wife Pregnant with BP Stable | 45 | 54 | ____ |
| New baby healthy | 45 | 54 | ____ |
| Death of Baby/Teen/illness/OD | 70 | 84 | ____ |
| Living with family member BP- Stable | 25 | 30 | ____ |
| Living with family member BP Unstable | 55 | 66 | ____ |
| Living with siblings with mental illness | 45 | 54 | ____ |
| Living with siblings no mental illness | 35 | 42 | ____ |
| One or Both Parents with BP Unstable | 55 | 66 | ____ |
| One or Both Parents with BP Stable | 40 | 48 | ____ |
| Loss of family support rejected shunned | 55 | 66 | ____ |
| Family member illness | 50 | 60 | ____ |
| Death of a family member close friend | 70 | 84 | ____ |

Section 3 Marriage & Family

Section 3 WAVES Chart—Marriage and Family

# The Bipolar WAVES Stress Chart
## Personal Situations

*Find your Bipolar Stress Zone*
Taken from The Bipolar WAVES Workbook
Copyright © 2021 by Philip Van Ostrander

| Personal Situations | A | B | C |
|---|---|---|---|
| Homeless  Lost  Home/Room/Apt | 50 | 60 | |
| No Psychiatric care insurance | 40 | 48 | |
| Victim of childhood abuse Unworthy | 50 | 58 | |
| Bankruptcy / Foreclosure | 35 | 42 | |
| Outstanding Achievement -Phd | 50 | 60 | |
| Major legal Issues /court/jail/ lawsuits | 70 | 84 | |
| Death of a pet | 50 | 60 | |
| Large Dept Mortgage /College Loans | 35 | 42 | |
| Involuntary Hospital stay- Psychotic | 55 | 66 | |
| Business Failure | 45 | 54 | |
| Change stable/no meds to toxic meds | 70 | 84 | |
| Change stable meds to stopping meds | 65 | 78 | |
| Changes in activities, sleeping, eating | 30 | 36 | |
| Major changes--moving/retirement | 45 | 54 | |
| Vacations/Holidays/Social events | 25 | 30 | |
| Living - High Crime /violence | 35 | 42 | |
| | | | |
| **Stress Level Score (SLS)=Sum C** | | | |

**Section 4 Personal Situations**

Section 4 WAVES Chart—Personal Situations

*Philip Van Ostrander*

# The Bipolar WAVES Stress Chart
## The 7 WAVES Bipolar Stress Zone Levels

*Find your Bipolar Stress Zone*
Taken from The Bipolar WAVES Workbook
Copyright © 2021 by Philip Van Ostrander

| The 7 WAVES Bipolar Stress Zone Levels | Col C |
|---|---|
| **X-Emergency-Zone Level 7    700 --->999** | |
| Extremely high risk of a psychotic episode | |
| Air lift to a hospital trauma center | |
| **Emergency-Zone Level 6    600 --->699** | |
| Emergency at risk of a Psychotic Episode | |
| Rush to a hospital trauma center | |
| **X-Danger-Zone Level 5    500 --->599** | |
| Possible Psychotic Episode Extreme Danger | |
| Go to a Hospital | |
| **Danger-Zone Level 4    400 --->499** | |
| In Danger of a Psychotic Episode | |
| Go to a Hospital | |
| **X-Caution-Zone Level 3    300 --->399** | |
| Use Extreme Caution -Possible Psychotic | |
| Episode Contact your Psychiatrist | |
| **Caution-Zone Level 2    150 --->299** | |
| Moderate risk of a Psychotic Episode | |
| Contact your Psychiatrist | |
| **Safe-Zone Level 1    65--->149** | |
| Low risk of a psychiatric Episode | |
| Contact your Psychiatrist | |

**Section 5  The 7 WAVES Bipolar Stress Zone Levels**

Section 5 WAVES Chart—The 7 WAVES Stress Zones

## How to determine your Stress Level Score (SLS)

Are you stable or unstable? This is the first thing you need to determine. If you are not sure if you are stable or unstable, then use the unstable Column B on the WAVES Charts.

## Column A Stable (taking effective meds)

If you are stable (taking effective meds or other treatments), use column A to check off your life situations that apply in your life now and transfer your points to column C. Tally up all the stress points in column C on Sections 1,2,3 and 4 to get your stable Stress Level Score (SLS) and then refer to the explanations below to determine what Zone applies to your situation.

## Column B Unstable (not taking effective meds or in treatment)

If you are unstable (not taking effective meds or no meds), use COL B to check off your life situations that apply in your life over a year or more. Transfer your points to column C. Tally up all the stress points in column C on Sections 1,2,3 and 4 to get your unstable Stress Level Score (SLS), and then refer to the explanations below to determine what Zone applies to your lifestyle.

## Explanation of the Stress Level Score (SLS) and the 7 ZONE levels

The workbook has seven-point ranges and seven corresponding zone levels. Each level represents a higher level of stress.

The seven zones start from the Safe Zone Level 1 with very little chance of a psychotic episode to the X-Emergency zone Level 7, requiring immediate emergency treatment in a psychiatric trauma center.

> **Note: If you are unstable, you need to seek psychiatric help to become stable ASAP. If you are stable, you do not want to become unstable by stopping psychiatric meds or taking a chance on new toxic or harmful meds unless there is no other option.**

### 700-Plus Point Range X-Emergency Zone Level 7

Level 7-*If* you have enough stress to be in X-Emergency Zone, you are facing a life-threatening psychiatric situation. You may need to be Involuntary hospitalized (call 911) until treated effectively. This level of psychosis will require emergency trauma treatment.

If comatose, it may require you to be airlifted to a trauma unit of a hospital. At this level of psychosis, some people may lose all sense of reality and exhibit hallucinations and delusions.

> **Note: This level of psychiatric stress is analogous to someone on life support being airlifted to a trauma center by helicopter.**

### 600 699 Point Range Emergency Zone Level 6

If you are in Emergency Zone Level 6, you have an extremely high risk or are presently having a life-threatening psychiatric situation. You are in the Emergency Zone and may need to be Involuntary hospitalized (call 911) until treated effectively.

This level of psychosis may occur during a full-blown panic attack or a very severe depression.

At this level of stress, you should be Involuntarily hospitalized in an emergency.

> **Note: This level of psychiatric and/or physical stress is analogous to bringing someone suffering a heart attack to a hospital emergency room by ambulance.**

500-599 Point Range X-Danger Zone Level 5
If you are in the X-Danger Zone Level 5, you are in extreme danger of having a psychotic episode. (e.g., extreme danger of a severe manic or severe depressive episode)
You should call 911 or seek immediate treatment in an emergency room of a hospital or psychiatric hospital.

You also may be in extreme danger of physical injury shortly if not treated effectively—for example, auto accident, suicide, suicide by auto. You are at risk of injuring yourself or other people.

> **Note: If you are unstable, (no meds or harmful ineffective meds) you need to find a competent psychiatrist because you are in extreme danger of having a psychotic episode.**

400-499 Point Range Danger Zone Level 4
If you are in the Danger Zone Level 4, you are in danger of having a psychiatric condition; you may even have suicidal thoughts or actions. (e.g., the danger of a serious manic or depressive episode)
You should seek treatment in an emergency room or contact your psychiatrist's office or hospital very soon.

You also may have a very high risk of physical illness or injury shortly. (E.g., auto accident, bizarre, violent behavior on the job)

300-399 Point Range X-Caution Zone Level 3
If you are in the Extreme-Caution Zone Level 3, you should use extra caution and contact your psychiatrist before your Stress level goes any higher.
You need to use extra caution because you do not want to add more stress points to your score.

You have a high chance of having a serious psychiatric episode (e.g., manic or depressive episode).

You may have a high risk of physical illness or injury shortly.

150-299 Point Range Caution Zone Level 2
At Level 2, You have a moderate chance of having a serious psychiatric episode if you stay under good psychiatric care.
You need to use caution because you do not want to add more stress points to your score.

65-149 Point Range Safe Zone Level 1
At Level,1-You have only a low to moderate chance of having a serious psychiatric episode.

If you are stable and stay under good psychiatric care, you will be in the Safe Zone. You may have only just a few stressful life situations to cause mental and physical stress.

> **Note: If you are unstable, your Lifetime (LBLS) score is already at 130 points so just a minor stressor will place you in the Caution Zone. In addition, even if you are stable and have no stressful life situations you still have that that 65 points of stress. For all practical purposes very few people with Bipolar are in the Safe Zone**

*ATTENTION A DISCLAIMER*
I want to emphasize the WAVES Chart is NOT based on any scientific study and should only be used as a guide for people diagnosed with BD or who have an undiagnosed case of BD. I have based these stress points for each life situation on observations I have made after attending and participating in a very active bipolar disorder support BDS group for over 15 years. I have also based these points on my experience of living with BD for over 75 years.

> **Note: I am not a psychiatrist or a heath care professional. I have not sought help from any heath care professional to design and develop these charts.**

## Explanation of the WAVES Chart categories
I have based the Stress points on WAVES Chart on the Holmes and Rahe Stress Scores in Appendix B but have split the life situations into eight categories as defined below.

Several categories are unique to someone with BD. The first category is unique to the WAVES Stress Charts and is the lifetime of the stress from living with BD.

I based the stress points on having a lifetime physical illness like Cerebral Palsy. I developed one chart to cover both BD lifestyles.

The first Column (COL A) is for people that are stable on meds and have a good support system.

This is analogous to a Cerebral Palsy patient getting the best care for their illness.

The next column (COL B) is for people that are not stable on meds or not taking any meds.

Column C (COL C) is for the reader to score points on life situations that may apply to their lifestyle.

The WAVES Stress Chart has eight categories, as described below.

## The Bipolar lifestyle

Finding your bipolar lifestyle is important for someone with BD. I classify people with bipolar in one of two groups or lifestyles, stable or unstable. Of course, bipolar is a complex illness, but the WAVE Charts attempts to identify and calculate stresses on people with both types of BD.

## Lifetime Bipolar Stress Level (LBSL) for stable people with Bipolar

I have called this stress category the Lifetime Bipolar Stress Level (LBSL) or Lifetime LBSL for short. If people are stable with a BD. I assigned a stress point value above the Holmes & Rahe score of 53 points for a physical illness because BD is a lifelong incurable mental illness like Cerebral Palsy.

Also, I have increased the stress levels for every life situation to account for living with mental illness, especially BD. I assigned a Lifetime Bipolar Stress Level (LBSL) of 65 for someone getting good psychiatric care and having a good support system.

I call this lifestyle stable bipolar normal. Stable represents someone responsible enough to take psychiatric medications over the long term.

After my brother and I became stable on effective meds, we concluded our BD illness was the most significant factor in our lives.

Yes, we had other issues to deal with, like alcoholism, but treating our alcoholism did not significantly improve our quality of life until we got treatment for our bipolar disorders.

But to make our life's a little more complicated, I noticed being treated effectively on meds and having a good support system may not make our lives less stressful if we have other life situations that may cause abnormally high levels of stress.

For example, other factors like mental disorders, addictions, physical health, bad relationships, marriage, and other living conditions all contributed to a BD lifestyle.

I also added living with someone with a mental illness could be extremely stressful, especially if they are not under good psychiatric care.

Many common living conditions of many people with BD can cause stress, but the many unique complex combinations of stressors can trigger a BD episode.

## Lifetime Bipolar Stress Level {LBSL) for unstable people with Bipolar

I know it may be more difficult to refer to two BD lifestyles, but I think there is a major difference in lifestyles for someone under effective treatment and someone with no mental health care at all or is in denial of their mental health status. This person may refuse psychiatric treatment of any kind.

Why do we need a different stress chart for unstable people living with BD? Perhaps some background of our lives may explain the differences between these two stress charts.

Both my brother and I have lived with BD for over 75 years now. From a young age until about 50 years old, we lived what I call an unstable

BD lifestyle. Without proper treatment, we struggled through life with very severe depressions, followed by periods of mania. Our lives became chaotic, unmanageable, and at times, led to thoughts of suicide. Our relationships, family life, and careers suffered from irresponsible behavior and bouts of alcoholism and spending sprees.

Of course, there may be variations from person to person on what chart to use, but if someone is getting poor psychiatric care and is not stable, use COL B of the Bipolar WAVES Stress Chart.

Therefore, I think the first category (Bipolar Lifestyle) is the most important factor in determining the total Stress Level Score. Getting the BD person stable needs to be addressed first for someone with a diagnosis of BD to live what I call a Stable BD normal lifestyle.

Sadly, I claim most people with BD will never lead a "Normal" life, and that is why I call someone on effective meds to lead a BD normal lifestyle.

## Physical Illnesses

Of course, physical illness can cause extreme stress. Three subcategories are short-term, long-term, and terminal Illness.

## Mental Disorders

As described above, the most significant stressor for people with BD is the diagnosis of having a devastating lifelong incurable mental illness. BD could be compared to a lifelong physical illness like Cerebral Palsy, but many times, the diagnosis of mental illness is more complex.

After years of attending a BDS group, I saw many people attending our sessions had other serious mental health issues. That is the case for me; I have a personality disorder and several other mental disorders that add additional stress to my life. These mental disorders also needed to be identified and points added to determine my total stress chart score.

The mental illness category could include gambling, hoarding, learning, psychotic disorders, and other mood disorders.

I want to use the Cautionary Statement from the DSM IV-TR (Text Revision) [(American Psychiatric Association, 1987) manual.

The proper use of these criteria requires specialized clinical training that provides both a body of knowledge and clinical skills.

> *Note: I do not claim to have either clinical training or skills; I only have the experience of living with a Bipolar Disorder for over 70 years*

## Addictions

In addition to mental disorders, many people in the BDS group had to deal with addictions to drugs and alcohol.

This was also the case; my brother and I were both alcoholics by our late teens. We both struggled with alcoholism until we got effective treatment for our BD. Stu was sober before treatment for BD, but his quality of life did not improve until he was treated for BD. Drugs and alcohol can also interfere with psychiatric medicines and may cause someone stable on psychiatric meds to become unstable.

I remember talking to a guy named Randy at the BD group who told me he was being treated only for his addiction to alcohol, but his psychiatrist noticed his quality of life was not improving by just getting sober. His psychiatrist suspected he also was bipolar and needed to be treated for his BD illness; after just a few weeks on lithium, his quality of life improved greatly. His family began to accept and support his diagnosis of BD. He was attending the BDS group for additional support.

This is what I have observed many times unless you treat the underlying problem of BD, your quality of life may not improve even though you get treatment for addictions or other mental disorders.

I think a combination of having unstable BD and long-term addiction to drugs and/or alcohol can have devastating consequences for anyone with BD, especially if unstable.

To simplify the WAVE Stress Chart, I have not factored in long-term addictions to both alcohol and drugs into the total SLS score.

## Careers and Jobs

I have listed this category next because many people with BD struggle with finding and keeping jobs early in life. Even when people have good relationships with co-workers, most people with BD need to find work and have job-related issues that can last into old age.

There are countless stories of how stressful starting a career can be for someone with a mental illness. Getting and keeping jobs can be a concern for their entire working life. We had one woman come to the BDS group that had over 20 different jobs, and she was only 43 years old.

I have identified several life situations that apply to someone with BD, but there are probably many more.

Again, both my brother and I had very stressful careers before we became stable, and several jobs related issues caused enormous stress in our lives.

I remember my brother telling me he would sneak into his pharmacy through the back door to keep his mental illness a secret from his employer. I guess it is a bit different now, but the stigma of having BD is still a factor in getting and keeping a job.

## Fired because you have a bipolar disorder
Some employers take advantage of people with mental illnesses.

We had a woman named Erica attend our BDS group one night. She was very distraught over losing her job after she left a list of her medications on her desk, and someone gave it to her boss. She was harassed and followed closely for several months until she got fired. Erica's story is in Chapter 5.

The unique situations that people with BD endure, I am afraid, are more common now than in years past because a few people do commit violent acts.

It is estimated several million people live with BD, but only a very small percentage commit an act of violence. Acts of violence are tragic but could be prevented if the person with BD has proper treatment.

Years ago, I had a job where I was harassed for five years before I decided to quit before I got fired. Stress on the job is very common for people with BD.

## People with BD finding employment after a stay in a hospital
Finding a job with a serious illness is difficult for someone with a physical disability, but hiding your mental disability is necessary,

especially with a diagnosis of BD. The American with Disabilities Act (ADA) law is clear an employer cannot discriminate against someone with a mental disability.

Can you be honest on a job application and still get the job? I do not believe you can list a mental illness on a job application and get the job. We have a few people who get jobs after telling their employer of their mental condition. Very few employers want to hire someone with BD. Most employers treat people with mental illness as a liability.

We had one woman get the job because her future boss had BD, but this is rare.

Say you finally get the dream job you have wanted all your life. Therefore, you start a job by lying on the job application; most employers consider lying on a job application grounds for dismissal. Now you need to hide your diagnosis from everyone in the company, and this creates even more stress in your life.

These job-related situations are common to many people with BD have what I call the accumulative BD stress factors for most people with BD. Unique job situations all compound to cause extreme levels of stress. Writing resumes, going to job interviews, harassment, and threats of dismissal.

## The threat of being fired for bipolar behavior
The threat of being fired is a common experience for someone with BD.

We had a woman who had a mild episode of mania, and the management sent her several threatening memos. Management told her she would be terminated after another incident. This work environment is extremely stressful for someone struggling with any form of mental illness.

I could list several people with BD who also had similar experiences on the job. Of course, this is just one category of eight that may cause stress for someone with a mental illness.

## Job interviews with gaps in employment history

Gaps in employment history are a red flag for most employers that are evaluating you for a responsible position. Many people lie and tell the employer they took time off to start a business or help take care of a family member, but this explanation many times is counterproductive. The employer may believe the applicant could leave the company and not want to train the person for any position.

Many applicants have several job interviews with various levels of management before a job offer creating yet another source of stress.

## Can't find work - No job prospects

This situation can be devastating for someone with BD or any illness. Job success is generally a measure of self-worth and a way to gain self-confidence. When you cannot find work, it spreads to all categories of your life, including relationships, marriage issues, dating, and many other personal situations. Working provides a way to become independent and feel more confident to tackle other challenges in life.

Therefore, not finding work can have lasting stress in many people's lives with BD. The thought of writing resumes and the challenges of getting and keeping a job can be overwhelming for many people without a mental illness.

Many people come to the BD group after losing a job, are humiliated, and are very depressed. Most people are severely depressed when they cannot find work. Many times, new members are relieved; other people in the BD group also are discouraged when they cannot find work. Finding a job is a major stressor in their lives.

Extreme difficulty in finding a job is a fact of our BD lifestyles for us that most "Normal" people will never experience.

## Returning to work after a stay in a hospital
Returning to work after a stay in a hospital can be demoralizing and lead to being harassed or shunned by co-workers. The shame is amplified after a demotion or layoff.

## Layoffs and starting a new career
After quitting or getting a layoff notice some people, dread the accumulative BD stress factors.

These tasks include looking for work when depressed, filling out job applications, and other job-related issues, all occurring at about the same time.

## The accumulative BD stress factors of finding and keeping jobs
I believe the many tasks involved in keeping a job can be overwhelming for someone struggling with BD. Usually, these tasks may need to be repeated many times in the life of someone with BD, and these job-related tasks don't become easier with age. Some people endure years of being humiliated, harassed, and rejected by both employers and co-workers.

As I have stated before, many employers treat people with mental illness as a liability and not as a valuable asset or resource.

## Relationships and Dating
I have listed this category before Marriage & Family because most people with BD also struggle with relationships and dating issues before getting married and starting a family.

Many people struggling with BD do have difficulties forming friendships, especially if they have multiple mental disorders. This category can be difficult for someone diagnosed and stable on meds but can be overwhelming if not stable or not aware you have a mental illness.

If a person is not stable on good medications, dating can have tragic consequences. Being unstable can also result in fear of making mistakes or acting inappropriate while on a date.

The stigma of having a mental illness is a fact, and bias in the media is a sad truth for most people with mental illness, especially a BD mental illness.

## TV Show advises, "Don't marry someone with a mental illness."

Years ago, I was watching a daytime talk show about how to have a happy marriage. I remember the "first rule" to happy marriages was "Don't marry someone with a mental illness." When I saw that message in big letters across the TV screen, I felt very sad because I knew it was true in many cases.

The hosts and others on the panel made fun of this "First rule," but it was not humorous for me to hear and see in big, bold letters.

I know my wife has been unhappy in our marriage at times, many spouses would be long gone like the statistics show, but it is also sad from the perspective of the mentally ill. It means a person with bipolar will only have a 10 percent chance of having a happy and lasting marriage.

I do not bring up the dismal marriage statistics to the bipolar group. Again, I contend if a person with bipolar illness is not diagnosed and treated effectively, the chance of a long-term marriage or even a long-term relationship, for that matter, is even less than 10%.

Now, after you have watched that TV show, what would you do? Really, the words "Don't marry someone with a mental illness" were in big, bold letters across the TV screen. I do not think they would dare display the words "Don't marry someone with Cerebral Palsy," would they? Maybe I do resent having a mental illness, but I do not think I would trade my lifetime BD normal lifestyle for a lifetime with Cerebral Palsy.

## Dating anxiety telling dates about your Bipolar illness

So as far as relationships go, when do you reveal you have a serious mental illness, especially a diagnosis of bipolar? You probably should not bring up your mental state on the first date if you want a second date.

I was usually worried about inappropriate statements or exposing my temperamental disposition when on a date. I was afraid I would get angry, overreact over some unrelated minor incident, and expose all my personality defects; I meant disorders.

Often, I overreacted and blamed other people for my erratic insane behavior before I became stable. From what I know now, I took on too many tasks all at the same time. Preventing overload is what the WAVES Chart is trying to show, your overall stress level over the past year or more.

What if you have never had a diagnosis of BD or other mental disorders? I think many "Normal" people recognize if someone acts strangely and may have mental issues.

Other times our mental illness is hidden from plain view; people cannot understand why we cannot handle common everyday tasks. People think we are "Normal" until we show signs of erratic manic behavior or an abnormal cycle of depression.

Some people visualize someone screaming on the rooftop of some building wielding a machete about some demon coming to get them. Yes, some with BD do act strangely and out of their minds, but they cannot make rational decisions. If people get proper treatment, psychotic episodes can almost be eliminated. In my case, I have not had a psychotic episode since I was properly treated at 50 years old. I did have bizarre behavior when I missed doses of the mood stabilizer years ago by mistake.

Therefore, I would recommend when you tell your date you have a mental illness, but you are stable and on good medications. Explaining to your date the difference between stable and unstable may make this task less stressful. I do think dating and relationships are far better if people are stable.

### Loss of friends due to bipolar behavior

Losing friends due to BD behavior is a common situation for many people with BD, a display of bizarre behavior by someone with BD can end friendships. For example, before I was stable, I would commit to a future date when manic and then cancel our date when I entered a low cycle. This pattern of behavior ended several relationships.

We had a 30-year-old guy named Karl who came to the BDS group and told us he lost all his friends due to a humiliating psychotic episode. He was devastated because friends were his only support system for many years. He was very unstable because he never was diagnosed with BD.

He would not tell us what led to losing all his friends, although we were mildly interested in listening to a good BD story. Usually, people are glad to tell their stories because we usually accept their behavior as just another BD story.

We do not judge other people's actions or inactions because we may be telling our tragic BD story to the group at the next meeting. This was not surprising for the group to hear because we have heard many stories of irresponsible behavior that led to losing friends and family over the years.

His BD episode landed him in a psychiatric hospital for a few weeks. He told us while at the psychiatric hospital, he was diagnosed with BD and put on one dose of Depakote, a mood stabilizer that changed his life. He told us he was going back telling his friends what had happened. Then he hoped his former friends would take him back. He said if they did not accept him back, he was going to find new friends that would accept he had a mental illness.

That was the most inspirational BD story I heard in years; just one dose of the mood stabilizer Depakote completely changed his life. He went from a lifetime of being unstable to stable in just a few weeks after treatment.

I was still mildly, well, very interested in what Karl did to lose all his so-called friends. We encourage people in the BDS group to tell us these BD stories so we can learn from them but not be judgmental.

## Breakup after a long-term relationship or learning you have BD

The heartbreak of a breakup can lead to grief and sorrow for many people with BD illness. Feeling of hopelessness and despair can lead to suicidal thoughts or actions. Loss of self-confidence can lead to hopelessness and a feeling of worthlessness, especially if not stable on meds and have a good support system.

So, you have told your girl or guy you have a serious mental illness, and you are madly in love and want to have a long-term relationship. You are in a state of euphoria over the prospect of living a happy life. Happiness and the chance of living a "Normal" and productive life are at your doorsteps, but you go into a manic episode and spend thousands of dollars on your sweetheart's credit card.

You're admitted to a hospital and diagnosed as having a BD mental illness. Your long-term relationship ends. This tragic event and other similar situations can cause unbearable grief and sadness that can last a lifetime.

## Breakup after learning about your bipolar disorder

I was 22 years old, and a series of events led to a traumatic breakup with my first love.

For me, this was the most devastating experience of my young life. I felt I was almost married to my first love, and then I went into a psychotic episode and treated her badly. We broke up after a series of tragic circumstances after she witnessed firsthand my bizarre and abusive behavior. At the time, I was not diagnosed with BD; I was very unstable due to many life situations all occurring at the same time. I am sure she saw I was mentally ill and ended our relationship with a Dear John letter. She never talked to me again.

After the very traumatic breakup with my first love, I entered a state of shock and was very unstable. I was distraught over the breakup; I went into what I call a state of amnesia over the devastating loss of my 1st love. Now, doesn't that alone speak to the abnormal stresses on a person after a breakup?

I think it is even more painful and stressful after a breakup because you may feel you have done nothing wrong. You do not even know you have a mental illness. Isn't this a sad and tragic situation? You feel the people you love are punishing you.

This is the difference between mental and physical disability. I think people accept someone easier now with a mental disability, but it is a burden we all share in common. That is why the BDS group has been so important to me, and I am sure other people in the group. We try to accept each other with all our faults and BD issues.

I am still interested in what Karl did to lose all his so-called friends.

## Marriage and Family

I believe if someone is not stable, marriage and family issues can be the most stressful and destructive of all other issues. This category has many stressors for someone with mental illness, especially if not getting effective treatment.

This category has over 20 life situations that can cause enormous stress in someone's life with BD. The statistics bear this out; over 90 percent of marriages fail if one spouse has BD.

### Death of a spouse

Of course, the death of a spouse is the most stressful event that can happen in a marriage where one or both partners have BD. The loss of a spouse is catastrophic, but many times, it also means the loss of a friend and caregiver. The loss of a spouse may be the only support the spouse has if the other family members do not support the spouse with the BD Illness.

## Marriage, divorce, separation, and other issues

Marriage, divorce, and separation can cause enormous stress for anyone with BD. The expectations for a newly married couple to lead a "Normal" life are challenging for anyone with a mental illness, especially BD illness.

That was the case in our marriage. Before we married, I could sleep in; avoid communication and the responsibilities of being a long-term partner in marriage.

The complications in my life dramatically increased after we had children, but other ordinary marriage issues added even more stress. We purchased a home, had fertility issues, and started a family. Then I decided to work on three businesses at the same time. I was very unstable without proper medications.

Many common issues come up with your spouse, pregnancy issues, caring for a new baby, and further stress if both parents have BD. I have tried to list most of the issues dealing with spouses, but I am sure there are a lot more.

## Separations, Affairs, Desertion, abandonment

When you have extramarital affairs caused by your irresponsible BD behavior, it can produce enormous stress, especially if you are not stable.

If you have children and your spouse is mentally ill and has no contact with you, your life can become unbearable for you and your children.

Desertion, I feel, is different from separation or extramarital affairs, where both parents communicate with each other at some level. They may have joint custody of their children. Desertion also may have lasting harmful effects on the children.

A mentally well spouse may abandon or desert their spouse with BD when the spouse with BD exhibits extreme behavior. This may happen when the mentally well spouse cannot support the ill spouse any longer due to extreme exhaustion. Sometimes separation is a matter of survival for the mentally well spouse.

## Living with family members with BD

This category attempts to identify many common living conditions for someone married and has family members on both sides also struggling with mental illness. From my experience in the BDS group, many families have one family member that is mentally unstable. By unstable, I mean a close family member with an addiction, mental disorder, or BD. This may be the family member was never diagnosed or treated but shows obvious signs of having a mental illness.

By identifying and adding up all these stressors, it is not hard to understand many of these stressors lead to divorce or separation. As they say, you not only marry your spouse but also must blend two dysfunctional families.

If family members on either side of the family have mental health issues, it can compound the stress in the lives of everyone in the family. I listed several conditions that could happen, for example, living with siblings, family members, or parents. Of course, the stressor depends on the stability of these family members. All these living conditions can be very complex.

These are the accumulative BD stress factors I have mentioned several times in this workbook. Dealing with mental illness in the family can be extremely stressful when several family members also have BD or other emotional issues.

The WAVES Workbook attempts to illustrate people with BD have many unique and difficult issues to deal with throughout a lifetime.

BD is a very complex mental illness and can influence many stages of life, including; dealing with your own mental issue, careers, relationships, marriage, and other situations in life.

## Living with people with other illnesses
I think many of the situations listed are self-explanatory—for example, people living with you with physical disabilities, elderly people, young children, and in-laws.

I have simplified the chart by listing life situations caused by BD, but many other conditions would also affect a person's lifestyle, such as living with someone with addictions, physical disabilities, dementia, or other mental illnesses like schizophrenia.

## People not living with you
In-laws, siblings, and other family members not living with you can also be a source of constant strife and tension, especially if they have addictions and/or mental illness.

Time and energy dealing with people who require constant care can be overwhelming.

## Loss of family support rejected shunned
Loss of family support can be the most devastating situation in the life of someone with mental illness. If everyone, including your spouse, rejects you, it can be a life-threatening event, especially if unstable.

## Death (Suicide} illness of family member, caregiver, or friend
The death or illness of a baby, child, teen, and others can produce long-term grief and a source of hopelessness for many people struggling with mental illness. Of course, when young people die for any reason, the overwhelming grief can lead to enormous stress on someone with BD.

We have had several people die in our BD group by suicide. We accept people do commit suicide when in a severe prolonged depression, especially if unstable.

We had a 35-year-old guy named Stan come to our group one night; he was severely depressed and on government assistance. He was so depressed; he could hardly fill out the paperwork to apply for mental health care assistance. He got an appointment, but it was not for several weeks. The following week he committed suicide.

Members of our group were devastated by the tragic news; this makes me want to vent my frustration again with the disparity between physical health care and the mental health care system.

Stan had an emergency crisis, much like a heart attack, and should have been taken to the nearest mental hospital for observation and treatment regardless of his ability to pay. The people in the group thought Stan was going to get help soon, but perhaps we needed to take him directly from the BDS meeting to the psychiatric hospital.

An illness in the family can also cause a great deal of stress, especially if he or she is a caregiver.

Therefore, marriage and family issues are complex and the source of constant stress because most people cannot ignore family issues entirely.

Again, the marriage stats bear this out when 90 percent of marriages fail.

## Personal situations

Over 15 personal situations could apply to people with BD mental illness. Now many personal situations can happen to "Normal" people, but I claim people with BD have far greater stress for the same situations caused by the accumulative BD stress factors that compound stressful events.

### Homeless Lost Home/Room/Apt
Many people with BD lose their jobs and become homeless, especially if they have lost the support of their family and friends.

My brother, a successful salesman for a solid corporation, found himself homeless after the stock market crash in 1987. He lost his job, real estate, and family support, including his family home.

Of course, many "Normal" people can be on the brink of bankruptcy and become homeless.

I claim the stress and feeling of rejection can cause abnormal levels of stress for people with a mental illness.

### Mental healthcare care
A series of unfortunate events may occur after getting ill or losing an income. People can lose health care insurance and end up on government assistance or welfare. This leads to not having proper mental health care treatment and becoming unstable.

This happened to Keith, the guy that committed suicide when he had to wait several weeks to see a psychiatrist.

Lack of proper mental health care should not be a factor for Americans living in a free society. People with a physical disability often get treatment after they become severely disabled. People with mental issues often are not diagnosed, even if they are severely mentally ill. My brother and I are examples of this disparity in mental health care. We struggled for decades without effective mental health care.

My brother got free psychiatric care at a county health clinic in Florida, but the county had some very wealthy residents. The county could afford to support a mental health clinic.

## Victim of childhood abuse—my Unworthy Syndrome

After I became active in Rosie's BDS group, I discovered many people, including me, were struggling with yet another condition in addition to BD. After I came to terms with my childhood emotional and sexual abuse, I needed to find a name for it. I named my condition my unworthy syndrome. I scored the condition 50 points on My WAVES Chart. However, many victims of childhood abuse may score being a victim of childhood abuse on their WAVES Chart much higher than 50 points.

## Bankruptcy /Legal Issues / large debt/business failures

Bankruptcy is often a way out of debt after overspending and not being able to pay mortgages and bank loans.

Many people with mental illness eventually need to deal with legal issues. Being arrested for DUI, lawsuits, and time in jail are not uncommon for someone with BD, especially if they are unstable and not on effective medications.

We had one member of our BD group go to California and charge $8000 on his fiancé's credit card. That quickly ended the engagement.

Before I was married, I was unstable and failed to pay utility bills until I got a utility shutoff notice. Without Nicole's financial support, I would have no heat, electricity, or water. Business failures can produce stressful life situations and lead to bankruptcy or loss of family income.

### Outstanding achievement

Attending and graduating from college was an outstanding achievement for me, and it took four long years to complete. I continued to have stress over college, dating, and addiction to alcohol all through college. At times, my stress level was extremely high before taking final exams, and I believe I developed a stress disorder. At the end of my third year at college, I had a breakup with my college sweetheart. I was on the verge of a nervous breakdown many times and did not think I could graduate.

Now for many "Normal" people graduating from college would not be viewed as an outstanding achievement, but for me, at the time, it was a major accomplishment.

People may site and score their outstanding personal achievements that caused a great deal of stress in their lives.

### Death of a pet

The death of a pet can be a major stressor for people with BD.

My brother lost his dog in a tragic accident after 15 years of faithful service. The sadness and grief of losing his faithful friend and companion were overwhelming. He said his dog was by his side throughout many dark days and nights. No doubt, his dog was by his side after his divorce and loss of support from his family. At one point, he told me his friendship with his faithful friend was his only family support.

### Involuntary/voluntary stay in a Psychiatric Hospital

Any stay in any hospital is, of course, extremely stressful for anyone but can be a terrifying experience if Involuntary or voluntary admitted to a psychiatric hospital due to a psychotic episode,

Changing psychiatrists and medications can be disastrous if put on toxic meds that may harm a patient. These conditions can lead to prolonged stays in a psychiatric hospital.

## Minor Lifestyle changes

Minor stressors like changes in everyday living, for example, eating, sleeping and exercise, and other activities are also stressful. Someone entering a gay or lesbian lifestyle can also be stressful for many people. Many times, these changes can lead to mania or severe depression.

Vacations, holidays, and social events can become very challenging for many families but problematic for people with BD, addictions, personality, or other mental health issues.

## Major Lifestyle changes moving /college/retirement

Of course, changes in living arrangements are very stressful for someone with BD. Having relatives or siblings move in with your family can be very stressful, especially if they also have mental issues.

Moving out of state may cause changes in jobs, psychiatrists, and new schools for kids. I found a move very difficult after we moved to another state. I needed to find a family doctor, dentists, and even barbers. Our kids found it difficult to start in new schools and make new friends. Even getting a new state driver's license was a hassle. Many of these changes are difficult for "Normal" people but can be extremely difficult for those with BD. Again, these accumulative BD stress factors can all add up to produce a crisis.

My brother Stu led a very upscale lifestyle with friends and wealthy business clients. After he moved to Florida, the high-class lifestyle ended. Of course, he lost many of his high-flying friends at the yacht club along the way.

## Changes from stable or no meds to harmful/toxic meds

As we saw in the last section, staying on stable meds is critically important to lead a BD normal life. I believe a good psychiatrist should not take you off proven stable, proven meds for no reason.

Sometimes and for no good reason, a psychiatrist may change meds or try a new medication for no reason. If the med is harmful to the individual, it can have very harmful effects and cause extreme instability. I call this mistreatment, and unfortunately, it does happen.

Sometimes we have a research doctor from universities come to our group. They want to find people to test new medications on a trial basis. Some give out free meds and pay people to test the new medications. I understand some are blind tests where some people are given a placebo that has no therapeutic value.

I recommend to people not to go off stable meds to try unproven experimental meds. Sometimes it may be beneficial to someone that cannot get stable on any proven meds, but I argue they are at risk of getting mistreatment. I contend taking toxic meds is one of the most stressful and harmful to anyone with a BD illness.

This is just my opinion; I am not a psychiatrist. Taking unproven meds may be the only option for people that have run out of other options. It is a risk people do take, and perhaps a new drug could be the next miracle drug to cure bipolar.

## Changes from stable meds to stopping meds (unstable)

Sometimes someone on good stable meds with very few side effects just stops taking them for various reasons. Some people do not get along with their psychiatrist and just do not listen to their doctor's medication recommendations. Other people are fortunate to find a good psychiatrist that treats their illness with very effective meds. They quickly become stable and then decide to stop taking their good meds. Many believe they do not need any psychiatric meds any longer because they feel "Normal." Of course, this causes their BD normal lifestyle to go from stable to unstable.

It must be frustrating for the good psychiatrist now; he needs to re-treat from the same illness all over again for them to become stable again. All stress points are now higher due to being untreated for their illness.

I have seen this happen in our support group, especially when people have doubts about their diagnosis of even having any mental illness. Some people are still in denial of their illness even after good results with meds. It is what it is. Sometimes after several bad BD episodes, they realize it was the good meds that helped them stay stable and have a better quality of life.

After five decades in an unstable condition, both my brother and I do not want to go back to our unstable lifestyle, and we rarely miss a dose of our medications.

## Living in high crime areas

Before I was married, I lived in a good neighborhood in a major city for several years. When I moved into the neighborhood, people of all races lived together and respected each other's way of life.

As the crime rate increased, I became more stressed out after the house next door began to sell drugs. The drug traffic passed by my door all night long, and at times, I feared I would be robbed or even worse.

Honest and law-abiding neighbors began to move out, and then the drug users and dealers took over our block. Living in a high-crime area can produce a hidden level of stress, especially for someone with a mental illness. Threats of violence and living in poverty can be very nerve-racking when the crime is all around you.

I never realized my crime-ridden neighborhood caused so much stress until I moved to a safer neighborhood out in the suburbs.

# Appendix B

## The Holmes and Rahe Life Stress Scale

This table is taken from "The Social Readjustment Rating Scale," Thomas H. Holmes, and Richard H. Rahe,

Journal of Psychosomatic Research, Volume 11, Issue 2, August 1967

Copyright © 1967 Published by Elsevier Science Inc All rights reserved.

Permission to reproduce is granted by the publisher.

| | Holmes and Rahe Life Stress Scale | | |
|---|---|---|---|
| Page 1-2 | Life Event or Situation | Score | Check |
| 1 | Death of spouse | 100 | |
| 2 | Divorce | 73 | |
| 3 | Marital separation | 65 | |
| 4 | Jail term | 63 | |
| 5 | Death of close family member | 63 | |
| 6 | Personal injury or illness | 53 | |
| 7 | Marriage | 50 | |
| 8 | Fired at work | 47 | |
| 9 | Marital reconciliation | 45 | |
| 10 | Retirement | 45 | |
| 11 | Change health of family member | 44 | |
| 12 | Pregnancy | 40 | |
| 13 | Sex difficulties | 39 | |
| 14 | Gain of new family member | 39 | |
| 15 | Business readjustment | 39 | |
| 16 | Change in financial state | 38 | |
| 17 | Death of close friend | 37 | |
| 18 | Change to a different line of work | 36 | |
| 19 | Change- arguments with spouse | 35 | |
| 20 | A large mortgage or loan | 31 | |
| 21 | Foreclosure of mortgage or loan | 30 | |
| 22 | Change in responsibilities at work | 29 | |

**The Holmes and Rahe Life Stress Scale Page 1 of 2**

|  | Holmes and Rahe Life Stress Scale | Score | Check |
|---|---|---|---|
| Page 2-2 | | | |
| 23 | Son or daughter leaving home | 29 | |
| 24 | Trouble with in-laws | 29 | |
| 25 | Outstanding personal achievement | 28 | |
| 26 | Spouse begins or stops work | 26 | |
| 27 | Begin or end school/college | 26 | |
| 28 | Change in living conditions | 25 | |
| 29 | Revision of personal habits | 24 | |
| 30 | Trouble with boss | 23 | |
| 31 | Change in work hours or conditions | 20 | |
| 32 | Change in residence | 20 | |
| 33 | Change in school/college | 20 | |
| 34 | Change in recreation | 19 | |
| 35 | Change in church activities | 19 | |
| 36 | Change in social activities | 18 | |
| 37 | A moderate loan or mortgage | 17 | |
| 38 | Change in sleeping habits | 16 | |
| 39 | Change family get-togethers | 15 | |
| 40 | Change in eating habits | 15 | |
| 41 | Vacation | 13 | |
| 42 | Christmas | 12 | |
| 43 | Minor law violations | 11 | |

**The Holmes and Rahe Life Stress Scale Page 2 of 2**

## How to calculate your "Normal" stress score

Using the Holmes and Rahe Life Stress Scale on pages 1 and 2, total up the points and refer to the list below.

300+ Point Range. You have a high or very high risk of becoming ill in the near future.

150-299 Point Range. You have a moderate to high chance of becoming ill in the near future.

<150Point Range. You have only a low to moderate chance of becoming ill in the near future.

## Henrys "Normal" lifestyle

In this example, we are going to score Henrys' "Normal" stress using the Holmes and Rahe Life Stress Scale Chart in Appendix B.

In this example, Henry has no mental illness.

Henry's unstable BD life and stress chart is listed in Chapter 7.

Then we can compare Henry's "Normal" life situations to his unstable BD lifestyle situations back in Chapter 7.

If Henry has no mental illness and no mental illness in his family, we use the Holmes and Rahe Life Stress Scale Chart in Appendix B.

Let's assume Henry has similar life situations outlined in Chapter 7 but now does not have a mental illness or addiction.

Let's say Henry recently was married, bought a house with a large mortgage, and moved to the suburbs. Henry's wife got pregnant and left her job due to complications with her pregnancy. Henry's brother has cancer. Before Henry got married, he had more responsibility at work. Now Henry has longer hours, and he is now in trouble with his boss and coworkers because he cannot complete his work on time. Now he is arguing with his wife over their finances.

According to the Holmes and Rahe Chart [(Holmes & Rahe, 1967). Henry has a high or very high risk of becoming physically ill in the near future. Now all these life situations put his total stress scale to 318.

His total stress score is listed in Table A below.

|  | Holmes and Rahe Life Stress Scale |  |  |
|---|---|---|---|
| Line # | Life Event or Situation | Points | Score |
| 7 | Marriage | 50 | |
| 12 | Pregnancy | 40 | |
| 20 | A large mortgage or loan | 31 | |
| 26 | Spouse begins or stops work | 26 | |
| 31 | Change in work hours or conditions | 20 | |
| 22 | Change in responsibilities at work | 29 | |
| 32 | Change in residence | 20 | |
| 30 | Trouble with boss | 23 | |
| 11 | Change in health of family member | 44 | |
| 19 | Change- arguments with spouse | 35 | |
| Total | Holmes and Rahe Stress Score | 318 | |

Table A Henry's Score with no history of mental illness

In Chapter 7, we scored Henry's Stress test scores for similar life situations or conditions, but he had an undiagnosed BD.

Now, if you compare this chart to the WAVES Chart for Henrys' chart 4a in Chapter 7 before treatment, you see the major differences between having no mental Illness and unstable BD illness. Henry now has similar issues, but because he is "Normal," his total stress is much lower at 318 points. Henry has a score of over 600 on the Bipolar WAVES Stress Chart 4a with unstable BD, and places him in the Emergency Zone Level 6.

So, because Henry has unstable BD, his life stresses are about twice as stressful as Henry living a "Normal" lifestyle.

# Bibliography

American Psychiatric Association. (1987). *DSM-III-R American Psychiatric Association: Diagnostic and Statistical Manual (DSM) of Mental Disorders Fourth Edition, Text Revision.* Washington, DC, DC: American Psychiatric Association.

Ancient Aliens: Aliens and the Presidents (S15 Ep12)

Cory, C. (Director). (2020). *Superhuman:The Invisible Made Visible*

Nat Geo, N. G. (n.d.). Drugs Inc Series.

Hawk, L. (n.d.). *Little Hawk Native American Wisdom- Indigenous Storytelling.* Retrieved from Youtube.com.

Holmes, T. H., & Rahe, R. H. (1967, August 1967). The Holmes and Rahe Life Stress Scale. *Journal of Psychosomatic Research, Volume 11,*(Issue 2).

Inc, Drugs. (n.d.). Drugs Inc TV documentaries series.

Jerrod Brown, M. M. (n.d.). *Father-Absent Homes: Implications for Criminal Justice and Mental Health Professionals.* Retrieved from mnpsych.org: mnpsych.org

Lazar, B. (n.d.). *Bob Lazar.* Retrieved from boblazar.com.

Long, 2016 Alien Crash Retrieval

Managing Bipolar Disorder. (2003, November 2003 ). *Psychology Today.*

National Institute of Mental Health. (n.d.).

History channel *navy-confirms-ufo-videos-real.* (n.d.). Retrieved from History channel: https://www.history.com/.amp/news/navy-confirms-ufo-videos-real

North, G. (1983 ). *Government by Emergency.* Ft Worth Texas 76124: American Bureau of Economic Research.

OECD. (n.d.). *OECD Heath Statistics 2013 Life expectancy.* Retrieved from oecd.org.

*Patient Seventeen* (n.d.). [Motion Picture].

Sisarich, T. (Director). (n.d.). *Irreplaceable* [Motion Picture].

Suzanne, P. W. (n.d.). *Intelligent Trees – The Documentary.* Retrieved from Intelligent-Trees.com: Intelligent-Trees.com

The Depression & Bipolar Support Alliance (DBSA) dbsalliance.org. (n.d.). *Bipolar Disorder Statistics.* Retrieved September 2017, from http://dbsalliance.org: http://dbsalliance.org/site/pageserver?pagename=eduacation_statistics_biploar_disorder

Wood, 2019 How China Got Rich

End The Bipolar WAVES Workbook

Made in the USA
Middletown, DE
08 March 2022